Morris Minor 1000 Owners Workshop Manual

J H Haynes

Member of the Guild of Motoring Writers

Models covered:

All models of Saloon, Convertible and Estate.
948 cc and 1098 cc

ISBN 978 0 85733 585 2

(024-5N3)

J H Haynes & Co. Ltd.
Haynes North America, Inc

www.haynes.com

ACKNOWLEDGEMENTS

It would not have been possible to produce such a detailed work without the generous assistance of the British Motor Corporation, who, through supplying us with all the technical data and illustrations requested have made a considerable contribution to the accuracy of this publication.

Thanks are also due to 'Practical Motorist' for their generous provision of the majority of photographs used in Chapter Eight, and to the many enthusiastic private owners who have come forward with advice and encouragement. Special thanks are due to Dave Hyland, whose car proved to be the one that was stripped and rebuilt and who enthusiastically assisted the author in this task.

GENERAL INFORMATION

Although this manual deals specifically with the cars detailed on the cover, in certain places other models in the B.M.C. 'A' Series range are also covered. This is for the interest and benefit of the reader who may wish to replace old, worn components with improved or nearly new parts from much later, but different, 'A' Series models, found perhaps as insurance write-offs or in breaker's yards. The majority of mechanical components, including engines and rear axles, are interchangeable between the Sprite, Midget, A.35, A.40, and Morris Minor.

CONTENTS

Fig. 1. Morris Minor 1000 – 948 c.c.
Fig. 2. Morris Minor 1000 – 1,098 c.c.

INTRODUCTION

This manual describes in detail how the Morris Minor 1000 owner can remove, dismantle, overhaul, reassemble, and replace all the mechanical and electrical components that comprise his car, and how he can maintain it in first class condition to ensure maximum longevity and reliability.

The author has stripped and rebuilt all the major mechanical and electrical components himself. Only through doing it in this way is it possible to pass onto the private owner the solutions to various problems he may encounter, and to give other hints and tips which can only be obtained through practical experience.

The photographic strip and rebuild sequences show how each of the major assemblies were removed, taken apart, and rebuilt, and in conjunction with the text and exploded illustrations, should make all the operations described quite clear - even to the novice who has never attempted this type of work previously.

The Morris Minor 1000 is a model which has achieved great popularity since its initial introduction. In standard condition it is an excellent compromise between smooth, silent running, fair performance, low running costs, and a good rate of wear.

As these models grow older and become worn it is inevitable that their reliability will decrease and repairs and general reconditioning will become necessary. It is hoped that this workshop manual will prove here to be of maximum assistance, as it is the only workshop manual available directed specifically to assist Minor 1000 owners, as opposed to service operators and garage owners.

The manuals issued by the majority of vehicle manufacturers are splendid publications which contain much useful information, but naturally they are of most use to commercial garages. They are only of limited interest to the private owner who is more concerned with the correct way to dismantle and reassemble component parts, and in fault tracing and rectification, than in the use of welding, drilling, machining, dial gauge measuring, and other specialised garage equipment, the use of which is frequently referred to in the pages of the average manufacturer's manual.

It is fully appreciated that the majority of owners have a good basic set of tools but no more, and therefore wherever possible, ways are shown to get round the use of expensive garage tools - as for example in the Chapter on the rear axle.

Garage repairs are becoming increasingly a simple case of removing a worn component or assembly and replacing it with a new or reconditioned one. The old fashioned arts required by mechanics of yore, such as the ability to scrape bearings until a perfect fit, are now a thing of the past. There is no special skill involved in stripping and rebuilding mechanical and electrical components providing care is taken. It follows that there is no valid reason why the average owner should not be able to strip and rebuild worn components himself and so benefit from the considerable financial savings this invariably involves. However, he must know how to go about the job properly, and must obviously possess average manual dexterity and a liking for machinery.

Here then is a manual which will show the enthusiastic, mechanically inclined Minor 1000 owner, how he can best maintain and repair his car himself, without recourse to professional assistance or expensive tools and machinery.

ROAD TEST AND PERFORMANCE DATA

MAXIMUM SPEEDS IN M.P.H.

	Morris Minor 1000 - 948 c.c.	Morris Minor 1000 - 1,098 c.c.
Max. speed	75.1 m.p.h.	78.0 m.p.h.
Third gear	60.5 "	68.0 "
Second gear	35.2 "	41.5 "
First gear	23.4 "	27.5 "

ACCELERATION

0 - 30 m.p.h.	6.8 secs	6.4 secs
0 - 40 m.p.h.	12.1 "	9.8 "
0 - 50 m.p.h.	18.5 "	15.8 "
0 - 60 m.p.h.	30.0 "	24.2 "

TOP GEAR PETROL CONSUMPTION AT STEADY SPEEDS

30 m.p.h.	54.2 m.p.g.	56.4 m.p.g.
40 m.p.h.	53.5 "	48.5 "
50 m.p.h.	44.5 "	41.4 "
60 m.p.h.	40.1 "	35.7 "
Overall fuel Consumption	43.5 "	35.0 "

DIMENSIONS – WEIGHTS – CAPACITIES

	LENGTH	WIDTH	HEIGHT	WHEELBASE	GROUND CLEARANCE
Morris Minor 948 c.c.	12 ft. 5½ in.	5 ft.	4 ft. 10 in.	7 ft. 2 in.	6¾ ins.
Morris Minor 1,098 c.c.	12 ft. 5½ in.	5 ft.	4 ft. 10 in.	7 ft. 2 in.	6¾ ins.

	ENGINE WEIGHT	GEARBOX WEIGHT	REAR AXLE WEIGHT	KERB WEIGHT	WEIGHT'S DISTRIBUTION
Morris Minor 948 c.c.	245 lb.	35 lb.	83 lb.	1,695 lb.	57/43% F/R
Morris Minor 1,098 c.c.	252 lb.	44 lb.	83 lb.	1,708 lb.	57/43% F/R

	WATER CAPACITY	ENGINE & FILTER OIL	GEARBOX OIL	REAR AXLE OIL	FUEL TANK
Morris Minor 948 c.c.	9.75 pints	6.5 pints	2.25 pints	1.75 pints	5.0 gal.
Morris Minor 1,098 c.c.	9.75 pints	6.5 pints	2.25 pints	1.75 pints	6.5 gal.

ROUTINE MAINTENANCE

The maintenance instructions listed below are basically those recommended by the manufacturer. Details of how to perform the maintenance tasks not described below can be found on the page number shown against each task. In addition to the regular maintenance tasks detailed by the manufacturers, the author has found further maintenance tasks which, through practical experience, it is recommended are carried out at the intervals suggested.

These additional tasks are indicated by an asterisk, and are primarily of a preventative nature in that they will assist in eliminating the unexpected failure of a component due to fair wear and tear.

The levels of the engine oil, radiator cooling water, and the battery electrolyte should be checked weekly, or more frequently if experience dictates this necessary, at your local garage, together with the tyre pressures, when filling up with petrol. It is helpful to use the same garage for this work as they will get to know your individual preferences for the particular make of oil you use, and the pressures you like to run your tyres at.

MILEAGE	MAINTENANCE TASK	Key to Illus.	Described on Page
Every 3,000 miles			
1	Run the car until the engine has reached normal operating temperature, remove the drain plug on the rear right-hand side of the sump and allow the engine oil to drain into a suitable receptacle. Replace the drain plug and refill with 5½ pints of a recommended S.A.E. 30 lubricant.	5	10
2	Unscrew the gearbox filler plug and check the level of the gearbox oil which should be level with the bottom thread of the hole. Top up with one of the recommended S.A.E. 30 lubricants as required.	5	10
3	Remove the filler plug in the rear axle, and top up as necessary with Castrol Hypoy, or a similar Hypoid S.A.E. 90 lubricant, until the oil reaches the bottom of the filler plug hole.	2	10
4	Fill a grease gun with Castrolease L.M. or a similar recommended multi-purpose grease, and thoroughly lubricate the following through the appropriate grease nipple which should be carefully wiped clean.		
	a) Steering tie-rod ball joints (2 nipples)	6	10
	b) King pin upper and lower joints (4 nipples)	7	10
	c) Propeller shaft universal joints (2 nipples)	8	10
5	Oil the handbrake linkage joint with an oil can filled with a recommended S.A.E. 20 lubricant.		
6	Unscrew the top of the carburettor dashpot and top up with one of the recommended S.A.E. 20 lubricants.	10	10
7	Check the level of the hydraulic brake fluid in the brake master cylinder reservoir, and top up as necessary with Lockheed Super Heavy Brake Fluid.		117
8	Refill the windscreen washer bottle.		
9	Adjust the brakes. Check the hoses and pipes for loose joints, or leaks or wear caused by the suspension or tyres rubbing against the flexible piping. *		117, 118
10	Check and adjust the tyre pressures.		
11	Wash the bodywork and chromium fittings and clean out the interior. *		
12	Remove the sparking plugs, clean them, and adjust the electrode gaps. *		81
13	Check that all the lights are functioning correctly and replace blown bulbs as necessary. *		131
14	Examine the tyre threads for sharp objects such as stones and remove them with a screwdriver or penknife. *		

MILEAGE	MAINTENANCE TASK	Key to Illus.	Described on Page

Every 6,000 miles

1 Perform all the maintenance tasks listed for the 3,000 mile service with the exception of item 6.

2 Remove the oil filter, wash the bowl in petrol and fit a new element and rubber seal. Refill the sump and filter with 6½ pints of S.A.E. 30 oil. **3** **30**

3 Remove the gearbox drain plug and drain all the old oil. Refill with 2¼ pints of S.A.E. 30 oil. N.B. With the introduction of improved oils, in later B.M.C. sponsored manuals it is recommended that the oil is changed once every 12,000 miles. **5** **10**

4 Remove the rear axle drain plug and allow all the oil to drain. Refill with 1½ pints of a good S.A.E. 90 oil such as Castrol Hypoy. N.B. With the introduction of improved oils in later B.M.C. sponsored manuals it is recommended that the oil is changed only once every 12,000 miles. **4** **10**

5 Oil the door, bonnet, and boot hinges with an S.A.E. 20 oil and grease the door striker plates.

6 Repack the hubs with grease - wipe away any excess. *

7 Lubricate all the carburettor controls.

8 Lubricate the pivot point of the brake and clutch pedal shafts. *

9 Remove the air cleaners, and if of the wire mesh-type clean them in petrol, reoil them and replace. If of the paper element-type replace the paper element. **59**

10 Turning to the S.U. carburettor, clean the suction chambers and piston, and top up the piston damper with a recommended S.A.E. 20 oil

11 Check the fuel lines and the union joints for leaks and replace as necessary. * **10** **10**

12 Remove and clean the gauze filters in the carburettor and fuel pump where these are fitted.

13 Remove the distributor cap, pull off the rotor arm and apply three drops of S.A.E. 20 oil to the head of the large screw. **14, 13, 12** **10**

14 Check the condition of the contact breaker points, clean and regap them and, if necessary, fit a new set, and check the timing and advance and retard mechanism. **78**

15 On early models unscrew the dynamo lubricator cap, and take out the felt pad and spring, and half fill the cap with grease. Replace the pad spring and cap. On later models apply two drops of S.A.E. 20 oil to the lubricator hole in the rear of the dynamo. **11** **10, 129**

16 Check the specific gravity of the battery and top up with distilled water or electrolyte, as appropriate. Give the battery a full 24-hour charge. **129**

17 Wipe over the battery terminals, ensure they are free from corrosion and coat them with petroleum jelly (Vaseline). *

18 Check and adjust the fan belt tension. * **58**

19 Check and adjust the valve rocker clearances. **46**

20 Adjust the carburettor slow running and tune if necessary. * **68**

21 Change over the tyres to equalise wear and inspect the walls for damage.

22 Check and adjust the steering toe-in. **149**

23 Balance the front wheels to eliminate steering vibration as necessary. *

24 Check the tightness of the nuts and bolts on the universal joints, spring clips and shackles, and steering gear. *

25 Examine the exhaust system for holes and leaks and repair as required. *

26 Check the condition of the heater and cooling system hoses and replace as necessary. *

27 Check the level of the hydraulic fluid in the dampers and top up as required with Armstrong Super Thin Shock Absorber Oil. **145**

28 Wax polish the bodywork and also the chromium plating. Force wax polish into any joins in the bodywork which have not been properly filled to help prevent rust formation. *

8

MILEAGE	MAINTENANCE TASK	Key to Illus.	Described on Page

Every 12,000 miles

1. Perform all the maintenance tasks listed for the 3,000 and 6,000 mile services with the exception of 1 in the 3,000 mile service.
2. Drain the engine oil when hot, change the filter, drop and clean the sump, replace and refill with 6½ pints of S.A.E. 30 oil.
3. Fill the grease gun with an S.A.E. 90 Hypoy oil, apply it to the nipple on the steering rack housing and give ten strokes of the grease gun. — 9 — 145
4. Lubricate the water pump sparingly with grease. If the pump squeaks a few tablespoons of hydraulic fluid in the cooling water will silence the carbon sealing ring.
5. Remove the speedometer cable, clean, and lightly lubricate the inner cable with thin machine oil. *
6. Steam clean the underside of the body, and clean the engine and engine compartment. *
7. Remove the sparking plugs and fit new ones correctly gapped. — 81
8. Remove the old contact breaker points and fit new ones. Set the gap correctly and time the ignition. — 78, 80
9. Inspect the ignition leads for cracks and perishing and replace as necessary. * — 81
10. Remove the brake drums, blow out the brake dust and inspect the linings for wear. * — 118
11. Examine the dynamo brushes, replace them if worn, and clean the commutator. * — 129
12. Check the headlamp bulbs and renew them if slightly blackened or if the element sags. * — 131
13. Check the headlamp beam setting and adjust if necessary.
14. Renew the windscreen wiper blades. *

Every 24,000 miles

1. In addition to the maintenance tasks listed previously, carry out the following operations:-
2. Check and adjust the backlash and end float in the rack and pinion steering gear. * — 150
3. Examine ball joints and hub bearings for wear and replace as necessary. * — 148
4. Remove the starter motor, examine the brushes, replace as necessary and clean the commutator and starter drive. * — 134, 135
5. If necessary, decarbonise the engine, and fit new valve springs. * — 23, 34, 45
6. When the sump is dropped for cleaning (See '2' in the 12,000 mile service) remove the big end bearing caps, examine the shell bearings for wear, and renew as necessary. * — 28, 32
7. Check the universal joints for wear and renew if worn. * — 108
8. Check the tightness of the battery earth lead on the bodywork, and the tightness of the engine earth lead to the chassis frame. — 78
9. Renew the condenser in the distributor.

RECOMMENDED LUBRICANTS

ENGINE & GEARBOX	Energol S.A.E. 30; Shell X-100 S.A.E. 30; Filtrate Medium 30; Sternol W.W. 30; Duckhams NOL Thirty; Castrol X.L.; Esso Extra Motor Oil 20W/30; Mobiloil A; B.P. Energol Visco-Static; Shell X-100 Multigrade 10W/30; Filtrate 10W/30 Multigrade; Sternol Multiplec; Duckhams Q5500; Duckhams Q20/50; Castrolite; Mobiloil Special.
REAR AXLE & STEERING GEAR	Energol E.P. S.A.E. 90; Shell Spirax 90 E.P.; Filtrate Hypoid Gear 90; Ambroleum E.P. 90; Duckhams E.P. 90; Castrol Hypoy; Esso Gear Oil E.P. 90; Mobilube G.X. 90.
ALL GREASE POINTS	Energrease L.2; Shell Retinax A; Filtrate Super Lithium Grease; Ambroline L.H.T.; Duckhams L.B. 10 Grease; Castrolease L.M.; Esso Multipurpose Grease H; Mobilgrease M.P.
OILCAN & CARBURETTOR	Energol S.A.E. 20W; Shell X-100 20W; Filtrate Zero 20/20W; Sternol W.W. 20; Duckhams NOL Twenty; Castrolite; Esso Extra Motor Oil 20W/30; Mobiloil Artic.

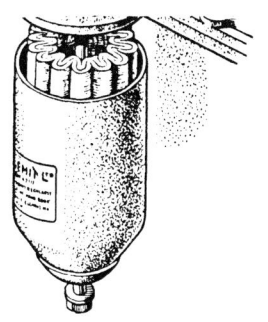

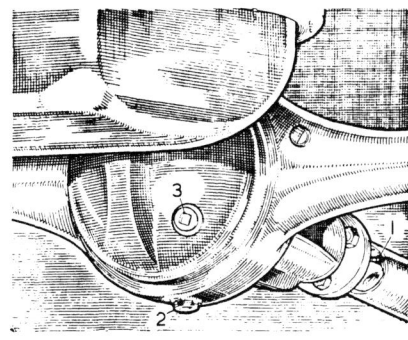

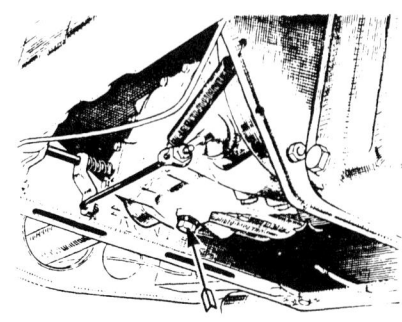

3. The filter body can be removed after the long centre bolt is unscrewed

4. 1 - Universal joint rear grease nipple 2 - Rear axle oil drain plug 3 - Rear axle oil filler plug

5. The gearbox oil drain plug (arrowed)

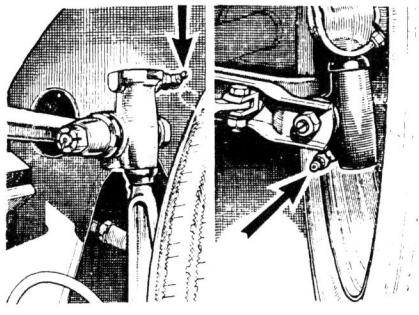

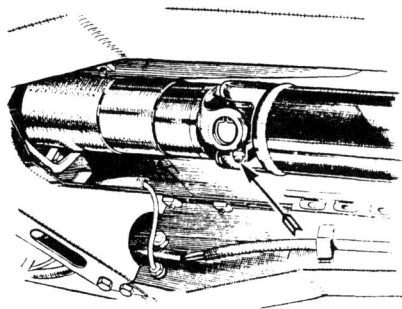

6. Each rack and pinion steering tie-rod has a grease nipple on the outer ball joint

7. Grease nipples are also fitted at the top and bottom of the kingpins

8. The location of the grease nipple at the front end of the propeller shaft universal joint

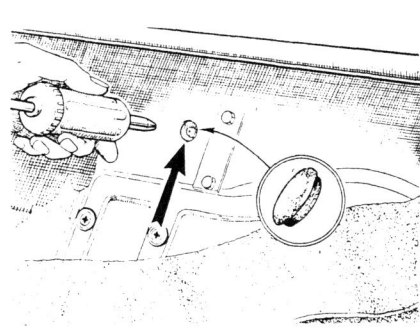

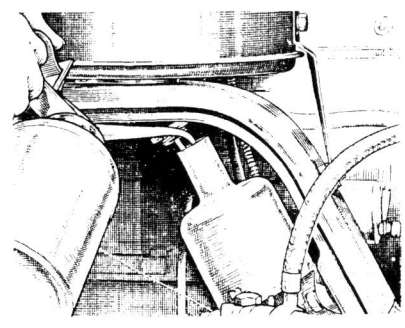

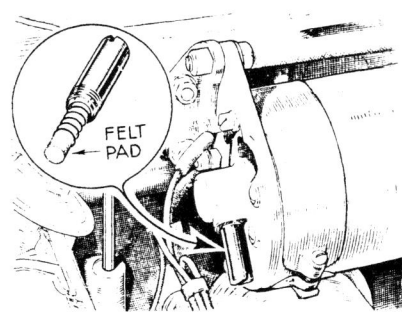

9. Access to the rack and pinion oil nipple is through the hole (normally covered with a rubber bung) in the toeboard on the passenger's side

10. The carburettor piston damper must be replenished as indicated

11. Early models make use of a wick lubric-ator for the dynamo. On later examples there is a small oil hole in the rear of the dynamo

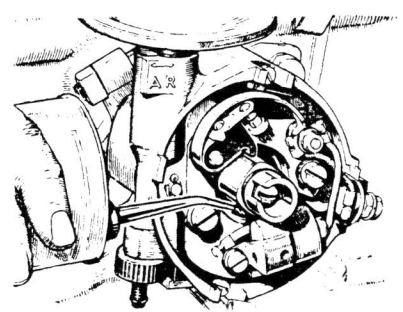

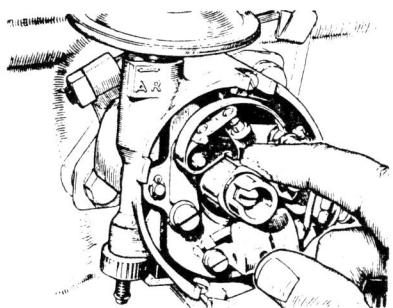

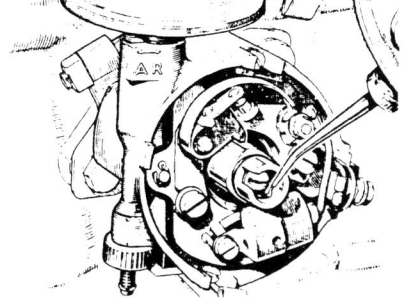

12. With the rotor arm removed, allow three drops of oil through the aperture round the cam to lubricate the automatic timing mechanism

13. A faint trace of grease should be smeared on the sides of the cam. Lubricate the points spindle at the same time

14. The cam bearing is lubricated with three drops of oil on the cam screw head

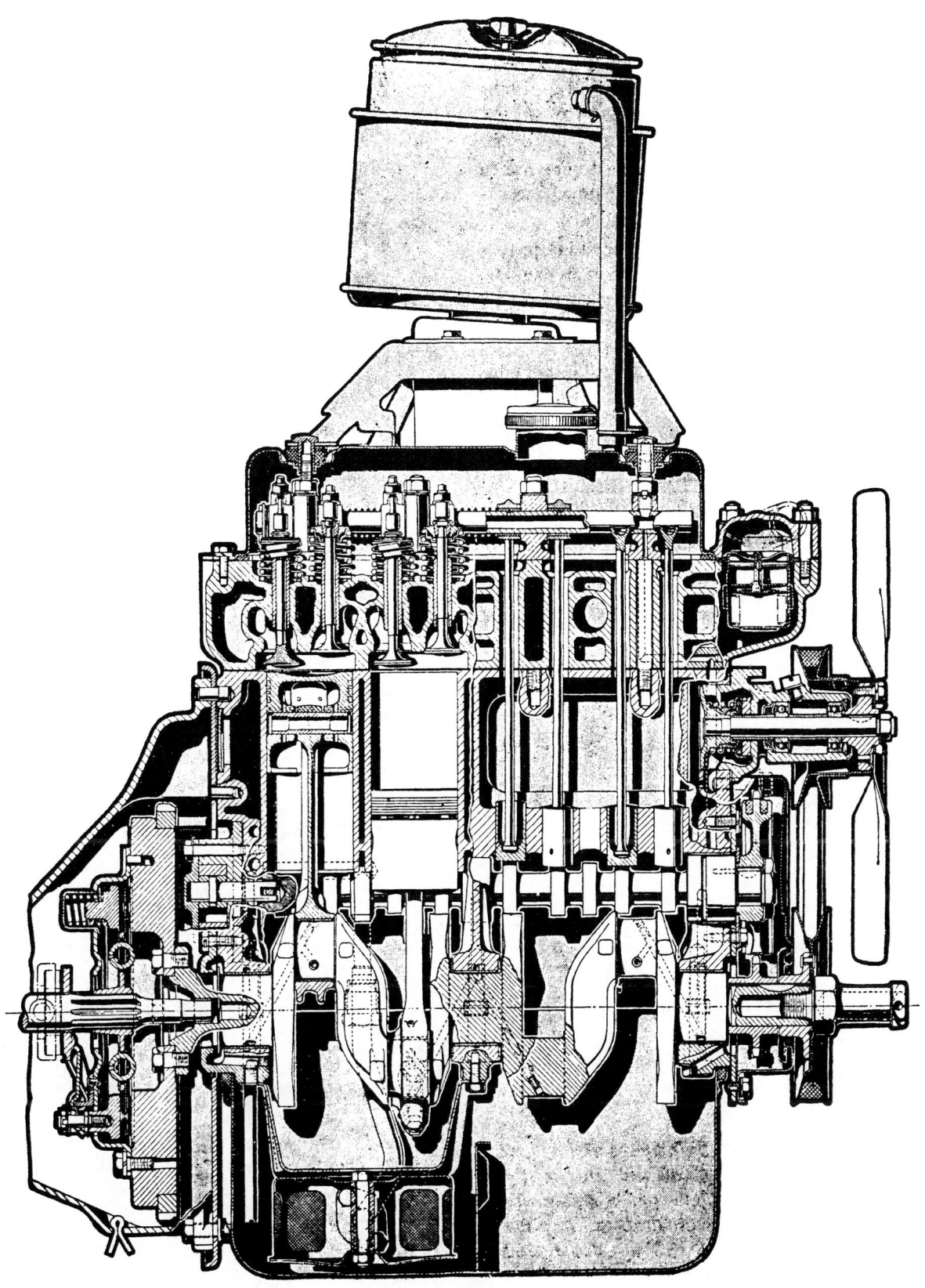

Sectioned view of the Morris Minor 948 c.c. engine

Fig. 16. Morris Minor 1000 engine compartment

CHAPTER ONE

ENGINE

ENGINE SPECIFICATION AND DATA – 948 c.c. TYPE 9

Engine

Type	4 cylinder in line O.H.V. pushrod operated.
Bore	2.478 in. (62.94 mm.).
Stroke	3.000 in. (76.2 mm.).
Cubic capacity	57.87 cu.in. (948 c.c.).
Compression ratio: High	8.3 : 1
Low	7.2 : 1
Capacity of combustion chamber (valves fitted)	24.5 c.c.
Oversize bore: 1st	.010 in. (.254 mm.).
2nd	.020 in. (.508 mm.).
3rd	.030 in. (.762 mm.).
Maximum torque	50 lbs/ft. at 2,500 r.p.m. (8.3 : 1 C.R.).
Firing order	1, 3, 4, 2
Location of No. 1 cylinder	Next to radiator.
Engine Mountings	3-point suspension rubber mountings, are each side of the forward half of the engine, and one under the gearbox.

Camshaft and Camshaft Bearings

The camshaft is driven from the crankshaft by a single roller chain with tensioner. Supported by 3 bearings.

Front bearing: Type	White metal lined - steel-backed.
Centre bearing: Type	Plain. (Running in block).
Rear bearing: Type	Plain. (Running in block).
Inside front bearing diameter reamed when fitted ..	1.667 to 1.6675 in. (42.342 to 42.355 mm.).
Front bearing clearance	.001 to .002 in. (.0254 to .0508 mm.).
Centre and rear bearing clearance	.00125 to .00275 in. (.032 to .07 mm.).
End float	.003 to .007 in. (.076 to .178 mm.).
Journal diameters: Front	1.6655 to 1.666 in. (42.304 to 42.316 mm.).
Centre	1.62275 to 1.62325 in. (41.218 to 41.231 mm.).
Rear	1.3725 to 1.3735 in. (34.862 to 34.887 mm.).

Connecting Rods and Big-End Bearings

Length between centres	5.75 in. (14.605 cm.).
Big end bearings	Steel backed, white metal or copper lead lined.
Side clearance	.008 to .012 in. (.203 to .305 mm.).
Bearing internal diameter clearance	.001 to .0025 in. (.025 to .063 mm.).

Crankshaft and Main Bearings

Main journal diameter	1.7505 to 1.7510 in. (44.46 to 44.47 mm.).
Minimum main journal regrind diameter	1.7105 in. (43.45 mm.).
Crankpin journal diameter	1.6254 to 1.6259 in. (41.28 to 41.30 mm.).
Minimum crankpin regrind diameter	1.5854 in. (40.27 mm.).
Main bearings	3 shell-type. Steel backed, lead bronze, lead-indium, copper-lead, or lead tin plated surfaces, or white metal on early models.
End float	.002 to .003 in. (.051 to .076 mm.).
Side thrust	Taken by thrust washers located on either side of centre main bearing.
Undersizes available	- .010 in. (-.254 mm.), - .020 in. (-.508 mm.), - .030 in. (-.762 mm.), - .040 in. (- 1.02 mm.).

Cylinder Block

Type	Cylinder cast integral with top half of crankcase.
Water jackets	Full length.

13

ENGINE

Cylinder Block

Type	Cylinder cast integral with top half of crankcase.
Water jackets	Full length .

Cylinder Head

Type   Cast iron with vertical valves. Siamised inlet ports, 2 separate and 1 siamised exhaust ports.

Combustion chamber capacity with valves fitted .. .. 24. 5 c. c.

Gudgeon Pin

Type	Semi-floating. Held by clamp bolt.
Fit to piston	. 0001 to . 00035 in. (. 0025 to . 009 mm.).
Fit in connecting rod	. 0001 to . 0006 in. (. 0025 to . 015 mm.).
Diameter (outer)	. 6244 to . 6246 in. (15. 86 to 15. 865 mm.).

Lubrication System

Type   Pressure feed.   Pressure fed bearings: Main, camshaft and connecting rods.   Reduced pressure to rocker shaft.   Piston pin and cylinder wall lubrication - splash.

Oil filter	Full flow.
Capacity of oil filter	1 pint (1. 2 U. S. pints. . 57 litre).
Crankcase ventilation	Directed flow via road draught tube on left-hand side of engine

Grade of oil Summer - Duckhams Q. 20/50, Castrol XL, Sternol W. W. 40, Mobiloil A. F. , Mobiloil B. B. , Esso Oil 40/50, Esso Oil 40, Esso Extra Oil 20W/40, Filtrate Heavy, Filtrate 20W/40, Energol S. A. E. 40, Shell X - 100 40, Shell X - 100, Shell Multigrade 20W/40

　　　　　　　Winter - Duckham's Q. 5500, Castrolite, Sternol W. W. Multigrade 10 / 30, Mobiloil Special, Esso Oil 20W/30, Esso Oil 20, Esso Extra Oil, Filtrate 10W/30, Filtrate Zero, Energol S. A. E. 20W, Visco-Static, Shell X - 100 20W, Shell X - 100, Multigrade 10W/30.

Sump capacity	5. 5 pints.
Sump & Filter capacity	6. 5 pints (7. 8 U. S. pints. 3. 7 litres).
Oil pump: Type	Eccentric rotor or vane.
Oil pump relief pressure	60 lb/sq. in.
Oil pressure: Normal	30 to 60 lbs/sq. in.
Idling	10 to 25 lbs/sq. in.
Relief valve spring: Free length	2. 859 in. (72. 63 mm.).
Fitted length	2. 156 in. (54. 77 mm.).

Pistons

Type .. .. .. Flat crown, anodised aluminium alloy. 3 compression rings, 1 oil control ring.

Clearance of piston: Top of skirt	. 0036 to . 0042 in.(.0914 to .1067 mm.).
Bottom of skirt	. 0016 to . 0022 in. (. 040 to . 056 mm.).
Piston Oversizes available	+ . 010 in. (+ . 254 mm.), + . 020 in. (+ . 508 mm.),
.. ..	+ . 030 in. (+ . 762 mm.), + . 040 in. (+ 1. 02 mm.).

Piston Rings

Top compression ring	Plain.
2nd and 3rd compression ring	Tapered.
Fitted gap	. 007 to . 012 in. (. 178 to . 30 mm.).
Groove clearance	. 0015 to . 0035 in. (. 038 to . 089 mm.).
Oil control ring	Slotted scraper.
Fitted gap	. 007 to . 012 in. (. 178 to . 30 mm.).
Clearance in groove	. 0015 to . 0035 in. (. 038 to . 089 mm.).

Tappets

Type	Bucket.
Length	1. 505 in. (38. 23 mm.).
Diameter	. 8120 in. (20. 62 mm.).

Valves

Head diameter: Inlet	1. 151 to 1. 156 in. (29. 23 to 29. 36 mm.).
Exhaust	1. 000 to 1. 005 in. (25. 4 to 25. 53 mm.).
Valve lift	. 28 in. (7. 14 mm.) Mk. I Sprite. All other models . 312 in. (7. 925 mm.).
Seat angle	Inlet and Exhaust 45°.
Valve clearance	. 012 in. (. 305 mm.) under normal conditions
.. ..	. 015 in. (. 381 mm.) for competition work

ENGINE

Valve rocker bush bore (reamed)	.5630 to .5635 in. (14.30 to 14.31 mm.).

Valve Guides

Length: Inlet and Exhaust	.. 1.687 in. (42.86 mm.).
Diameter: Inlet and Exhaust: Outside	.4695 to .470 in. (11.92 to 11.94 mm.).
Inside	.2813 to .2818 in. (7.145 to 7.177 mm.).
Fitted height above head	19/32nd in. (15.1 mm.).

Valve Timing

Inlet valve: opens 5° B.T.D.C.	Exhaust valve: opens 40° B.B.D.C.
closes 45° A.B.D.C.	closes 10° A.T.D.C.
Valve timing marks..	Dimples on crankshaft and camshaft sprockets.
Chain pitch and number of pitches	.. 3/8th in. (9.52 mm.). 52 pitches.
Valve rocker clearance: timing	.019 in. (.48 mm.).

Valve Springs

Type	.. Single valve springs.
Free length	.. 1.625 in. (1⅝th in. 41.275 mm.).
Fitted length	.. 1¹⁹⁄₆₄th in. (3.3 cm.).
Valve spring pressure with valves open	.. 70 lb.
Valve spring pressure with valves closed	.. 37.5 lb. + or - 2 lb.

TORQUE WRENCH SETTINGS

Connecting rod bolts	35 lb/ft.
Crankshaft pulley nut	70 lb/ft.
Cylinder head nuts	40 lb/ft.
Flywheel bolts	40 lb/ft.
Main bearing bolts	60 lb/ft.
Manifold nuts	15 lb/ft.
Oil filter retaining nut	16 lb/ft.
Oil pump retaining nut	9 lb/ft.
Rocker cover retaining bolts	4 lb/ft.
Rocker pedestal nuts	25 lb/ft.
Sump retaining bolts	6 lb/ft.
Tappet chest side covers	2 lb/ft.
Thermostat housing nuts	8 lb/ft.
Timing cover ¼ in. bolts	6 lb/ft.
Timing cover 5/16 in. bolt	14 lb/ft.
Water pump nuts	17 lb/ft.

ENGINE SPECIFICATION AND DATA – 1,098 c.c. TYPE 10

The engine specification is identical to the type 9 specification except for the differences detailed below.

Engine

Bore	2.543 in. (64.58 mm.).
Stroke	3.296 in. (83.72 mm.).
Capacity	67 cu.in. (1,098 c.c.).
Compression ratio: High	8.5 : 1
Low	7.5 : 1
Capacity of combustion chamber (valves fitted)	1.95 cu.in. (32 c.c.). (7.5 : 1 C.R.).
Oversize bore: 1st.	+ .010 in. (.254 mm.).
Max.	+ .020 in. (.508 mm.).

Camshaft and Camshaft Bearings

Bearings: Number & Type:	3 white metal lined, steel-backed shell bearings
Inside bearing diameter reamed when fitted: Front	.. 1.667 to 1.6675 in. (42.342 to 42.355 mm.).
Centre	.. 1.6242 to 1.6247 in. (41.256 to 41.269 mm.).
Rear	.. 1.3745 to 1.3750 in. (34.912 to 34.925 mm.).

ENGINE

Big-End Bearings
Material .. .. Steel-backed copper-lead
Bearing side clearance .. .. .008 to .012 in. (.203 to .305 mm.).
Bearing diametral clearance .. .. .001 to .0025 in. (.025 to .063 mm.).

Gudgeon Pin
Type .. .. Fully floating.
Fit in piston .. .. Hand push fit.

Main Bearings
Number & Type .. .. 3 shell-type.
Material .. .. Steel-backed copper-lead
Length .. .. $1\frac{1}{16}$ in. (27 mm.).
Diametral clearance .. .. .001 to .0027 in. (.025 to .070 mm.).
Undersizes .. .. - .010 in. (- .254 mm.)., - .020 in. (- .508 mm.)., - .030 in. (- .762 mm.).,
- .040 in. (- 1.016 mm.).

Pistons
Type .. .. Solid skirt.
Clearances: Bottom of skirt .. .. .0005 to .0011 in. (.013 to .028 mm.).
Top of skirt .. .. .0021 to .0037 in. (.053 to .094 mm.).
Oversizes .. .. + .010 in. (+ .254 mm.), + .020 in. (+ .508 mm.).

Piston Rings
Compression Rings: Type: Top ring .. .. .. Plain internally chamfered (chrome-faced).
Second and third rings .. .. Tapered.
Width (top ring) .. .. .. .062 to .0625 in. (1.575 to 1.587 mm.).
(second and third rings) .. .. .0615 to .0625 in. (1.558 to 1.587 mm.).
Thickness .. .. .106 to .112 in. (2.69 to 2.84 mm.).
Fitted gap .. .. .007 to .012 in. (.178 to .305 mm.).
Clearance in groove .. .. .002 to .004 in. (.051 to .102 mm.).
Oil control: Type .. .. Slotted scraper.
Width .. .. .124 to .125 in. (3.15 to 3.175 mm.).
Thickness .. .. .106 to .112 in. (2.69 to 2.84 mm.).
Fitted gap .. .. .007 to .012 in. (.178 to .305 mm.).
Clearance in groove .. .. .0015 to .0035 in. (.038 to .089 mm.).

Valves
Head diameter: Inlet .. .. 1.156 in. (29.37 mm.).
Exhaust .. .. 1.000 in. (25.40 mm.).
Stem diameter: Inlet .. .. .2793 to .2798 in. (7.094 to 7.107 mm.).
Exhaust .. .. .2788 to .2793 in. (7.081 to 7.094 mm.).
Valve lift .. .. .312 in. (7.925 mm.).
Valve stem to guide clearance: Inlet .. .. .. .0015 to .0025 in. (.038 to .064 mm.).
Exhaust .. .. .. .002 to .003 in. (.051 to .076 mm.).
Valve rocker clearance: Running .. .. .012 in. (.305 mm.) (cold).
Timing .. .. .021 in. (.53 mm.)
Valve rocker bush bore (reamed) .. .. .5630 to .5635 in. (14.30 to 14.312 mm.).

Valve Guides
Length .. .. 1.531 in. (38.89 mm.).
Diameter: Outside .. .. .469 in. (11.91 mm.).
Inside .. .. .2813 to .2818 in. (7.145 to 7.157 mm.).

Valve Springs
Free length .. .. 1.750 in. (44.45 mm.).
Number of working coils .. .. $4\frac{1}{2}$.
Pressure: Valve open .. .. 85 lb. (38.6 kg.).
Valve closed .. .. 52.5 lb. (23.8 kg.).

Valve Timing
Inlet valve: Opens 5° B.T.D.C.)
Closes 45° A.B.D.C.) With .021 in. (.53 mm.) valve rocker clearance (for checking
Exhaust valve: Opens 51° B.B.D.C.) purposes only).
Closes 21° A.T.D.C.)

ENGINE

GENERAL DESCRIPTION

The engine is a four cylinder, overhead valve, type of either 948 c.c. or 1,098 c.c., depending on the model and its year of manufacture. It is supported by rubber mountings in the interests of silence and lack of vibration.

Two valves per cylinder are mounted vertically in the cast iron cylinder head and run in pressed in valve guides. They are operated by rocker arms and pushrods from the camshaft which is located at the base of the cylinder bores in the left-hand side of the engine.

The cylinder head has all five inlet and exhaust ports on the left-hand side. Cylinders 1 and 2 share a siamised inlet port and also cylinders 3 and 4. Cylinders 1 and 4 have individual exhaust ports and cylinders 2 and 3 share a siamised exhaust port.

The cylinder block and the upper half of the crankcase are cast together. The bottom half of the crankcase consists of a pressed steel sump.

The pistons are made from anodised aluminium alloy with either split or solid skirts, depending on the model. Three compression rings and a slotted oil control ring are fitted to both types. The gudgeon pin is retained in the little end of the connecting rod by a pinch bolt on earlier models, and by means of two circlips on later models, which have fully floating gudgeon pins. Renewable white metal, lead-indium, or lead-tin big end bearings are fitted.

At the front of the engine a single row chain drives the camshaft via the camshaft and crankshaft chain wheels. On early models the chain is tensioned by a ring tensioner, while later models make use of two rubber rings either side of the gearwheel teeth. The camshaft is supported in three bearings, two being bored directly in the crankcase while a white metal bearing is fitted at the chain wheel end which is renewable.

On later model 948 c.c. engines and 1,098 c.c. units (9CG, 10MA, 10CG) three steel-backed white metal camshaft bearings were fitted. These later engines also had no water passages between cylinders one and two, and three and four. The design of the water pump was also different and alumilited aluminium alloy pistons were fitted. The oil filter and oil sump gauze strainer location and design were also changed.

The statically and dynamically balanced forged steel crankshaft is supported by three renewable main bearings. Crankshaft end float is controlled by four semi-circular thrust washers, two of which are located on either side of the centre main bearing.

The centrifugal water pump and radiator cooling fan are driven together with the dynamo from the crankshaft pulley wheel by a rubber/fabric belt. The distributor is mounted towards the rear of the right-hand side of the cylinder block and advances and retards the ignition timing by mechanical and vacuum means. The distributor is driven at half crankshaft speed by a short shaft and skew gear from a skew gear on the camshaft. The oil pump is driven from the rear of the camshaft and this unit also actuates a mechanical fuel pump on Austin models via a cam and lever arrangement.

MAJOR OPERATIONS WITH ENGINE IN PLACE

The following major operations can be carried out to the engine with it in place in the body frame:-
1. Removal and replacement of the cylinder head assembly.
2. Removal and replacement of the sump.
3. Removal and replacement of the big end bearings.
4. Removal and replacement of the pistons and connecting rods.
5. Removal and replacement of the timing chain and gears.
6. Removal and replacement of the camshaft.

MAJOR OPERATIONS WITH ENGINE REMOVED

The following major operations can be carried out with the engine out of the body frame and on the bench or floor:-
1. Removal and replacement of the main bearings.
2. Removal and replacement of the crankshaft.
3. Removal and replacement of the oil pump.
4. Removal and replacement of the flywheel.

METHODS OF ENGINE REMOVAL

There are two methods of engine removal. The engine can either be removed complete with gearbox, or the engine can be removed without the gearbox by separation at the gearbox bellhousing. Both methods are detailed below.

ENGINE REMOVAL WITHOUT GEARBOX

The engines on all 'A' series models, excluding transverse engined variants, can be removed by the system detailed below. Where slight variations occur between one model and another, these are detailed.

On all models of the Sprite, Midget, A.40, and Morris Minor 1000, the engine is lifted out of the engine compartment. On the A.35 the engine has to be lowered out underneath the car.

Practical experience has proved that the engine can be removed easily and quickly in about four hours by adhering to the following sequence of operations in the order given:-
1. Turn on the water drain taps found at the bottom of the radiator and on the side of the cylinder block. Do not drain the water in your garage or the place where you will remove the engine if receptacles are not available to catch the water.
2. Disconnect the battery by removing the earth lead. For safety from electrical shocks it is best to remove the battery from the engine compartment.
3. With a suitable container in position unscrew the drain plug at the bottom right-hand corner of the sump and drain off the engine oil. When the oil is drained screw the plug back in lightly to ensure it is not mislaid.
4. Remove or lift back the bonnet as detailed below:-
   a) All models except the Sprite Mk. I and Morris Minor - Remove the set bolts and spring washers from each of the two bonnet hinges on the bonnet side of the hinge. The bonnet can then be lifted away.

4. b) Austin Healey Sprite Mk. I - The bonnet and wings lift off together as one unit. First, disconnect the wiring harness to the lights and traffic flasher indicators at the snap connectors. Remember to mark each side of each connection as otherwise it is easy to reconnect them incorrectly and find that the headlamps flash when the flashing direction indicator switch is turned on, and so on. The wiring harness must also be disconnected from its securing clip located on the right-hand hinge. Remove the four set bolts from each bonnet hinge on the bonnet side of the hinge. Remove the screw at the top of each of the two telescopic bonnet supports and, with the aid of a friend, lift the bonnet away. The bonnet is too heavy and cumbersome to be lifted away by one person only.

c) Morris Minor - To allow the bonnet to be fully opened remove the clevis pin which holds the bonnet to the bonnet support.

5. Unscrew the clip on the lower radiator hose, at the radiator pipe outlet, and remove the hose off the pipe. Unscrew the clip on the upper radiator hose at the thermostat housing outlet pipe, and remove the hose off the pipe. Also disconnect the heater unit inlet and outlet hoses (On models fitted with heater units), by releasing the securing clips on the control valve and heater return pipe located on the inlet side of the water pump.

6. Remove the four bolts from the caged nuts (two on each side of the radiator) which secures the radiator to the body and lift the radiator out. Close the drain tap.

7. Disconnect the throttle linkage and the choke control at the carburettor end. It is necessary to remove the carburettor and air cleaner from the inlet manifold on all models except for the Sprite and Midget. (For further details see Chapter 3).

8. Unscrew the two exhaust pipe clamp bolts at the joint between the exhaust manifold and the exhaust pipe, and remove the exhaust pipe support from the bellhousing if one is fitted, by releasing the appropriate bellhousing bolt. Pull the exhaust pipe away from the manifold.

9. Disconnect the low tension lead from the distributor, and the leads from the dynamo, starter motor, and oil pressure warning bulb switch (where fitted).

10. In the case of the Austin Healey Sprite and M.G. Midget fitted with tachometers, it is necessary to remove the reduction drive and cable from the rear of the dynamo. Alternatively, remove the cable by unscrewing the cable securing cap.

11. Unscrew the two bolts securing the starter motor in position and remove the motor.

12. To gain better access to the right-hand engine mounting bracket it is helpful to remove the dynamo. Unscrew the securing bolts (two at the front and one at the rear) and lift off the fan belt, and then the dynamo. If the coil is mounted on the dynamo it will also be necessary to remove

the high tension lead to the distributor, and the two low tension leads at the markings SW (switch) and CB (contact breaker). If the dynamo is not removed and the coil is mounted on it then it is only necessary to remove the low tension wire from the SW terminal.

13. If a sling is to be placed round the engine then it is sound practice to remove the distributor cap and rotor arm. The cap is made from plastic and therefore fragile and can be easily damaged while the engine is being lifted out. To remove the cap, first unscrew the high tension lead from the coil centre terminal. Pull the high tension leads away from the sparking plugs carefully marking which lead terminates at which plug. It may be possible to determine the correct lead order by the different length of each lead, with the longest lead to the plug furthest from the distributor, and the shortest to the closest. There is no need to mark the leads in this case.

14. On Austin models with a mechanical fuel pump unscrew the inlet fuel pipe at the fuel pump. On models with an S.U. fuel pump release the fuel inlet pipe at the carburettor end.

15. On models fitted with an oil pressure gauge, remove the pipe from its union at the rear left-hand side of the block by unscrewing the retaining nut.

16. A more convenient method of lifting the engine out than of using a sling is to fit the special lifting hooks, available from most B.M.C. garages, which fit under the rocker cover securing nuts.

17. Where fitted, disconnect the clutch lever return spring from the rear engine plate.

18. Release the nuts and bolts securing the gearbox bellhousing to the engine rear plate and at the same time free the earth strap attached to the bottom right bellhousing bolt where this is fitted.

19. For all versions of the Sprite, Midget, A.40, and Minor 1000, proceed as follows:-

a) Remove the two nuts securing the engine front plate to the engine mounting bracket on the right-hand side of the engine in the case of R.H.D. cars, and the left-hand side of the engine in the case of L.H.D. cars. Disconnect the complete engine mounting bracket from the body frame on the opposite side. For R.H.D. cars this will be the left-hand side. If wished, for ease of manipulation, the complete engine mounting bracket can be removed from the front plate by unscrewing the two nuts and spring washers.

b) With lifting tackle connected to the lifting hooks, or with slings fitted round the engine front and rear, lift the engine forwards and up out of the car. If no lifting tackle is available, four strong men can lift the engine out. On the Morris Minor it is necessary to turn the engine sideways before lifting it out as otherwise it is necessary to remove the radiator grille assembly.

20. For all models of the Austin A.35 proceed as follows, noting that the front wheels must be chocked up so that the engine can be removed

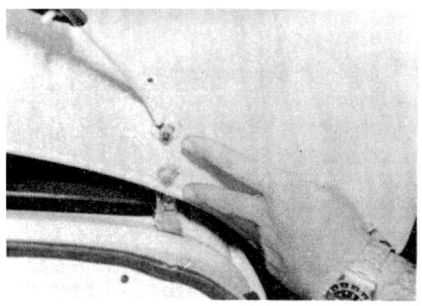

Release the two nuts on each hinge which hold the bonnet to the hinge

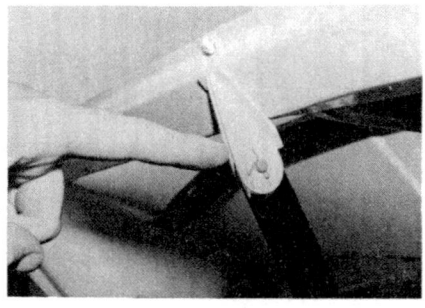

The bonnet can be removed only after the split pin has been extracted from the bonnet support strut peg, so freeing the support

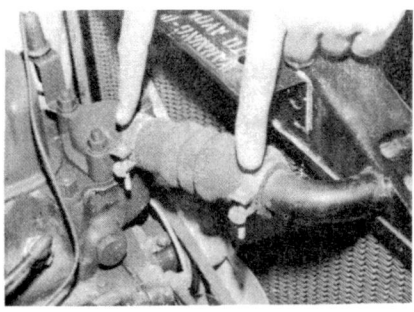

Release both clips on the upper radiator hose and pull the hose free prior to removing the radiator

The bottom clip on the lower radiator hose must also be released. After undoing the two bolts on either side of the radiator, it is easily lifted out

Do not forget to remove the engine support steady

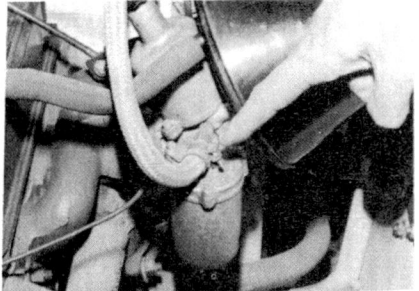

The petrol pipe to the carburettor will have to be disconnected at the float chamber

The lucar connector to the low pressure oil warning light must be carefully pulled off the sender unit

On one side undo the four nuts and bolts which hold the engine support bracket to the subframe. On the other side it is only necessary to release the nuts from the support rubber

Ensure the nut holding the lead to the starter motor is undone, and the lead removed

An important point to watch when reassembling the engine is that the earth strap is properly connected. Otherwise the engine may not start

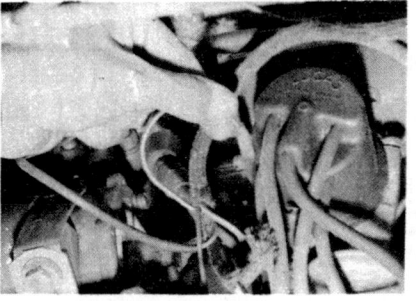

The wire leading to the side of the distributor is disconnected by simply pulling the lucar connector away

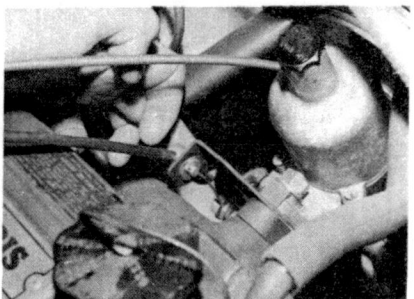

Remember to release the S.U. carburettor accelerator cable from its clamp on the throttle arm if the engine is being removed complete with carburettor

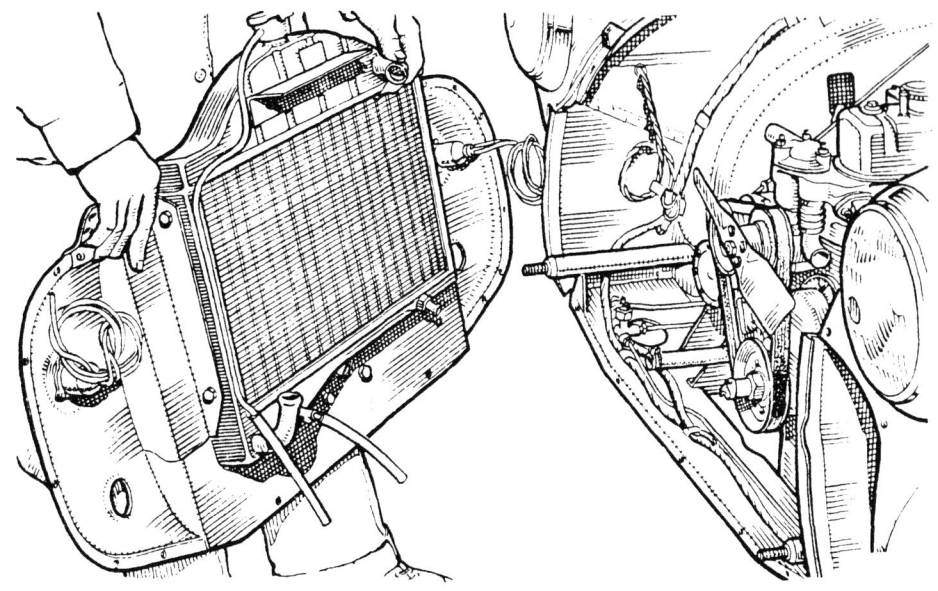

Above: The radiator and radiator surround can be completely removed
Below: .The engine and gearbox coming out with the aid of suitable lifting tackle

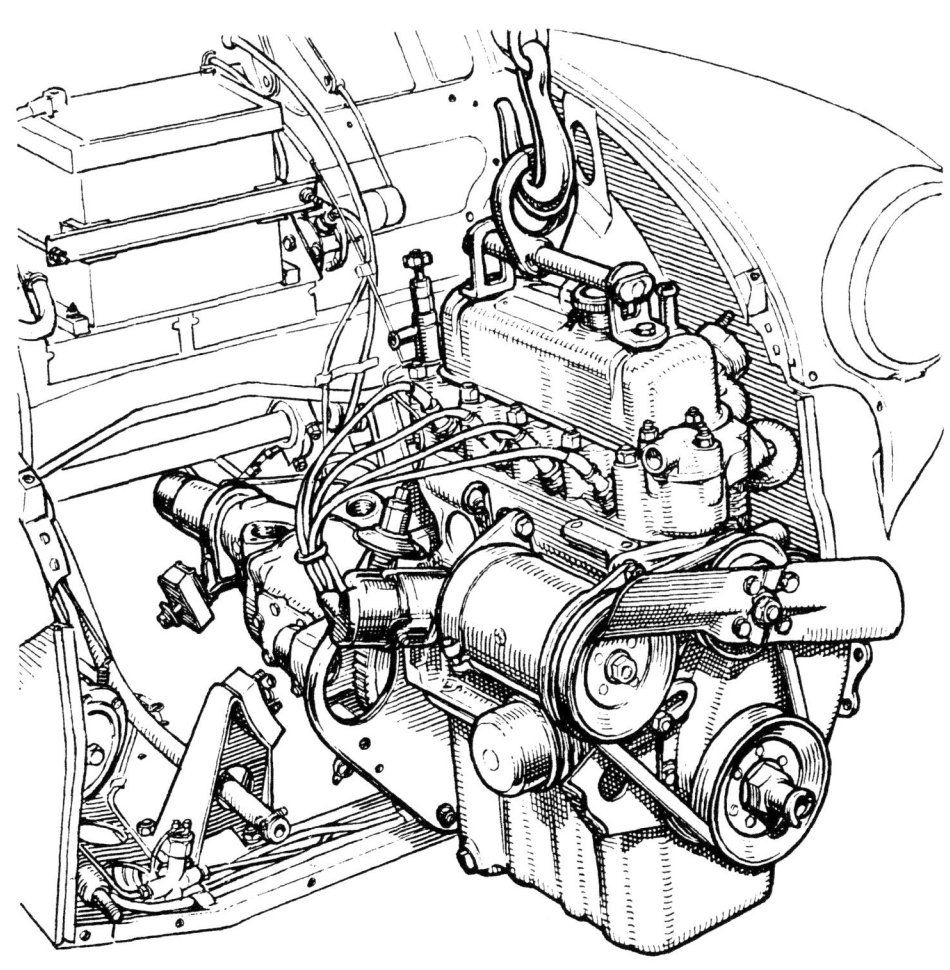

from beneath the car.

a) Unscrew the securing nut and washer holding each of the two engine mounting rubbers to the engine mounting bracket.

b) Lift the engine approximately an inch and unscrew the four bolts holding each of the engine mounting brackets to the chassis frame. Remove the two brackets.

c) Move the engine forward to free the gearbox first motion shaft and then lower the engine onto a suitable trolley and pull it out from under the car.

21 Practical experience has proved that it is often helpful to remove the oil cleaner by unscrewing the centre bolt, as the cleaner easily fouls the steering column, except on the Morris 1000.

ENGINE REMOVAL WITH GEARBOX

The procedure for removing the engine and gearbox together is the same as for removing the engine without the gearbox up to para. 16 in the preceeding section. There is one alteration, and this is that there is no necessity to remove the starter motor. The following additional sequence should now be applied to all models:-

1. Drain the oil from the gearbox by removing the drain plug on the underside of the gearbox. It is essential that this operation is not skipped as failure to drain the gearbox will result in oil pouring out from the rear gearbox extension when the propeller shaft is removed and the gearbox is tilted for removal.

2. Unscrew the speedo. cable from the gearbox.

3. The following sequence of operations applies to all models of the Sprite, Midget, and A.40. See para. 4 for details for Morris Minor 1000, and para. 5 for A.35. :-

a) Remove the carpeting from around the gearbox tunnel and remove the gearlever cover by unscrewing the securing set screws. Unscrew the bolts retaining the gearlever plate and the anti-rattle plunger and then lift out the gearlever.

b) Release the gearbox mounting bracket from the bodyframe by removing the four set bolts and spring washers which retain it in place. Two are located one on each side of the propeller shaft tunnel, and two underneath it.

c) While underneath the car, remove the two bolts and spring washers which secure the clutch operating cylinder to the bell housing or if difficulty is experienced here, release the hydraulic pipe at the operating cylinder end. Lose as little hydraulic fluid as possible by immediately plugging the open end of the pipe.

d) Also, while under the car, examine the accessability of the propeller shaft at the gearbox end. If the propeller shaft tunnel is boxed in it will not be possible to slide the propeller shaft onto the gearbox drive shaft when the engine and gearbox is refitted in the car. In this case mark the flange of the propeller

shaft to the rear axle flange to ensure assembly in the same relative position, remove the four nuts and bolts holding the flanges together and remove the propeller shaft rearwards.

e) With lifting tackle connected to the lifting hooks or slung round the engine firmly and securely, raise the engine slightly and then pull forwards and up. The engine and gearbox will then come out together with the gearbox mounting bracket still attached to the gearbox nosepiece. On the Austin A.40 it is helpful to have a trolley-jack under the gearbox as the power unit comes out at a very steep angle in order to clear the top front body cross member, which is not removable.

4. The following applies to the Morris Minor 1000:-

a) Release the two nuts which hold the front bumper in place and remove the bumper.

b) It is necessary to remove the complete radiator grille and surrounds. First, remove the chromium-plated grille surround by releasing the three 2 B.A. nuts found on the inside of the wings. This will expose the nuts and bolts which hold the grille assembly and surround in place. Release them, disconnect the operating rod from the bonnet catch arm by removing the split pin and spring washer, and separate the snap connectors on the wiring harness to the sidelights, found in the wings.

c) The radiator grille and surrounds can now be lifted away.

d) As the clutch is not hydraulically actuated it is necessary to remove the clutch mechanical linkage. First, remove the clutch return spring from the engine rear plate. Extract the split pins and washers from the two rods and remove them from the clutch levers. Remove the relay lever bracket from the body by releasing the two bolts and spring washers which hold it in place. Remove the relay clutch shaft by releasing the two bolts which hold it in place against the gearbox.

e) Support the engine with lifting tackle connected to the lifting hooks or slung round the power unit.

f) Pull back the carpet over the gearbox, release the screws holding the gearbox cover in place, lift off the cover, remove the gearlever retaining plate by unscrewing the three retaining bolts and lift away the gearlever.

g) Cars after chassis number 264013 will have an engine steady cable connected from the rear cross member to a bracket on the gearbox flange held by three bolts. To remove the cable which provides longitudinal support to the engine and gearbox, first unscrew the locking and adjusting nuts on the cable from the bracket on the cross member. The opposite end of the cable is mated to a cast screw thread which screws into the engine steady bracket. Unscrew the cable by means of the flats on the cast cable end.

h) Unscrew the nuts and spring and flat washers from each of the two gearbox mounting rubbers which secure the mounting rubbers to the cross members.

i) Remove the four bolts which hold the cross member to the bodyframe and NOTE that the front bolt on the left-hand side also supports the engine earthing cable. Lower the gearbox and remove the cross member.

j) Remove the two nuts and spring washers on either side of the engine which secure the engine front plate to the engine mounting rubbers. Remove the four nuts and spring washers which hold the left-hand engine mounting bracket to the bodyframe, and lift the engine up and slightly to the left to clear the studs in the rubber engine mounting on the right, and lift away the left-hand bracket.

k) Lift the engine and gearbox forward out of the car.

NB. The propeller shaft tunnel is not enclosed under the car and there is, therefore, no need to remove the propeller shaft.

5. The following applies to the Austin A.35:-

a) As the clutch is not hydraulically operated, it is necessary to remove the clutch mechanical linkage. Unscrew the two nuts and bolts from the clutch pedal shaft support flange, and the two bolts from the inner flange. Remove the pin in the outer spherical bush and free the shaft by sliding it away from the gearbox. Release the engine mounting brackets as detailed in para. 20 of the preceeding section.

b) Mark the flange of the propeller shaft to the rear axle flange to ensure reassembly in the same relative position, remove the four nuts and bolts holding the flanges together and remove the propeller shaft rearwards.

c) Remove the two bolts which secure the gearbox mounting bracket to the bodyframe (one each side of the propeller shaft tunnel) and unscrew the nuts securing the cross member.

d) Lower the engine and gearbox onto a suitable trolley and pull it out from under the car.

DISMANTLING THE ENGINE - GENERAL

It is best to mount the engine on a dismantling stand, but as this is frequently not available, then it is best to stand the engine on a strong bench so as to be at a comfortable working height. Failing this, it can be stripped down on the floor. During the dismantling process the greatest care should be taken to keep the exposed parts free from dirt. As an aid to achieving this aim, it is a very sound scheme to thoroughly clean down the outside of the engine, removing all traces of oil and congealed dirt. A good grease solvent such as 'Gunk' will make the job much easier, as, after the solvent has been applied and allowed to stand for a time, a vigorous jet of water will wash off the solvent and all the grease and dirt. If the dirt is thick and deeply embedded, work the solvent into it with a wire brush.

Finally wipe down the exterior of the engine with a clean rag and only then, when it is finally quite free from dirt, should the dismantling process begin. As the engine is stripped, clean each part in a bath of paraffin or petrol. Never immerse parts with oilways in paraffin, i.e. the crankshaft, but to clean wipe down carefully with a petrol damped rag. Oilways can be cleaned out with pipe cleaners. If an air line is present all parts can be blown dry and the oilways blown through as an added precaution.

Re-use of old engine gaskets ia a false economy and can give rise to oil and water leaks, if nothing worse. To avoid the possibility of trouble after the engine has been reassembled always use new gaskets throughout. Do not throw the old gaskets away as it sometimes happens that an immediate replacement cannot be found and the old gasket is then very useful as a template. Hang up the old gaskets as they are removed on a suitable hook or nail.

To strip the engine it is best to work from the top down. The sump provides a firm base on which the engine can be supported in an upright position. When the stage where the sump must be removed is reached, the engine can be turned on its side and all other work carried out with it in this position.

Wherever possible, replace nuts and bolts and washers finger-tight from wherever they were removed. This helps avoid later loss and muddle. If they cannot be replaced then lay them out in such a fashion that it is clear from where they were removed.

REMOVING ANCILLIARY ENGINE COMPONENTS

Before basic engine dismantling begins it is necessary to strip it of ancilliary components and these are as follows:-

Dynamo
Distributor
Thermostat
Oil filter assembly and pipe
Inlet manifold and carburettor/s
Exhaust manifold
Mechanical fuel pump (where fitted)

It is possible to strip all these items with the engine in the car if it is merely the individual items that require attention. Presuming the engine to be out of the car on the bench, starting on the right-hand side of the unit, follow the procedure detailed below:-

1. Slacken off the dynamo retaining bolts and remove the unit with its support brackets.

2. To remove the distributor first disconnect the manifold vacuum advance/retard pipe which leads from the small securing clip at the rear of the cylinder head. Unscrew the clamp bolt at the base of the distributor and lift the distributor away from its base plate and drive shaft.

3. Remove the thermostat cover by releasing the three nuts and spring washers which hold it in position and then remove the gasket and thermostat unit.

4. Unscrew the bolts on the oil pipe leading from the filter to the block and remove the pipe. Mask

over the hole left in the block with masking tape or block it with a clean piece of rag.

5. Remove the oil filter assembly by unscrewing the two retaining bolts which hold it to the block. The right-hand side of the engine is now stripped of all ancilliary equipment.

6. Inlet manifold and carburettors. Moving to the left - hand side of the engine, remove the inlet manifold complete w i t h carburettor/s if this item has not already been removed, by unscrewing the brass nuts and washers holding the manifolds to the cylinder head.

7. Mechanical fuel pump. Remove the mechanical fuel pump by unscrewing the two retaining bolts which hold it to the block and release it from the petrol feed pipe to the carburettor. In the case of Morris cars fitted with an S. U. electrical fuel pump the hole in the block will be blanked over with a masking plate.

The engine is now stripped of all ancilliary comonents and is ready for major dismantling to begin.

CYLINDER HEAD REMOVAL - ENGINE ON BENCH

Remove cylinder head in the following manner: -

1. Release the clips on the small hose between the water pump and the cylinder head and remove the hose. In cases of extreme difficulty, and providing a replacement hose is available, cut the hose in half.

2. Unscrew the two rocker cover bolts and lift the rocker cover and gasket away.

3. Unscrew the rocker pedestal nuts (four) and the nine main cylinder head nuts half a turn at a time in the order shown in the Fig. No. 1 : 10. When all the nuts are no longer under tension they may be screwed off the cylinder head one at a time.

4. Remove the rocker assembly complete, and place it on one side.

5. Remove the push rods, keeping them in the relative order in which they were removed. T h e easiest way to do this is to push them through a sheet of thick paper or thin card in the correct sequence.

6. The cylinder head can now be removed by lifting upwards. If the head is jammed, try to rock it to break the seal. Under no circumstances try to prise it apart from the block with a screwdriver or cold chisel as damage may be done to the faces of the head or block. If the head will not readily free, turn the engine over by the flywheel as the compression in the cylinders will often break the cylinder head joint. If this fails to work, strike the head sharply with a plastic headed hammer, or with a wooden hammer, or with a metal hammer with an intersposed piece of wood to cushion the blows. Under no circumstances hit the head directly with a metal hammer as this may cause the iron casting to fracture. Several sharp taps with the hammer at the same time pulling upwards should free the head. Lift the head off and place on one side.

CYLINDER HEAD REMOVAL - ENGINE IN CAR

To remove the cylinder head with the engine still in the car the following additional procedure to that above must be followed. This procedure should be carried out before that listed above.

1. Disconnect the battery by removing the lead from the positive terminal.

2. Drain the water by turning the taps at the base of the radiator, and at the bottom left-hand corner of the cylinder block.

3. Loosen the clip at the thermostat housing end on the top water hose, and pull the hose from the thermostat housing pipe.

4. Remove the small water pump to cylinder head by-pass hose.

5. Remove the heater / demister unit inlet hose by releasing the clip securing it to the cylinder head (on cars with heater/demister units.).

6. If twin carburettors are fitted it is easier to leave them in position and release the accelerator and choke cables at the carburettor end. For the Morris Minor, A. 35, and A. 40 it is easier to remove the air cleaner and carburettor by removing the securing bolts to the inlet manifold.

The procedure is now the same as for removing the cylinder head when on the bench. One tip worth noting is that should the cylinder head refuse to free easily, the battery can be reconnected up, and the engine turned over on the solenoid switch. Under no circumstances turn the ignition on where an S.U. electrical fuel pump is fitted unless the wire to the pump is disconnected, and ensure that the distributor cap is removed as otherwise the engine might fire.

VALVE REMOVAL

The valves can be removed from the cylinder head by the following method. With a pair of pliers remove the spring circlips holding the two halves of the split tapered collets together. Compress each spring in turn with a valve spring compressor until the two halves of the collets can be removed. Release the compressor and remove the spring, shroud, and valve.

If, when the valve spring compressor is screwed down, the valve spring retaining cap refuses to free and expose the split collet, do not continue to screw down on the compressor as there is a likelihood of damaging it. Gently tap the top of the tool directly over the cap with a light hammer. This will free the cap. To avoid the compressor jumping off the valve spring retaining cap when it is tapped, hold the compressor firmly in position with one hand.

Slide the rubber oil control seal off the top of each valve stem and then drop out each valve through the combustion chamber.

It is essential that the valves are kept in their correct sequence unless they are so badly worn that they are to be renewed. If they are going to be kept and used again, place them in a sheet of card having eight holes numbered 1 to 8 corresponding with the relative positions the valves were in when fitted. Also keep the valve springs, washers, etc. in the correct order.

Fig. 1:1. KEY TO MAIN STATIC ENGINE COMPONENTS

1 Block—cylinder
2 Plug—core hole
3 Plug—oil relief valve passage
4 Plug—oil gallery
5 Stud—long—cylinder head
6 Stud—short—cylinder head
7 Stud—blanking plate
8 Stud—rear dynamo bracket
9 Stud—long—water pump body
10 Stud—short—water pump body
11 Restrictor—camshaft oil feed
12 Dowel—main bearing cap
13 Plug—rear main bearing cap
14 Pipe—rear main bearing cap drain
15 Bolt—main bearing cap
16 Lock washer—bolt
17 Cover—rear
18 Joint—cover
19 Screw—cover
20 Tap—water drain
21 Washer—tap
22 Plug—oil priming
23 Washer—copper—plug
24 Union—oil gauge pipe
25 Washer—copper—union
26 Cylinder head
27 Plug—oil hole
28 Stud—long—rocker bracket
29 Stud—short—rocker bracket
30 Washer—rocker bracket stud
31 Spring washer—rocker bracket stud
32 Nut—rocker bracket stud
33 Stud—water outlet elbow
34 Stud—short—exhaust manifold
35 Stud—medium—exhaust manifold
36 Stud—long—exhaust manifold
37 Stud—heater tap hole plate
38 Joint—cylinder head
39 Washer—cylinder head stud
40 Nut—cylinder head stud
41 Cover—cylinder block front
42 Felt—cover
43 Joint—cover
44 Screw—to front bearer plate

45 Washer—plain—screw
46 Spring washer—screw
47 Screw—to bearer plate and block
48 Washer—plain—screw
49 Spring washer—screw
50 Cover with elbow—front—block side
51 Cover—rear—block side
52 Joint—covers
53 Screw—to block
54 Washer—fibre—screw
55 Pipe—with clip—fume vent
56 Screw—clip
57 Spring washer—screw
58 Plate—blanking
59 Joint—to block
60 Spring washer—stud
61 Nut—stud
62 Cover—rocker gear
63 Cap with cable
64 Joint—cover
65 Cap nut
66 Bush—rubber—cap nut
67 Cup washer—nut
68 Washer—bracket—height adjusting
69 Cover plate—heater control tap
70 Joint—cover plate
71 Spring washer—cover plate stud
72 Nut—stud
73 Housing—distributor
74 Screw—to block
75 Washer—shakeproof—screw
76 Screw—distributor to housing
78 Pipe—ignition control
79 Olive—pipe
80 Nut—pipe—carburettor end
81 Nut—pipe—distributor end
82 Clip—pipe
83 Valve—oil relief
84 Spring—valve
85 Cap—valve
86 Washer—fibre—cap
87 Screw—to bearing cap
88 Washer—shakeproof—screw

89 Sump
90 Joint—R.H.—sump
91 Joint—L.H.—sump
92 Plug—drain
93 Washer—plug
94 Seal—main bearing cap
95 Indicator—oil level
96 Screw—to block
97 Washer—screw
98 Elbow—water outlet
99 Joint—elbow
100 Spring washer—stud
101 Nut—stud
102 Thermostat
103 Joint—thermostat
104 Adaptor—by-pass
105 Connection—adaptor
106 Clip—connection
107 Body—water pump
108 Plug—body
109 Washer—fibre—plug
110 Spindle with vane
111 Spring
112 Cup—spring locating
113 Seal—rubber
114 Distance piece
115 Seal
116 Retainer—outer—for felt
117 Felt
118 Retainer—inner—for felt
119 Bearing
120 Distance piece—bearing
121 Retainer—bearing grease
122 Circlip—retainer
123 Pulley
124 Key—pulley
125 Washer—spindle
126 Nut—spindle
127 Joint—to block
128 Spring washer—pump stud
129 Nut—pump stud
130 Blade—fan
131 Screw—to pulley
132 Spring washer—screw

133 Belt—fan
134 Bracket—dynamo—rear
135 Spring washer—bracket stud
136 Nut—bracket stud
137 Pillar—adjusting link
138 Spring washer—pillar
139 Nut—pillar
140 Link—dynamo adjusting
141 Screw—link to dynamo
142 Spring washer—screw
143 Washer—link to pillar
144 Spring washer—link to pillar
145 Nut—link to pillar
146 Bolt—dynamo to bracket
147 Spring washer—bolt
148 Nut—bolt
149 Bolt—dynamo to water pump body
150 Spring washer—bolt
151 Nut—bolt
152 Pulley—dynamo
153 Fan—dynamo
163 Washer—large—clamping
164 Washer—small
165 Nut—stud
168 Plate—front bearer
169 Joint—to block
170 Screw—to block
171 Spring washer—screw
172 Screw—to main bearing cap
173 Plate—locking—cap screw
174 Block—rubber—front mounting
175 Nut—to plate
176 Spring washer—nut
177 Nut—to front mounting bracket
178 Spring washer—nut
185 Plate—rear bearer—gearbox
186 Dowel—top—to block
187 Dowel—bottom—to block
188 Joint—to block
189 Screw—to block
190 Spring washer—screw

24

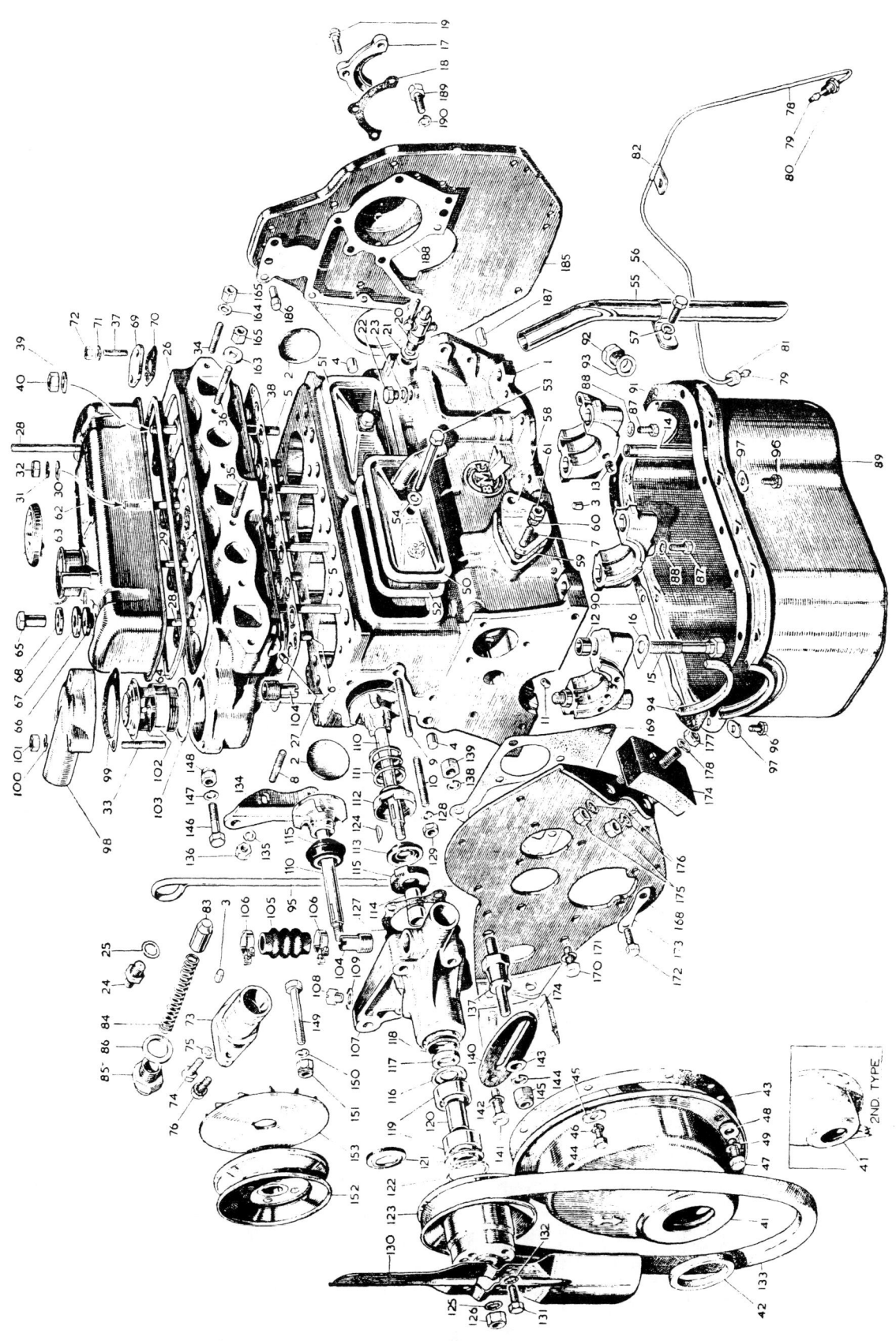

Fig. 1:2. KEY TO MAIN MOVING ENGINE COMPONENTS

1   Liner—front camshaft bearing
2   Bearing—crankshaft main
3   Thrust washer—upper—crankshaft
4   Thrust washer—lower—crankshaft
5   Piston assembly
6   Ring—compression—piston—first and third
7   Ring—scraper—piston—bottom
8   Pin—gudgeon
9   Guide—inlet valve
10 Guide—exhaust valve
11 Valve—inlet
12 Valve—exhaust
13 Spring—valve
14 Oil seal—valve
15 Cup—valve spring
16 Retainer—valve cap
17 Circlip—valve retainer
18 Shroud—guide and oil seal retainer
19 Shaft—valve rocker
20 Ring—compression—piston—second
21 Plug—screwed—rocker shaft
22 Bracket—tapped hole—shaft
23 Bracket—shaft
24 Rocker—valve
25 Bush—rocker
26 Screw—tappet adjusting
27 Locknut—adjusting screw
28 Spring—rocker
29 Washer—D/C—rocker
30 Washer—plain—rocker

31 Split pin—rocker
32 Screw—rocker locating
33 Plate—locating screw
34 Tappet—valve
35 Push rod—tappet
36 Crankshaft
37 Restrictor—crankshaft—oil
38 Bush—drive gear
39 Gear—crankshaft
40 Key—gear and pulley
41 Washer—gear packing
42 Thrower—crankshaft oil
43 Pulley—crankshaft
45 Lock washer—nut
46 Rod and cap—connecting—1 and 3
47 Rod and cap—connecting—2 and 4
48 Bolt—cap
49 Lock washer—cap bolt
50 Bearing—connecting rod
51 Screw—gudgeon pin clamp
52 Spring washer—clamp screw
53 Flywheel
54 Ring—flywheel starter
55 Dowel—flywheel to clutch
56 Screw—flywheel to crankshaft
57 Lock washer—screw
58 Camshaft
59 Pin—oil pump drive
60 Plate—camshaft locating
61 Screw—plate to block

62 Washer—shakeproof—screw
63 Gear—camshaft
64 Ring—gear tensioner
65 Key—gear
66 Nut—camshaft
67 Lock washer—nut
68 Chain—timing
69 Spindle—distributor drive
70 Body—oil pump
71 Shaft with inner rotor—pump
73 Cover—pump
74 Screw—pump cover
75 Spring washer—screw
76 Joint—pump to block
77 Bolt—pump to block
78 Lock washer—bolt
96 Plug—plain
97 Plate—rocker bracket stud
98 Washer—lock
99 Body
100 Rotor
101 Vanes
102 Sleeve—rotor
103 Cover
104 Bolt—cover
105 Washer—bolt
106 Bolt—body
107 Washer—bolt
108 Washer—lock—oil pump

26

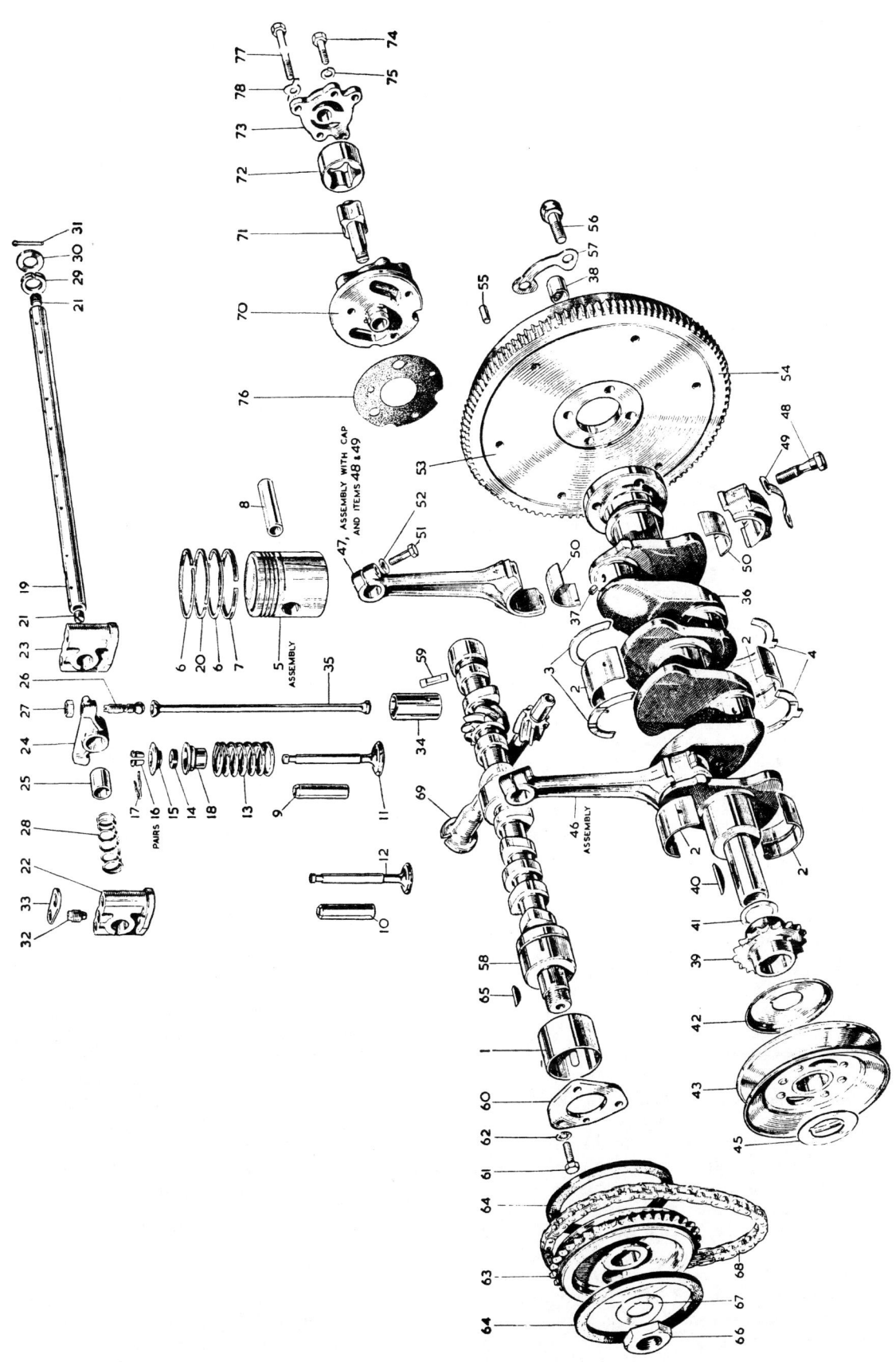

VALVE GUIDE REMOVAL

If it is wished to remove the valve guides they can be removed from the cylinder head in the following manner. Place the cylinder head with the gasket face on the bench and with a suitable hard steel punch drift the guides out of the cylinder head.

DISMANTLING THE ROCKER ASSEMBLY

To dismantle the rocker assembly, release the rocker shaft locating screw, remove the split pins, flat washers, and spring washers from each end of the shaft and slide from the shaft the pedestals, rocker arms, and rocker spacing springs.

TIMING COVER, GEARS & CHAIN REMOVAL

The timing cover, gears, and chain can be removed with the engine in the car providing the radiator and fan belt are removed. The procedure for removing the timing cover, gears and chain is otherwise the same irrespective of whether the engine is in the car or on the bench, and is as follows:-

1. Bend back the locking tab of the crankshaft pulley locking washer under the crankshaft pulley retaining bolt, or the starter handle dog in the case of the Morris Minor, and with a large spanner remove the bolt and locking washer.

2. Placing two large screwdrivers behind the camshaft pulley wheel at 180° to each other, carefully lever the wheel off. It is preferable to use a proper pulley extractor if this is available, but large screwdrivers or tyre levers are quite suitable, providing care is taken not to damage the pulley flange.

3. Remove the woodruff key from the crankshaft nose with a pair of pliers and note how the channel in the pulley is designed to fit over it. Place the woodruff key in a glass jam jar as it is a very small part and can easily become lost.

4. Unscrew the bolts holding the timing cover to the block. NOTE That four of the bolts are larger than the others, and that each bolt makes use of a large flat washer as well as a spring washer.

5. Pull off the timing cover and gasket.

6. With the timing cover off, take off the oil thrower. NOTE That the concave side faces forward.

7. Bend back the locking tab on the washer under the camshaft retaining nut and unscrew the nut noting how the locking washer locating tag fits in the camshaft gearwheel keyway.

8. To remove the camshaft and crankshaft timing wheels complete with chain, ease each wheel forward a little at a time levering behind each gearwheel in turn with two large screwdrivers at 180° to each other. If the gearwheels are locked solid then it will be necessary to use a proper gearwheel and pulley extractor, and if one is available this should be used anyway in preference to screwdrivers. With both gearwheels safely off, remove the woodruff keys from the crankshaft and camshaft with a pair of pliers and place them in the jam jar for safe keeping. Note the number of very thin packing washers behind the crankshaft gearwheel and remove them very carefully.

CAMSHAFT REMOVAL

The camshaft can be removed with the engine in place in the car, or with the engine on the bench. If the camshaft is to be removed with the engine in the car, the radiator and fan belt must be removed after the cooling system has been drained. The timing cover, gears and chain, must be removed as detailed in the previous section. It is also necessary to remove the distributor drive gear as detailed in the following section. With the drive gear out of the way, proceed in the following manner:-

1. Remove the three bolts and spring washers which hold the camshaft locating plate to the block. The bolts are normally covered by the camshaft gearwheel.

2. Remove the plate. The camshaft can now be withdrawn. Take great care to remove the camshaft gently, and in particular ensure that the cam peaks do not damage the camshaft bearings as the shaft is pulled forward.

DISTRIBUTOR DRIVE REMOVAL

To remove the distributor drive with the sump still in position it is first necessary to remove one of the tappet cover bolts. With the distributor and the distributor clamp plate already removed, this is achieved as follows:-

1. Unscrew the single retaining bolt and lock washer to release the distributor housing.

2. With the distributor housing removed, if the sump is still in position screw into the end of the distributor drive shaft a $5/16$th in. U. N. F. bolt. A tappet cover bolt is ideal for this purpose. The drive shaft can then be lifted out, the shaft being turned slightly in the process to free the shaft skew gear from the camshaft skew gear.

3. If the sump has already been removed then it is a simple matter to push the drive shaft out from inside the crankcase.

SUMP, PISTON, CONNECTING ROD & BIG END

BEARING REMOVAL

The sump, pistons, and connecting rods can be removed with the engine still in the car or with the engine on the bench. If in the car, proceed as for removing the cylinder head with the engine in the car. If on the bench proceed as for removing the cylinder head with the engine in this position. The pistons and connecting rods are drawn up out of the top of the cylinder bores.

1. Remove the bolts and washers holding the sump in position. Remove the sump and the sump gasket.

2. Unscrew the oil suction pipe at the cylinder block.

3. The two bolts holding the oil cleaner support bracket (one on the centre and one on the rear main bearing caps) should now be unscrewed. The bracket complete with the strainer can now be lifted away giving clear access to the big end bolts.

4. Knock back with a cold chisel the locking tabs on the big end retaining bolts, and remove the bolts and locking tabs.

5. Remove the big end caps one at a time, taking care to keep them in the right order and the correct way round. Also ensure that the shell bearings are also kept with their correct connecting rods and caps unless they are to be renewed. Normally, the numbers 1 to 4 are stamped on adjacent sides of the big end caps and connecting rods, indicating which cap fits on which rod and which way round the cap fits. If no numbers or lines can be found then with a sharp screwdriver scratch mating marks across the joint from the rod to the cap. One line for connecting rod No. 1, two for connecting rod No. 2, and so on. This will ensure there is no confusion later as it is most important that the caps go back in the correct position on the connecting rods from which they were removed.

6. If the big end caps are difficult to remove they may be gently tapped with a soft hammer.

7. To remove the shell bearings, press the bearing opposite the groove in both the connecting rod, and the connecting rod caps and the bearings will slide out easily.

8. Withdraw the pistons and connecting rods upwards and ensure they are kept in the correct order for replacement in the same bore. Refit the connecting rod caps and bearings to the rods if the bearings do not require renewal to minimise the risk of getting the caps and rods muddled.

GUDGEON PIN

Two different types of gudgeon pin retention are employed, depending on the age of the engine.

To remove the gudgeon pin to free the piston from the connecting rod on early models, it is merely necessary to remove the little end bolt and lockwasher. With the bolt removed the gudgeon pin should push out through either side of the piston. If it shows reluctance to move, then on no account force it out, as this could damage the piston. Immerse the piston in a pan of boiling water for three minutes. On removal the expansion of the aluminium should allow the gudgeon pin to slide out easily.

On later engines, fully floating gudgeon pins are fitted, and these are retained in the pistons by circlips at each end of the pin. To extract the pin, remove the circlips at one end and push the pin out, immersing it in boiling water if it appears reluctant to move. Make sure the pins are kept with the same piston for ease of refitting.

PISTON RING REMOVAL

To remove the piston rings, slide them carefully over the top of the piston, taking care not to scratch the aluminium alloy. Never slide them off the bottom of the piston skirt. It is very easy to break the piston rings if they are pulled off roughly so this operation should be done with extreme caution. It is helpful to make use of an old hacksaw blade, or better still,

an old .020 in. feeler gauge. Lift one end of the piston ring to be removed out of its groove and insert the end of the feeler gauge under it. Turn the feeler gauge slowly round the piston and as the ring comes out of its groove apply slight upward pressure so that it rests on the land above. It can then be eased off the piston with the feeler gauge stopping it from slipping into any empty grooves if it is any but the top piston ring that is being removed.

FLYWHEEL & ENGINE END PLATE REMOVAL

Having removed the clutch (see Chapter 5) the flywheel and engine end plate can be removed. It is only possible for this operation to be carried out with the engine out of the car.

1. Bend back the locking tabs from the four bolts which hold the flywheel to the flywheel flange on the rear of the crankshaft.

2. Unscrew the bolts and remove them, complete with the two locking plates.

3. Lift the flywheel away from the crankshaft flange. NOTE - Some difficulty may be experienced in removing the bolts by the rotation of the crankshaft every time pressure is put on the spanner. The only answer is to lock the crankshaft in position while the bolts are removed. To lock the crankshaft a wooden wedge can be inserted between the crankshaft and the side of the block inside the crankcase.

4. The engine end plate is held in position by a number of bolts and spring washers of varying size. Release the bolts noting where different sizes fit and place them together to ensure none of them become lost. Lift away the end plate from the block complete with the paper gasket.

CRANKSHAFT & MAIN BEARING REMOVAL

Drain the engine oil, remove the timing gears and remove the sump, the oil gauze filter, and suction pipe, and the big end bearings, flywheel and engine end plate as had already been detailed. Removal of the crankshaft can only be attempted with the engine on the bench.

1. Release the locking tabs from the six bolts which hold the three main bearing caps in place.

2. Unscrew the bolts and remove them together with the locking plates.

3. Remove the two bolts which hold the front main bearing cap against the engine front plate.

4. Remove the main bearing caps and the bottom half of each bearing shell, taking care to keep the bearing shells in the right caps.

5. When removing the centre bearing cap, NOTE the bottom semi-circular halves of the thrust washers, one half lying on either side of the main bearing. Lay them with the centre bearing along the correct side.

6. Slightly rotate the crankshaft to free the upper halves of the bearing shells and thrust washers which should now be extracted and placed over the correct bearing cap.

7. Remove the crankshaft by lifting it away from the crankcase.

LUBRICATION SYSTEM

A forced feed system of lubrication is fitted with oil circulated round the engine from the sump below the block. The level of engine oil in the sump is indicated on the dipstick which is fitted on the right hand side of the engine. It is marked to indicate the optimum level which is the maximum mark. The level of oil in the sump, ideally, should not be above or below this line. Oil is replenished via the filler cap on the front of the rocker cover.

The oil pump is mounted at the end of the crankcase and is driven by the camshaft. Three different types of oil pump have been fitted at different times. These are the Burman rotary vane type, or the Hobourn Eaton or Concentric (Engineering) Ltd. concentric rotor type. All are of the non-draining variety to allow rapid pressure build-up when starting from cold.

Oil is drawn from the sump through a gauze screen in the oil strainer and is sucked up the pick-up pipe and drawn into the oil pump. From the oil pump it is forced under pressure along a gallery on the right-hand side of the engine, and through drillings to the big end, main and camshaft bearings. A small hole in each connecting rod allows a jet of oil to lubricate the cylinder wall with each revolution.

From the camshaft front bearing oil is fed through drilled passages in the cylinder block and head to the front rocker pedestal where it enters the hollow rocker shaft. Holes drilled in the shaft allow for the lubrication of the rocker arms, and the valve stems and push rod ends. This oil is at a reduced pressure to the oil delivered to the crankshaft bearings. Oil from the front camshaft bearing also lubricates the timing gears and the timing chain. Oil returns to the sump by various passages, the tappets being lubricated by oil returning via the push rod drillings in the block.

On all models a full flow oil filter is fitted, and all oil passes through this filter before it reaches the main oil gallery. The oil is passed directly from the oil pump across the block to an external pipe on the right-hand side of the engine which feeds into the filter head.

OIL FILTER REMOVAL & REPLACEMENT

The full flow oil filter fitted to all engines is located three quarters of the way down the right-hand side of the engine towards the front. It is removed by unscrewing the long centre bolt which holds the filter bowl in place. With the bolt released (use a 9/16 A.F. spanner) carefully lift away the filter bowl which contains the filter and will also be full of oil. It is helpful to have a large basin under the filter body to catch the amount which is bound to spill.

Throw the old filter element away and thoroughly clean down the filter bowl, the bolts and associated parts with petrol and when perfectly clean wipe dry with a non-fluffy rag.

A rubber sealing ring is located in a groove round the head of the oil filter and forms an effective leak-proof joint between the filter head and the filter

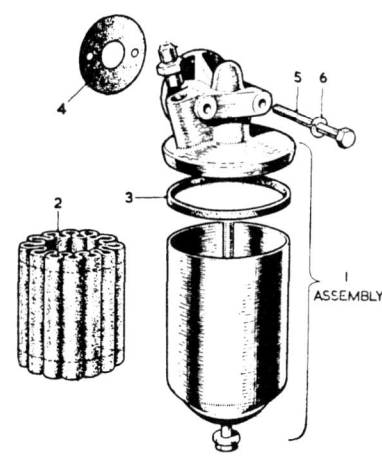

Fig. 1:2A. The component parts of the oil filter assembly. 1 Oil filter. 2 Element. 3 Joint washer. 4 Joint-Filter to cylinder block. 5 Screw. 6 Spring washer.

bowl. A new rubber sealing ring is supplied with each new filter element.

Carefully prise out the old sealing ring from the locating groove. If the ring has become hard and is difficult to move take great care not to damage the sides of the sealing ring groove.

With the old ring removed, fit the new ring in the groove at four equidistant points and press it home a segment at a time. Do not insert the ring at just one point and work round the groove pressing it home as, using this method, it is easy to stretch the ring and be left with a small loop of rubber which will not fit into the locating groove.

Reassemble the oil filter assembly by first passing up the bolt through the hole in the bottom of the bowl, with a steel washer under the bolts head and a rubber or felt washer on top of the steel washer and next to the filter bowl.

Slip the spring over the bolt inside the bowl, then the other steel washer, the remaining rubber or felt washer and lastly the filter seating plate with the concave face downwards. Slip in a new filter element and with the bolt pressed hard up against the filter bowl body (to avoid leakage) three quarter fill the bowl with engine oil.

Offer up the bowl to the rubber sealing ring and before finally tightening down the centre bolt, check that the lip of the filter bowl is resting squarely on the rubber sealing ring and is not offset and off the ring. If the bowl is not seating properly, rotate it until it is. Run the engine and check the bowl for leaks.

OIL PRESSURE RELIEF VALVE - REMOVAL & REPLACEMENT

To prevent excessive oil pressure - for example when the engine is cold - an oil pressure relief valve is built into the right-hand side of the engine at the rear just below the oil pressure unit take-off point.

The relief valve is identified externally by a

Fig. 1:3. The component parts of the oil pressure relief valve

large $^9/16$ in. domed hexagon nut. To dismantle the unit unscrew the nut and remove it, complete with the two fibre or copper sealing washers. The relief spring and the relief spring cup can then be easily extracted.

In position, the metal cup fits over the opposite end of the relief valve spring resting in the dome of the hexagon nut, and bears against a machining in the block. When the oil pressure exceeds 60 lb/sq.in. the cup is forced off its seat and the oil by-passes it and returns via a drilling directly to the sump.

Check the tension of the spring by measuring its length. If it is shorter than $2^7/8$ in. it should be replaced with a new spring. Reassembly of the relief valve unit is a reversal of the above procedure.

OIL PUMP REMOVAL & DISMANTLING

Oil pump removal is an operation which can only be carried out with the engine out of the car. Prior to removing the pump it is necessary to remove the clutch, flywheel, and engine rear plate. The oil pump engages via a lip and slot with the rear of the camshaft from which it is directly driven.

1. Bend back the locking tabs on the three securing bolts which hold the pump to the block.
2. Unscrew the bolts and remove them complete with washers.
3. The oil pump cover can now be removed, complete with drive shaft and inner rotor.
4. To dismantle either the Burman or Hobourn Eaton type of pump, merely unscrew the two bolts holding the pump end plate in position.
5. The Concentric (Engineering) Ltd. pump must not be dismantled and if suspect must be exchanged for a rebuilt unit.

A modified Hobourn Eaton oil pump was fitted to later engines and is fully interchangeable with the earlier type. The later type can be recognised by the words 'Hobourn Eaton' round the cover flange rather than round the cover centre. The new pump is identified by Part No. 2A 692 and is fully interchangeable with the old pump, identified by Part No. 2A 341.

Before engine No. 194195, only the Hobourn Eaton concentric rotor pump was used. After this engine, either the Hobourn Eaton or the Burman rotary vane type may be fitted. If it is wished to remove the vanes from the rotor on the Burman pump it should be noted that the rotor sleeve is a press fit on the rotor and should be gently prised off when the vanes can be removed.

EXAMINATION & RENOVATION - GENERAL

With the engine stripped down and all parts thoroughly cleaned, it is now time to examine everything for wear. The following items should be checked and where necessary renewed or renovated as shown below:-

CRANKSHAFT EXAMINATION & RENOVATION

Examine the crankpin and main journal surfaces for signs of scoring or scratches. Check the ovality of the crankpins at different positions with a micrometer. If more than 0.001 in. out of round, the crankpins will have to be reground. It will also have to be reground if there are any scores or scratches present. Also check the journals in the same fashion. On highly tuned engines the centre main bearing has been known to break up. This is not always immediately apparent, but slight vibration in an otherwise normally smooth engine and a very slight drop in oil pressure under normal conditions are clues. If the centre main bearing is suspected of failure it should be immediately investigated by dropping the sump and removing the centre main bearing cap. Failure to do this will result in a badly

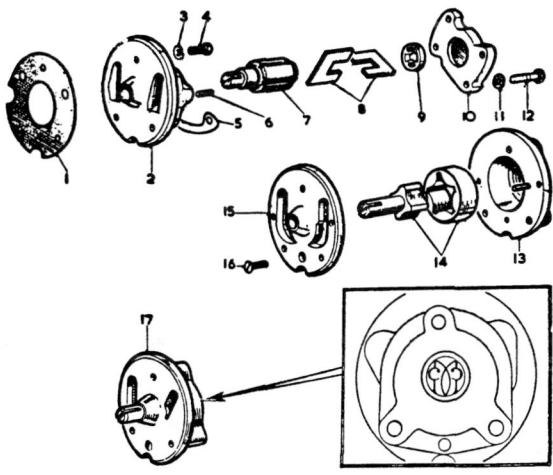

Fig. 1:4. The component parts of the three types of oil pump which may be fitted

Burman Pump		Hoburn Eaton Pump	Concentric (Engineering)
1. Joint washer	7. Rotor		17. Pump
2. Pump body	8. Vane	13. Body	Serviced
3. Washer	9. Sleeve	14. Rotor & Shaft	as an
4. Set screw	10. Body cover	15. Cover	assembly
5. Lock plate	11. Shakeproof washer	16. Screw	only
6. Dowel	12. Screw		

scored centre main journal. The following is the standard crankpin and main journal diameter with the regrind sizes available:-

	948 c.c. and 1,098 c.c.
Crankpin diameter (Standard)	1.6254 to 1.6259 in. or 41.285 to 41.298 mm.
Regrind sizes:-	-.010 in. (.254 mm.), -.020 in. (.508 mm.), -.030 in. 762 mm.). -.040 in. (1.016 mm.).
Main journal diameter (Standard)	1.7505 to 1.751 in. or 44.46 to 44.47 mm.

Regrind sizes are the same as for the crankpin regrind sizes. The crankpin and main journal diameters for both engines should not be ground less than as listed below. If it is necessary to grind below the permitted diameters a new crankshaft should be fitted.

Minimum crankpin regrind diameter	1.5854 in. (40.27 mm.).
Minimum main journal regrind diameter	1.7105 in. (43.45 mm.).

BIG END & MAIN BEARINGS - EXAMINATION & RENOVATION

Big end bearing failure is accompanied by a noisy knocking from the crankcase, and a slight drop in oil pressure. Main bearing failure is accompanied by vibration which can be quite severe as the engine speed rises and falls and a drop in oil pressure.

Bearings which have not broken up, but are badly worn will give rise to low oil pressure and some vibration. Inspect the big ends, main bearings, and thrust washers for signs of general wear, scoring, pitting, and scratches. The bearings should be mat grey in colour. With lead-indium bearings should a trace of copper colour be noticed the bearings are badly worn as the lead bearing material has worn away to expose the indium underlay. Renew the bearings if they are in this condition or if there is any sign of scoring or pitting.

Main bearings are not interchangeable between the 948 c.c. and 1,098 c.c. engines as the main journals are of a different length. The undersizes available are designed to correspond with the regrind sizes, i.e. -.010 bearings are correct for a crankshaft reground -.010 undersize. The bearings are in fact, slightly more than the stated undersize as running clearances have been allowed for during their manufacture.

Very long engine life can be achieved by changing big end bearings at intervals of 30,000 miles and main bearings at intervals of 50,000 miles, irrespective of bearing wear. Normally, crankshaft wear is infinitesimal and regular changes of bearings will ensure mileages of between 100,000 to 150,000 miles before crankshaft regrinding becomes necessary. Crankshafts normally have to be reground because of scoring due to bearing failure.

CYLINDER BORES - EXAMINATION & RENOVATION

The cylinder bores must be examined for taper, ovality, scoring and scratches. Start by carefully examining the top of the cylinder bores. If they are at all worn a very slight ridge will be found on the thrust side. This marks the top of the piston ring travel. The owner will have a good indication of the bore wear prior to dismantling the engine, or removing the cylinder head. Excessive oil consumption accompanied by blue smoke from the exhaust is a sure sign of worn cylinder bores and piston rings.

Measure the bore diameter just under the ridge with a micrometer and compare it with the diameter at the bottom of the bore, which is not subject to wear. If the difference between the two measurements is more than .006 in. then it will be necessary to fit special piston rings or to have the cylinders rebored and fit oversize pistons and rings. If no micrometer is available remove the rings from a piston and place the piston in each bore in turn about 3/4 in. below the top of the bore. If an 0.010 feeler gauge can be slid between the piston and the cylinder wall on the thrust side of the bore then remedial action must be taken. Oversize pistons are available in the following sizes:-

+.010 in. (.254 mm.), +.020 in. (.508 mm.), for 1,098 c.c. engines
+.010 in. (.254 mm.), +.020 in. (.508 mm.), +.030 in. (.762 mm.), +.040 in. (1.016 mm.) for 948 c.c. engines

These are accurately machined to just below these measurements so as to provide correct running clearances in bores bored out to the exact oversize dimensions.

If the bores are slightly worn but not so badly worn as to justify reboring, then special oil control rings can be fitted to the existing pistons which will restore compression and stop the engine burning oil. Several different types are available and the manufacturers instructions concerning their fitting must be followed closely.

PISTONS & PISTON RINGS - EXAMINATION & RENOVATION

If the old pistons are to be refitted, carefully remove the piston rings and then thoroughly clean them. Take particular care to clean out the piston ring grooves. At the same time do not scratch the aluminium in any way. If new rings are to be fitted to the old pistons then the top ring should be stepped so as to clear the ridge left above the previous top ring. If a normal but oversize new ring is fitted, it will hit the ridge and break, because the new ring will not have worn in the same way as the old, which will have worn in unison with the ridge.

Before fitting the rings on the pistons each should be inserted approximately 3 in. down the cylinder bore and the gap measured with a feeler gauge. This should be between .006 in. and .010 in. It is essential that the gap should be measured at the bottom of the ring travel, as if it is measured at the top of a worn bore and gives a perfect fit, it could easily seize at the bottom. If the ring gap is too small rub down the ends of the ring with a very fine file until the gap, when fitted, is correct. To keep the rings square in the bore for measurement line each up in turn by inserting an old piston in the bore upside down, and use the piston to push the ring down about 3 in. Remove the piston and measure the piston ring gap.

When fitting new pistons and rings to a rebored engine the piston ring gap can be measured at the top of the bore as the bore will not now taper. It is not necessary to measure the side clearance in the piston ring grooves with the rings fitted as the groove dimensions are accurately machined during manufacture. When fitting new oil control rings to old pistons it may be necessary to have the grooves widened by machining to accept the new wider rings. In this instance the manufacturers representative will make this quite clear and will supply the address to which the pistons must be sent for machining.

When new pistons are fitted, take great care to fit the exact size best suited to the particular bores in your engine. B.M.C. go one stage further than merely specifying one size of piston for all standard bores. Because of very slight differences in cylinder machining during production it is necessary to select just the right piston for the bore. Five different sizes are available for the standard bore as well as the four oversize dimensions already shown.

Examination of the cylinder block face will show adjacent to each bore a small diamond shaped box with a number stamped in the metal. Careful examination of the piston crown will show a matching diamond and number. These are the standard piston sizes and will be the same for all four bores. If standard pistons are to be refitted or standard low compression pistons changed to standard high compression pistons, then it is essential that only pistons with the same number in the diamond are used. With larger pistons, the amount oversize is stamped in an ellipse in the piston crown.

On engines with tapered second and third compression rings, the top narrow side of the ring is marked with a 'T'. Always fit this side uppermost and carefully examine all rings for this mark before fitting.

CAMSHAFT & CAMSHAFT BEARINGS - EXAMINATION & RENOVATION

Carefully examine the camshaft bearings for wear. NOTE on early engines that only the front camshaft bearing is renewable. If the bearings are obviously worn or pitted or the metal underlay is showing through, then they must be renewed. This is an operation for your local B.M.C. dealer or the local engineering works as it demands the use of specialised equipment. The bearings are removed with a special drift after which new bearings are pressed in, care being taken to ensure the oil holes in the bearings line up with those in the block. With a special tool the bearings are then reamered in position.

The camshaft itself should show no sign of wear, but, if very slight scoring on the cams is noticed, the score marks can be removed by very gentle rubbing down with very fine emery cloth. The greatest care should be taken to keep the cam profiles smooth.

VALVES & VALVE SEATS - EXAMINATION & RENOVATION

Examine the heads of the valves for pitting and burning, especially the heads of the exhaust valves. The valve seatings should be examined at the same time. If the pitting on valve and seat is very slight the marks can be removed by grinding the seats and valves together with coarse, and then fine, valve grinding paste. Where bad pitting has occured to the valve seats it will be necessary to recut them and fit new valves. If the valve seats are so worn that they cannot be recut, then it will be necessary to fit new valve seat inserts. These latter two jobs should be untrusted to the local B.M.C. agent or engineering works. In practice it is very seldom that the seats are so badly worn that they require renewal. Normally, it is the valve that is too badly worn for replacement, and the owner can easily purchase a new set of valves and match them to the seats by valve grinding.

Valve grinding is carried out as follows:-

Smear a trace of coarse carborundum paste on the seat face and apply a suction grinder tool to the valve head. With a semi-rotary motion, grind the valve head to its seat, lifting the valve occasionally to redistribute the grinding paste. When a dull matt even surface finish is produced on both the valve seat and the valve, then wipe off the paste and repeat the process with fine carborundum paste, lifting and turning the valve to redistribute the paste as before. A light spring placed under the valve head will greatly ease this operation. When a smooth unbroken ring of light grey matt finish is produced, on both valve and valve seat faces, the grinding operation is completed.

Scrape away all carbon from the valve head and the valve stem. Carefully clean away every trace of grinding compound, taking great care to leave none in the ports or in the valve guides. Clean the valves and valve seats with a paraffin soaked rag then with a clean rag, and finally, if an air line is available, blow the valves, valve guides and valve ports clean.

TIMING GEARS & CHAIN - EXAMINATION & RENOVATION

Examine the teeth on both the crankshaft gear wheel and the camshaft gearwheel for wear. Each tooth forms an inverted 'V' with the gearwheel periphery, and if worn the side of each tooth under tension will be slightly concave in shape when compared with the other side of the tooth, i.e. one side of the inverted 'V' will be concave when compared with the other. If any sign of wear is present the gearwheels must be renewed.

Examine the links of the chain for side slackness and renew the chain if any slackness is noticeable when compared with a new chain. It is a sensible precaution to renew the chain at about 60,000 miles and at a lesser mileage if the engine is stripped down for a major overhaul. The actual rollers on a very badly worn chain may be slightly grooved.

ROCKERS & ROCKER SHAFT - EXAMINATION & RENOVATION

Remove the threaded plug with a screwdriver from the end of the rocker shaft and thoroughly clean out the shaft. As it acts as the oil passage for the valve gear also ensure the oil holes in it are quite clear after having cleaned them out. Check the shaft for straightness by rolling it on the bench. It is most unlikely that it will deviate from normal, but, if it does, then a judicious attempt must be made to straighten it. If this is not successful purchase a new shaft. The surface of the shaft should be free from any worn ridges caused by the rocker arms. If any wear is present, renew the shaft. Wear is only likely to have occured if the rocker shaft oil holes have become blocked.

Check the rocker arms for wear of the rocker bushes, for wear at the rocker arm face which bears on the valve stem, and for wear of the adjusting ball ended screws. Wear in the rocker arm bush can be checked by gripping the rocker arm tip and holding the rocker arm in place on the shaft, noting if there is any lateral rocker arm shake. If shake is present, and the arm is very loose on the shaft, remedial action must be taken. Pressed steel valve rockers cannot be renovated by renewal of the rocker arm bush. It is necessary to fit new rocker arms. Forged rocker arms which have worn bushes may be taken to your local B. M. C. agent or engineering works to have the old bush drawn out and a new bush fitted. Forged rockers and pressed steel rockers are interchangeable in sets of eight, but, where one or two pressed steel rockers only require renewal it is not advised to replace them with the forged type.

Check the tip of the rocker arm where it bears on the valve head for cracking or serious wear on the case hardening. If none is present reuse the rocker arm. Check the lower half of the ball on the end of the rocker arm adjusting screw. On high performance B. M. C. engines wear on the ball and top of the pushrod is easily noted by the unworn 'pip' which fits in the small central oil hole on the ball. The larger this 'pip' the more wear has taken place to both the ball and the pushrod. Check the pushrods for straightness by rolling them on the bench. Renew any that are bent.

TAPPETS - EXAMINATION & RENOVATION

Examine the bearing surface of the tappets which lie on the camshaft. Any indentation in this surface or any cracks indicate serious wear and the tappets should be renewed. Thoroughly clean them out, removing all traces of sludge. It is most unlikely that the sides of the tappets will prove worn, but, if they are a very loose fit in their bores and can readily be rocked, they should be exchanged for new units. It is very unusual to find any wear in the tappets, and any wear present is likely to occur only at very high mileages.

FLYWHEEL STARTER RING - EXAMINATION & RENOVATION

If the teeth on the flywheel starter ring are badly worn, or if some are missing, then it will be nec-

essary to remove the ring. This is achieved by splitting the ring with a cold chisel. The greatest care should be taken not to damage the flywheel during this process.

To fit a new ring heat it gently and evenly with an oxy-acetylene flame until a temperature of approximately 350°C is reached. This is indicated by a light metalic blue surface colour. With the ring at this temperature, fit it to the flywheel with the front of the teeth facing the flywheel register. The ring should be tapped gently down onto its register and left to cool naturally when the shrinkage of the metal on cooling will ensure that it is a secure and permanent fit. Great care must be taken not to overheat the ring, as if this happens the temper of the ring will be lost.

Alternatively, your local B. M. C. agent or local engineering works may have a suitable oven in which the flywheel can be heated. The normal domestic oven will only give a temperature of about 250°C at the very most and, although it may just be possible to fit the ring with it at this temperature, it is unlikely and no great force should have to be used.

OIL PUMP - EXAMINATION & RENOVATION

It is unlikely that the oil pump will be worn, but, if the engine is fully stripped down it is only sensible to check the pump for wear. With the pump dismantled, if it is the Hobourn Eaton unit, check the rotor internally and also the drive shaft lobes for any signs of excessive wear or scoring. If wear is found, renew the worn components.

If it is the Burman pump, examine the inside of the pump body in which the vanes rotate and also the edges of the vanes for signs of scoring. If any is found renew the worn components.

CYLINDER HEAD - DECARBONISATION

This can be carried out with the engine either in or out of the car. With the cylinder head off carefully remove with a wire brush and blunt scraper all traces of carbon deposits from the combustion spaces and the ports. The valve head stems and valve guides should also be freed from any carbon deposits. Wash the combustion spaces and ports down with petrol and scrape the cylinder head surface free of any foreign matter with the side of a steel rule, or a similar article.

Clean the pistons and top of the cylinder bores. If the pistons are still in the block then it is essential that great care is taken to ensure that no carbon gets into the cylinder bores as this could scratch the cylinder walls or cause damage to the pistons and rings. To ensure this does not happen, first turn the crankshaft so that two of the pistons are at the top of their bores. Stuff rag into the other two bores or seal them off with paper and masking tape. The waterways should also be covered with small pieces of masking tape to prevent particles of carbon entering the cooling system and damaging the water pump.

There are two schools of thought as to how much carbon should be removed from the piston crown. One school recommends that a ring of carbon should

Although the engine is fairly heavy it is not difficult to carry short distances. In this case it was carried up four flights of steps to the author's workshop

Thoroughly clean the engine externally before stripping it down. Take off the rocker cover, tappet chest covers, rocker gear, and pushrods and lift off the head

The crankshaft fan belt pulley wheel can be gently eased off after the retaining bolt has been removed

The crankshaft can be prevented from turning by placing a length of wood such as a hammer handle between the crankshaft and the side of the block

The gearwheels can be removed by judicious levering with spanners or broad screwdrivers as illustrated. Move each wheel a little in turn so as not to strain the chain

The next step is to thoroughly clean the block internally. Check that the oilways are clear, and remove all traces of old gaskets

The camshaft is inserted from the front of the block. Make sure the peaks of the cams do not damage the white metal bearings

These are the component parts of the vane type oil pump. 1 - Pump body. 2 - Vanes and rotor. 3 - Cover plate. 4 - Securing bolts and lockwashers

The vanes and rotor seat in the recess in the cover. They should be fitted first to the pump body

Make sure a new gasket is properly positioned between the pump and the block. The slot in the rotor engages a raised lip in the end of the camshaft

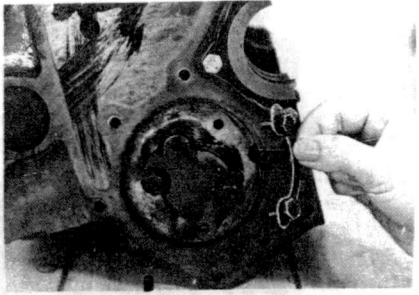

With the pump in place, fit the securing bolts and remember to turn up the tabs on the lockwasher

The pump is now securely fitted and the engine endplate can be replaced

The next step is to fit the distributor drive. This can be inserted and removed by hand providing the sump is off

The lower end of the drive fits into a recess in the block and the skew gear meshes with a similar gear on the camshaft

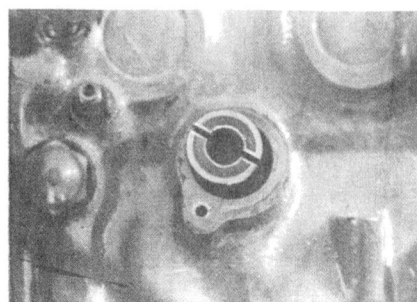

The drive head should initially be in this position to allow for rotation when fitted. N.B. On all B.M.C. 'A' Series engines except Sprite Mk. I rotate the shaft 180°

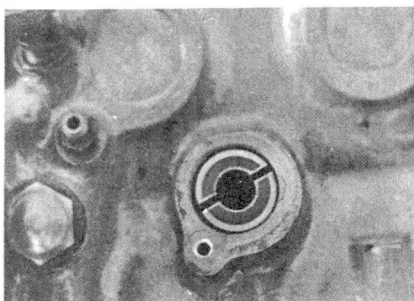

With the drive pulley home the slots should be in the 'twenty to two' position. N.B. On all B.M.C. 'A' Series engines except the Sprite Mk. I the larger segment is at the top

Next the distributor drive retaining plate is placed in position with the recessed hole lining up with the threaded hole in the flange on the block

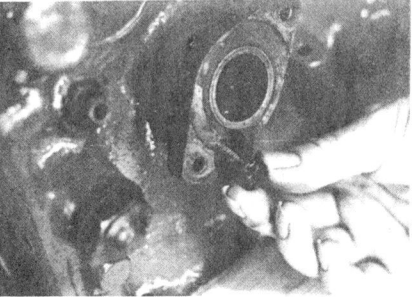

Screw in the retaining bolt and lock washer to secure the plate

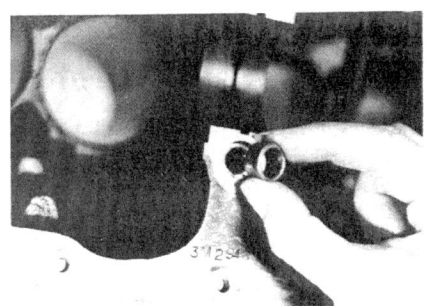

Before fitting the main bearings and crankshaft make sure the bearing cap locating dowels are in place

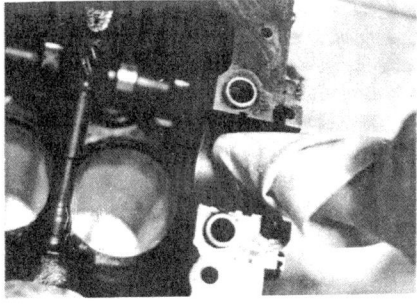

Thoroughly clean the bearing housings and the oilways in the block

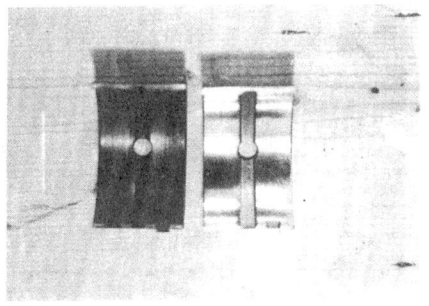

The shell bearing on the left is worn and scored. Compare it with the condition of the new bearing on the right! Renew the bearing if worn

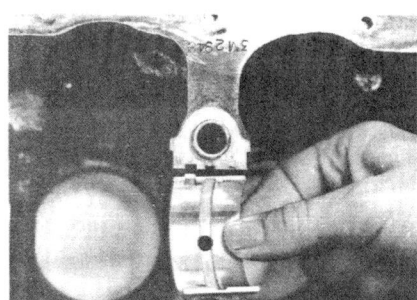

The next step is to fit the main bearing so that the lip on each shell engages with the machined slot in each bearing housing

With the new shells fitted to the block, lubricate them generously with S.A.E. 20/30 engine oil. An old plastic detergent bottle makes a handy oilcan

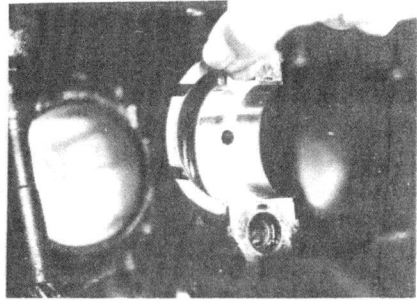

Next place a thrust washer, grooves facing outwards, on either side of the centre main bearing housing. Hold the washer to the block by a dab of oil

be left round the edge of the piston and on the cylinder bore wall as an aid to low oil consumption. Although this is probably true for early engines with worn bores, on later engines the thought of the second school can be applied; which is that for effective decarbonisation all traces of carbon should be removed.

If all traces of carbon are to be removed, press a little grease into the gap between the cylinder walls and the two pistons which are to be worked on. With a blunt scraper carefully scrape away the carbon from the piston crown, taking great care not to scratch the aluminium. Also scrape away the carbon from the surrounding lip of the cylinder wall. When all carbon has been removed, scrape away the grease which will now be contaminated with carbon particles, taking care not to press any into the bores. To assist prevention of carbon build-up the piston crown can be polished with a metal polish such as Brasso. Remove the rags or masking tape from the other two cylinders and turn the crankshaft so that the two pistons which were at the bottom are now at the top. Place rag or masking tape in the cylinders which have been decarbonised and proceed as just described.

If a ring of carbon is going to be left round the piston then this can be helped by inserting an old piston ring into the top of the bore to rest on the piston and ensure that carbon is not accidentally removed. Check that there are no particles of carbon in the cylinder bores. Decarbonising is now complete.

VALVE GUIDES - EXAMINATION & RENOVATION

Examine the valve guides internally for wear. If the valves are a very loose fit in the guides and there is the slightest suspicion of lateral rocking, then new guides will have to be fitted. If the valve guides have been removed compare them internally by visual inspection with a new guide as well as testing them for rocking with the valves.

SUMP - EXAMINATION & RENOVATION

Thoroughly wash out the sump with petrol and then inspect the cork packings in the semi-circular crankshaft seal housings. If they are at all flattened new ones should be fitted. Remove the old packing pieces, carefully pushing them right down into the grooves. Should the packing material stand out more than $1/16$ in. above the sump flange it must be cut back to this figure.

ENGINE REASSEMBLY - GENERAL

To ensure maximum life with minimum trouble from a rebuilt engine, not only must everything be correctly assembled, but everything must be spotlessly clean, all the oilways must be clear, locking washers and spring washers must always be fitted where indicated and all bearing and other working surfaces must be thoroughly lubricated during assembly. Before assembly begins renew any bolts or studs the threads of which are in any way damaged, and whenever possible use new spring washers. Apart from your normal tools, a supply of clean rag, an oil can filled with engine oil (an empty plastic detergent bottle thoroughly cleaned and washed out, will invariably do just as well), a new supply of assorted spring washers, a set of new gaskets, and preferably a torque spanner, should be collected together.

CRANKSHAFT REPLACEMENT

Ensure that the crankcase is thoroughly clean and that all oilways are clear. A thin-twist drill is useful for cleaning them out. If possible, blow them out with compressed air. Treat the crankshaft in the same fashion, and then inject engine oil into the crankshaft oilways.

Commence work on rebuilding the engine by replacing the crankshaft and main bearings:-

1. If the old main bearing shells are to be replaced, (a false economy unless they are virtually as new), fit the three upper halves of the main bearing shells to their location in the crankcase, after wiping the locations clean.

2. NOTE that at the back of each bearing is a tab which engages in locating grooves in either the crankcase or the main bearing cap housings.

3. If new bearings are being fitted, carefully clean away all traces of the protective grease with which they are coated.

4. With the three upper bearing shells securely in place, wipe the lower bearing cap housings and fit the three lower shell bearings to their caps ensuring that the right shell goes into the right cap if the old bearings are being refitted.

5. Wipe the recesses either side of the centre main bearing which locate the upper halves of the thrust washers.

6. Generously lubricate the crankshaft journals and the upper and lower main bearing shells and carefully place the crankshaft in position.

7. Introduce the upper halves of the thrust washers (the halves without tabs) into their grooves either side of the centre main bearing, rotating the crankshaft in the direction towards the main bearing tabs (so that the main bearing shells do not slide out). At the same time feed the thrust washers into their locations with their oil grooves outwards away from the bearing.

8. Ensure that all six tubular locating dowels are firmly in place, one on each side of the upper halves of the three main bearings, and then fit the main bearing caps in position ensuring they locate properly on the dowels. The mating surfaces must be spotlessly clean or the caps will not seat properly.

9. When replacing the centre main bearing cap, ensure the thrust washers, generously lubricated, are fitted with their oil grooves facing outwards and the locating tab of each washer is in the slot in the bearing cap.

10. Replace the one-piece locking tabs over the main bearing caps and replace the main bearing cap bolts screwing them up finger-tight.

11. Test the crankshaft for freedom of rotation. Should it be very stiff to turn or possess high spots a most careful inspection must be made,

11. preferably by a qualified mechanic with a micrometer to get to the root of the trouble. It is very seldom that any trouble of this nature will be experienced when fitting the crankshaft.

12. Tighten the main bearing bolts to a torque of 60 lb/ft. and turn up the locking tabs with a cold chisel.

OIL PUMP REASSEMBLY & REPLACEMENT

The oil pump must be fitted before the engine end plate in early models. On later models with an exposed pump this is not of importance.

To reassemble the Hobourn Eaton oil pump replace the outer rotor, inner rotor and drive shaft in the pump body and secure the end cover in place with the two bolts and spring washers.

To reassemble the Burman oil pump, replace the vanes in the rotor and fit the rotor to the pump body. Secure the pump end cover in place with the two bolts and spring washers.

To replace either oil pump or the Concentric (Engineering) Ltd. oil pump to the crankcase, fill the pump being fitted with engine oil, correctly place the paper gasket in position on the pump body flange, ensuring that the gasket does not cover the inlet or exhaust ports, and firmly bolt the pump unit to the crankcase using a spring washer under the head of each bolt, which should be tightened to a torque of 9 lb/ft.

Because of the disposition of the three bolt holes it is impossible to fit the oil pump the wrong way round.

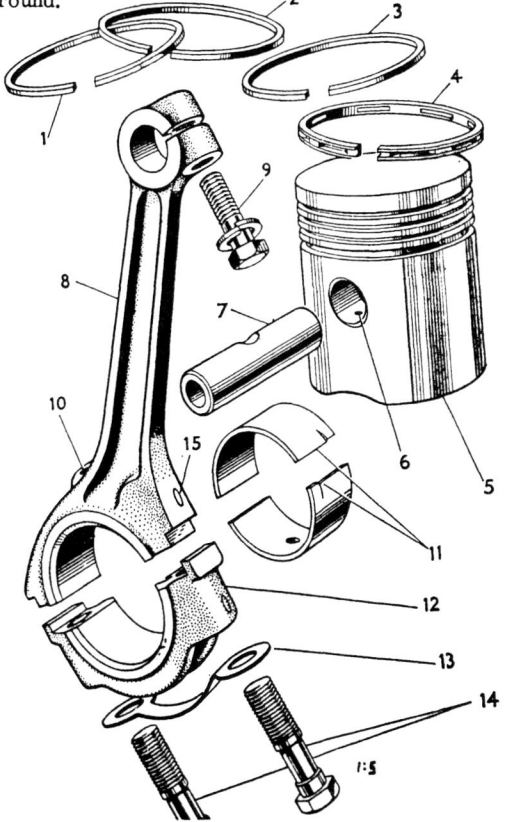

Fig. 1 : 5. Early-type piston and connecting rod assembly (948 c.c.). 1 Piston ring—parallel. 2 Piston ring—taper. 3 Piston ring—taper. 4 Piston ring—scraper. 5 Piston. 6 Gudgeon pin lubricating hole. 7 Gudgeon pin. 8 Connecting rod. 9 Clamping screw and washer. 10 Cylinder wall lubricating jet. 11 Connecting rod bearings. 12 Connecting rod cap. 13 Lockwasher. 14 Bolts. 15 Connecting rod and cap marking.

PISTON & CONNECTING ROD REASSEMBLY

If the same pistons are being used, then they must be mated to the same connecting rod with the same gudgeon pin. If new pistons are being fitted it does not matter which connecting rod they are used with, but, the gudgeon pins should be fitted on the basis of selective assembly.

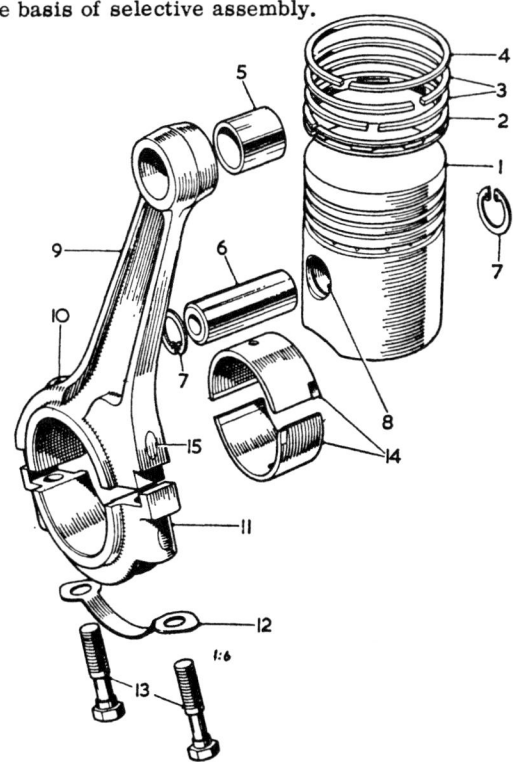

Fig. 1 : 6. Later-type piston and connecting rod assembly (1,098 c.c.). 1 Piston 2 Piston ring—scraper. 3 Piston rings—taper. 4 Piston ring—parallel. 5 Small-end bush. 6 Gudgeon pin. 7 Circlip. 8 Gudgeon pin lubricating hole . 9 Connecting rod. 10 Cylinder wall lubricating jet. 11 Connecting rod cap. 12 Lockwasher. 13 Bolts. 14 Connecting rod bearings. 15 Connecting rod and cap marking.

This involves trying each of the pins in each of the pistons in turn and fitting them to the ones they fit best as is detailed below.

Because aluminium alloy, when hot, expands more than steel, the gudgeon pin may be a very tight fit in the piston when they are cold on the variety which use a little end clamp bolt. To avoid any damage to the piston it is best to heat it in boiling water when the pin will slide in easily.

Lay the correct piston adjacent to each connecting rod and remember that the same rod and piston must go back into the same bore. If new pistons are being used it is only necessary to ensure that the right connecting rod is placed in each bore.

To assemble the pistons to the connecting rods or engines where the gudgeon pin is held in the little end by a clamp bolt, proceed as follows:-

1. Locate the small end of the connecting rod in the piston, with the marking 'FRONT' on the piston crown towards the front of the engine, and the hole for the gudgeon pin bolt in the connecting rod towards the camshaft.

2. NOTE The indentation in the centre of the gudgeon pin and insert the pin in the connecting rod so that the indentation lines up with the clamp bolt

Check that everything is scrupulously clean. Lubricate the main journals with engine oil before fitting the crankshaft to the crankcase

With the crankshaft in place the next job is to fit the main bearing caps

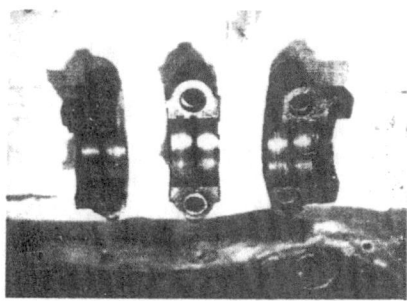

The three main bearing caps are each different. The one on the right is fitted at the front, and the other two at the middle and rear, respectively

Thoroughly clean the main bearing cap and fit the shell bearing so the notch lies in the groove in the cap

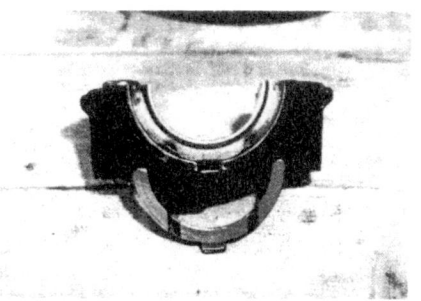

With the shell bearing in place in the centre main bearing cap, fit the lower halves of the thrust washer, grooves facing outwards

With the main bearing caps fitted check the camshaft end float between the thrust washers and the crank with a feeler gauge. .003 in. end float is correct

Tighten down the main bearing caps to a torque of 60 lb./ft., and then lock the bolts by knocking up the locking tabs

If the original crankshaft is being fitted check the washers are in place on the crankshaft nose. They ensure the gearwheels lie in the same plane

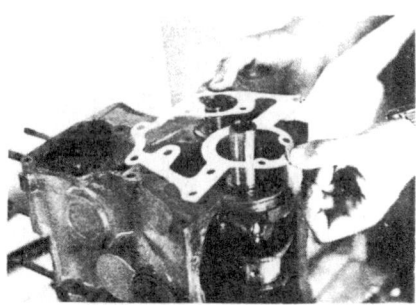

The next step is to thoroughly clean the face of the block and fit a new front end plate gasket

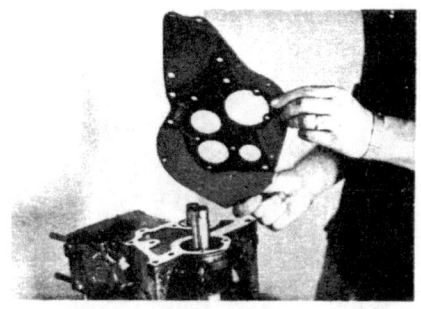

The front end plate must be carefully cleaned and then fitted to the block. Hold it in place with several bolts screwed in finger tight

With the front end plate in place the camshaft retaining plate can be fitted

Fit the locking tab to the end plate as shown, and fit the two bolts. Turn up the tabs on the locking plate

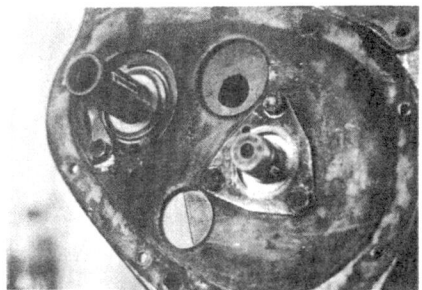

Fit and tighten down the three camshaft retaining plate bolts. Remember to fit spring washers

When refitting the chain round the gear wheels and to the engine, the two 'dots' must be adjacent to each other on an imaginary line passing through each wheel centre

With the engine on its side, set the crankshaft and camshaft so the woodruff keys are at 2 o'clock and 4 o'clock respectively

Next, place the camshaft locking washer with its tag in the gearwheel keyway. Then fit the securing nut

Tighten the camshaft gearwheel nut, holding the crankshaft stationary with a spanner as shown. Make sure plenty of rag is placed between the spanner and the crankshaft

The gearwheels and timing chain are now in place and correctly positioned

Next bend back the camshaft locking washer to lock the camshaft gearwheel nut in place

The flange on the timing gear case must be carefully cleaned and scraped and a new gasket laid on the front endplate

Place the oil thrower, concave side down, on the nose of the crankshaft. Remember to position the thrower so it fits over the crankshaft key

The timing chain and gearwheels nearly ready for replacement of the timing gear case

A new felt washer should be positioned on the oil thrower as indicated

The next step is to refit the timing case and replace the bolts and lockwashers

hole in such a way that the bolt will pass through without touching the gudgeon pin.

3. For the gudgeon pin to fit correctly it should slide in three quarters of its travel quite freely and for the remaining quarter have to be tapped in with a plastic or wooden headed hammer, or the piston heated in water so the pin will slide in the remaining quarter easily.

4. Fit a new spring washer under the head of the connecting rod bolt and screw it into position using a torque figure of 25 lb/ft.

To assemble the piston to the connecting rod on engines where the gudgeon pin is fully floating proceed as follows:-

1. Fit a gudgeon pin circlip in position at one end of the gudgeon pin hole in the piston.

2. Locate the connecting rod in the piston with the marking 'FRONT' on the piston crown towards the front of the engine, and the connecting rod caps towards the camshaft side of the engine.

3. Slide the gudgeon pin in through the hole in the piston and through the connecting rod little end until it rests against the previously fitted circlip. NOTE that the pin should be a push fit.

4. Fit the second circlip in position. Repeat this procedure for all four pistons and connecting rods.

PISTON RING REPLACEMENT

Check that the piston ring grooves and oilways are thoroughly clean and unblocked. Piston rings must always be fitted over the head of the piston and never from the bottom. The easiest method to use when fitting rings is to wrap a .020 feeler gauge round the top of the piston and place the rings one at a time, starting with the bottom oil control ring, over the feeler gauge.

The feeler gauge, complete with ring, can then be slid down the piston over the other piston ring grooves until the correct groove is reached. The piston ring is then slid gently off the feeler gauge into the groove.

An alternative method is to fit the rings by holding them slightly open with the thumbs and both of your index fingers. This method requires a steady hand and great care as it is easy to open the ring too much and break it.

PISTON REPLACEMENT

The pistons, complete with connecting rods, can be fitted to the cylinder bores in the following sequence:-

1. With a wad of clean rag wipe the cylinder bores clean.

2. The pistons, complete with connecting rods, are fitted to their bores from above.

3. As each piston is inserted into its bore ensure that it is the correct piston/connecting rod assembly for that particular bore and that the connecting rod is the right way round, and that the front of the piston is towards the front of the bore, i.e. towards the front of the engine.

4. The piston will only slide into the bore as far as the oil control ring. It is then necessary to

compress the piston rings into a clamp and to gently tap the piston into the cylinder bore with a wooden or plastic hammer. If a proper piston ring clamp is not available then a suitable jubilee clip does the job very well.

CONNECTING ROD TO CRANKSHAFT RE-ASSEMBLY

As the big ends on the connecting rods are offset it will be obvious if they have been inserted the wrong way round as they will not fit over the crankpins. The centre two connecting rods should be fitted with the offset part of the rods adjacent, and the connecting rods at each extremity of the engine should have the offset part of the rods facing outwards.

1. Wipe the connecting rod half of the big end bearing cap and the underside of the shell bearing clean, and fit the shell bearing in position with its locating tongue engaged with the corresponding groove in the connecting rod.

2. If the old bearings are nearly new and are being refitted then ensure they are replaced in their correct locations on the correct rods.

3. Generously lubricate the crankpin journals with engine oil, and turn the crankshaft so that the crankpin is in the most advantageous position for the connecting rod to be drawn onto it.

4. Wipe the connecting rod bearing cap and back of the shell bearing clean and fit the shell bearing in position ensuring that the locating tongue at the back of the bearing engages with the locating groove in connecting rod cap.

5. Generously lubricate the shell bearing and offer up the connecting rod bearing cap to the connecting rod.

6. Fit the connecting rod bolts with the one-piece locking tab under them and tighten the bolts with a torque spanner to 35 lb/ft. With a cold chisel knock up the locking tabs against the bolt head.

7. When all the connecting rods have been fitted, rotate the crankshaft to check that everything is free, and that there are no high spots causing binding.

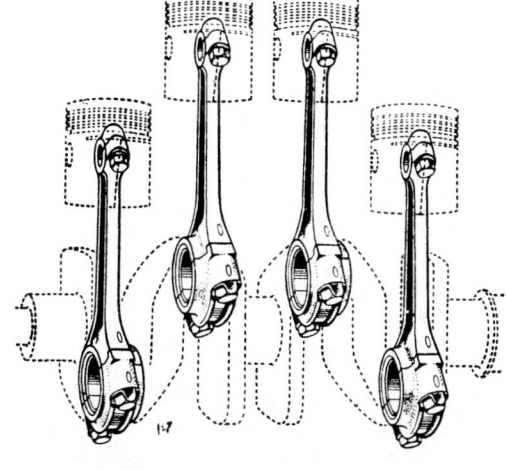

Fig. 1:7. Showing the correct positions of the offsets on the connecting rod big-ends

41

GAUZE STRAINER & SUCTION PIPE REASSEMBLY

The gauze strainer and suction pipe should be thoroughly cleaned in petrol, and then blown dry with a compressed air line. Reassembly consists of re-fitting the gauze strainer to the strainer bracket with the two small bolts and star washers, and then re-fitting the bracket to the crankcase. One leg rests on the centre main bearing cap, while the other rests on the rear main bearing cap. With spring washers under their heads, tighten down the two support bracket bolts. Reconnect the oil suction pipe to the threaded drilling in the crankcase.

FLYWHEEL REPLACEMENT

When replacing the flywheel it is important to ensure that it is placed in the correct relative position with the crankshaft.

To do this, turn the crankshaft until piston Nos. 1 and 4 are at the top of their bores and lock the crankshaft in this position with a wedge of wood between the crankshaft and the crankcase.

Wipe the mating surfaces of the crankshaft flange and flywheel clean, and then fit the flywheel so the marks '1/4' on the flywheel periphery are at the top.

Screw in the four bolts and locking plates and tighten the bolts to a torque of 40 lb/ft. Bend up the locking tabs on the locking plates and replace the clutch as detailed in Chapter 5.

SUMP REPLACEMENT

After the sump has been thoroughly cleaned, scrape all traces of the old sump gasket from the sump flange, and fit new main bearing cap oil seals as detailed on page 37.

Wipe down the inside of the crankcase, including the camshaft bearing surfaces, clean. Thoroughly clean and scrape the crankshaft to sump flange.

With a new sump gasket held lightly in position offer up the sump to the crankcase.

Bolt the sump in position with the large flat washer next to the sump flange and the starred or spring washer under the bolt head.

Take care not to over-tighten the sump bolts as they strip their threads very easily. The correct torque that they should be tightened to is 6 lb/ft.

CAMSHAFT REPLACEMENT

With the sump in position the engine can be stood upright and the following operations, including camshaft replacement, will be found easier with the engine in this position.

Wipe the camshaft bearing journals clean and lubricate them generously with engine oil.

Insert the camshaft into the crankcase gently, taking care not to damage the camshaft bearings with the cams.

With the camshaft inserted into the block as far as it will go, rotate it slightly to ensure the slot in the oil pump drive has mated with the camshaft flange. If it has not yet mated the camshaft will go a further 1/4 in. into the block as the flange and slot line up.

Replace the camshaft locating plate and tighten down the three retaining bolts and washers.

TIMING GEARS, CHAIN & COVER REPLACEMENT

Before reassembly begins check that the packing washers are in place on the crankshaft nose. If new gearwheels are being fitted it may be necessary to fit additional washers (please see para. 6). These washers ensure that the crankshaft gearwheel lines up correctly with the camshaft gearwheel.

1. Replace the woodruff keys in their respective slots in the crankshaft and camshaft and ensure that they are fully seated. If their edges are burred they must be cleaned with a fine file.

2. Lay the camshaft gearwheels on a clean surface so that the two timing dots are adjacent to each other. Slip the timing chain over them and pull the gearwheels back into mesh with the chain so that the timing dots, although further apart, are still adjacent to each other.

3. Rotate the crankshaft so that the woodruff key is at top dead centre (The engine should be standing upright on its sump).

4. Rotate the camshaft so that when viewed from the front the woodruff key is at the two o'clock position.

5. Fit the timing chain and gearwheel assembly onto the camshaft and crankshaft, keeping the timing marks adjacent. If the camshaft and crankshaft have been positioned accurately it will be found that the keyways on the gearwheels will match the position of the keys, although it may be necessary to rotate the camshaft a fraction to ensure accurate lining-up of the camshaft gearwheel.

6. Press the gearwheels into position on the crankshaft and camshaft as far as they will go.
   NOTE If new gearwheels are being fitted they should be checked for alignment before being finally fitted to the engine. Place the gearwheels in position without the timing chain and place the straight edge of a steel ruler from the side of the camshaft gearteeth to the crankshaft gearwheel, and measure the gap between the steel rule and the gearwheel. If a gap exists a suitable number of packing washers must be placed on the crankshaft nose to bring the crankshaft

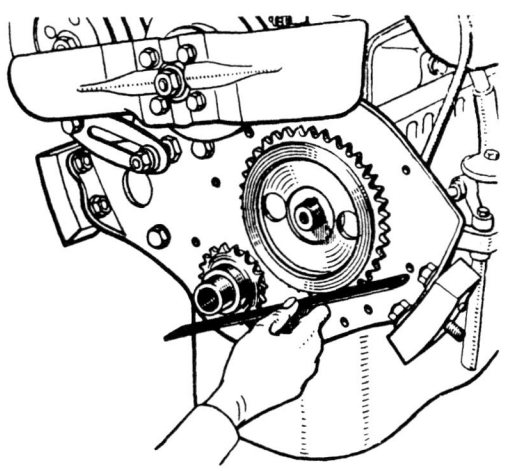

Fig. 1:8. Use the straight edge of a steel rule to line up the gearwheel teeth

The crankshaft pulley wheel can now be fitted over the nose of the crankshaft

With the pulley wheel in place replace the retaining bolt and lock washer and tighten to a torque of 70 lb./ft. Tap up the tab on the lock washer

The component parts of the piston and connecting rod assembly. Later pistons have fully floating little ends

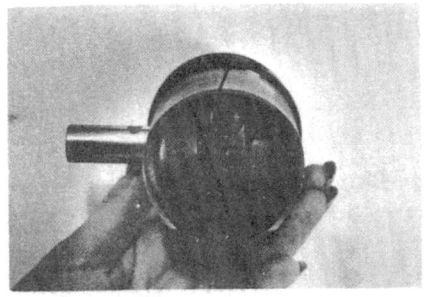

When the piston is assembled to the connecting rod, ensure the cut-out on the gudgeon pin lines up with the hole for the clamping bolt in the little end

Each piston is clearly marked "FRONT". Fit it this way round. The '3' in the diamond stamped on the block and piston crown indicates the grade of piston fitted

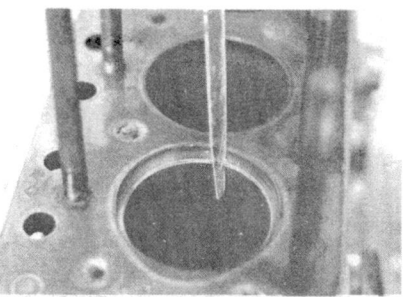

Measure each piston ring gap in turn, with a feeler gauge, with the rings fitted in the bore. The gap should be .007 to .012 in.

The next step is to fit the piston and connecting rod assemblies. The bores must be perfectly clean before the pistons are fitted

When compressing the piston rings there is no need to use an expensive piston ring compressor. A jubilee clip is just as good

Tap the piston lightly with a plastic-headed hammer until it is fully entered into the cylinder bore

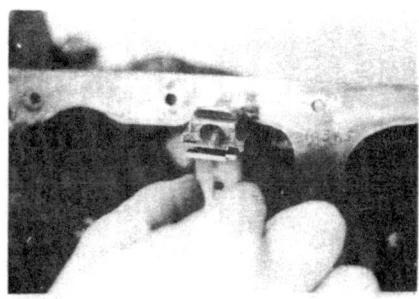

The connecting rod big end cap must be perfectly clean. The bearing shell can then be fitted with its lip locating in the groove in the rod

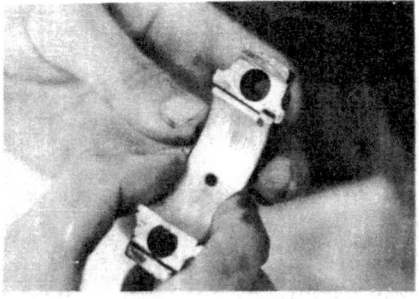

Fit the big end cap bearing shell in the same way and make sure you replace the big end cap to the same connecting rod from which it was removed

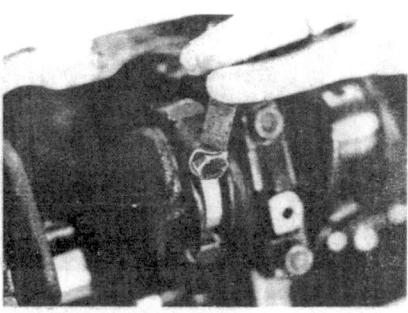

The next step is to tighten the big end bolts to a torque of 35 lb./ft. and then knock up the tab on the locking washer

Then turn to the rear of the engine and fit a new end plate gasket after ensuring the block is quite clean. The gasket is held by two locating studs

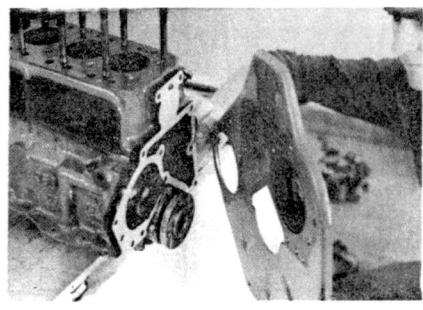

Fit the engine end plate with the flange pointing away from the block

Fit and tighten up the seven bolts and spring washers which hold the end plate to the block

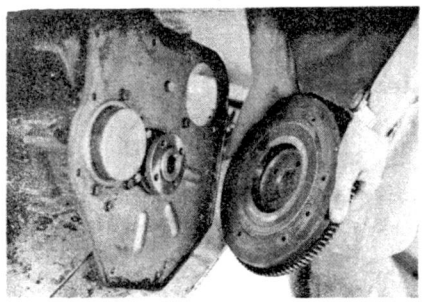

Turn the crankshaft so that piston 1 and 4 are at T.D.C. The flywheel is fitted with the flat face towards the crankshaft

The mark $\frac{1}{4}$ on the flywheel periphery must be at the top when it is fitted. Screw in the four flywheel retaining bolts. Remember to fit the locking washers

Tighten the flywheel bolts to a torque of 40 lb./ft. To prevent the crankshaft from turning place a blunt cold chisel in the position shown

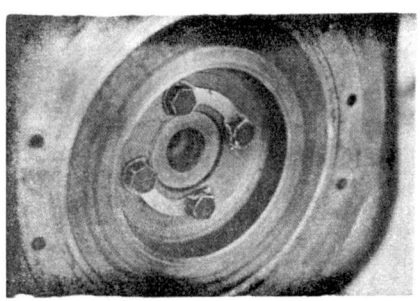

When the bolts are fully tightened remember to turn up the tabs on the joined lockwashers

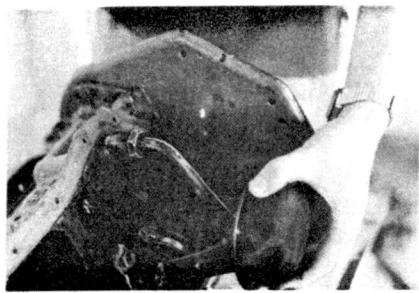

The pick-up pipe from the gauze strainer fits in a threaded hole on the inside of the sump flange

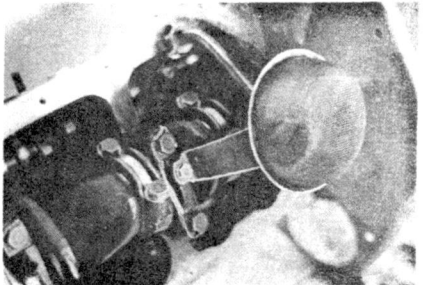

The strainer is held in place by a bracket which is secured to the centre and rear main bearing caps by two bolts and spring washers

Tighten the two bolts down securely. The next step is to fit the sump, so thoroughly clean the sump flange on the block

To prevent oil leaks renew the cork sump seals, front and rear. The seal when fully pushed into the retaining dowel should not stand more than approx. $\frac{1}{16}$ in. proud

The sump gasket should now be fitted. Note that it comes in two halves. Never use an old sump gasket as oil leaks may result

gearwheel onto the same plane as the camshaft gearwheel.

7. Fit the oil thrower to the crankshaft with the concave side forward.

8. Fit the locking washer to the camshaft gearwheel with its locating tab in the gearwheel keyway.

9. Screw on the camshaft gearwheel retaining nut and tighten securely.

10. Bend up the locking tab of the locking washer to securely hold the camshaft retaining nut.

11. Generously oil the chain and gearwheels.

12. Ensure the interior of the timing cover and the timing cover flange is clean and generously lubricate the felt washer in the timing cover. Then, with a new gasket in position, fit the timing cover to the block.

13. Screw in the timing cover retaining bolts with the flat washer next to the cover flange and under the spring washer. The 1/4 in. bolts should be tightened with a torque spanner to 6 lb/ft., and the 5/16 in. bolts to 14 lb/ft.

14. Fit the crankshaft pulley to the nose of the crankshaft ensuring that the keyway engages with the woodruff key.

15. Fit the crankshaft retaining bolt locking washer in position and screw on either the crankshaft pulley retaining bolt or the crankshaft pulley retaining dog, depending on whether or not a starting handle is fitted. Tighten both to a torque of 70 lb/ft.

VALVE & VALVE SPRING REASSEMBLY

To refit the valves and valve springs to the cylinder head, proceed as follows:-

1. Rest the cylinder head on its side, or if the manifold studs are still fitted, with the gasket surface downwards.

2. Fit each valve and valve spring in turn, wiping down and lubricating each valve stem as it is inserted into the same valve guide from which it was removed.

3. As each valve is inserted slip the oil control

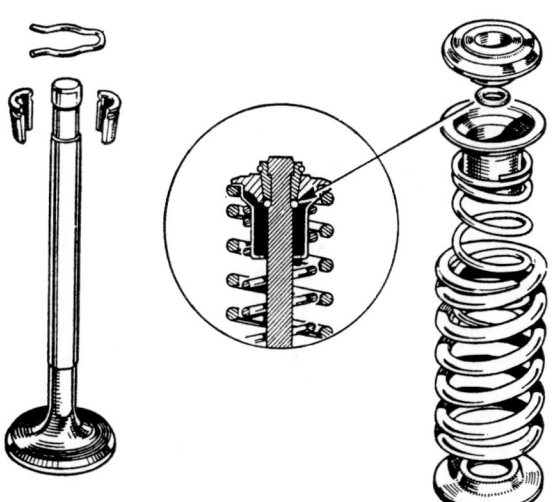

Fig. 1 : 9. Showing how the component parts of the valve assembly fit together. NOTE the position of the oil seal (arrowed)

rubber ring into place just under the bottom of the cotter groove.

4. Move the cylinder head towards the edge of the work bench if it is facing downwards and slide it partially over the edge of the bench so as to fit the bottom half of the valve spring compressor to the valve head.

5. Slip the valve spring, shroud and cap over the valve stem.

6. With the base of the valve compressor on the valve head compress the valve spring until the cotters can be slipped into place in the cotter grooves. Gently release the compressor and fit the circlip in position in the grooves in the cotters.

7. Repeat this procedure until all eight valves and valve springs are fitted.

ROCKER SHAFT REASSEMBLY

To reassemble the rocker shaft fit the split pin, flat washer, and spring washer at the rear end of the shaft and then slide on the rocker arms, rocker shaft pedestals, and spacing springs in the same order in which they were removed.

With the front pedestal in position, screw in the rocker shaft locating screw and slip the locating plate into position. Finally, fit to the front of the shaft the spring washer, plain washer, and split pin, in that order.

TAPPET & PUSHROD REPLACEMENT

Generously lubricate the tappets internally and externally and insert them in the bores from which they were removed through the tappet chest.

With the cylinder head in position fit the pushrods in the same order in which they were removed. Ensure that they locate properly in the stems of the tappets, and lubricate the pushrod ends before fitment.

CYLINDER HEAD REPLACEMENT

After checking that both the cylinder block and cylinder head mating faces are perfectly clean, generously lubricate each cylinder with engine oil.

1. Always use a new cylinder head gasket as the old gasket will be compressed and not capable of giving such a good seal. It is also easier at this stage to refit the small hose from the water pump to the cylinder head.

2. Never smear grease on either side of the gasket as when the engine heats up the grease will melt and may allow compression leak to develop. Personally, I never like using gasket cement as if a new gasket is used and the head and block faces are true there should be no requirement for it. (The most successful racing engines never use gasket cement.).

3. The cylinder head gasket is marked 'FRONT' and 'TOP' and should be fitted in position according to the markings.

4. With the gasket in position carefully lower the cylinder head onto the cylinder block.

5. With the head in position fit the cylinder head nuts and washers finger tight to the five cylinder

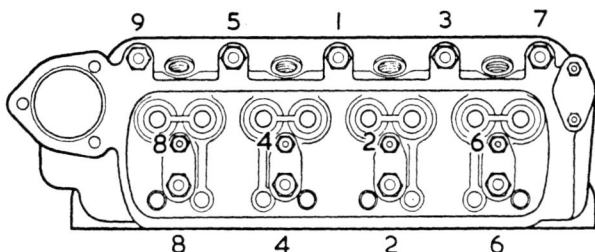

Fig. 1:10. Loosen and tighten the cylinder head nuts in the order shown

Valve fully open	Check & Adjust
Valve No. 8	Valve No. 1
" " 6	" " 3
" " 4	" " 5
" " 7	" " 2
" " 1	" " 8
" " 3	" " 6
" " 5	" " 4
" " 2	" " 7

head holding down studs, which remain outside the rocker cover. It is not possible to fit the remaining nuts to the studs inside the rocker cover until the rocker assembly is in position.

6. Fit the pushrods as detailed in the previous section.

7. The rocker shaft assembly can now be lowered over its eight locating studs. Take care that the rocker arms are the right way round. Lubricate the ball joints, and insert the rocker arm ball joints in the pushrod cups.
   NOTE Failure to place the ball joints in the cups can result in the ball joints seating on the edge of a pushrod or outside it when the head and rocker assembly is pulled down tight.

8. Fit the four rocker pedestal nuts and washers, and then the four cylinder head stud nuts and washers which also serve to hold down the rocker pedestals. Pull the nuts down evenly, but without tightening them right up.

9. When all is in position, the nine cylinder head nuts and the four rocker pedestal nuts can be tightened down in the order shown in Fig. 1:10 above. Turn the nuts a quarter of a turn a time and tighten the four rocker pedestal nuts to 25 lb/ft. and the nine cylinder head nuts to 40 lb/ft.

ROCKER ARM/VALVE ADJUSTMENT

The valve adjustments should be made with the engine cold. The importance of correct rocker arm/ valve stem clearances cannot be overstressed as they vitally affect the performance of the engine. If the clearances are set too open, the efficiency of the engine is reduced as the valves open late and close earlier than was intended. If, on the other hand the clearances are set too close there is a danger that the stems will expand upon heating and not allow the valves to close properly which will cause burning of the valve head and seat and possible warping. If the engine is in the car to get at the rockers it is merely necessary to remove the two holding down studs from the rocker cover, and then to lift the rocker cover and gasket away.

It is important that the clearance is set when the tappet of the valve being adjusted is on the heel of the cam, (i. e. opposite the peak). This can be effected by carrying out the adjustments in the following order (which also avoids turning the crankshaft more than necessary.).

The correct valve clearance of .012 in. (.305 mm.) is obtained by slackening the hexagon locknut with a spanner while holding the ball pin against rotation with the screwdriver. Then, still pressing down with the screwdriver, insert a feeler gauge in the gap between the valve stem head and the rocker arm and adjust the ball pin until the feeler gauge will just move in and out without nipping. Then, still holding the ball pin in the correct position, tighten the locknut. An alternative method is to set the gaps with the engine running, and although this may be faster it is no more reliable.

DISTRIBUTOR & DISTRIBUTOR DRIVE REPLACEMENT

It is important to set the distributor drive correctly as otherwise the ignition timing will be totally incorrect. It is easy to set the distributor drive in apparently the right position, but, exactly 180° out by omitting to select the correct cylinder which must not only be at T. D. C. but must also be on its firing stroke with both valves closed. The distributor drive should therefore not be fitted until the cylinder head is in position and the valves can be observed. Alternatively, if the timing cover has not been replaced, the distributor drive can be replaced when the dots on the timing wheels are adjacent to each other.

1. Rotate the crankshaft so that No. 1 piston is at T. D. C. and on its firing stroke (the dots in the timing gears will be adjacent to each other). When No. 1 piston is at T. D. C. the inlet valve on No. 4 cylinder is just opening and the exhaust valve closing.

2. When the marks '1/4' on the flywheel are at T. D. C., or when the dimple on the crankshaft pulley wheel is in line with the pointer on the timing gear cover, then Nos. 1 and 4 pistons are at T. D. C.

3. Screw the tappet cover bolt into the head of the distributor drive (any 5/16 in. U. N. F. bolt will do).

4. Insert the distributor drive into its housing so that when fully home the smaller half of the offset distributor drive head is in the eleven o'clock position. To allow for the rotation of the distributor drive as its skew gear meshes with the skew gear on the camshaft the drive should be inserted with the slot vertical and the smaller offset towards the front of the engine. As the drive is pushed right home the skew gears will turn the drive shaft anti-clockwise to the eleven o'clock position.

Thoroughly clean out the sump and replace and tighten the drain plug. Then fit the sump to the crankcase

Tighten down the sump securing screws (bolts are sometimes used) to a torque of 6 lb./ft. Ensure the large 'load spreader' washers are fitted under the spring washer

With the sump fitted, stand the engine upright. This will make the fitting of the valve gear and cylinder head much easier

When the small recess in the pulley wheel is in line with the long pointer the engine is at T.D.C. Each of the two smaller pointer indicates 5° advance

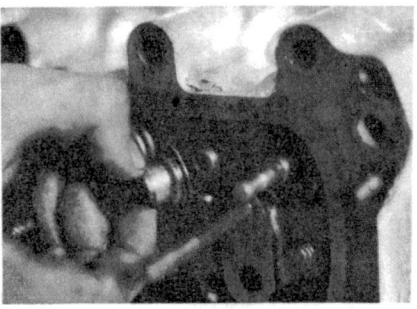

The next step is to fit the valves and valve springs to the cylinder head. Start by fitting the valve guide shroud in place

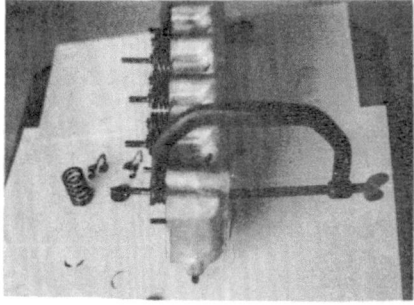

Next fit each valve, oil seal, and valve spring. Compress the spring with a compressor and make sure the head of the compressor does not slip

Now fit the split collets. A trace of grease will help hold them to the valve stem recess. This job calls for care as the items are small and easily dropped

Slacken off the spring compressor until the collets are firmly held by the valve spring cup. Fit a circlip to the collets to make sure they stay together

This is what the completed built-up valve and valve spring assembly should look like

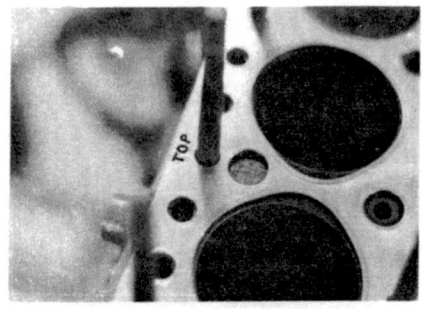

The next step is to thoroughly clean the face of the block and cylinder head. Fit a new cylinder head gasket with the side marked 'top' upwards

The cylinder head can now be fitted. Keep the head and block parallel to each other so the head does not bind on the cylinder head studs

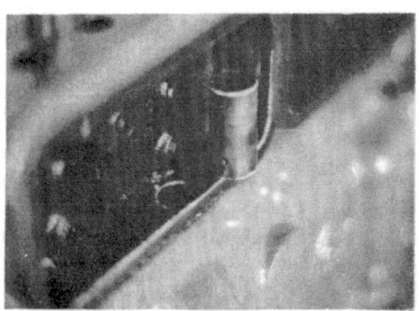

Make sure the oil holes in the tappets are clear, and replace them through the tappet chest apertures. Fit the clutch assembly

47

Next fit the push rods with the mushroom shaped end fed into the block first. Make sure the push rods seat properly in the tappets

Next reassemble the rocker gear on the rocker shaft and fit to the cylinder head. Make sure that the oil holes are clear in the rocker shaft

Make sure that the rocker pedestal locking plate is fitted before replacing the rocker pedestal and cylinder head nuts

The cylinder head and rocker bracket washers and nuts are now fitted. Tighten the cylinder head nuts to a torque of 40 lb./ft. in the order shown in Illus. 1:10

The next step is to set the valve clearance to .015 in. Unlock the nut and screw the tappet adjusting screw up or down until the arm just nips the blade

Clean the thermostat housing flange and then fit a new gasket in place

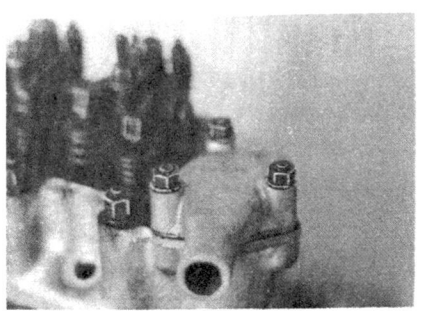

Then fit the thermostat and thermostat cover and replace the spring washer and do up the three nuts

The oil pressure relief valve fits into the threaded hole on the right-hand side of the engine at the rear

The next step is to clean the tappet chest flanges and refit the tappet chest covers using a new cork gasket. Tighten the bolts to 2 lb./ft. Then fit the petrol pump

Make sure the hole at the rear of the block is covered by the flat plate, and remember to use a new gasket

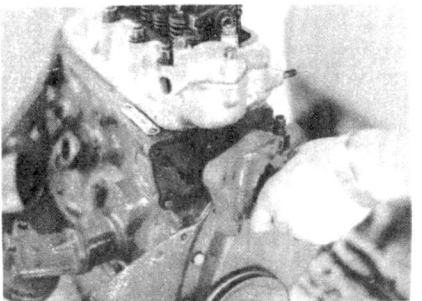

Now fit the water pump to the front of the engine. Make sure the mating surfaces are clean and that a new gasket is fitted

Fit the by-pass hose at the same time as the pump is fitted. It is very difficult to fit the hose after the pump is in place

5. Remove the tappet cover bolt from the drive shaft.

6. Replace the distributor housing and lock it in position with the single bolt and lockwasher.

7. The distributor can now be replaced and the two securing bolts and spring washers which hold the distributor clamping plate to the distributor housing, tightened. If the clamp bolt on the clamping plate was not previously loosened and the distributor body was not turned in the clamping plate, then the ignition timing will be as previously. If the clamping bolt has been loosened, then it will be necessary to retime the ignition as in Chapter 4.

FINAL ASSEMBLY

The rocker cover can now be fitted, using a new cork gasket. Fit the two tappet cover plates, using new gaskets, and tighten the tappet chest bolts to a torque of 2 lb/ft. Do not exceed this figure or the covers will distort and leak oil. Reconnect the ancilliary components to the engine in the reverse order to which they were removed.

It should be noted that in all cases it is best to reassemble the engine as far as possible before refitting it to the car. This means that the inlet and exhaust manifolds, carburettor, dynamo, water thermostat, oil filter, distributor, and mechanical fuel pump (where fitted), should all be in position. Ensure that the oil filter is filled with engine oil, as otherwise on engines with a full flow lubrication scheme there will be a delay in the oil reaching the bearings while the oil filter refills.

ENGINE REPLACEMENT WITHOUT GEARBOX

Although the engine can be replaced with one man and a suitable winch, it is easier if two are present. One to lower the engine into the engine compartment and the other to guide the engine into position and to ensure it does not foul anything. Generally speaking, engine replacement is a reversal of the procedures used when removing the engine. The sequence is not quite the same however, and the following order will be found the easiest and quickest to follow.

1. Connect the lifting tackle to the lifting hooks, or place suitable slings round the front and rear of the engine.

2. Raise the engine, and if using a fixed hoist, roll the car under it and lower the engine into the engine compartment. With the Morris Minor it is necessary to lower the engine in sideways and then turn it round in the engine compartment (unless the radiator and grille have been removed).

3. When the engine is nearly at rest on the engine mountings, roll the car forward a little so that the main drive shaft from the gearbox enters the spigot in the centre of the clutch plate cleanly. Do not yet release the engine slings or tighten down the engine mounting bolts.

4. Replace the nuts, bolts, and spring washers which hold the engine end plate to the gearbox bellhousing and remember to refit the earth strap to the bottom right bellhousing bolt where the earth strap is fitted in this position. (It is sometimes taken from off the gearbox mounting bolt).

5. Do not yet insert the bellhousing bolt, which also serves as the attachment point for the exhaust pipe bracket.

6. While under the car securing the bottom bellhousing bolts refit the starter motor by the two bolts and lockwashers.

7. To line up the mounting bracket holes it may be necessary to move the engine about slightly and this will be found much easier to do if the slings are still in position and taking most of the strain. Replace the nuts, bolts, and spring washers to the engine mounting brackets and tighten them finger tight.

8. Remove the sling from the engine and with the full weight of the power unit on the engine mounting brackets, tighten the nuts and bolts down securely.

9. Refit the exhaust manifold down pipe to the exhaust pipe, replace the clamp, and secure the joint with the two clamp bolts.

10. Refit the exhaust pipe support bracket to its attachment point on the appropriate bellhousing nut and bolt.

11. Reconnect the fuel inlet pipe to the mechanical fuel pump on early models using this type of pump. With models using an S.U. electrical fuel pump, connect the inlet pipe from the pump to the carburettor/s.

12. Refit the distributor cap and reconnect the high tension leads to the appropriate sparking plugs.

13. Reconnect the high tension lead from the centre of the distributor cap to the coil, and the low tension lead from the terminal 'C' on the coil to the terminal on the side of the distributor.

14. Reconnect the leads to the dynamo. The different sized terminals ensure that no mistake can be made. Also reconnect the starter motor cable to the starter motor.

15. On cars fitted with rev. counters, refit the rev. counter drive.

16. Reconnect the accelerator and choke cables and replace the air cleaner/s on the carburettor/s.

17. Reconnect the oil pressure sender unit, or the oil pressure gauge pipe line to the threaded take off point at the right-hand near side of the engine.

18. If the small by-pass hose between the cylinder head and the water pump was not replaced when the head was refitted then this must be done now. This can sometimes be a difficult operation but should be carried out fairly easily if the small jubilee clips are slipped over each end of the tube which is then squeezed in a vice, and is quickly fitted before the hose has time to expand to its normal length again.

19. Refit the radiator, heater, and radiator hoses. Always use new hoses if the old hoses show signs of internal or external cracking or flaking.

20. Reconnect the water temperature gauge sender unit to the tapped hole at the front right-hand

The next step is to fit the rocker cover using a new cork gasket. Then fit a new exhaust gasket over the manifold studs

Next clean the flanges of the exhaust manifold and fit the manifold over the retaining studs

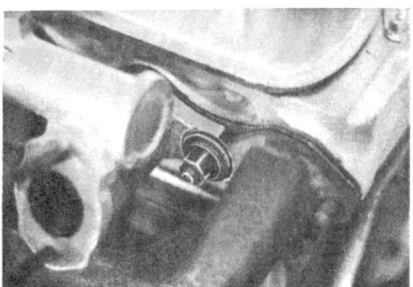

Fit the inlet manifold and place the large retaining washer under the spring washer on each common inlet and exhaust manifold stud

Tighten down the manifold nuts to a torque of 15 lb./ft.

The inlet and exhaust manifolds fitted in place. The inlet manifold differs between various 'A' series models but all are interchangeable

Four bolts secure the fan blades and the fan pulley wheel to the water pump

Next, fit the heat protection shield over the carburettor studs where this is a standard fitting

The rear dynamo support bracket is held to the block by two bolts. Remember to fit spring washers

At the front the dynamo is held by an adjustable link and three lock nuts

The nut which holds the bolt which supports the adjustable link is located on the engine side of the front plate

Fit the distributor, oil filter, and fan belt and then offer up and attach the gearbox bell housing to the engine rear plate

The engine now rebuilt, and, complete with gearbox which has also been rebuilt (See Chapter 6), is ready for replacing in your car

side of the engine where a water temperature gauge is fitted.

21. Replace the bonnet (easier with two people), and reconnect the lights (where applicable).

22. Reconnect the battery.

23. Check that the drain taps are closed and refill the cooling system with water and the engine with the correct grade of oil. Start the engine and carefully check for oil or water leaks. There should be no oil or water leaks if the engine has been reassembled carefully, all nuts and bolts tightened down correctly, and new gaskets and joints used throughout.

ENGINE REPLACEMENT WITH GEARBOX

The procedure for replacing the engine and gearbox together as a unit is the same as for replacing the engine by itself. Except that it is easier to fit the starter motor before the power unit is lowered into the engine compartment and of course all the bellhousing bolts (except the one for the earth lead and the one for the exhaust pipe bracket) will be already tightened into place.

Generally, replacement is a reversal of the removal sequence, but as an aid to rapid replacement, the following notes are made :-

1. On cars such as the Austin Healey Sprite with an enclosed propeller shaft tunnel, the propeller shaft must be mounted on the gearbox mainshaft splines before the rear end of the gearbox enters the transmission tunnel.

2. On cars where the propeller shaft can be slid over the gearbox mainshaft splines with the shaft bolted in place to the pinion flange on the rear axle because of an unboxed in transmission tunnel, it is helpful to roll the car forward an inch or two to allow the splines to mate easily.

3. For all models except the Morris Minor 1000, (See para. 4), and the Austin A. 35 (See para. 5), the additional procedure to follow is :-
   a) With the gearbox mounting bracket in position in the body frame replace the four set bolts and spring washers which hold it in place. Do this while the engine is still supported in the slings and before the engine support mounting brackets are tightened down.
   b) Rescrew the speedometer cable to the side of the gearbox.
   c) Refit the clutch operating cylinder to the bellhousing with the two set bolts and spring washers and bleed the system as detailed in Chapter 5.
   d) Replace the gearlever, anti-rattle plunger, gearbox retaining plate, and the gearlever

cover. Refit the carpeting round the transmission tunnel.
   e) Refill the gearbox with the correct grade of oil.

4. The following sequence applies to the Morris Minor 1000.
   a) Replace the cross member to the gearbox, and replace the four bolts and spring washers which hold the cross member to the body frame. Ensure that the front bottom left-hand bolt is connected to the earthing strap.
   b) Replace the nuts, spring, and flat washers which secure the gearbox mounting rubbers to the cross member.
   c) Reconnect the mechanically actuated clutch mechanism. (See Chapter 5 for further details).
   d) Reconnect the engine mountings, remove the slings, and tighten the securing bolts firmly.
   e) Replace the gearlever, anti-rattle plunger, gearbox cover, and carpeting.
   f) Screw the speedometer cable into its drive housing on the side of the gearbox.
   g) After chassis No. 264013 reconnect the engine steady cable. This is a direct reversal of the dismantling process. The correct tension on the cable should be such that the engine and gearbox will not move forward in the chassis. If the cable is overtensioned the engine will vibrate and feel rough. It is very important not to twist the cable while increasing the tension, and to preclude this happening, the cable should be held with a suitably sized spanner over the flats found at the rear end of the cable.
   h) Refill the gearbox with the correct grade of oil.

5. In the case of the A. 35, proceed as follows :-
   a) Raise the front of the car and slide the engine and gearbox into place on a trolley.
   b) Lower the front of the body and jack the engine and gearbox up into position.
   c) Replace the cross member and do up the two bolts (one on each side of the propeller shaft tunnel) which hold the gearbox mounting bracket to the bodyframe.
   d) Reconnect the propeller shaft and the engine mounting brackets.
   e) Replace the component parts of the clutch mechanical linkage in the reverse order to that given on page 22, para. 5.
   f) Reconnect the speedometer cable to the gearbox.
   g) Replace the gearlever as previously described in para. 3 (e) on this page.

ENGINE FAULT FINDING CHART

Cause	Trouble	Remedy
SYMPTOM:	ENGINE MISFIRES OR IDLES UNEVENLY	
Intermittent sparking at sparking plug	Ignition leads loose	Check and tighten as necessary at spark plug and distributor cap ends.
	Battery leads loose on terminals	Check and tighten terminal leads.
	Battery earth strap loose on body attachment point	Check and tighten earth lead to body attachment point.
	Engine earth lead loose	Tighten lead.
	Low tension leads to SW and CB terminals on coil loose	Check and tighten leads if found loose.
	Low tension lead from CB terminal side to distributor loose	Check and tighten if found loose.
	Dirty, or incorrectly gapped plugs	Remove, clean, and regap.
	Dirty, incorrectly set, or pitted contact breaker points	Clean, file smooth, and adjust.
	Tracking across inside of distributor cover	Remove and fit new cover.
	Ignition too retarded	Check and adjust ignition timing.
	Faulty coil	Remove and fit new coil.
Fuel shortage at engine	Mixture too weak	Check jets, float chamber needle valve, and filters for obstruction. Clean as necessary. Carburettor(s) incorrectly adjusted.
	Air leak in carburettor(s)	Remove and overhaul carburettor.
	Air leak at inlet manifold to cylinder head, or inlet manifold to carburettor	Test by pouring oil along joints. Bubbles indicate leak. Renew manifold gasket as appropriate.
Mechanical wear	Incorrect valve clearances	Adjust rocker arms to take up wear.
	Burnt out exhaust valves	Remove cylinder head and renew defective valves.
	Sticking or leaking valves	Remove cylinder head, clean, check and renew valves as necessary.
	Weak or broken valve springs	Check and renew as necessary.
	Worn valve guides or stems	Renew valve guides and valves.
	Worn pistons and piston rings	Dismantle engine, renew pistons and rings.
SYMPTOM:	LACK OF POWER & POOR COMPRESSION	
Fuel/air mixture leaking from cylinder	Burnt out exhaust valves	Remove cylinder head, renew defective valves.
	Sticking or leaking valves	Remove cylinder head, clean, check, and renew valves as necessary.
	Worn valve guides and stems	Remove cylinder head and renew valves and valve guides.
	Weak or broken valve springs	Remove cylinder head, renew defective springs.
	Blown cylinder head gasket (Accompanied by increase in noise)	Remove cylinder head and fit new gasket.
	Worn pistons and piston rings	Dismantle engine, renew pistons and rings.
	Worn or scored cylinder bores	Dismantle engine, rebore, renew pistons & rings.
Incorrect Adjustments	Ignition timing wrongly set. Too advanced or retarded	Check and reset ignition timing.
	Contact breaker points incorrectly gapped	Check and reset contact breaker points.
	Incorrect valve clearances	Check and reset rocker arm to valve stem gap.
	Incorrectly set sparking plugs	Remove, clean and regap.
	Carburation too rich or too weak	Tune carburettor(s) for optimum performance.
Carburation and ignition faults	Dirty contact breaker points	Remove, clean, and replace.
	Fuel filters blocked causing top end fuel starvation	Dismantle, inspect, clean, and replace all fuel filters.
	Distributor automatic balance weights or vacuum advance and retard mechanisms not functioning correctly	Overhaul distributor.
	Faulty fuel pump giving top end fuel starvation	Remove, overhaul, or fit exchange reconditioned fuel pump.

(See also page 84)

ENGINE

Cause	Trouble	Remedy
SYMPTOM:	EXCESSIVE OIL CONSUMPTION	
Oil being burnt by engine	Badly worn, perished or missing valve stem oil seals	Remove, fit new oil seals to valve stems.
	Excessively worn valve stems and valve guides	Remove cylinder head and fit new valves and valve guides.
	Worn piston rings	Fit oil control rings to existing pistons or purchase new pistons.
	Worn pistons and cylinder bores	Fit new pistons and rings, rebore cylinders.
	Excessive piston ring gap allowing blow-by	Fit new piston rings and set gap correctly.
	Piston oil return holes choked	Decarbonise engine and pistons.
Oil being lost due to leaks	Leaking oil filter gasket	Inspect and fit new gasket as necessary.
	Leaking rocker cover gasket	" " " " " " "
	Leaking tappet chest gasket	" " " " " " "
	Leaking timing case gasket	" " " " " " "
	Leaking sump gasket	" " " " " " "
	Loose sump plug	Tighten, fit new gasket if necessary.
SYMPTOM:	UNUSUAL NOISES FROM ENGINE	
Excessive clearances due to mechanical wear	Worn valve gear (Noisy tapping from rocker box)	Inspect and renew rocker shaft, rocker arms, and ball pins as necessary.
	Worn big end bearing (Regular heavy knocking)	Drop sump, if bearings broken up clean out oil pump and oilways, fit new bearings. If bearings not broken but worn fit bearing shells.
	Worn timing chain and gears (Rattling from front of engine)	Remove timing cover, fit new timing wheels and timing chain.
	Worn main bearings (Rumbling and vibration)	Drop sump, remove crankshaft, if bearings worn but not broken up, renew. If broken up strip oil pump and clean out oilways.
	Worn crankshaft (Knocking, rumbling and vibration)	Regrind crankshaft, fit new main and big end bearings.

CHAPTER TWO

COOLING SYSTEM

SPECIFICATION

Type .. .. Pressurised radiator.	Thermo-siphon, pump assisted, and fan cooled.
Thermostat setting 948 c.c. models	65° to 70°C. (149° to 158°F.).
1,098 c.c. models	Standard 82°C. (180°F.).
.. ..	Hot climates 74°C. (165°F.).
.. ..	Cold climates 88°C. (190°F.).
Blow-off pressure of radiator cap	7 lb/sq. in. (.49 Kg./cm^2).

GENERAL DESCRIPTION

The engine cooling water is circulated by a thermo-siphon, water pump assisted system, and the coolant is pressurised. This is to both prevent the loss of water down the overflow pipe with the radiator cap in position and to prevent premature boiling in adverse conditions. The radiator cap is pressurised to 7 lb/sq.in. and increases the boiling point to 225°F. If the water temperature exceeds this figure and the water boils, the pressure in the system forces the internal part of the cap off its seat, thus exposing the overflow pipe down which the steam from the boiling water escapes thus relieving the pressure. It is, therefore, important to check that the radiator cap is in good condition and that the spring behind the sealing washer has not weakened. Most garages have a special machine in which radiator caps can be tested.

The cooling system comprises the radiator, top and bottom water hoses, by-pass hose to return water to the block when the thermostat is closed, heater hoses (if heater/demister fitted), the impeller water pump, (mounted on the front of the engine it carries the fan blades and is driven by the fan belt), the thermostat and the two drain taps.

The system functions in the following fashion. Cold water in the bottom of the radiator circulates up the lower radiator hose to the water pump where it is pushed round the water passages in the cylinder block, helping to keep the cylinder bores and pistons cool.

The water then travels up into the cylinder head and circulates round the combustion spaces and valve seats absorbing more heat, and then, when the engine is at its proper operating temperature, travels out of the cylinder head, past the open thermostat into the upper radiator hose, and so into the radiator header tank. The water travels down the radiator where it is rapidly cooled by the in-rush of cold air through the radiator core, which is created by both the fan and the motion of the car. The water, now cold, reaches the bottom of the radiator, when the cycle is repeated.

When the engine is cold the thermostat (which is a valve which opens and closes according to the temperature of the water) maintains the circulation of the same water in the engine by returning it via the by-pass hose to the cylinder block. Only when the correct minimum operating temperature has been reached, as shown in the specification, does the thermostat begin to open, allowing water to return to the radiator. On 948 c.c. models with a thermostat that opens at 65°C it is advantageous to fit the later model thermostat designed to open at 82°C.

COOLING SYSTEM - DRAINING

With the car on level ground drain the system as follows:-

1. If the engine is cold remove the filler cap from the radiator by turning the cap anti-clockwise. If the engine is hot having just been run, then turn the filler cap very slightly until the pressure in the system has had time to disperse. Use a rag over the cap to protect your hand from escaping steam. If, with the engine very hot, the cap is released suddenly the drop in pressure can result in the water boiling. With the pressure released the cap can be removed.

2. If anti-freeze is in the radiator drain it into a clean bucket or bowl for re-use.

3. Open the two drain taps. When viewed from the front the radiator drain tap is on the bottom right-hand side of the radiator, and the engine drain tap is halfway down the rear right-hand side of the cylinder block. A short length of rubber tubing over the radiator drain tap nozzle will assist draining the coolant into a container without splashing.

4. When the water has finished running, probe the drain tap orifices with a short piece of wire to dislodge any particles of rust or sediment which may be blocking the taps and preventing all the water draining out.

COOLING SYSTEM - FLUSHING

With time the cooling system will gradually lose its efficiency as the radiator becomes choked with rust scales, deposits from the water, and other sediment. To clean the system out, remove the radiator cap and the drain tap and leave a hose running in the

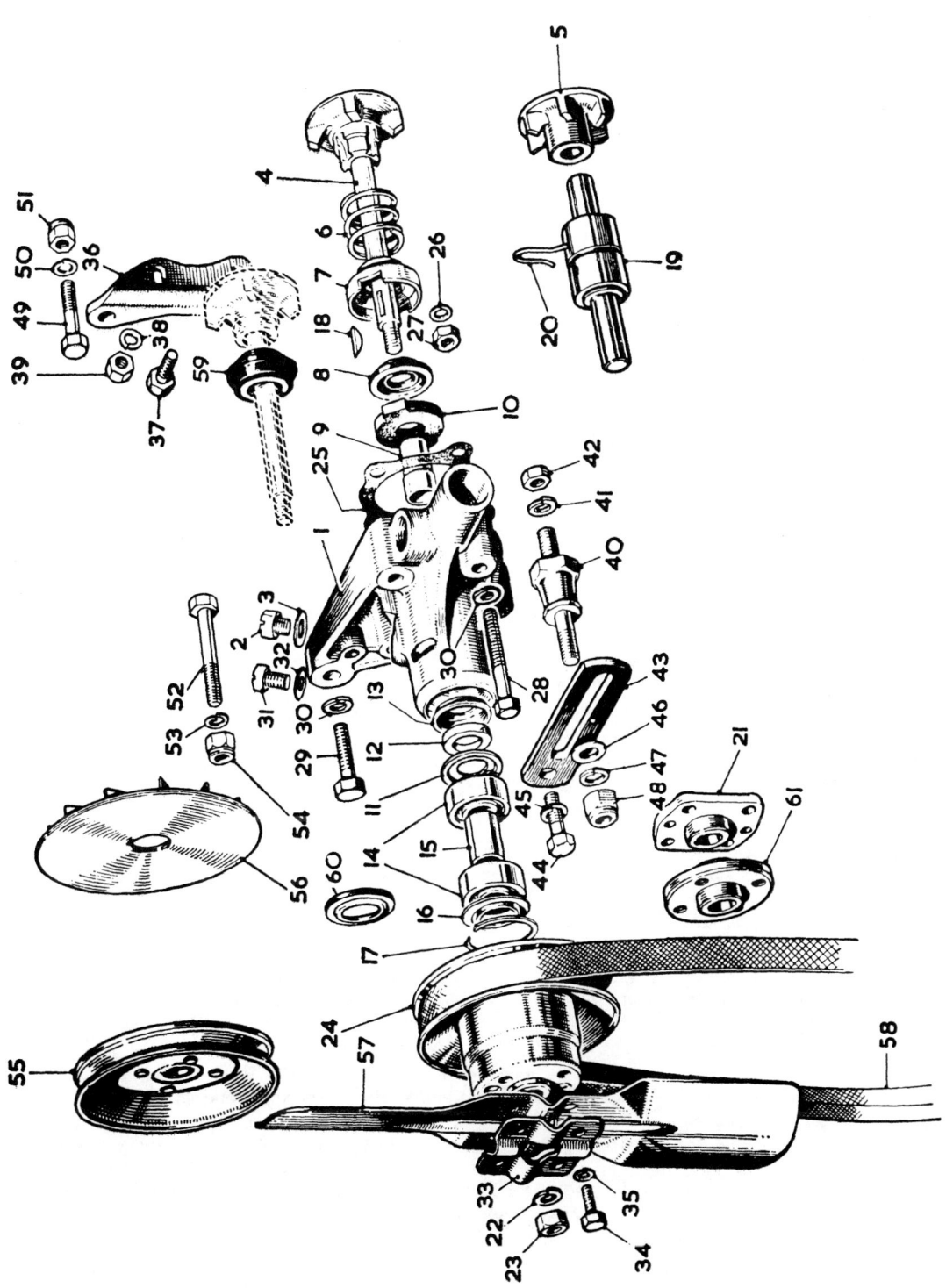

Fig. 2:1. Exploded view of the component parts of both early and late type water pumps. 1 Pump body. 2 Plug-pump body. 3 Washer (fibre). 4 Early type spindle with vane. 5 Later type vane. 6 Spring. 7 Spring locating cup. 8 Rubber seal. 9 Distance piece. 10 Seal. 11 Outer felt retainer. 12 Felt. 13 Inner felt retainer. 14 Bearing. 15 Bearing distance piece. 16 Bearing grease retainer. 17 Retainer circlip. 18 Key pulley. 19 Later type bearing and spindle assembly. 20 Bearing retaining clip. 21 Pulley hub. 22 Washer. 23 Hub nut. 24 Pulley (early type). 25 Washer. 26 Spring washer. 27 Pump stud nut. 28 Screw. 29 Short screw. 30 Spring washer. 31 Screw. 32 Fibre washer. 33 Fan blade plate stiffener. 34 Fan pulley screw. 35 Spring washer. 36 Dynamo rear bracket. 37 Screw. 38 Washer. 39 Nut. 40 Adjusting link pillar. 41 Spring washer. 42 Nut. 43 Dynamo adjusting link. 44 Screw. 45 Spring washer. 46 Washer. 47 Spring washer. 48 Nut. 49 Dynamo bolt. 50 Spring washer. 51 Nut. 52 Bolt. 53 Spring washer. 54 Nut. 55 Pulley (later type). 56 Dynamo fan. 57 Fan blade. 58 Fan belt. 60 Bearing grease retainer. 61 Pulley hub.

55

radiator cap orifice for ten to fifteen minutes.

In very bad cases the radiator should be reversed flushed. This can be done with the radiator in position. The cylinder block tap is closed and a hose placed over the open radiator drain tap. Water, under pressure, is then forced up through the radiator and out of the header tank filler orifice.

The hose is then removed and placed in the filler orifice and the radiator washed out in the usual fashion.

COOLING SYSTEM - FILLING
1. Close the two drain taps.
2. Fill the system slowly to ensure that no air locks develop. If a heater unit is fitted, check that the valve to the heater unit is open, otherwise an air lock may form in the heater. The best type of water to use in the cooling system is rain water, so use this whenever possible.
3. Do not fill the system higher than within ½ in. of the filler orifice. Overfilling will merely result in wastage which is especially to be avoided when anti-freeze is in use.
4. Only use anti-freeze mixture with a glycerine or ethylene base.
5. Replace the filler cap and turn it firmly clockwise to lock it into position.

RADIATOR REMOVAL - INSPECTION & CLEANING
The radiator is removed by the system detailed on page 18. With the radiator out of the car any leaks can be soldered up or repaired with a substance such as "calaloy". Clean out the inside of the radiator by flushing as detailed in the section before last. When the radiator is out of the car it is advantageous to turn it upside down for reverse flushing. Clean the exterior of the radiator by hosing down the radiator matrix with a strong jet or water to clear away road dirt, dead flies, etc.

Inspect the radiator hoses for cracks, internal or external perishing, and damage caused by overtightening of the securing clips. Replace the hoses as necessary. Examine the radiator hose securing clips and renew them if they are rusted or distorted. The drain taps should be renewed if leaking, but ensure the leak is not because of a faulty washer behind the tap. If the tap is suspected try a new washer to see if this clears the trouble first.

RADIATOR REPLACEMENT
To replace the radiator proceed as follows:-
1. Fit the radiator bottom hose to the bottom pipe but do not tighten the clip completely. (For the Austin Healey Sprite and M.G. Midget, fit the bottom hose to the water pump first). Fit the top hose in position on the top radiator pipe and again do not completely tighten the clip.
2. Replace the radiator in the bodyshell and check that the rubbing strips (where fitted) are also replaced.
3. Screw in the four bolts and spring washers which hold the radiator in place, finger tight.
4. Fit the upper radiator hose to the thermostat outlet pipe, and the lower hose to the input side of the water pump. (For the Austin Healey Sprite

and M.G. Midget fit the bottom hose under the rack and pinion steering gear to the radiator).
5. Fully tighten down the radiator securing bolts and tighten up the radiator hose clips.
6. Fill the system with water, start the engine to pressurise the system, and check for leaks.

THERMOSTAT REMOVAL, TESTING & REPLACEMENT
To remove the thermostat partially drain the cooling system (4 pints is enough), loosen the upper radiator hose at the thermostat elbow end and pull it off the elbow. Unscrew the three set bolts and spring washers from the thermostat housing and lift the housing and paper gasket away. Take out the thermostat.

Test the thermostat for correct functioning, by immersing it in a saucepan of cold water together with a thermometer. Heat the water and note when the thermostat begins to open. Early thermostats opened between 68°C and 72°C, and later ones at 82°C. It is preferable to change the early type for a later unit. It is advantageous in winter to fit a thermostat that does not open until 88°C and will obviate any need to fit a radiator blind. Discard the thermostat if it opens too early. Continue heating the water until the thermostat is fully open. Then let it cool down naturally. If the thermostat will not open fully in boiling water, or does not close down as the water cools, then it must be exchanged for a new one. If the thermostat is stuck open when cold this will be apparent when removing it from the housing.

Replacing the thermostat is a reversal of the removal procedure. Remember to use a new paper gasket between the thermostat housing elbow and the thermostat. Renew the thermostat elbow if it is badly eaten away.

WATER PUMP REMOVAL
The standardised water pump fitted now to all models was not fitted on early versions of the O.H.V. Morris Minor and the Austin A.35. Both types of water pump are removed in exactly the same way.
1. Drain the cooling system, remove the top and bottom radiator hoses, and lift out the radiator.
2. Remove the dynamo and fan belt. (See chapter 12).
3. Unscrew the four bolts which hold the pump body to the front of the cylinder block, release the jubilee clip on the upper end of the by-pass hose, release the heater hose (if fitted), and remove the water pump complete with by-pass hose.

WATER PUMP DISMANTLING & REPLACEMENT EARLY TYPE
To dismantle the water pump fitted to early versions of the Morris Minor and Austin A.35, proceed as follows:-
1. Unscrew the four bolts and spring washers which hold the fan blades and fan pulley in place.
2. Remove the large nut and spring washer on the end of the water pump spindle.
3. Remove the hub from the spindle either by judicious levering, or by using a suitable hub puller.

4. Pull out the woodruff key from the slot in the spindle. Remove the circlip which retains the oil seal washer, and remove it with the oil seal.

5. With a plastic or wooden hammer, gently tap the complete spindle and water pump impeller out of the rear of the water pump body.

6. Inspect the rubber seal and the hard moulded seal located behind the impeller and renew them if required.

7. If it is necessary to renew either the front or rear bearings pull the front bearing off the spindle with a suitable bearing extractor, or tap it off evenly. To remove the rear bearing, the distance piece between the front and rear bearing can be slipped off the spindle and the rear bearing removed.

8. The felt washer and retainers behind the rear bearing can now be slipped forwards off the spindle. The rear distance piece can now be removed.

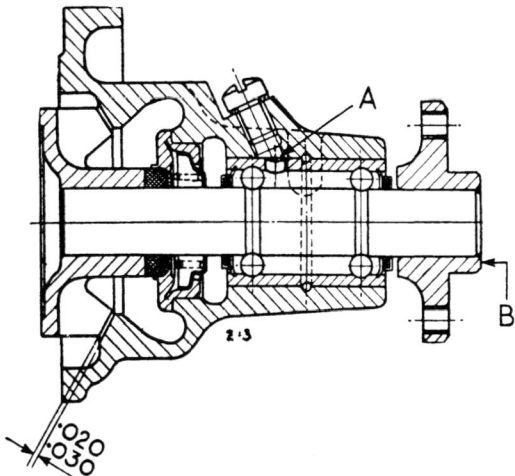

Fig. 2:3. A section through the water pump showing the location of the components. When assembled, the hole in the bearing must coincide with the lubricating hole in the water pump (A) and the face of the hub (B) must be flush with the end of the spindle

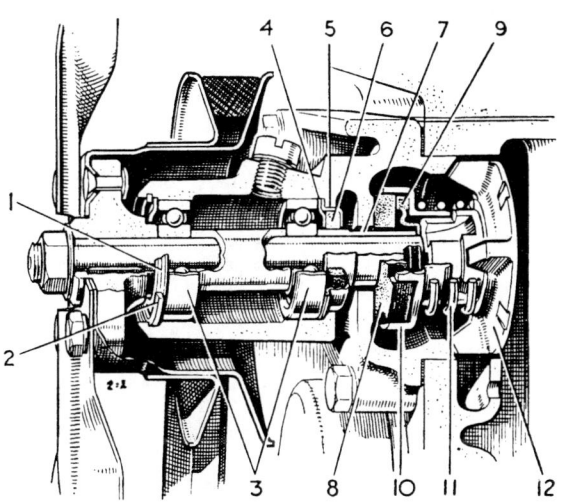

Fig. 2:2. A sectioned view of the water pump. 1 Bearing grease retainer. 2 Circlip. 3 Bearing. 4 Outer felt retainer. 5 Inner felt retainer. 6 Felt. 7 Distance piece. 8 Seal. 9 Rubber seal. 10 Spring locating cup. 11 Water seal spring. 12 Vane with spindle.

To reassemble the water pump and replace it in position is a reversal of the above procedure. New oil seals should be fitted if any are suspect and it is a sound idea to replace the felt washer automatically. The pump bearings should be repacked with Castrolease LM or a similar grease.

WATER PUMP DISMANTLING & REPLACEMENT LATER TYPE

The simpler water pump now fitted to all 'A' series engines is removed from the front of the block in exactly the same way as the earlier pump. To dismantle it proceed as follows:-

1. Remove the four bolts and spring washers which hold the fan blades and fan pulley in place. With these removed, pull or tap off the hub from the end of the spindle, taking great care not to damage it.

2. Then pull out the bearing retaining wire.

3. The spindle and bearing assembly are combined (and are only supplied on exchange as a complete unit), and should now be gently tapped out of the rear of the water pump.

4. The oil seal assembly and the impeller will also come out with the spindle and bearing assembly.

5. The impeller vane is removed from the spindle by judicious tapping and levering, or preferably, to ensure no damage and for ease of operation, with an extractor. The oil seal assembly can then be slipped off.

Reassembly of the water pump and replacement on the front of the block is a reversal of the above sequence. Four points should be noted which have not already been covered:-

1. If the oil seal assembly shows any sign of damage or wear it should be renewed, and the gasket between the water pump and the cylinder block should be renewed every time the pump is removed.

2. There is a small hole in the bearing body cover. When assembled it is vital that this hole lines up with the lubrication hole in the pump body. To check that this is so, prior to reassembly remove the greasing screw and check visually that the hole is in the correct position directly below the greasing aperture.

3. Regrease the bearing by pushing a small amount of grease into the greaser and then screwing in the greasing screw. Under no circumstances should grease be applied under pressure as it could ruin the efficiency of the oil seal.

4. The fan belt tension must be correct when all is reassembled. If the belt is too tight undue strain will be placed on the water pump and dynamo bearings, and if the belt is too loose it will slip and wear rapidly as well as giving rise to low electrical output from the dynamo.

TEMPERATURE GAUGE

On the Austin Healey Sprite and M.G. Midget a

COOLING SYSTEM

temperature gauge is fitted as standard. On other cars it is possible to fit a temperature gauge with a take-off from the top radiator hose, the actual instrument being mounted on a special instrument holder just below the fascia.

The temperature gauge fitted as standard to the above mentioned models comprises a thermal indicator, a wire protected pipe filled with mercury, and a dial type of temperature gauge.

The gauge is held to the instrument panel by a small bracket behind the dial body and this bracket must be released if it is wished to remove the gauge. The thermal indicator is secured to the radiator header tank with a gland nut. If the gauge ceases to function it is necessary to renew the complete assembly as a unit.

FAN BELT ADJUSTMENT

The fan belt tension is correct when there is $\frac{1}{2}$ in. of lateral movement at the midpoint position of the belt between the crankshaft pulley wheel and the water pump pulley wheel.

To adjust the fan belt, slacken the dynamo securing bolts and move the dynamo either in or out until the correct tension is obtained. It is easier if the dynamo bolts are only slackened a little so it requires some force to move the dynamo. In this way the tension of the belt can be arrived at more quickly than by making frequent adjustments. If difficulty is experienced in moving the dynamo away from the engine a long spanner placed behind the dynamo and resting against the block serves as a very good lever and can be held in this position while the dynamo bolts are tightened.

FAULT FINDING CHART

Cause	Trouble	Remedy
SYMPTOM:	OVERHEATING	
Heat generated in cylinder not being successfully disposed of by radiator	Insufficient water in cooling system	Top up radiator
	Fan belt slipping (Accompanied by a shrieking noise on rapid engine acceleration	Tighten fan belt to recommended tension or replace if worn.
	Radiator core blocked or radiator grill restricted	Reverse flush radiator, remove obstructions.
	Bottom water hose collapsed, impeding flow	Remove and fit new hose.
	Thermostat not opening properly	Remove and fit new thermostat.
	Ignition advance and retard incorrectly set (Accompanied by loss of power, and perhaps, misfiring)	Check and reset ignition timing.
	Carburettor(s) incorrectly adjusted (mixture too weak)	Tune carburettor(s).
	Exhaust system partially blocked	Check exhaust pipe for constrictive dents and blockages.
	Oil level in sump too low	Top up sump to full mark on dipstick.
	Blown cylinder head gasket (Water/steam being forced down the radiator overflow pipe under pressure)	Remove cylinder head, fit new gasket.
	Engine not yet run-in	Run-in slowly and carefully.
	Brakes binding	Check and adjust brakes if necessary.
SYMPTOM:	UNDERHEATING	
Too much heat being dispersed by radiator	Thermostat jammed open	Remove and renew thermostat.
	Incorrect grade of thermostat fitted allowing premature opening of valve	Remove and replace with new thermostat which opens at a higher temperature.
	Thermostat missing	Check and fit correct thermostat.
SYMPTOM	LOSS OF COOLING WATER	
Leaks in system	Loose clips on water hoses	Check and tighten clips if necessary.
	Top, bottom, or by-pass water hoses perished and leaking	Check and replace any faulty hoses.
	Radiator core leaking	Remove radiator and repair.
	Thermostat gasket leaking	Inspect and renew gasket.
	Radiator pressure cap spring worn or seal ineffective	Renew radiator pressure cap.
	Blown cylinder head gasket (Pressure in system forcing water/steam down overflow pipe	Remove cylinder head and fit new gasket.
	Cylinder wall or head cracked	Dismantle engine, dispatch to engineering works for repair.

CHAPTER THREE

FUEL SYSTEM AND CARBURATION

SPECIFICATIONS

Morris Minor 1000 – 948 c.c.

Carburettor:	Make and type	S.U. H2 type. $1\frac{1}{4}$ in. (31.75 mm.) throttle.
	Needle 1957/8	BXI (standard). S (rich). MO (weak).
	1957/8 (paper air cleaner) ..	M (standard).
	Later models	M (standard). AH2 (rich). EB (weak).
	Make and type (later models) ..	S.U. HS2 type. $1\frac{1}{4}$ in. (31.75 mm.) throttle.
	Carburettor needle	M (standard). AH2 (rich). EB (weak).
	Carburettor spring	Red.
Air Cleaner:	Make and type .. A.C.	Early models CL oil bath.
	.. .. ..	Later models Coopers dry type with paper element.

Morris Minor 1000 – 1,098 c.c.

Carburettor:	Make and type	S.U. HS2 type. $1\frac{1}{4}$ in. (31.75 mm.) throttle.
	Jet	.090 in. (2.29 mm.).
	Needle	AN (standard). H6 (rich). EB (weak).
	Spring	Red.

GENERAL DESCRIPTION

The fuel system on the Morris Minor Series II and 1000 are basically the same and comprise a fuel tank mounted under the boot (the boot floor has to be removed to get at it), an S.U. electric fuel pump mounted on the scuttle, the fuel line between the tank and the pump, and a semi-downdraught $1\frac{1}{4}$ in. H2 S.U. carburettor.

Later models, after engine Nos. 9M-U-H353600 and 9M-U-L353449, make use of the improved and simplified HS2 carburettor which is not readily interchangeable with the previous type. The differences between these two carburettors are listed under the heading 'S.U. Carburettor - Description' on page 64.

Early models use an oil bath air cleaner, while later models make use of two types of dry type air cleaners with paper elements. The earlier type of dry paper element air cleaner was fitted from car Nos. 698137 and 693918 (Traveller) for the home market, and from car No. 720666 for the export market. The later type of dry air cleaner was fitted with the introduction of the 10MA 1,098 c.c. engine.

OIL BATH AIR CLEANERS - REMOVAL, REPLACEMENT & SERVICING

Early examples of the Morris Minor 1000 used an oil wetted or oil bath type of air cleaner. To remove either type, unscrew the clamp support bolt from the side of the cleaner, release the securing clip from the breather pipe, and lift away the assembly.

Dismantling for servicing merely consists of unscrewing the wing nut and removing the strainer. Wash the strainer in petrol and re-oil it in the case of the oil wetted-type, and empty and clean out the oil container and wash the strainer in petrol in the case of the oil bath type. Fill the oil bath type with fresh engine oil to the oil level mark. There is no need to oil the mesh with the oil bath type as the inrush of air over the oil will carry oil up into the mesh.

DRY TYPE AIR CLEANERS - REMOVAL, REPLACEMENT & SERVICING

Dry type renewable element air cleaners of identical design are fitted to later versions, and the design of these were changed with the introduction of the 1,098 c.c. engines.

On the earlier version fitted to '9' series engines the element can be removed after first screwing off the cover retaining wing nut and prising off the air cleaner cover with a screwdriver inserted in one of the two slots provided for this purpose. Thoroughly clean the container and fit a new paper element, throwing the old element away. If it is wished to remove the air cleaner base completely, then the two securing bolts to the carburettor flange must be removed, together with the breather pipe. Replacement is a reversal of this procedure.

The cleaners fitted to the 1,098 c.c. engines are removed by screwing off the wing nut from the top of the cleaner and then removing the cleaner body, element, cleaner base and rubber washer. If it is wished to remove the cleaner casting to which the cleaner body is attached, unscrew the retaining bolts which hold it to the carburettor flange and lift away together with the flange washer.

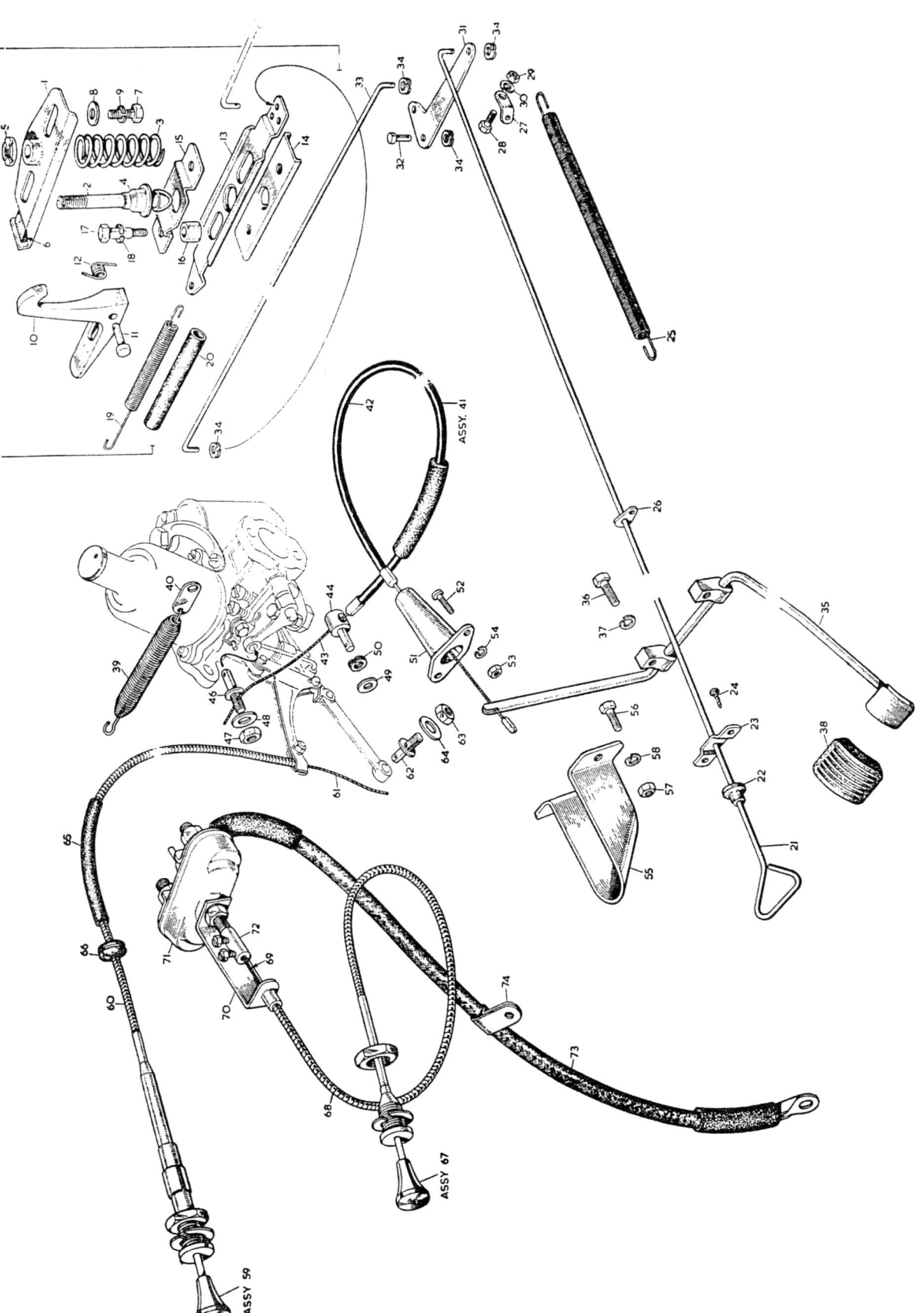

Fig. 3:1. Key to the carburettor and starter control components. 1 Bracket—lower. 2 Pin—lock striker. 3 Spring—striker pin. 4 Cup—spring retaining. 5 Ring—pin locking. 6 Buffer —safety hook. 7 Screw—pin assembly to bonnet. 8 Washer—pin screw. 9 Washer—spring. 10 Catch assembly. 11 Pin—safety catch. 12 Spring—safety catch. 13 Slide —bonnet lock. 14 Support—lock slide. 15 Plate—slide guide. 16 Tube—distance—slide. 17 Bolt—slide to cowl. 18 Washer—spring. 19 Spring—slide tension. 20 Sleeve—rubber—tension spring. 21 Rod—bonnet lock control. 22 Grommet—rod through dash. 23 Retainer—grommet. 24 Screw—retainer to dash. 25 Spring—anti-rattle. 26 Link—spring to control rod. 27 Link—spring to body. 28 Screw—link to body. 29 Nut—link screw. 30 Washer—spring—link screw. 31 Lever—control rod. 32 Pin—lever pivot. 33 Rod—lever to lock slide. 34 Washer—spring—rods and lever pin. 35 Pedal assembly. 36 Bolt—pedal to dash. 37 Washer—spring—pedal return. 38 Pad—rubber. 39 Spring—pedal return. 40 Link—spring to cable. 41 Cable assembly—accelerator. 42 Cable—outer. 43 Cable—inner. 44 Ferrule pin. 46 Pin—cable to carburettor lever. 47 Nut—lever pin. 48 Washer—lever pin nut. 49 Washer—ferrule pin to bracket. 50 Washer—spring—ferrule pin. 51 Guide—cable through dash. 52 Screw—guide to dash. 53 Nut—guide to dash. 54 Washer—spring. 55 Guard —pedal. 56 Screw—guard to dash. 57 Nut—guard screw. 58 Washer—spring. 59 Control assembly—mixture. 60 Cable—outer. 61 Cable—inner. 62 Pin—cable to carburettor lever. 63 Nut—lever pin. 64 Washer—lever pin. 65 Tube—rubber. 66 Grommet through dash. 67 Control assembly. 68 Cable—inner. 69 Cable—outer. 70 Bracket—cable. 71 Switch—

ASSY. 41

ASSY 67

ASSY 59

60

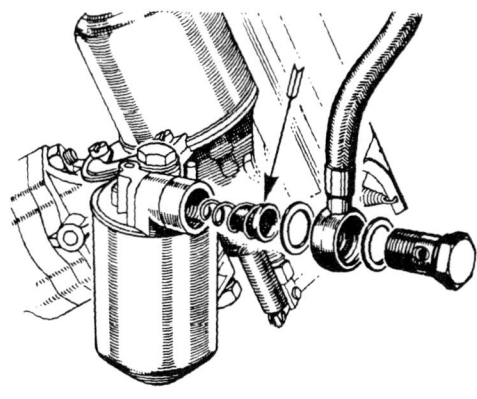

Fig. 3:2A. Remove and clean the carburettor filter at the specified intervals

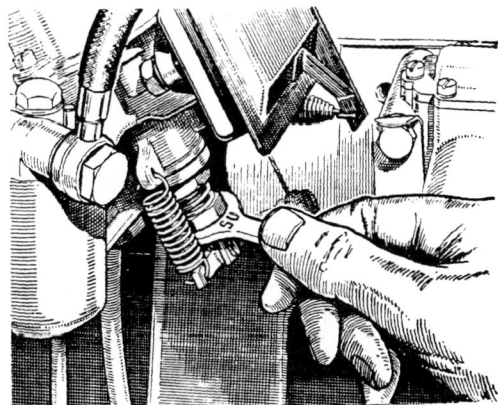

Fig. 3:2B. The jet is adjusted as shown above

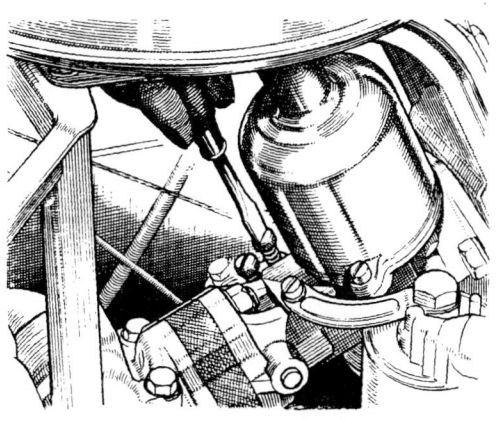

Fig. 3:2C. Turn the screw shown to alter the gap between the throttle interconnecting and operating levers

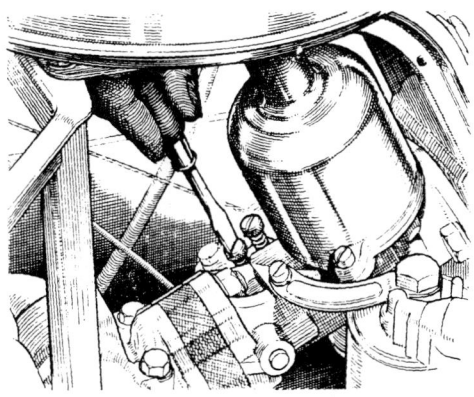

Fig. 3:2D. To alter the slow running turn the slow running screw indicated above

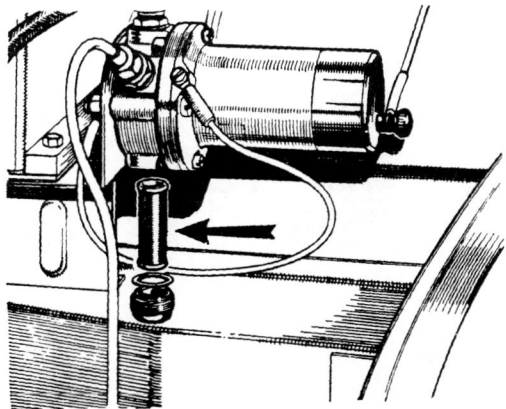

Fig. 3:2E. Check the filter in the petrol pump at the recommended intervals

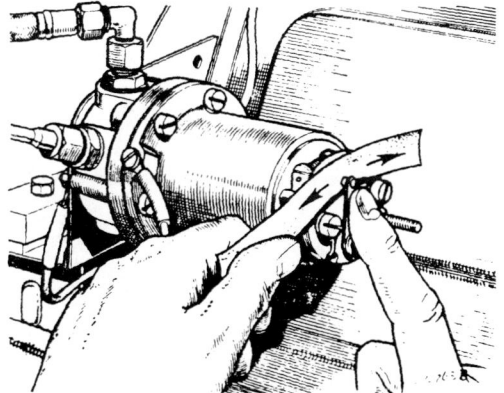

Fig. 3:2F. Keep the contact breaker points clean by drawing a strip of paper between them as indicated above

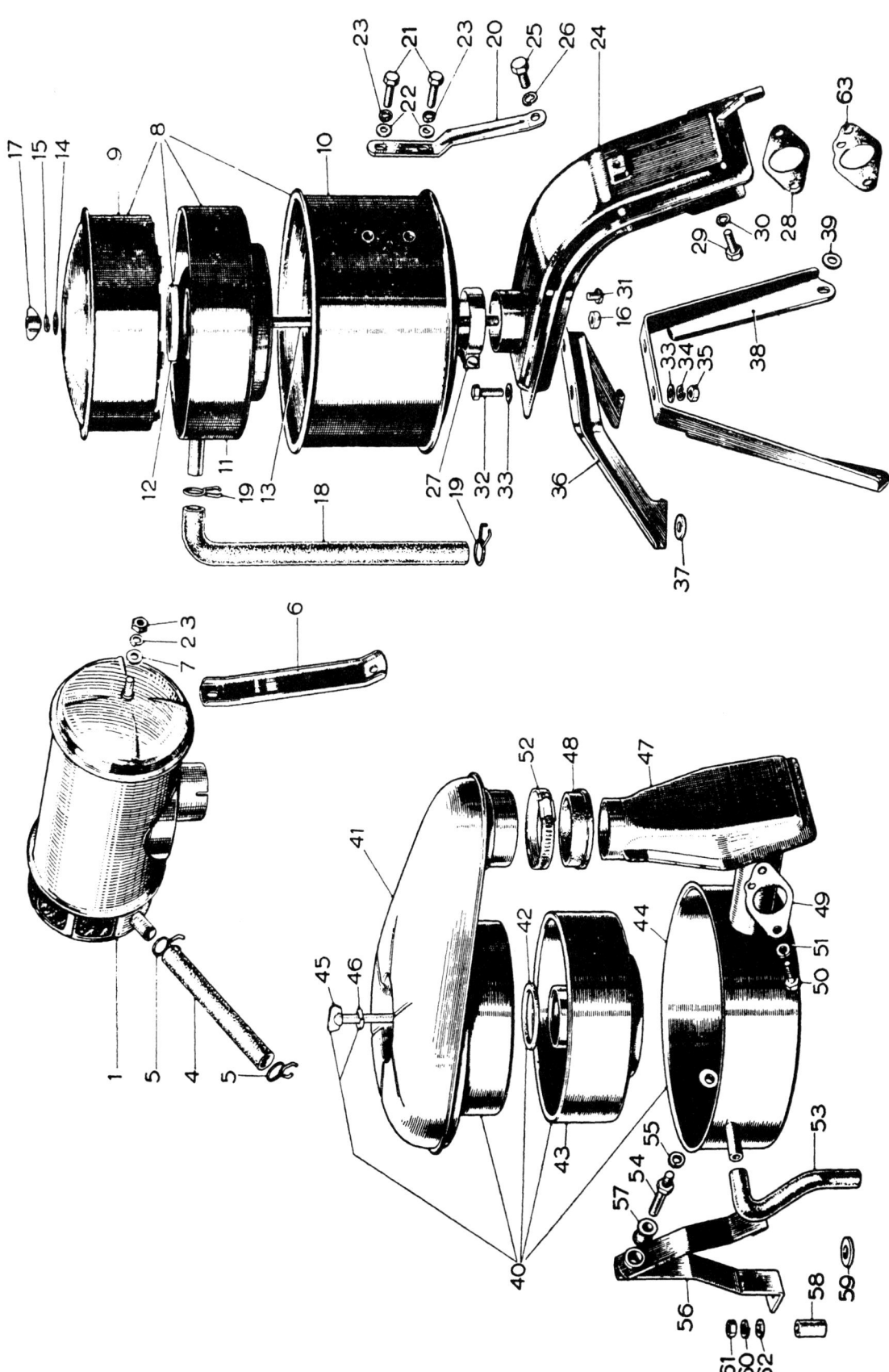

Fig. 3 : 3. Component parts of three of the various air silencers/cleaners which may be fitted. 1 Air silencer. 2 Spring washer. 3 Nut. 4 Hose. 5 Hose clip. 6 Silencer steady bracket. 7 Plain washer. 8 Export air cleaner. 9 Cover and element. 10 Silencer chamber. 11 Oil container. 12 Cover washer. 13 Centre stud. 14 Washer. 15 Spring washer. 16 Locknut. 17 Wing nut. 18 Hose. 19 Hose clip. 20 Cleaver bracket. 21 Screw. 22 Washer. 23 Spring washer. 24 Air pipe. 25 Screw. 26 Spring washer. 27 Clip. 28 Joint. 29 Screw. 30 Spring washer. 31 Blanking screw. 32 Screw. 33 Plain washer. 34 Spring washer. 35 Nut. 36 Bracket. 37 Washer. 38 Bracket. 39 Washer. 40 Air cleaner. 41 Cover and element assembly. 42 Gasket. 43 Oil container. 44 Silencer chamber. 45 Wing nut. 46 Spring washer. 47 Air pipe. 48 Rubber sleeve. 49 Gasket. 50 Screw. 51 Washer. 52 Clip. 53 Breather pipe. 54 Stud. 55 Spring washer. 56 Steady bracket. 57 Bush. 58 Adaptor. 59 Washer. 60 Washer. 61 Nut. 62 Washer. 63 Joint.

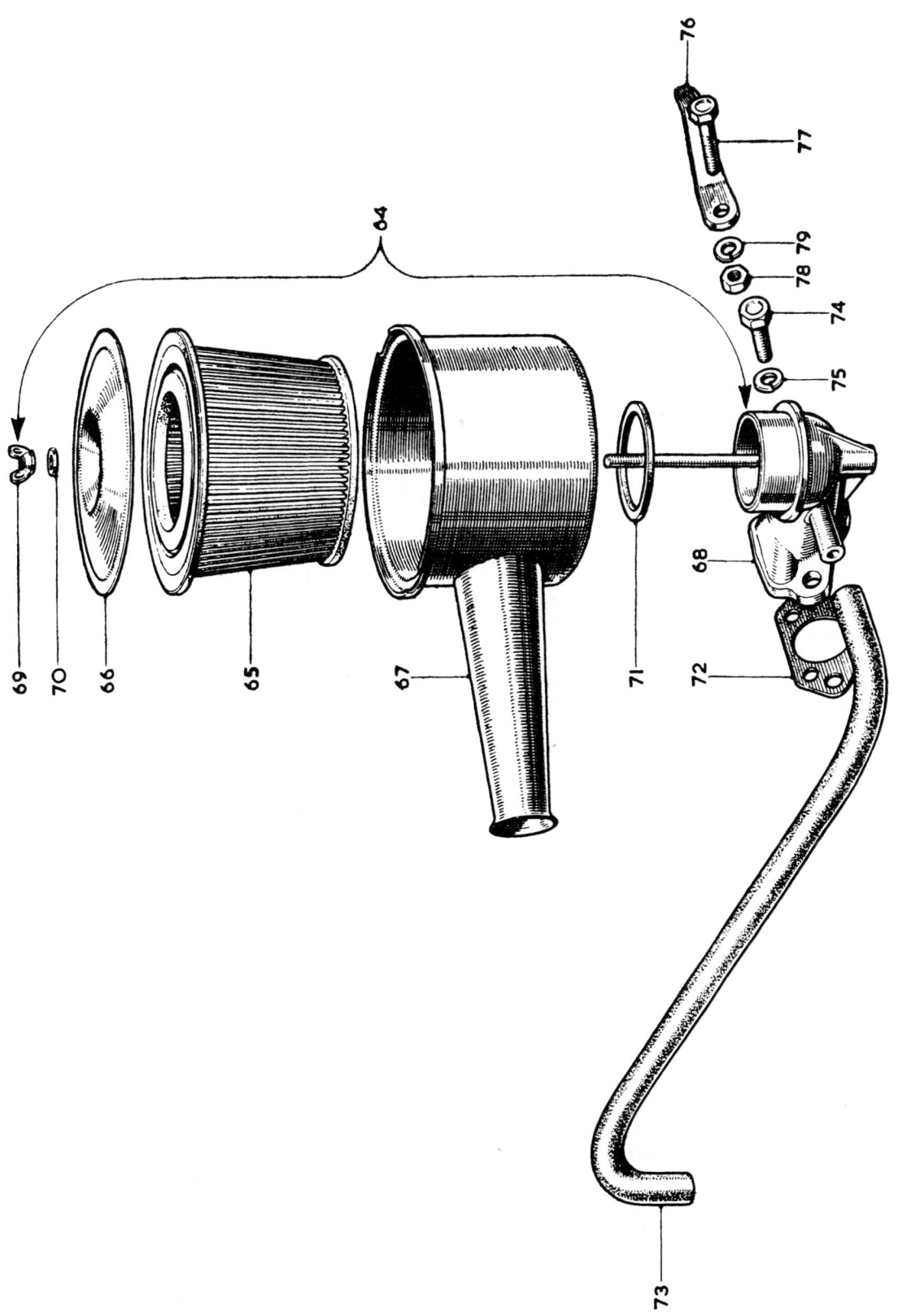

Fig. 3:4. Component parts of the paper element air cleaner and silencer. 64 Air cleaner. 65 Paper element. 66 Lid. 67 Body assembly. 68 Casting and tie-rod assembly. 69 Wing nut. 70 Fibre washer. 71 Rubber washer. 72 Gasket. 73 Hose. 74 Screw. 75 Washer. 76 Anchor bracket. 77 Bracket. 78 Nut. 79 Spring washer.

FUEL SYSTEM AND CARBURATION

S.U. CARBURETTORS - DESCRIPTION

The variable choke S.U. carburettor is a relatively simple instrument and is basically the same irrespective of its size and type. It differs from most other carburettors in that instead of having a number of various sized fixed jets for different conditions, only one variable jet is fitted to deal with all possible conditions.

Although the alterations are few it is as well to know the differences between the early H1/H2 type S.U. carburettor fitted to certain of the 'A' Series engines and the later HS2 type. The H2 carburettor has a thimble gauze filter in the float chamber inlet union, the fuel is carried from the float chamber to the jet in a casting which is part of the float chamber, and the float chamber is secured to the carburettor body by a float chamber holding up bolt which passes through the float chamber extension casting, and is surrounded on either side with rubber grommets. (These grommets frequently wear, allowing fuel to leak. Regular renewal is recommended at intervals of 12,000 miles.) Under the head of the holding up bolt is a metal washer. The jet bearings are in two halves and are held apart with a spring.

The HS2 carburettor is a simplified version of the H2 type. As well as modifications to the mixture control and ignition control advance and retard pipe, there is no gauze filter in the float chamber inlet union, the fuel is carried from the float chamber to the base of the jet head by a nylon pipe, the float chamber is secured to the carburettor body by a horizontally positioned bolt with rubber cushioning washers and grommets, and the jet bearing assembly is far simpler, consisting of one long bearing. These alterations result in a more reliable and efficient carburettor with less likelihood of developing faults.

Air passing rapidly through the carburettor choke draws petrol from the jet so forming the petrol/air mixture. The amount of petrol drawn from the jet depends on the position of the tapered carburettor needle, which moves up and down the jet orifice according to engine load and throttle opening, thus effectively altering the size of the jet so that exactly the right amount of fuel is metered for the prevailing road conditions.

The position of the tapered needle in the jet is determined by engine vacuum. The shank of the needle is held at its top end in a piston which slides up and down the dashpot in response to the degree of manifold vacuum. This is directly controlled by the position of the throttle.

With the throttle fully open, the full effect of inlet manifold vacuum is felt by the piston which has an air bleed into the choke tube on the outside of the throttle. This causes the piston to rise fully, bringing the needle with it. With the accelerator partially closed only slight inlet manifold vacuum is felt by the piston (although, of course, on the engine side of the throttle the vacuum is now greater), and the piston only rises a little, blocking most of the jet orifice with the metering needle.

To prevent the piston fluttering and to give a richer mixture when the accelerator is suddenly

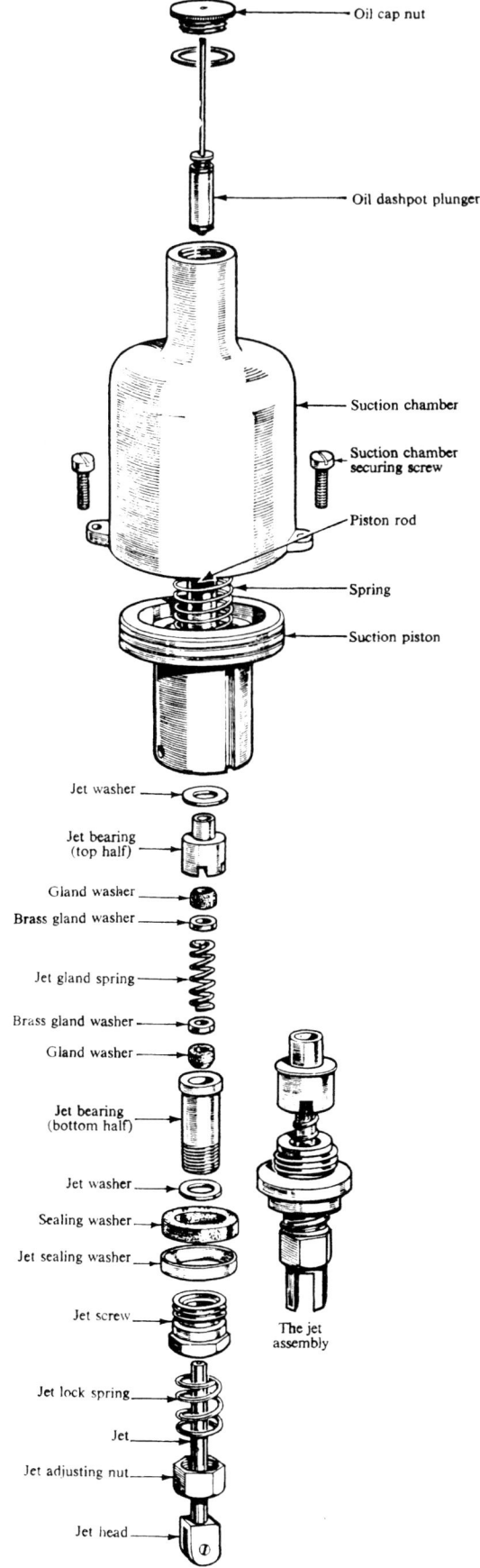

- Oil cap nut
- Oil dashpot plunger
- Suction chamber
- Suction chamber securing screw
- Piston rod
- Spring
- Suction piston
- Jet washer
- Jet bearing (top half)
- Gland washer
- Brass gland washer
- Jet gland spring
- Brass gland washer
- Gland washer
- Jet bearing (bottom half)
- Jet washer
- Sealing washer
- Jet sealing washer
- Jet screw
- Jet lock spring
- Jet
- Jet adjusting nut
- Jet head
- The jet assembly

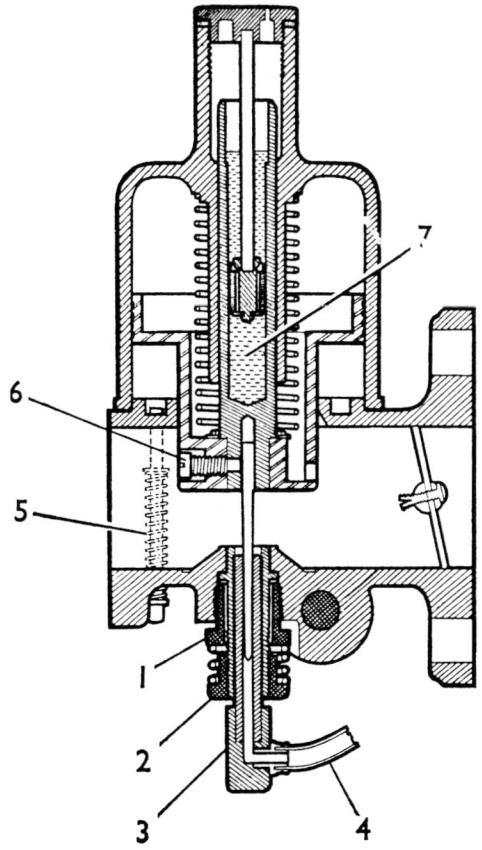

Fig. 3:6. A section through the HS2 carburettor showing—1 Jet locking nut. 2 Jet adjusting nut. 3 Jet head. 4 Nylon fuel pipe. 5 Piston lifting pin. 6 Needle securing screw. 7 Piston damper oil well.

depressed, an oil damper and light spring are fitted inside the dashpot.

The only portion of the piston assembly to come into contact with the piston chamber or dashpot is the actual central piston rod. All the other parts of the piston assembly, including the lower choke portion, have sufficient clearances to prevent any direct metal to metal contact which is essential if the carburettor is to work properly.

The correct level of the petrol in the carburettor is determined by the level of the float in the float chamber. When the level is correct the float rises and by means of a lever resting on top if it closes the needle valve in the cover of the float chamber. This closes off the supply of fuel from the pump. When the level in the float chamber drops as fuel is used in the carburettor, so the float sinks and as it does, so the float needle comes away from its seat so allowing more fuel to enter the float chamber to restore the level to normal.

S.U. CARBURETTORS - REMOVAL & REPLACEMENT

1. Release the clip which secures the breather hose to the rocker cover, and pull the hose from the rocker cover pipe.
2. Unscrew the union which holds the vacuum advance pipe to the carburettor body.
3. Remove the air cleaner complete by releasing the two securing bolts and lockwashers from the carburettor flange.

4. Unscrew the union or clip securing the fuel inlet pipe to the float chamber and pull away the pipe.
5. Remove the choke and accelerator cables from the carburettor linkages.
6. Remove the two nuts and lockwashers which hold the S.U. carburettor to the inlet manifold. The bottom nut is sometimes difficult to unscrew, but merely requires patience. Lift the carburettor away from the inlet manifold together with the inlet manifold gasket. If twin carburettors are being removed then the procedure is exactly the same as above but both carburettors will have to be lifted off together as they are joined by a common spindle.

To replace the carburettor/s reverse the above procedure using new gaskets where required. Do not omit to fit the spring washers.

S.U. CARBURETTORS - DISMANTLING

The S.U. carburettor with only two normally moving parts - the throttle valve and the piston assembly - makes it a straightforward instrument to service, but at the same time it is a delicate unit and clumsy handling can cause much damage. In particular it is easy to knock the finely tapering needle out of true, and the greatest care should be taken to keep all the parts associated with the dashpot scrupulously clean.

1. Remove the oil dashpot plunger nut from the top of the dashpot.
2. Unscrew the two set screws holding the dashpot to the carburettor body, and lift away the dashpot, light spring, and piston and needle assembly.
3. To remove the metering needle from the choke portion of the piston unscrew the sunken retaining screw from the side of the piston choke and pull out the needle. When replacing the needle ensure that the shoulder is flush with the underside of the piston.
4. Release the float chamber from the carburettor by releasing the clamping bolt and sealing washers from the carburettor base. (The bolt is removed from the side in the case of the H2 instrument).
5. Normally, it is not necessary to dismantle the carburettor further, but if because of wear or for some other reason it is wished to remove the jet, this is easily accomplished by removing the clevis pin holding the jet operating lever to the jet head, and then just removing the jet by extracting it from the base of the carburettor. The jet adjusting screw can then be unscrewed together with the jet adjusting screw locking spring.
6. If the larger jet locking screw above the jet adjusting screw is removed, then the jet will have to be recentred when the carburettor is reassembled. With the jet screws removed on HS2 carburettors it is a simple matter to release the jet bearing. On the H1/H2 type of carburettor, dismantling is more complex. With the jet locking screw removed, take out the sealing washer, jet gland spring, brass

gland washer, gland washer, and the top half of the jet bearing in this order.

7. To remove the throttle and actuating spindle release the two screws holding the throttle in position in the slot in the spindle, slide the throttle out of the spindle and then remove the spindle.

S.U. CARBURETTOR FLOAT CHAMBER DISMANTLING, EXAMINATION & REASSEMBLY

To dismantle the float chamber, first disconnect the inlet pipe from the fuel pump at the top of the float chamber cover. On early cars a fuel filter was fitted in the inlet union. This consisted of a spring loaded thimble of fine gauze. On removal of the securing screw and the fuel pipe banjo the backing spring will force the filter half out of its housing in the float chamber cover, making removal for cleaning simple. If the gauze does not come forward in this fashion, judicious levering round its rim with a small screwdriver will free it. Clean the gauze in petrol with a toothbrush. Never try and clean the gauze with a piece of rag.

On the H1/H2 carburettor unscrew the nut in the middle of the float chamber cover and lift away the cover. NOTE that there is a fibre washer under the nut and a larger washer between the cover and the float chamber body. On the HS2 carburettor the cover is held in position by three set screws.

If it is not wished to remove the float chamber completely and the carburettor is still attached to the engine, carefully insert a thin piece of bent wire under the float and lift the float out. To remove the float chamber from the carburettor body on H1/H2 instruments, release the hexagon headed retaining bolt at the base of the carburettor that passes through the float chamber extension casting. On the HS2 instrument, release the bolt which runs horizontally through the carburettor. Make a careful note of the rubber grommets and washers and on reassembly ensure they are replaced in the correct order. If the float chamber is removed completely it is a simple matter to turn it upside down to drop the float out. Check that the float is not cracked or leaking. If it is it must be repaired or renewed.

The float chamber cover contains the needle valve assembly which regulates the amount of fuel which is fed into the float chamber.

One end of the float lever rests on top of the float, rising and falling with it, while the other end pivots on a hinge pin which is held by two lugs. On the float cover side of the float lever is a needle which rises and falls in its brass seating according to the movement of the lever.

With the cover in place the hinge pin is held in position by the walls of the float chamber. With the cover removed the pin is easily pushed out so freeing the float lever and the needles.

Examine the tip of the needle and the needle seating for wear. Wear is present when there is a discernible ridge in the chamfer of the needle. If this is evident then the needle and seating must be renewed. This is a simple operation and the hexagon head of the needle housing is easily screwed out.

Never renew either the needle or the seating without renewing the other part as otherwise it will not be possible to get a fuel tight joint.

Clean the fuel chamber out thoroughly. Reassembly is a reversal of the dismantling procedure detailed above. Before replacing the float chamber cover, check that fuel level setting is correct.

S.U. CARBURETTOR FLOAT CHAMBER FUEL LEVEL ADJUSTMENT

It is essential that the fuel level in the float chamber is always correct as otherwise excessive fuel consumption may occur. On reassembly of the float chamber check the fuel level before replacing the float chamber cover, in the following manner:

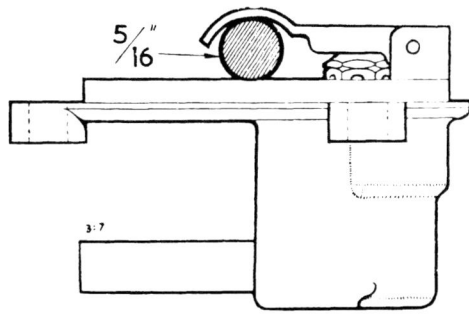

Fig. 3:7. The method of setting the correct clearance of the float lever on early carburettors

Invert the float chamber so that the needle valve is closed. On early cars with H1 carburettors it should be possible to just slide a $7/16$ in. bar between the curved portion of the float lever and the machined lip of the float chamber cover. On later models with H2 carburettors, a $5/16$ in. bar should be used.

If the bar lifts the lever or if the lever stands proud of the bar then it is necessary to bend the lever at the bifurcation point between the shank and the curved portion until the clearance is correct. Never bend the flat portion of the lever. On later cars with

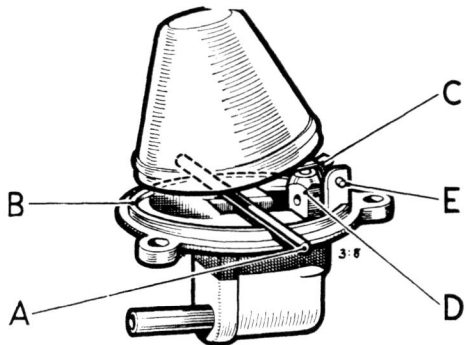

Fig. 3:8. The method of setting the correct clearance of the float lever on later cars. A $1/8$ to $3/16$ in. B Machined lip. C Angle of float lever. D Float needle and seat assembly. E Lever hinge pin.

a conical float use a $1/8$ in. bar and place it parallel to the float lever hinge pin and in the centre of the float chamber cover. Reset the angle of the float by bending the lever as necessary.

S. U. CARBURETTOR EXAMINATION & REPAIR

The S.U. carburettor generally speaking, is most reliable, but even so it may develop one of several faults which may not be readily apparent unless a careful inspection is carried out. The common faults the carburettor is prone to are:-

1. Piston sticking.
2. Float needle sticking.
3. Float chamber flooding.
4. Water and dirt in the carburettor.

In addition the following parts are susceptible to wear after long mileages and as they vitally affect the economy of the engine should be checked and renewed, where necessary, every 24,000 miles.

a) The Carburettor Needle. If this has been incorrectly assembled at some time so that it is not centrally located in the jet orifice, then the metering needle will have a tiny ridge worn on it. If a ridge can be seen then the needle must be renewed. S.U. carburettor needles are made to very fine tolerances and should a ridge be apparent no attempt should be made to rub the needle down with fine emery paper. If it is wished to clean the needle it can be polished lightly with metal polish.

b) The Carburettor Jet. If the needle is worn it is likely that the rim of the jet will be damaged where the needle has been striking it. It should be renewed as otherwise fuel consumption will suffer. The jet can also be badly worn or ridged on the outside from where it has been sliding up and down between the jet bearings everytime the choke has been pulled out. Removal and renewal is the only answer here as well.

c) Check the edges of the throttle and the choke tube for wear. Renew if worn.

d) The washers fitted to the base of the jet, to the float chamber, and to the petrol inlet union may all leak after a time and can cause much fuel wastage. It is wisest to renew them automatically when the carburettor is stripped down.

e) After high mileages the float chamber needle and seat are bound to be ridged. They are not an expensive item to replace and should be renewed as a set. They should never be renewed separately.

PISTON STICKING - The hardened piston rod which slides in the centre guide tube in the middle of the dashpot is the only part of the piston assembly (which comprises the jet needle, suction disc, and piston choke) that should make contact with the dashpot. The piston rim and the choke periphery are machined to very fine tolerances so that they will not touch the dashpot or the choke tube walls.

After high mileages wear in the centre guide tube (especially on semi-downdraught S.U.s) may allow the piston to touch the dashpot wall. This condition is known as sticking.

If piston sticking is suspected or it is wished to test for this condition, rotate the piston about the centre guide tube at the same time sliding it up and down inside the dashpot. If any portion of the piston makes contact with the dashpot wall then that portion of the wall must be polished with metal polish until clearance exists. In extreme cases, fine emery cloth can be used.

The greatest care should be taken to remove only the minimum amount of metal to provide the clearance, as too large a gap will cause air leakage and will upset the functioning of the carburettor. Clean down the walls of the dashpot and the piston rim and ensure that there is no oil on them. A trace of oil may be judiciously applied to the piston rod.

If the piston is sticking under no circumstances try to clear it by trying to alter the tension of the light return spring.

FLOAT NEEDLE STICKING - If the float needle sticks the carburettor will soon run dry and the engine will stop despite there being fuel in the tank.

The easiest way to check a suspected sticking float needle is to remove the inlet pipe at the carburettor, and where a mechanical fuel pump is fitted, turn the engine over on the starter motor by pressing the solenoid. Where an electrical fuel pump is fitted turn on the ignition. If fuel spurts from the end of the pipe (direct it towards the ground or into a wad of cloth or jar), then the fault is almost certain to be a sticking float needle.

Remove the float chamber and dismantle the valve as detailed on page 66 and clean the housing and float chamber out thoroughly.

FLOAT CHAMBER FLOODING - If fuel emerges from the small breather hole in the cover of the float chamber this condition is known as flooding. It is caused by the float chamber needle not seating properly in its housing; normally because a piece of dirt or foreign matter has become jammed between the needle and the needle housing. Alternatively the float may have developed a leak or be maladjusted so that it is holding open the float chamber needle valve even though the chamber is full of petrol. Remove the float chamber cover, clean the needle assembly, check the setting of the float as detailed on page 66, and shake the float to verify if any petrol has leaked into it.

WATER & DIRT IN CARBURETTOR - Because of the size of the jet orifice, water or dirt in the carburettor is normally easily cleared. If dirt in the carburettor is suspected lift the piston assembly and flood the float chamber. The normal level of fuel should be about $1/16$ in. below the top of the jet and on flooding the carburettor the fuel should well up out of the jet hole.

If very little or no petrol appears, start the engine (the jet is never completely blocked) and with the throttle fully open, blank off the air intake. This will create a partial vacuum in the choke tube and help to suck out any foreign matter from the jet tube. Release the throttle as soon as the engine starts to race. Repeat this procedure several times, stop the engine, and then check the carburettor as detailed in the first paragraph.

If this has failed to do the trick then there is no alternative but to remove and blow out the jet (see page 65 for details).

S.U. H1/H2 CARBURETTOR JET CENTRING

The carburettor metering needle is used as a pilot for centring the jet. The piston should therefore be in position, with the dashpot in place, before the jet is centred.

On the H1/H2 carburettor with the adjusting screw spring removed, screw the adjusting hexagon up into its highest position. The adjusting hexagon is the lower of the two nuts.

Slide the jet up into position until it is as high as it will go with the base of the jet head against the underside of the adjusting screw.

The larger hexagon jet screw located above the adjusting nut should now be unscrewed two turns, when it will be found that by gripping the base of the jet and jet adjusting screw that the jet can be moved very slightly laterally.

Move the jet until the carburettor needle will enter into it fully, and can also be lifted up and will fall under its own weight with a soft click, so entering fully into the jet without any trace of fouling. The jet is now centralised.

Tighten the large jet screw slightly and check that the needle is still quite free to slide in the jet orifice without binding. Tighten down the jet screw firmly and recheck that the jet is still centralised.

Remove the jet and the adjusting screw, replace the set screw retaining spring, and return the jet screw and the jet to their positions. It will now be necessary to adjust the carburettor for correct mixture strength.

S.U. HS2 CARBURETTOR JET CENTRING

The procedure adopted is very similar to that used for the H1/H2 carburettor and is as follows: Remove the union holding the nylon feed tube to the base of the jet, together with the jet and jet adjusting nut securing spring, after removing the link between the jet head and lever.

Replace the jet and nylon feed tube and press them up under the head of the large hexagonal jet locking nut. Unscrew this nut slightly until the jet bearing can be turned.

Remove the damper securing nut and damper from the top of the dashpot and push the piston assembly right down so that the metering needle enters fully into the jet.

Tighten the jet locking nut and test the piston assembly to check that the needle is still quite free to slide in the jet orifice. On lifting the piston and then releasing it the piston should hit the inside jet bridge with a soft metallic click, and the intensity of the click should be the same whether the jet is in its normal position or is fully lowered.

If the sound is different when the jet is fully lowered then the jet is not yet properly centralised and the process must be repeated.

When all is correct, remove the jet, replace the jet adjusting nut securing spring, the adjusting nut and jet, and the link between the jet head and the lever.

S.U. CARBURETTOR REASSEMBLY

When dealing with the H1/H2 carburettor, start by reassembling the jet assembly. Replace the copper jet washer on the neck of the upper half of the jet bearing and insert the bearing in position at the top of the jet orifice in the carburettor base.

Position the gland sealing washer in the upper jet bearing with its bevelled edge uppermost (towards the jet orifice). Then fit the small brass washer and the spring.

Position the gland sealing washer in the lower jet bearing with its bevelled edge downwards and then fit the small brass washer.

Insert the copper jet washer under the head of the bottom half of the jet bearing, fit the jet sealing washers over the large jet securing screw, which can now be screwed into position. The jet must now be centred as described in the previous section.

Reassembly of the carburettor is now quite straightforward and is merely a reversal of the dismantling instructions.

When dealing with the HS2 carburettor matters are much simplified as both halves of the H2 jet bearing have been changed to one long bearing with no washers or springs and it is merely necessary to place the jet bearing in position, and then fit the washer and locking nut. Reassembly then continues as a reversal of the dismantling instructions.

S.U. CARBURETTOR - ADJUSTMENT & TUNING

To adjust and tune the S.U. carburettor proceed in the following manner: Check the colour of the exhaust at idling speed with the choke fully in. If the exhaust tends to be black, and the tailpipe interior is also black it is a fair indication that the mixture is too rich. If the exhaust is colourless and the deposit in the exhaust pipe is very light grey it is likely that the mixture is too weak. This condition may also be accompanied by intermittent misfiring, while too rich a mixture will be associated with 'hunting'. Ideally the exhaust should be colourless with a medium grey pipe deposit.

Once the engine has reached its normal operating temperature, detach the carburettor/s air intake cleaner. With twin carburettors disconnect the throttle linkage between them by loosening the small nut on the folded metal clamp.

Only two adjustments are provided on the S.U. carburettor. Idling speed is governed by the throttle adjusting screw, and the mixture strength by the jet adjusting screw. The S.U. carburettor is correctly adjusted for the whole of its engine revolution range when the idling mixture strength is correct.

Idling speed adjustment is effected by the idling adjusting screw. To adjust the mixture set the engine to run at about 1,000 r.p.m. by screwing in the idling screw. If twin S.U. carburettors are fitted repeat this procedure for each instrument in turn.

Check the mixture strength by lifting the piston of the carburettor approximately $1/32$ in. (8 mm.)

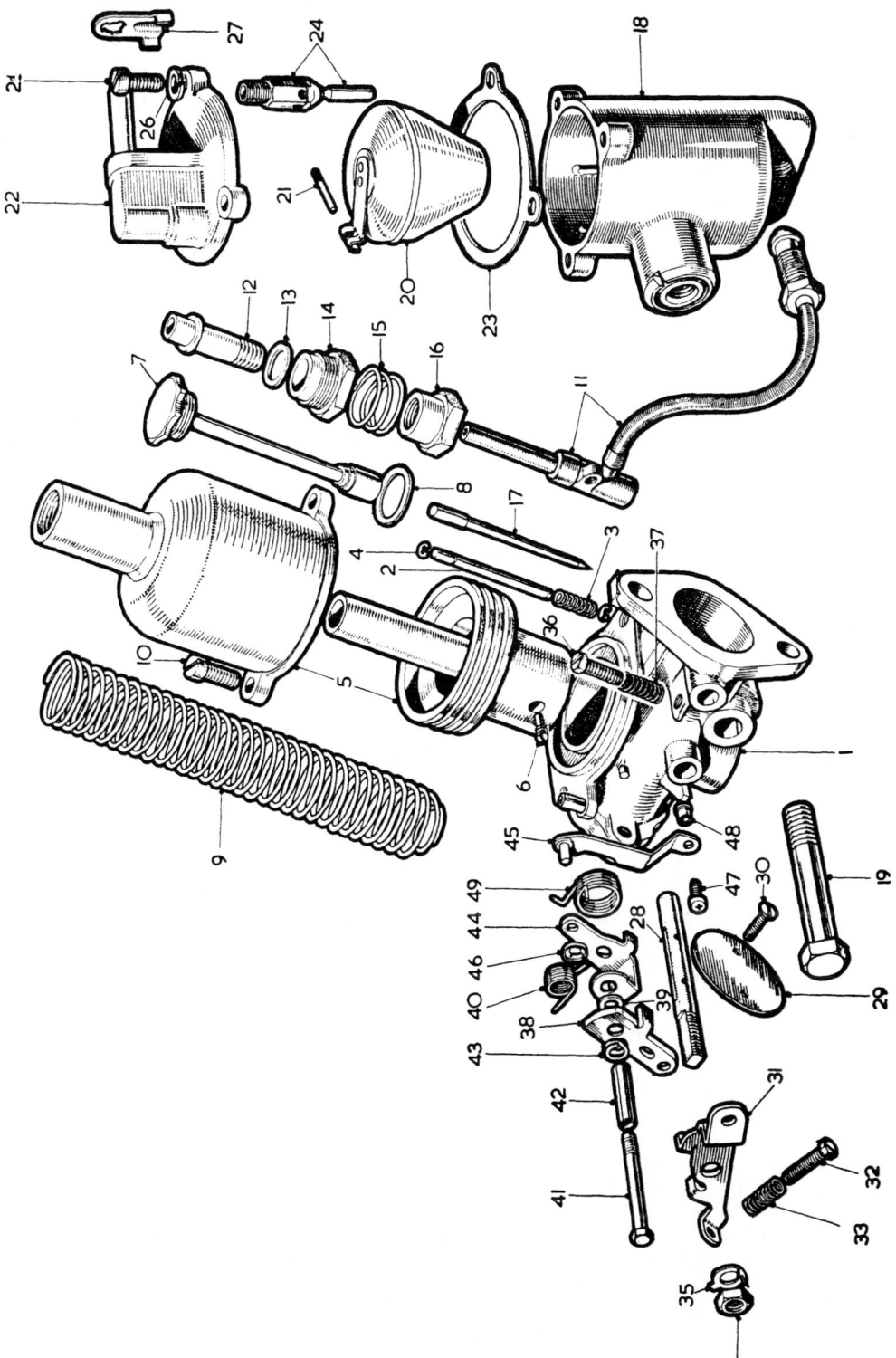

Fig. 3:9. The component parts of the S.U. type HS2 carburettor. 1 Body. 2 Piston lifting pin. 3 Spring for pin. 4 Circlip for pin. 5 Suction chamber and piston assembly. 6 Needle locking screw. 7 Piston damper assembly. 8 Washer for damper cap (fibre). 9 Piston spring. 10 Screw—suction chamber to body. 11 Jet assembly. 12 Jet bearing. 13 Washer for jet bearing (brass). 14 Lock screw for jet bearing. 15 Lock spring. 16 Jet adjusting nut. 17 Jet needle. 18 Float chamber body. 19 Float chamber lid assembly. 20 Float and lever assembly. 21 Lever hinge pin. 22 Float chamber lid assembly. 23 Washer for lid. 24 Needle and seat assembly. 25 Screw—float chamber lid to body. 26 Spring washer. 27 Baffle—overflow. 28 Throttle spindle. 29 Throttle disc. 30 Screw—throttle disc. 31 Throttle lever. 32 Cam stop screw. 33 Spring for stop screw. 34 Throttle spindle nut. 35 Tab washer for nut. 36 Idling stop screw. 37 Spring for stop screw. 38 Cam lever. 39 Washer. 40 Cam lever spring. 41 Cam lever pivot bolt. 42 Pivot bolt tube. 43 Spring washer. 44 Pick-up lever assembly. 45 Jet link. 46 Jet link retaining clip. 47 Jet link securing screw. 48 Bush. 49 Spring for pick-up lever.

69

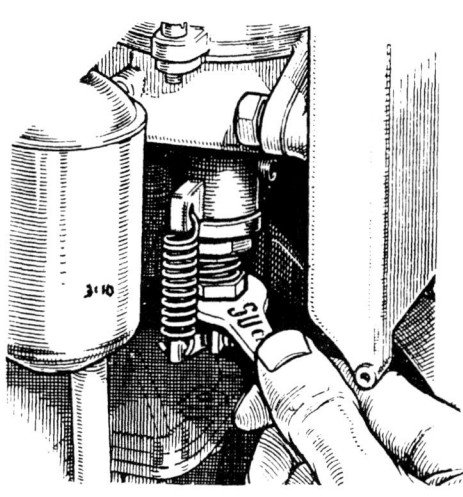

Fig. 3:10. To adjust the jet, the jet adjusting nut must be turned in the appropriate direction, as shown

with a thin wire spoke or small screwdriver so as to disturb the airflow as little as possible, when if:

a) the speed of the engine increases appreciably the mixture is too rich.

b) the engine speed immediately decreases the mixture is too weak.

c) the engine speed increases very slightly the mixture is correct.

To enrich the mixture rotate the adjusting screw, which is the screw at the bottom of the carburettor, in an anti-clockwise direction, i.e. downwards. To weaken the mixture rotate the jet adjusting screw in a clockwise direction, i.e. upwards. Only turn the adjusting screw a flat at a time and check the mixture strength between each turn. It is likely that there will be a slight increase or decrease in r.p.m. after the mixture adjustment has been made so the throttle idling adjusting screw should now be turned so that the engine idles at between 600 and 700 r.p.m.

SYNCHRONISATION OF TWIN S.U. CARBURETTORS

The Austin Healey Sprite and M.G. Midget are fitted with twin S.U. carburettors as standard and many other models are modified to take twin S.U.s. The procedure for synchronising them is as follows:-

First ensure that the mixture is correct in each instrument. With twin S.U. carburettors, in addition to the mixture strength being correct for each instrument, the idling suction must be equal on both. It is best to use a vacuum synchronising device such as the Motor Meter synchro tester. If this is not available it is possible to obtain fairly accurate synchronisation by listening to the hiss made by the air flow into the intake throats of each carburettor.

The aim is to adjust the throttle butterfly disc so that an equal amount of air enters each carburettor. Loosen the screw on the folded clamp which connects the two throttle disc spindles. Listen to the hiss from each carburettor and if a difference in intensity

is noticed between them, then unscrew the throttle adjusting screw on the other carburettor until the hiss from both the carburettors are the same.

With vacuum synchronisation device all that it is necessary to do is to place the instrument over the mouth of each carburettor in turn and adjust the adjusting screws until the reading on the gauge is identical for both carburettors.

Tighten the screw on the folded clamp to connect the throttle disc of the two carburettors together, at the same time holding down the throttle adjusting screws against their idling stops. Synchronisation of the two carburettors is now complete.

S.U. FUEL PUMPS - DESCRIPTION

Basically all S.U. fuel pumps are identical in concept and differ only in detail. The S.P. pump is fitted to the A.40 Mk. II, the S.U. type 'L' pump to the Morris Minor, and the latest type of pump, the type 'AUF' to the Mk. III Sprite and Mk. II Midget.

As the pumps are so similar it is quite possible that a non-standard one has been fitted on an exchange basis, and for this reason the differences between the pumps will be listed in the text as they occur, so that if a later type of pump has been fitted it will create no difficulty. The following can be taken to apply equally to all three types of pump except where otherwise stated.

The S.U. 12-volt electric fuel pump consists of a long outer body casing housing the diaphragm, armature and solenoid assembly, with at one end the contact breaker assembly protected by a bakelite cover, and at the other end a short casting containing the inlet and outlet ports, filter, valves, and pumping chamber. The joint between the bakelite cover and the body casing is protected with a rubber sheath.

The pump operates in the following manner. When the ignition is switched on current travels from the terminal on the outside of the bakelite cover through the coil located round the solenoid core which becomes energised and acting like a magnet draws the armature towards it. The current then passes through the points to earth.

When the armature is drawn forward it brings the diaphragm with it against the pressure of the diaphragm spring. This creates sufficient vacuum in the pump chamber to draw in fuel from the tank through the fuel filter and non-return inlet valve.

As the armature nears the end of its travel a 'throw over' mechanism operates which separates the points so breaking the circuit.

The diaphragm return spring then pushes the diaphragm and armature forwards into the pumping chamber so forcing the fuel in the chamber out to the carburettor through the non-return outlet valve. When the armature is nearly fully forward the throw over mechanism again functions, this time closing the points and re-energising the solenoid, so repeating the cycle.

S.U. FUEL PUMP - REMOVAL & REPLACEMENT

1. Disconnect the earth lead from the battery. (Positive terminal).

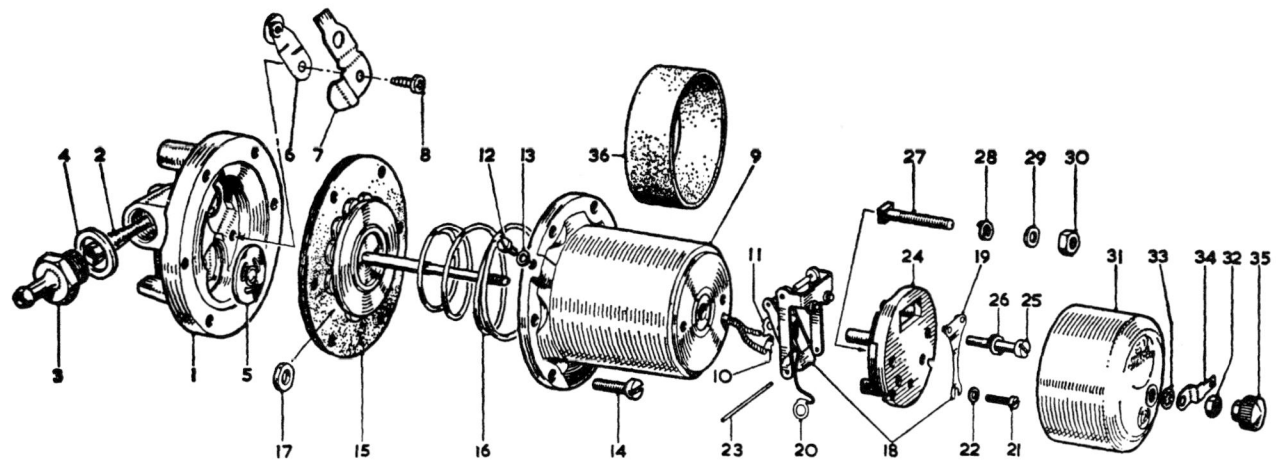

Fig. 3 : 11A. An exploded view of the SP type fuel pump

1 Body
2 Filter
3 Nozzle inlet
4 Washer for nozzle
5 Valve—outlet
6 Valve—inlet
7 Retainer—valve

8 Screw for retainer
9 Housing—coil
10 Tag—5 B.A. terminal
11 Tag—2 B.A. terminal
12 Screw—earth
13 Washer—spring
14 Screw—housing to body

15 Diaphragm assembly
16 Spring
17 Roller
18 Rocker and blade
19 Blade
20 Tag—2 B.A. terminal
21 Screw for blade
36 Sleeve—rubber

22 Washer—dished
23 Spindle for contact breaker
24 Pedestal
25 Screw—pedestal to housing
26 Washer—spring
27 Screw for terminal
28 Washer—spring

29 Washer—lead—for screw
30 Nut for screw
31 Cover—end
32 Nut for cover
33 Washer—shakeproof
34 Connector—Lucar
35 Knob—terminal

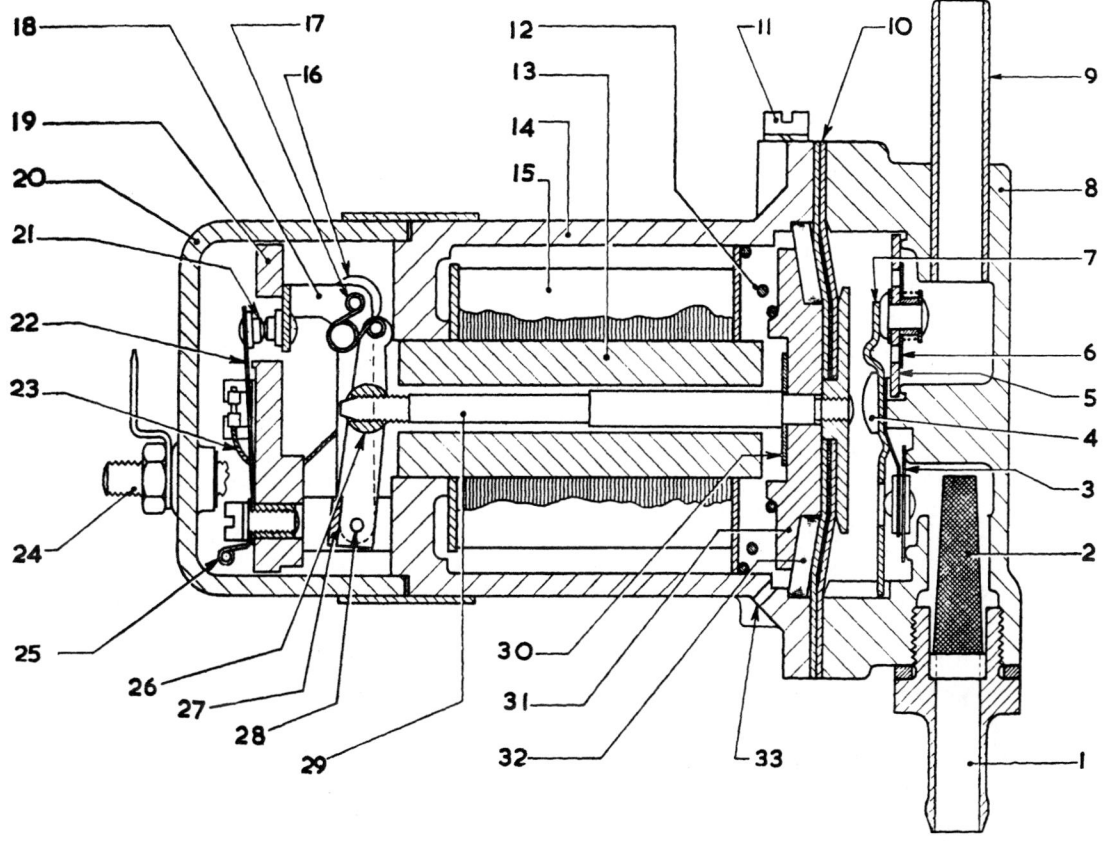

Fig. 3 : 11B. A sectioned view of the SP type fuel pump

1 Feed nozzle
2 Filter
3 Inlet valve
4 Screw—valve retainer
5 Carrier plate

6 Delivery valve
7 Valve retainer
8 Body
9 Outlet connection
10 Diaphragm

11 Earth screw
12 Feed spring
13 Solenoid core
14 Coil housing
15 Coil

16 Fibre rollers
17 Toggle spring
18 Outer rocker
19 Pedestal
20 End cap

21 Contact points
22 Spring blade
23 Braided earth wire
24 Terminal screw
25 Coil lead tag

26 Trunnion
27 Inner rocker
28 Rocker hinge pin
29 Armature spindle
30 Impact washer

31 Armature
32 Brass
   rollers
33 Air vent

2. Disconnect the earth and the supply wires from their terminals on the pump body.

3. Remove the fuel inlet and outlet pipes by undoing the union nuts or the clip screws. (Remove the vent pipe connector where fitted, at this stage).

4. Unscrew the two bolts and spring washers which hold the pump in position and remove the pump.

5. Replacement of the pump is a reversal of the above process. Two particular points to watch are that:
   a) The fuel inlet and outlet pipes are connected up the right way round.
   b) A good electrical earth connection is made.

S.U. FUEL PUMP - DISMANTLING

1. The filter and inlet and outlet arrangements differ between the three pumps and for this reason it is necessary to deal with them individually at this stage:-
   a) Type S.P. Remove the inlet nozzle by unscrewing it, and take out the filter from the inlet port. NOTE the fibre washer under the nozzle head. The outlet nozzle is pressed into the end casting and cannot be removed.
   b) Type A.U.F. Release the inlet and outlet nozzles, valves, sealing washers, and filter by unscrewing the two screws from the spring clamp plate which hold them all in place.
   c) Type L - Unscrew the hexagon headed plug from the underside of the fuel pump and remove the sealing washers and inlet and outlet valves. If it is wished to dismantle the valve cage, remove the circlip from the cage so freeing the valve.

2. Mark the flanges adjacent to each other and separate the housing holding the armature and solenoid assembly from the pumping chamber casting by unscrewing the six screws holding both halves of the pump together. Take great care not to tear or damage the diaphragm as it may stick to either of the flanges as they are separated. On the S.P. pump, remove the pan-headed screw which holds the valve retainer in place to the floor of the pumping chamber, and remove the retainer and the inlet and outlet valves which have already been removed on the A.U.F. and L pumps.

3. The armature spindle which is attached to the armature head and diaphragm is unscrewed anti-clockwise from the trunnion at the contact breaker end of the pump body. Lift out the armature, spindle, and diaphragm, and remove the impact washer from under the head of the armature. (This washer quietens the noise of the armature head hitting the solenoid core), and the diaphragm return spring.

4. Slide off the protective rubber sheath and unscrew the terminal nut, connector (where fitted), and washer from the terminal screw, and remove the bakelite contact breaker cover.

5. Unscrew the 5 B.A. screws which hold the contact spring blade in position and remove it with the blade and screw washer.

6. Remove the cover retaining nut on the terminal screw, and cut through the lead washer under the nut on the terminal screw with a pocket knife,

7. Remove the two bakelite pedestal retaining screws complete with spring washers which hold the pedestal to the solenoid housing, remove the braided copper earth lead, and the coil lead from the terminal screw.

8. Remove the pin on which the rockers pivot by pushing it out sideways and remove the rocker assembly. The pump is now fully dismantled. It is not possible to remove the solenoid core and coil and the rocker assembly must not be broken down, as it is only supplied on exchange as a complete assembly.

S.U. FUEL PUMP - INSPECTION & SERVICING

Although not given in the official manufacturers servicing charts, I consider it a very sound scheme to service the S.U. fuel pump every 12,000 miles to minimise the possibility of failure.

Remove the filter as has already been detailed and thoroughly clean it in paraffin. At the same time clean the points by gently drawing a piece of thin card between them. Do this very carefully so as not to disturb the tension of the spring blade. If the points are burnt or pitted they must be renewed and a new blade and rocker assembly fitted.

If the filter is coated with a gum-like substance very like varnish, serious trouble can develop in the future unless all traces of this gum (formed by deposits from the fuel) are removed.

To do this boil all steel and brass parts in a 20% solution of caustic soda, then dip them in nitric acid and clean them in boiling water. Alloy parts can be cleaned with a clean rag after they have been left to soak for a few hours in methylated spirits.

With the pump stripped right down, wash and clean all the parts thoroughly in paraffin and renew any that are worn, damaged, fractured, or cracked. Pay particular attention to the gaskets and diaphragm.

S.U. FUEL PUMP - REASSEMBLY

1. Fit the rocker assembly to the bakelite pedestal and insert the rocker pivot pin. The pin is case hardened and wire or any other substitute should never be used if the pin is lost.

2. Place the spring washer, wiring tag from the short lead from the coil, a new lead washer, and the nut on the terminal screw, and tighten the nut down.

3. Attach the copper earth wire from the outer rocker immediately under the head of the nearest pedestal securing screw, and fit the pedestal to the solenoid housing with the two pedestal securing screws and lockwashers. It is unusual to fit an earth wire immediately under the screw head but this is because in practice the spring washer has been found to be a not particularly good conductor.

4. Fit the lockwasher under the head of the spring blade contact securing screw, then the last lead from the coil, and then the spring blade so that

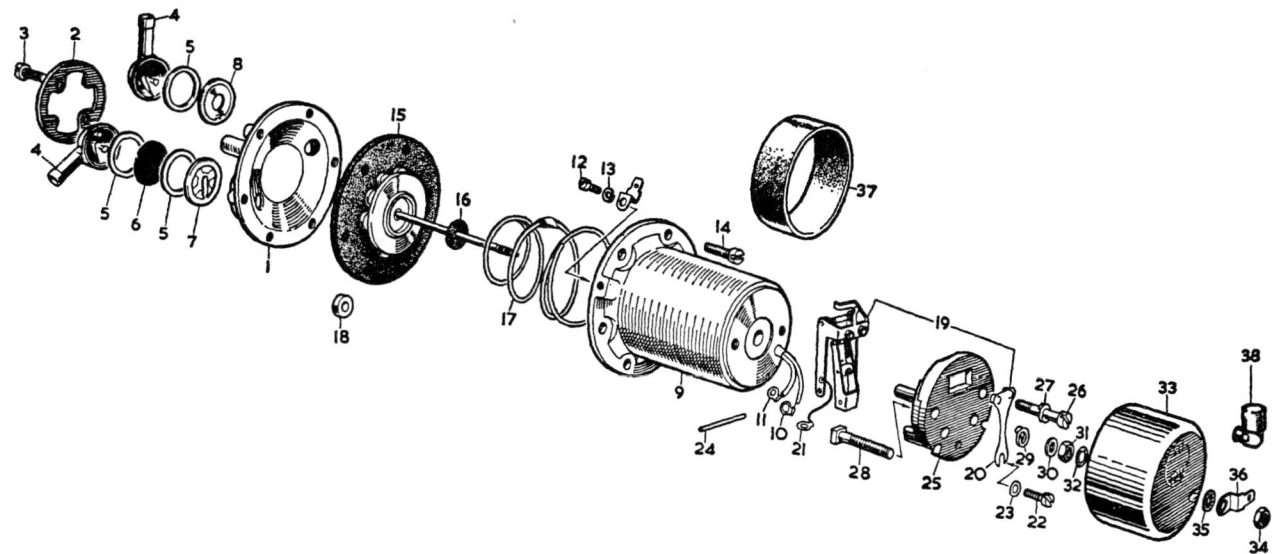

Fig. 3:12. The S.U. type A.U.F. electric petrol pump. Key to component parts. 1 Body. 2 Spring clamp plate. 3 Screw. 4 Nozzle—inlet/outlet. 5 Sealing washer. 6 Filter. 7 Valve—inlet. 8 Valve—outlet. 9 Housing coil. 10 Tag 5 BA terminal. 11 Tag 2 BA terminal. 12 Screw earth. 13 Washer spring. 14 Screw—housing to body. 15 Diaphragm assembly. 16 Impact washer. 17 Spring. 18 Roller. 19 Rocker and blade. 20 Blade. 21 Tag—2 BA terminal. 22 Screw for blade. 23 Washer—dished. 24 Spindle for contact breaker. 25 Pedestal. 26 Screw—pedestal to housing. 27 Washer—spring. 28 Screw for terminal. 29 Washer—spring. 30 Washer—lead—for screw. 31 Nut for screw. 32 Spacer—nut to cover. 33 Cover—end. 34 Nut for cover. 35 Washer—shakeproof. 36 Connector—Lucar. 37 Packing sleeve. 38 Non-return valve.

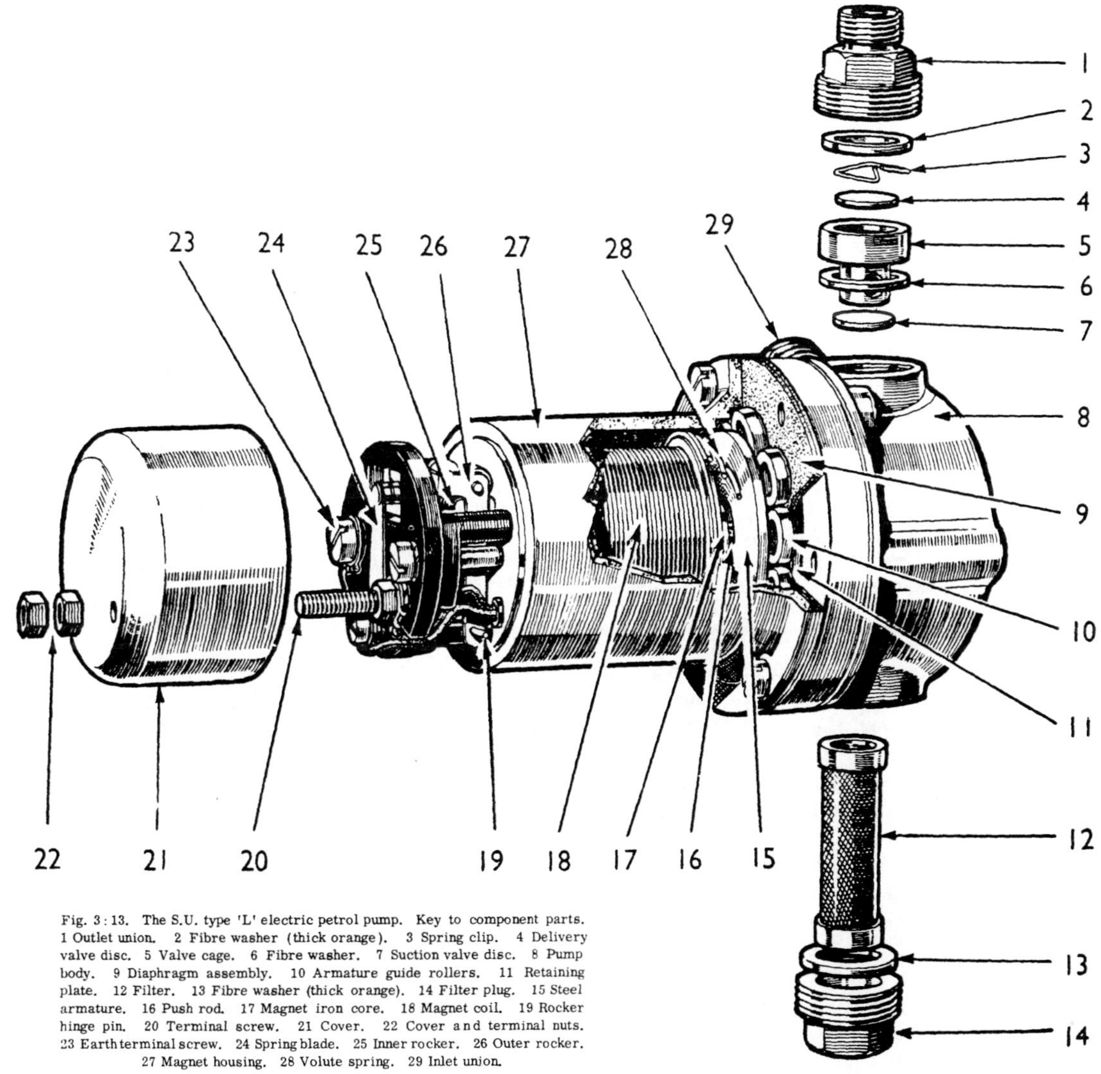

Fig. 3:13. The S.U. type 'L' electric petrol pump. Key to component parts. 1 Outlet union. 2 Fibre washer (thick orange). 3 Spring clip. 4 Delivery valve disc. 5 Valve cage. 6 Fibre washer. 7 Suction valve disc. 8 Pump body. 9 Diaphragm assembly. 10 Armature guide rollers. 11 Retaining plate. 12 Filter. 13 Fibre washer (thick orange). 14 Filter plug. 15 Steel armature. 16 Push rod. 17 Magnet iron core. 18 Magnet coil. 19 Rocker hinge pin. 20 Terminal screw. 21 Cover. 22 Cover and terminal nuts. 23 Earth terminal screw. 24 Spring blade. 25 Inner rocker. 26 Outer rocker. 27 Magnet housing. 28 Volute spring. 29 Inlet union.

there is nothing between it and the bakelite pedestal. It is important that this order of assembly is adhered to. Lightly tighten the screw.

5. The static position of the pump when it is not in use is with the contact points making firm contact and this forces the spring blade to be bent slightly back. Move the outer rocker arm up and down and position the spring blade so that the contacts on the rocker or blade wipe over the centre line of the other points. NOTE that with the 'L' type of pump only one set of points are fitted. When open the blade should rest against the small ledge on the bakelite pedestal just below the points (This also applies to the A.U.F. and S.P. pumps). The points should come into contact with each other when the rocker is halfway forward. To check that this is correct press the middle of the blade gently so that it rests against the ridge with the points just having come into contact. It should now be possible to slide a .030 in. feeler gauge between the rocker rollers and the solenoid housing. If the clearance is not correct bend the tip of the blade very carefully until it is.

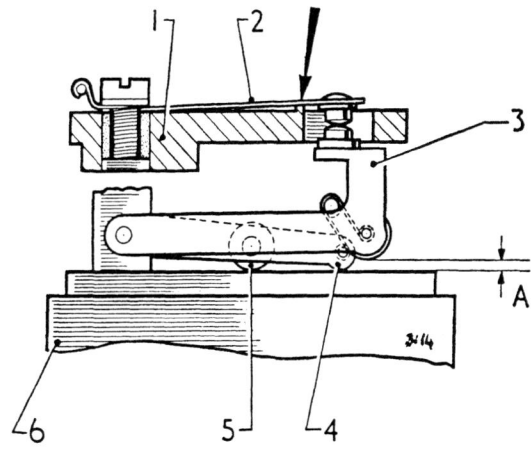

Fig. 3:14. The contact gap setting 'A' on early-type rocker assemblies should be .030 in. (.8 mm.)

On the A.U.F. and S.P. pumps with the outer rocker against the coil housing and the spring blade contact resting against the pedestal, the gap between the points should be .030 in.

6. Tighten down the blade retaining screw, and check that with A.U.F. and S.P. models a considerable gap exists between the underside of the spring blade and the pedestal ledge, with the rocker contact bearing against the blade contact and the rocker fully forward in the normal static position. With the rocker arm down, ensure that the underside of the blade rests on the ledge of the pedestal. If not, remove the blade and very slightly bend it until it does.

7. Place the impact washer on the underside of the armature head, fit the diaphragm return spring with the wider portion of the coil against the solenoid body, place the brass rollers in position

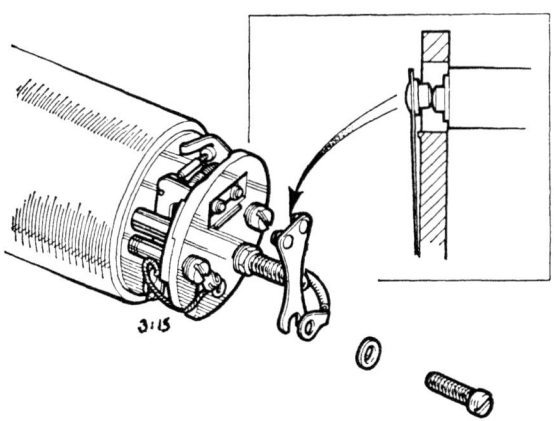

Fig. 3:15. The correct position of the blade and rocker contact points

under the diaphragm and insert the armature spindle through the centre of the solenoid core, and screw the spindle into the rocker trunnion.

8. It will be appreciated that the amount the spindle is screwed into the rocker trunnion will vitally affect the functioning of the pump. To set the diaphragm correctly, turn the steel blade to one side, and screw the armature spindle into the trunnion until if the spindle was screwed in a further sixth of a turn the throw-over rocker would not operate the points closed to points open position. Now screw out the armature spindle four holes ($^2/_3$ of a turn) to ensure that wear in the points will not cause the pump to stop working. Turn the blade back into its normal position.

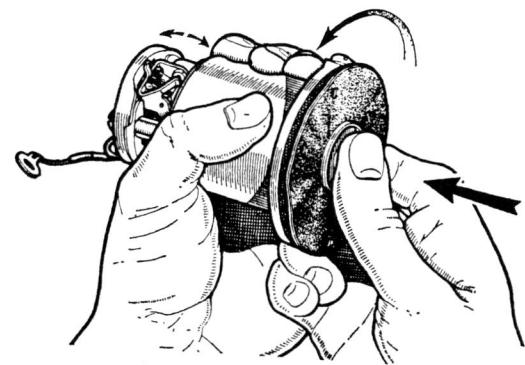

Fig. 3:16. Unscrew the diaphragm until the rocker just throws over

9. Reassembly of the valves, filters, and nozzles into the pumping chamber is a reversal of the dismantling process. Use new washers and gaskets throughout.

10. With the pumping chamber reassembled, replace it carefully on the solenoid housing, ensuring that the previously made mating marks on the flanges line up with each other. Screw the six

screws in lightly on the 'L' model, and firmly on the A.U.F. and S.P. models

11. For the best results on the 'L' type pump it is necessary to have the diaphragm in the fully forward position, i.e. at the end of the induction stroke when the fuel chamber would be full of fuel. To achieve this, connect up the pump to a battery and with a matchstick behind the rollers to hold the points closed, electrical current will hold the armature against the return spring in the fully forward position. Tighten down the six screws.

12. Fit the bakelite cover and replace the shake-proof washer, lucar connector, cover nut, and terminal knob to the terminal screw in the case of S.P. and A.U.F. models, and the terminal nut to the terminal screw in the case of the 'L' type model. Then, replace the terminal lead and cover nut, so locking the lead between the cover nut and the terminal nut. Assembly of all three types is now complete.

FUEL TANK - REMOVAL & REPLACEMENT

1. Remove the filler cap and from underneath the car unscrew the drain plug from the tank, draining the contents into a suitable container. When drained, replace the plug and washer securely.
2. While still underneath the car disconnect the fuel outlet pipe by undoing the union nut.
3. Disconnect the hose clip and pull off the filler tube from the petrol tank neck.
4. Disconnect the earth lead from the battery (positive terminal) and remove the petrol gauge wires from their attachments to the fuel gauge sender unit mounted in the side of the tank.
5. Unscrew the screws which hold the tank unit in place and remove the tank. Note the packing strip under the flange and take care not to damage it. At this stage it is sometimes helpful to

position a jack under the tank so that it does not pull away as the bolts are released. It is also sometimes found easier to partially move the tank before releasing the sender gauge unit leads, as with the tank half removed they are more accessible.

6. Replacing the tank is a reversal of the above process. Three particular points to watch are that:
   a) The packing strip is correctly in place.
   b) The union nut is securely tightened and does not weep when the tank is filled with petrol.
   c) The drain plug and washer are securely replaced.
   d) The rubber ferule beneath the filler cap makes an efficient seal with the body.

FUEL TANK GAUGE UNIT - REMOVAL & REPLACEMENT

1. Remove the fuel tank as previously described.
2. Unscrew the screws which hold the gauge unit to the tank carefully, and lift the complete unit away, ensuring that the float lever is not bent or damaged in the process.
3. Replacement of the unit is a reversal of the above process. To ensure a fuel tight joint, scrape both the tank and sender gauge mating flanges clean, and always use a new joint washer and a suitable gasket cement.

FUEL TANK CLEANING

With time it is likely that sediment will collect in the bottom of the fuel tank. Condensation, resulting in rust and other impurities, will usually be found in the fuel tank of any car more than three or four years old.

When the tank is removed it should be vigorously flushed out and turned upside down, and if facilities are available, steam cleaned.

FUEL SYSTEM AND CARBURATION

FAULT FINDING CHART

Cause	Trouble	Remedy
SYMPTOM:	FUEL CONSUMPTION EXCESSIVE	
Carburation and ignition faults	Air cleaner choked and dirty giving rich mixture	Remove, clean and replace air cleaner.
	Fuel leaking from carburettor(s), fuel pumps, or fuel lines	Check for and eliminate all fuel leaks. Tighten fuel line union nuts.
	Float chamber flooding	Check and adjust float level.
	Generally worn carburettor(s)	Remove, overhaul and replace.
	Distributor condenser faulty	Remove, and fit new unit.
	Balance weights or vacuum advance mechanism in distributor faulty	Remove, and overhaul distributor.
Incorrect adjustment	Carburettor(s) incorrectly adjusted mixture too rich	Tune and adjust carburettor(s).
	Idling speed too high	Adjust idling speed.
	Contact breaker gap incorrect	Check and reset gap.
	Valve clearances incorrect	Check rocker arm to valve stem clearances and adjust as necessary.
	Incorrectly set sparking plugs	Remove, clean, and regap.
	Tyres under-inflated	Check tyre pressures and inflate if necessary.
	Wrong sparking plugs fitted	Remove and replace with correct units.
	Brakes dragging	Check and adjust brakes.
SYMPTOM:	INSUFFICIENT FUEL DELIVERY OR WEAK MIXTURE DUE TO AIR LEAKS	
Dirt in system	Petrol tank air vent restricted	Remove petrol cap and clean out air vent.
	Partially clogged filters in pump and carburettor(s)	Remove and clean filters.
	Dirt lodged in float chamber needle housing	Remove and clean out float chamber and needle valve assembly.
	Incorrectly seating valves in fuel pump	Remove, dismantle, and clean out fuel pump.
Fuel pump faults	Fuel pump diaphragm leaking or damaged	Remove, and overhaul fuel pump.
	Gasket in fuel pump damaged	Remove, and overhaul fuel pump.
	Fuel pump valves sticking due to petrol gumming	Remove, and thoroughly clean fuel pump.
Air leaks	Too little fuel in fuel tank (Prevalent when climbing steep hills)	Refill fuel tank.
	Union joints on pipe connections loose	Tighten joints and check for air leaks.
	Split in fuel pipe on suction side of fuel pump	Examine, locate, and repair.
	Inlet manifold to block or inlet manifold to carburettor(s) gasket leaking	Test by pouring oil along joints - bubbles indicate leak. Renew gasket as appropriate.

CHAPTER FOUR

IGNITION SYSTEM

SPECIFICATION

Morris Minor 1000 – 948 c.c.

Distributor: Rotation	Anti-clockwise (viewed from above).
Manual advance	None.
Automatic advance	Vacuum control 7 to 9°; centrifugal 17 to 19°.
Advance starts at	400 to 650 r.p.m.
Contact breaker gap	.014 to .016 in. (.36 to .40 mm.).
Contact spring tension	20 to 24 oz. (567 to 680 gm.).
Condenser or capacitor capacity	.2 mf.
Sparking plug	Champion N5 (was code NA8), 14 mm., 3/4 in. reach.
Ignition timing: Low compression	4° B.T.D.C. (3/16 in. (4.76 mm.) on the periphery of the crankshaft pulley.
High compression	5° B.T.D.C.

Morris Minor 1000 – 1,098 c.c.

Sparking plugs	Champion N5.
Size	14 mm.
Plug gap	.025 in. (.64 mm.).
Coil	LA12
Distributor	25D4
Distributor contact points gap	.014 to .016 in. (.36 to .40 mm.).
Timing	3° B.T.D.C.

GENERAL DESCRIPTION

In order that the engine can run correctly it is necessary for an electrical spark to ignite the fuel/air mixture in the combustion chamber at exactly the right moment in relation to engine speed and load. The ignition system is based on feeding low tension voltage from the battery to the coil where it is converted to high tension voltage. The high tension voltage is powerful enough to jump the sparking plug gap in the cylinders many times a second under high compression pressures, providing that the system is in good condition and that all adjustments are correct.

The ignition system is divided into two circuits. The low tension circuit and the high tension circuit.

The low tension (sometimes known as the primary) circuit consists of the battery, lead to the control box, lead to the ignition switch, lead from the ignition switch to the low tension or primary coil windings (terminal SW), and the lead from the low tension coil windings (coil terminal CB) to the contact breaker points and condenser in the distributor.

The high tension circuit consists of the high tension or secondary coil windings, the heavy ignition lead from the centre of the coil to the centre of the distributor cap, the rotor arm, and the sparking plug leads and sparking plugs.

The system functions in the following manner.

Low tension voltage is changed in the coil into high tension voltage by the opening and closing of the contact breaker points in the low tension circuit. High tension voltage is then fed via the carbon brush in the centre of the distributor cap to the rotor arm of the distributor. The rotor arm revolves inside the distributor cap, and each time it comes in line with one of the four metal segments in the cap, which are connected to the sparking plug leads, the opening and closing of the contact breaker points causes the high tension voltage to build up, jump the gap from the rotor arm to the appropriate metal segment and so via the sparking plug lead to the sparking plug, where it finally jumps the spark plug gap before going to earth.

The ignition is advanced and retarded automatically, to ensure the spark occurs at just the right instant for the particular load at the prevailing engine speed.

The ignition advance is controlled both mechanically and by a vacuum operated system. The mechanical governor mechanism comprises two lead weights, which move out from the distributor shaft as the engine speed rises due to centrifugal force. As they move outwards they rotate the cam relative to the distributor shaft, and so advance the spark. The weights are held in position by two light springs and it is the tension of the springs which is largely responsible for correct spark advancement.

The vacuum control consists of a diaphragm, one side of which is connected via a small bore tube to the carburettor, and the other side to the contact breaker plate. Depression in the inlet manifold and carburettor, which varies with engine speed and throttle opening, causes the diaphragm to move, so moving the contact breaker plate, and advancing or retarding the spark. A fine degree of control is achieved by a spring in the vacuum assembly.

CONTACT BREAKER ADJUSTMENT

To adjust the contact breaker points to the correct gap, first pull off the two clips securing the distributor cap to the distributor body, and lift away the cap. Clean the cap inside and out with a dry cloth. It is unlikely that the four segments will be badly burned or scored, but if they are the cap will have to be renewed.

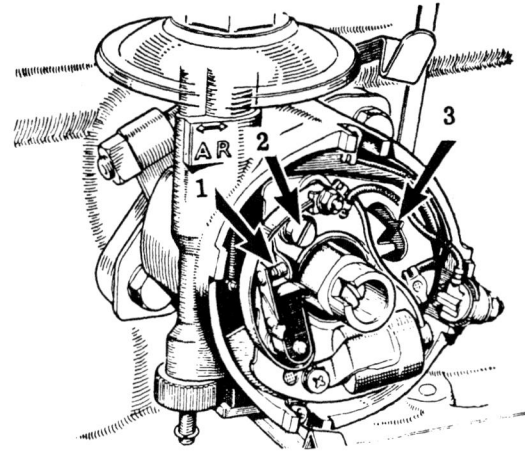

Fig. 4 : 1. The DM2 distributor with the cover and rotor arm removed showing '1' Contact breaker points. '2' Securing screw. '3' Slot for screwdriver to vary point gap.

Push in the carbon brush located in the top of the cap once or twice, to make sure that it moves freely.

Gently prise the contact breaker points open to examine the condition of their faces. If they are rough, pitted, or dirty, it will be necessary to remove them for resurfacing, or for replacement points to be fitted.

Presuming the points are satisfactory, or that they have been cleaned and replaced, measure the gap between the points by turning the engine over until the contact breaker arm is on the peak of one of the four cam lobes. A 0.015 in. feeler gauge should now just fit between the points.

If the gap varies from this amount, slacken the contact plate securing screw, and adjust the contact gap by inserting a screwdriver in the notched hole at the end of the plate. Turning clockwise to decrease and anti-clockwise to increase the gap. Tighten the securing screw and check the gap again.

Replace the rotor arm and distributor cap and clip the spring blade retainers into position.

REMOVING & REPLACING CONTACT BREAKER POINTS

If the contact breaker points are burned, pitted or badly worn, they must be removed and either replaced, or their faces must be filed smooth.

To remove the points unscrew the terminal nut and remove it together with the steel washer under its head. Remove the flanged nylon bush and then the condenser lead and the low tension lead from the terminal pin. Lift off the contact breaker arm and then remove the large fibre washer from the terminal pin.

The adjustable contact breaker plate is removed by unscrewing the one holding down screw and removing it, complete with spring and flat washer.

To reface the points, rub their faces on a fine carborundum stone, or on fine emery paper. It is important that the faces are rubbed flat and parallel to each other so that there will be complete face to face contact when the points are closed. One of the points will be pitted and the other will have deposits on it.

It is necessary to completely remove the built-up deposits, but not necessary to rub the pitted point right down to the stage where all the pitting has disappeared, though obviously if this is done it will prolong the time before the operation of refacing the points has to be repeated.

To replace the points, first position the adjustable contact breaker plate, and secure it with its screw spring and flat washer. Fit the fibre washer to the terminal pin, and fit the contact breaker arm over it. Insert the flanged nylon bush with the condenser lead immediately under its head, and the low tension lead under that, over the terminal pin. Fit the steel washer and screw on the securing nut.

The points are now reassembled and the gap should be set as detailed in the previous section.

CONDENSER REMOVAL, TESTING & REPLACEMENT

The purpose of the condenser, (sometimes known as a capacitor) is to ensure that when the contact breaker points open there is no sparking across them which would waste voltage.

The condenser is fitted in parallel with the contact breaker points, and if it develops a short circuit, will cause ignition failure as the points will be prevented from interrupting the low tension circuit.

If the engine becomes very difficult to start or begins to miss after several miles running and the breaker points show signs of excessive burning, then the condition of the condenser must be suspect. A further test can be made by separating the points by hand with the ignition switched on. If this is accompanied by a flash it is indicative that the condenser has failed.

Without special test equipment the only sure way to diagnose condenser trouble is to replace a suspected unit with a new one and note if there is any improvement.

To remove the condenser from the distributor, remove the distributor cap and the rotor arm. Unscrew the contact breaker arm terminal nut, and remove the nut, washer, and flanged nylon bush and release the condenser lead from the bush. Unscrew the condenser retaining screw from the breaker plate and remove the condenser. Replacement of the condenser is simply a reversal of the removal process. Take particular care that the condenser lead does not short circuit against any portion of the breaker plate.

DISTRIBUTOR LUBRICATION

It is important that the distributor cam is lubricated with petroleum jelly at the specified mileages, and that the breaker arm, governor weights, and cam spindle, are lubricated with engine oil once every 1,000 miles. In practice it will be found that lubrication every 2,000 miles is adequate, although this is not recommended by the factory.

Great care should be taken not to use too much lubricant, as any excess that might find its way onto the contact breaker points could cause burning and misfiring.

To gain access to the cam spindle, lift away the rotor arm. Drop no more than two drops of engine oil onto the screw head. This will run down the spindle when the engine is hot and lubricate the bearings. No more than ONE drop of oil should be applied to the pivot post.

DISTRIBUTOR REMOVAL & REPLACEMENT

1. To remove the distributor from the engine, start by pulling the terminals off each of the sparking plugs. Release the nut securing the low tension lead to the terminal on the side of the distributor and unscrew the high tension lead retaining cap from the coil and remove the lead.

2. Unscrew the union holding the vacuum tube to the distributor vacuum housing.

3. Remove the distributor body clamp bolts which hold the distributor clamp plate to the engine and remove the distributor. NOTE if it is not wished to disturb the timing then under no circumstances should the clamp pinch bolt, which secures the distributor in its relative position in the clamp, be loosened. Providing the distributor is removed without the clamp being loosened from the distributor body, the timing will not be lost.

4. Replacement is a reversal of the above process providing that the engine has not been turned in the meantime. If the engine has been turned it will be best to retime the ignition. This will also be necessary if the clamp pinch bolt has been loosened.

DISTRIBUTOR DISMANTLING

1. With the distributor removed from the car and on the bench, remove the distributor cap and lift off the rotor arm. If very tight, lever it off gently with a screwdriver.

2. Remove the points from the distributor as detailed in the section 'Removing and replacing contact breaker points' on page 78.

3. Remove the condenser from the contact breaker

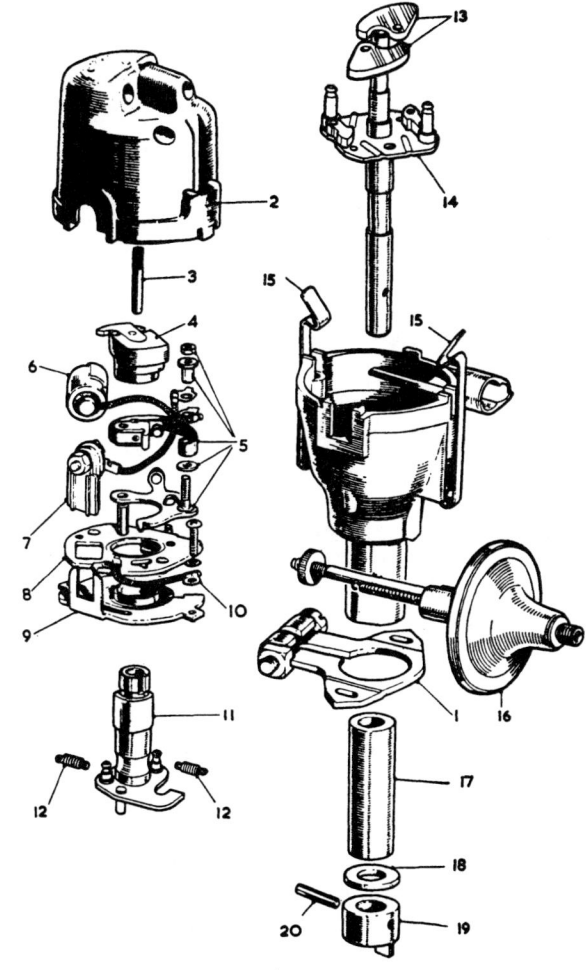

Fig. 4 : 2. Exploded view of the distributor showing the component parts. 1 Clamping plate. 2 Moulded cap. 3 Brush and spring. 4 Rotor arm. 5 Contacts (set). 6 Capacitor. 7 Terminal and lead (low-tension). 8 Moving contact breaker plate. 9 Contact breaker base plate. 10 Earth lead. 11 Cam. 12 Automatic advance springs. 13 Weight assembly. 14 Shaft and action plate. 15 Cap-retaining clips. 16 Vacuum unit. 17 Bush. 18 Thrust washer. 19 Driving dog. 20 Parallel pin.

plate by releasing its securing screw.

4. Unhook the vacuum unit spring from its mounting pin on the moving contact breaker plate.

5. Remove the contact breaker plate.

6. Unscrew the two screws and lockwashers which hold the contact breaker base plate in position and remove the earth lead from the relevant screw. Remember to replace this lead on reassembly.

7. Lift out the contact breaker base plate.

8. NOTE the position of the slot in the rotor arm drive in relation to the offset drive dog at the opposite end of the distributor. It is essential that this is reassembled correctly as otherwise the timing may be 180° out.

9. Unscrew the cam spindle retaining screw, which is located in the centre of the rotor arm drive, and remove the cam spindle.

10. Lift out the centrifugal weights together with their springs.

11. To remove the vacuum unit, spring off the small circlip which secures the advance adjustment nut which should then be unscrewed. With the micrometer adjusting nut removed, release the spring and the micrometer adjusting nut lock spring clip. This is the clip that is responsible for the 'clicks' when the micrometer adjuster is turned, and it is small and easily lost as is the circlip, so put them in a safe place. Do not forget to replace the lock spring clip on reassembly.

12. It is only necessary to remove the distributor drive shaft or spindle if it is thought to be excessively worn. With a thin punch drive out the retaining pin from the driving tongue collar on the bottom end of the distributor drive shaft. The shaft can then be removed. The distributor is now completely dismantled.

DISTRIBUTOR INSPECTION & REPAIR

Check the points as has already been detailed on page 78. Check the distributor cap for signs of tracking, indicated by a thin black line between the segments. Replace the cap if any signs of tracking are found.

If the metal portion of the rotor arm is badly burned or loose, renew the arm. If slightly burnt clean the arm with a fine file.

Check that the carbon brush moves freely in the centre of the distributor cover.

Examine the fit of the breaker plate on the bearing plate and also check the breaker arm pivot for looseness or wear and renew as necessary.

Examine the balance weights and pivot pins for wear, and renew the weights or cam assembly if a degree of wear is found.

Examine the shaft and the fit of the cam assembly on the shaft. If the clearance is excessive compare the items with new units, and renew either, or both, if they show excessive wear.

If the shaft is a loose fit in the distributor bushes and can be seen to be worn, it will be necessary to fit a new shaft and bushes. The old bushes in the early distributor, or the single bush in later ones, are simply pressed out. NOTE that before inserting new bushes they should be stood in engine oil for 24 hours.

Examine the length of the balance weight springs and compare them with new springs. If they have stretched they must be renewed.

DISTRIBUTOR REASSEMBLY

Reassembly is a straight reversal of the dismantling process, but there are several points which should be noted in addition to those already given in the section on dismantling.

Lubricate with S.A.E. 20 engine oil the balance weights and other parts of the mechanical advance mechanism, the distributor shaft, and the portion of the shaft on which the cam bears, during assembly. Do not oil excessively but ensure these parts are adequately lubricated.

On reassembling the cam driving pins with the centrifugal weights, check that they are in the correct position so than when viewed from above, the rotor arm should be at the six o'clock position, and the small offset on the driving dog must be on the right.

Check the action of the weights in the fully advanced and fully retarded positions and ensure they are not binding.

Tighten the micrometer adjusting nut to the middle position on the timing scale.

Finally, set the contact breaker gap to the correct clearance of .015 in.

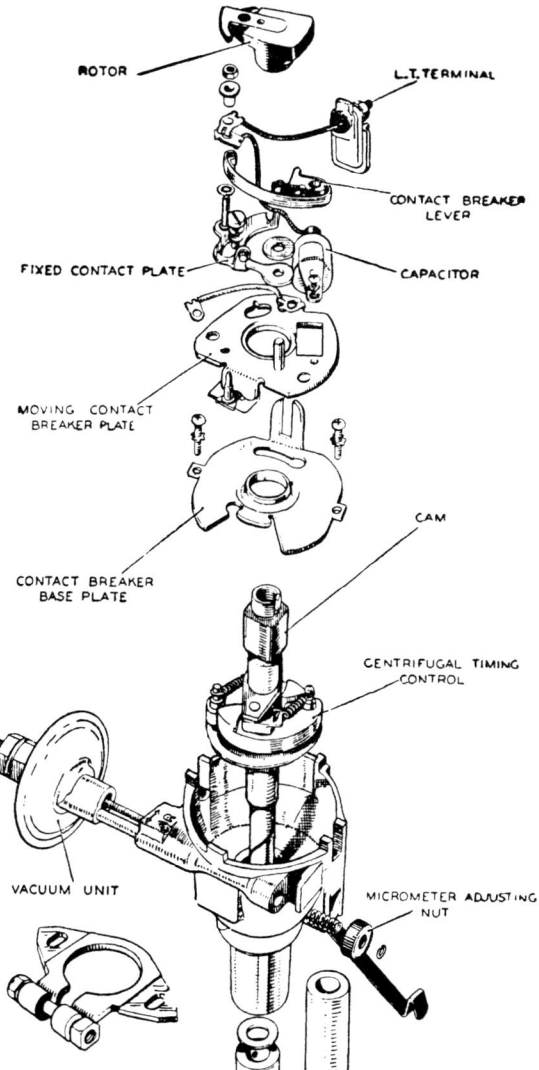

Fig. 4:3. An exploded view of the DM2 distributor showing the centrifugal timing control in the assembled position

IGNITION TIMING

If the clamp plate pinch bolt has been loosened on the distributor and the static timing lost, or if for any other reason it is wished to set the ignition timing, proceed as follows:

The static advance is checked at the exact moment of opening of the points with regards to the position of the dimple in the crankshaft pulley in relation to the pointers on the bottom of the timing gear cover case. The longest pointer indicates T.D.C. and each of the two shorter pointers indicate 5° B.T.D.C. and 10° B.T.D.C., repectively.

Check the 'Ignition specification' for the correct

position of the crankshaft pulley wheel when the points should be just beginning to open. This is shown as the 'static setting'.

Having determined whether your engine possesses a high or low compression ratio (by checking the engine number) turn the engine over so that No. 1 piston is coming up to T.D.C. on the compression stroke. (This can be checked by removing No. 1 sparking plug and feeling the pressure being developed in the cylinder, or by removing the rocker cover and noting when the valves in No. 4 cylinder are rocking, i.e. the inlet valve just opening and exhaust valve just closing. If this check is not made it is all too easy to set the timing 180° out, as both No. 1 and 4 cylinders come up to T.D.C. at the same time but only one is on the firing stroke.

Continue turning the engine until the dimple on the crankshaft pulley is in line with the correct timing mark on the timing cover, or is in the correct position with regards to the pointers.

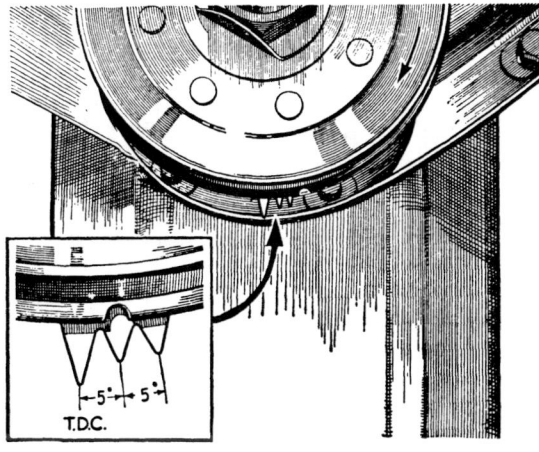

Fig. 4:4. The ignition timing is initially set with the aid of the three pointers and the notch in the crankshaft pulley

Remove the distributor cover, slacken off the distributor body clamp bolt, and with the rotor arm pointing towards the No. 1 terminal (check this position with the distributor cap and lead to No. 1 sparking plug), insert the distributor into the distributor housing. The dog on the drive shaft should match up with the slot in the distributor driving spindle.

Insert the two bolts holding the distributor in position.

With the engine set in the correct position and the rotor arm opposite the correct segment for No. 1 cylinder, turn the advance/retard knob on the distributor until the contact points are just beginning to open. Eleven clicks of the knurled micrometer adjuster nut represent 1° of timing movement.

If the range of adjustment provided by this adjuster is not sufficient, then, if the clamp bolt is not already slackened, it will be necessary to slacken it, and turn the distributor body half a graduation as marked on the adjusting spindle barrel. (Each graduation represents 5° timing movement or 55 clicks of the micrometer adjuster). Sufficient adjustment will normally be found available using the distributor

micrometer adjuster. When this has been achieved the engine is statically timed.

Difficulty is sometimes experienced in determining exactly when the contact breaker points open. This can be ascertained most accurately by connecting a 12-volt bulb in parallel with the contact breaker points (one lead to earth and the other from the distributor low tension terminal). Switch on the ignition, and turn the advance and retard adjuster until the bulb lights up indicating that the points have just opened.

If a stroboscopic timing light is being used, attach one lead to No. 1 sparking plug, and attach the other lead into the free end of No. 1 plug ignition cable leading from the distributor. Start the engine and shine the light on the crankshaft pulley and timing indicators. If the engine idles at more than 400 r.p.m. then the correct static timing will not be obtained as the centrifugal weights will have started to advance. On the 1,098 c.c. versions of the Sprite/Midget this has been allowed for in the 8° B.T.D.C. setting.

If the light shows the dimple in the pulley wheel to be to the right of the timing marks, then the ignition is too far advanced. If the dimple appears to the left of the timing marks, then the ignition is too far retarded. Turn the distributor body or micrometer adjuster until the timing dimple appears in just the right position in relation to the timing marks.

Tighten the clamp bolt and recheck that the timing is still correct, making any small correction necessary with the micrometer adjuster.

SPARKING PLUG & LEADS

The correct functioning of the sparking plugs are vital for the correct running and efficiency of the engine.

At intervals of 6,000 miles the plugs should be removed, examined, cleaned, and if worn excessively replaced. The condition of the sparking plug will also tell much about the overall condition of the engine.

If the insulator nose of the sparking plug is clean and white, with no deposits, this is indicative of a weak mixture, or too hot a plug (A hot plug transfers heat away from the electrodes slowly - a cold plug transfers it away quickly).

The plugs fitted as standard are the Champion N5 14 mm type. If the tip and insulator nose is covered with hard black-looking deposits, then this is indicative that the mixture is too rich. Should the plug be black and oily, then it is likely that the engine is fairly worn, as well as the mixture being too rich.

If the insulator nose is covered with light tan to greyish brown deposits, then the mixture is correct and it is likely that the engine is in good condition.

If there are any traces of long brown tapering stains on the outside of the white portion of the plug, then the plug will have to be renewed, as this shows that there is a faulty joint between the plug body and the insulator, and compression is being allowed to leak away.

Plugs should be cleaned by a sand blasting machine, which will free them from carbon more thoroughly than cleaning by hand. The machine will also test the condition of the plugs under compression. Any plug that fails to spark regularly at the recommended pressure should be renewed.

The sparking plug gap is of considerable importance, as if it is too large or too small, the size of the spark and its efficiency will be seriously impaired. The sparking plug gap should be set to 0.025 in. for the best results.

This is done by measuring the gap with a feeler gauge, and then bending open, or closed, the outer plug electrode until the correct gap is achieved. The centre electrode should never be bent as bending it will crack the insulation and cause plug failure if nothing worse.

When replacing the plugs, remember to use new plug washers, and replace the leads from the distributor in the correct firing order, which is 1, 2, 4, 3, No. 1 cylinder being the one nearest the radiator.

The plug leads require no routine attention other than being kept clean and wiped over regularly. Also at intervals of 6,000 miles, pull each lead off the plug in turn, and also remove them from the distributor by unscrewing the knurled moulded terminal knobs. Water can seep down into these joints giving rise to a white corrosive deposit, which must be carefully removed from the brass washer at the end of each cable, through which the ignition wires pass.

IGNITION SYSTEM FAULT-FINDING

By far the majority of breakdown and running troubles are caused by faults in the ignition system either in the low tension or high tension circuits.

IGNITION SYSTEM FAULT SYMPTOMS

There are two main symptoms indicating ignition faults. Either the engine will not start or fire, or the engine is difficult to start and misfires. If it is a regular misfire, so that the engine is only running on two or three cylinders, the fault will almost sure to be in the secondary, or high tension, circuit. If the misfiring is intermittent, the fault could be in either the high or low tension circuits. If the car stops suddenly, or will not start at all, it is likely that the fault is in the low tension circuit. Loss of power and overheating, apart from faulty carburation settings, are normally due to faults in the distributor or incorrect ignition timing.

FAULT DIAGNOSIS - Engine fails to start

If the engine fails to start it is likely that the fault is in the low tension circuit. It will be known whether there is a good charge in the battery by the way the starter motor spins over. If the battery is evidently in good condition, then check the distributor.

Remove the distributor cap and rotor arm, and check that the contact points are not burnt, pitted or dirty. If the points are badly pitted, or burnt or dirty, clean and reset them as has already been detailed on page 78.

If the engine still refuses to fire check the low tension circuit further. Check the condition of the condenser as detailed under 'Condenser removal, testing and replacement' on page 78. Switch on the ignition and turn the crankshaft until the contact breaker points have fully opened. With either a voltmeter or bulb, and length of wire, connect the contact breaker plate terminal to earth on the engine. If the bulb lights, the low tension circuit is in order, and the fault is in the points. If the points have been cleaned and reset, and the bulb still lights, then the fault is in the high tension circuit.

If the bulb fails to light, connect it to the ignition coil terminal CB and earth. If it lights, it points to a damaged wire or loose connection in the cable from the CB terminal to the terminal on the contact breaker plate.

If the bulb fails to light, connect it between the ignition coil terminal SW and earth. If the bulb lights it indicates a fault in the primary winding of the coil, and it will be necessary to fit a replacement unit.

Should the bulb not light at this stage, then check the cable to SW for faults or a loose connection. Connect the bulb from the negative terminal of the battery to the SW terminal of the coil. If the bulb lights, then the fault is somewhere in the switch, or wiring and control box. Check further as follows:

a) Check the white cable leading from the control box A.3 terminal to the ignition switch. If the bulb fails to light, then this indicates that the cable is damaged, or one of the connections loose, or that there is a fault in the switch.

b) Connect the bulb between the ignition switch white terminal cable and earth. If the bulb fails to light, this indicates a fault in the switch or in the wiring leading from the control box.

c) Connect the bulb to the other ignition switch terminal and then to earth. If the bulb fails to light, this indicates a fault or loose connection in the wiring leading from the control box.

d) Connect the bulb between the lighting and ignition terminal in the control box, and then to earth. If the bulb fails to light this indicates a faulty control box.

e) Connect the bulb from the fuse unit terminal to earth. If the bulb fails to light this indicates a fault or loose connection in the wire leading from the starter solenoid to the control box.

f) Connect the bulb from the input terminal of the solenoid switch to earth. If the bulb fails to light then there is a fault in the cable from the battery to the solenoid switch, or the earth lead of the battery is not properly earthed, and the whole circuit is dead.

If the fault is not in the low tension circuit, check the high tension circuit. Disconnect each plug lead in turn at the sparking plug end, and hold the end of the cable about $3/16$ in. away from the cylinder block. Spin the engine on the starter motor by pressing the rubber button on the starter motor solenoid switch (under the bonnet). Sparking between the end of the cable and the block should be fairly strong with a regular blue spark. (Hold the lead with rubber to avoid electric shocks).

Should there be no spark at the end of the plug leads, disconnect the lead at the distributor cap, and hold the end of the lead about $1/4$ in. from the block. Spin the engine as before, when a rapid succession of blue sparks between the end of the lead and the block, indicate that the coil is in order, and that either the distributor cap is cracked, or the carbon brush is stuck or worn, or the rotor arm is faulty.

Check the cap for cracks and tracking, and the rotor arm for cracks or looseness of the metal portion and renew as necessary.

If there are no sparks from the end of the lead from the coil, then check the connections of the lead to the coil and distributor head, and if they are good, and the low tension side is without fault, then it will be necessary to fit a replacement coil.

FAULT DIAGNOSIS - Engine Misfires

If the engine misfires regularly, run it at a fast idling speed, and short out each of the plugs in turn by placing a short screwdriver across from the plug terminal to the cylinder. Ensure that the screwdriver has a WOODEN or PLASTIC INSULATED HANDLE.

No difference in engine running will be noticed when the plug in the defective cylinder is short circuited. Short circuiting the working plugs will accentuate the misfire.

Remove the plug lead from the end of the defective plug and hold it about $3/16$ in. away from the block. Restart the engine. If the sparking is fairly strong and regular the fault must lie in the sparking plug.

The plug may be loose, the insulation may be cracked, or the points may have burnt away giving cracked, or the points may have burnt away giving too wide a gap for the spark to jump. Worse still, one of the points may have broken off. Either renew the plug, or clean, gap, and test it.

If there is no spark at the end of the plug lead, or if it is weak and intermittent, check the ignition lead from the distributor to the plug. If the insulation is cracked or perished, renew the lead. Check the connections at the distributor cap.

If there is still no spark, examine the distributor cap carefully for tracking. This can be recognised by a very thin black line running between two or more electrodes, or between an electrode and some other part of the distributor. These lines are paths which now conduct electricity across the cap thus letting it run to earth. The only answer is a new distributor cap.

Apart from the ignition timing being incorrect, other causes of misfiring have already been dealt with under the section dealing with the failure of the engine to start. To recap - these are that:

a) The coil may be faulty giving an intermittent misfire.

b) There may be a damaged wire or loose connection in the low tension circuit.

c) The condenser may be short circuiting.

d) There may be a mechanical fault in the distributor (Broken driving spindle or contact breaker spring).

If the ignition timing is too far retarded, it should be noted that the engine will tend to overheat, and there will be a quite noticeable drop in power. If the engine is overheating and the power is down, and the ignition timing is correct, then the carburettor should be checked, as it is likely that this is where the fault lies. See Chapter 3 for further details on this.

Cause	Trouble	Remedy
SYMPTOM:	ENGINE FAILS TO TURN OVER WHEN STARTER BUTTON PULLED	
No current at starter motor	Flat or defective battery	Charge or replace battery. Push-start car.
	Loose battery leads	Tighten both terminals and earth ends of earth lead.
	Defective starter solenoid or switch or broken wiring	Run a wire direct from the battery to the starter motor or by-pass the solenoid.
	Engine earth strap disconnected	Check and retighten strap.
Current at starter motor	Jammed starter motor drive pinion	Place car in gear and rock from side to side. Alternatively, free exposed square end of shaft with spanner.
	Defective starter motor	Remove and recondition.
SYMPTOM:	ENGINE TURNS OVER BUT WILL NOT START	
No spark at sparking plug	Ignition damp or wet	Wip dry the distributor cap and ignition leads.
	Ignition leads to spark plugs loose	Check and tighten at both spark plug and distributor cap ends.
	Shorted or disconnected low tension leads	Check the wiring on the CB and SW terminals of the coil and to the distributor.
	Dirty, incorrectly set, or fitted contact breaker points	Clean, file smooth, and adjust.
	Faulty condenser	Check contact breaker points for arcing, remove and fit new.
	Defective ignition switch	By-pass switch with wire.
	Ignition leads connected wrong way round	Remove and replace leads to spark plugs in correct order.
	Faulty coil	Remove and fit new coil.
	Contact breaker point spring earthed or broken	Check spring is not touching metal part of distributor. Check insulator washers are correctly placed. Renew points if the spring is broken.
No fuel at carburettor float chamber or at jets	No petrol in petrol tank	Refill tank!
	Vapour lock in fuel line (In hot conditions or at high altitude)	Blow into petrol tank, allow engine to cool, or apply a cold wet rag to the fuel line.
	Blocked float chamber needle valve	Remove, clean, and replace.
	Fuel pump filter blocked	Remove, clean, and replace.
	Choked or blocked carburettor jets	Dismantle and clean.
	Faulty fuel pump	Remove, overhaul, and replace. Check CB points on S.U. pumps.
Excess of petrol in cylinder or carburettor flooding	Too much choke allowing too rich a mixture to wet plugs	Remove and dry sparking plugs or with wide open throttle, push-start the car.
	Float damaged or leaking or needle not seating	Remove, examine, clean and replace float and needle valve as necessary.
	Float lever incorrectly adjusted	Remove and adjust correctly.
SYMPTOM:	ENGINE STALLS & WILL NOT START	
No spark at sparking plug	Ignition failure - Sudden	Check over low and high tension circuits for breaks in wiring
	Ignition failure - Misfiring precludes total stoppage	Check contact breaker points, clean and adjust. Renew condenser if faulty.
	Ignition failure - In severe rain or after traversing water splash	Dry out ignition leads and distributor cap.
No fuel at jets	No petrol in petrol tank	Refill tank.
	Petrol tank breather choked	Remove petrol cap and clean out breather hole or pipe.
	Sudden obstruction in carburettor(s)	Check jets, filter, and needle valve in float chamber for blockage
	Water in fuel system	Drain tank and blow out fuel lines

CHAPTER FIVE

CLUTCH AND ACTUATING MECHANISM

SPECIFICATION

Morris Minor 1000 – 948 c.c.

Type	Borg & Beck $6\frac{1}{4}$ in. (158.7 mm.) dry plate.
Free length of pressure springs	1.58 in. (40.1 mm.).
Pedal free movement	$\frac{3}{4}$ in. (20 mm.).
Facing	Wound yarn.
Spring identification colour: Pressure:	Early models 3 dark blue, 3 yellow and green.
.. ..	Later models 6 yellow and green.
Plate:	Light grey.

Morris Minor 1000 – 1,098 c.c.

Type	Single dry plate.
Diameter	$7\frac{1}{4}$ in. (184 mm.).
Facing material	Wound yarn.
Pressure springs	6.
Colour	Yellow.
Pedal free movement	$1\frac{3}{8}$ to $1\frac{1}{2}$ in. (35 to 38 mm.).

GENERAL DESCRIPTION

The earlier 948 c.c. models are fitted with a Borg & Beck single dry plate clutch of $6\frac{1}{4}$ in. diameter. Later, 1,098 c.c. models are fitted with a basically similar, but redesigned unit with a diameter of $7\frac{1}{4}$ in.

The clutch consists of a steel clutch cover containing the pressure plate, pressure springs, release levers, and clutch disc (sometimes called the driven plate), the cover being bolted and dowelled onto the rear face of the flywheel.

The pressure plate, pressure springs, and release levers are all attached to the clutch assembly cover. The clutch disc is held in position between the flywheel and the pressure plate by the pressure plate springs, and is free to slide along the splined main drive shaft.

Friction lining material is rivetted to each side of the disc and it has a spring cushioned hub to absorb transmission shocks and to help ensure a smooth take-off.

The clutch is actuated by a mechanical linkage. Depressing the clutch pedal turns the clutch pedal shaft and a lever at one end of the shaft, which pulls back the clutch operating rod. The opposite end of the clutch operating rod is attached to the clutch withdrawal lever, sometimes known as the release arm.

The opposite end of the release arm is forked and is located behind the release bearing. As the pivoted clutch withdrawal lever moves backwards it bears against the release bearing pushing if forward to bear against the three clutch release levers. These levers move the pressure plate backwards against the pressure of the pressure springs, in this way disengaging the pressure plate from the clutch disc.

When the clutch pedal is released, the pressure plate springs force the pressure plate into contact with the high friction lining on one side of the clutch disc, and press the disc forwards so the friction linings on the other side of the disc come into contact with the flywheel face, this way sandwiching the plate and taking up the drive.

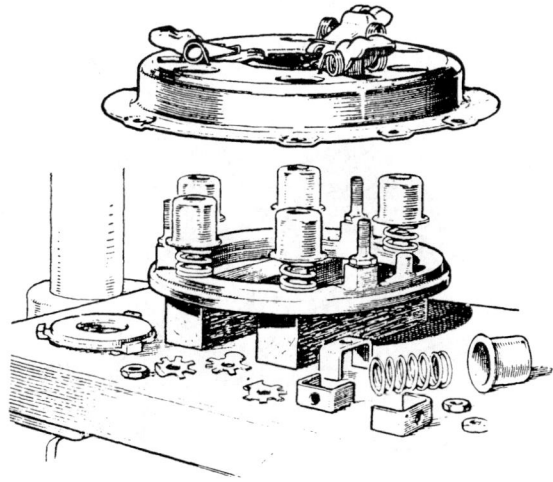

Fig. 5:1. The component parts of the clutch ready for final reassembly. The springs and cups must be in place before the cover plate is lowered into place

CLUTCH AND ACTUATING MECHANISM

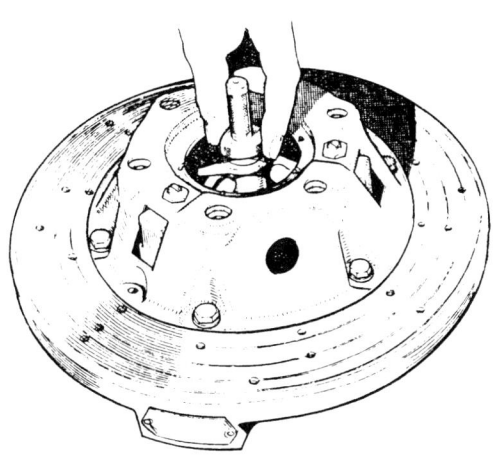

Fig.

Checking the setting of the release levers

As the friction linings on the clutch disc wear, the pressure plate automatically moves closer to the disc to compensate. This makes the inner ends of the release levers travel further towards the gearbox which decreases the release bearing clearance and the free clutch pedal movement which must be periodically restored to standard.

MAINTENANCE

The only maintenance required by the clutch for the life of the clutch disc linings is for the free movement of the clutch pedal to be periodically restored. It is vital that this is done at intervals of 6,000 miles as too little clearance can cause clutch slip, and too much clearance can make the clutch impossible to disengage.

Adjustment consists of altering the effective length of the clutch pedal rod.

Fig. 5:3A. Adjust the clutch by means of the spherical adjusting nut behind the locknut (arrowed)

Unscrew the lock nut at the clutch withdrawal lever end of the operating rod, and screw in or out the larger adjusting nut until there is the following free travel at the clutch pedal.

Morris Minor 9M Engine: $6\frac{1}{4}$ in. diameter clutch.
Pedal Free Movement $\frac{3}{4}$ in.
Morris Minor 10M Engine: $7\frac{1}{4}$ in. diameter clutch.
Pedal Free Movement $1\frac{1}{4}$ in.

Free travel is the distance the clutch pedal will move under the pressure of one finger before the resistance of the pressure plate springs are met. When this point is reached a pressure of about 50 lbs. per sq./in. is required to depress the clutch pedal further.

When the clutch free travel has been correctly set, tighten the lock nut onto the adjusting nut, without disturbing the position of the latter.

CLUTCH PEDAL LINKAGE - REMOVAL & REPLACEMENT

1. Remove the clutch return spring from the engine rear plate.
2. Extract the split pins and washers from the two rods and remove them from the clutch levers.
3. Remove the relay lever bracket from the body by releasing the two bolts and spring washers which hold it in place.

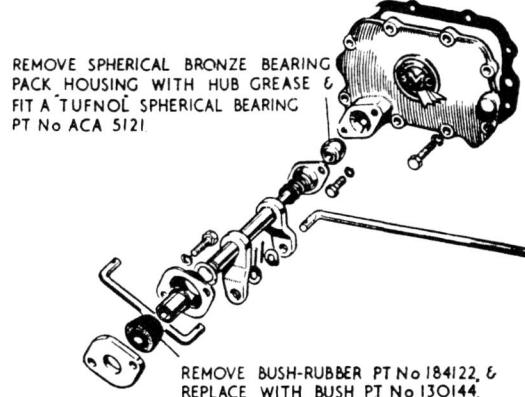

REMOVE SPHERICAL BRONZE BEARING PACK HOUSING WITH HUB GREASE & FIT A TUFNOL SPHERICAL BEARING PT No ACA 5121

REMOVE BUSH-RUBBER PT No 184122, & REPLACE WITH BUSH PT No 130144.

Fig. 5:3B. On earlier models check the spherical bronze bearing and the bush rubber and replace with new components if worn

4. Remove the relay clutch shaft by releasing the two bolts and spring washers which hold it in place against the gearbox.
5. Reassembly is a reversal of this process.

CLUTCH REMOVAL

The clutch can be removed after dropping the gearbox as detailed in Chapter 6. This is the easiest method. Other ways to remove the clutch are to first remove the engine as detailed in Chapter 1, or to remove the engine and gearbox together and then split to give access to the clutch.

Before the clutch can be serviced the gearbox must be removed. This involves removal of the longitudinal member under the rear of the gearbox. It is held in place by two bolts on either side

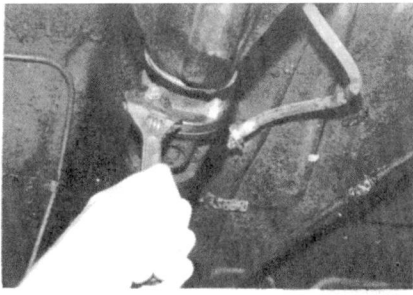

Mark the propeller shaft to rear axle flanges and undo the four securing nuts and bolts. Disengage the propeller shaft by lowering it and pulling it away from the mainshaft splines

The clutch release mechanism must be disconnected prior to undoing the gearbox bellhousing bolts

Undo the bolts holding the clutch cover assembly in place. In this instance the pressure plate was broken which meant buying a new pressure plate assembly

It is a false economy not to renew the carbon thrust bearing in the clutch release fork during a clutch overhaul (unless the bearing is nearly new)

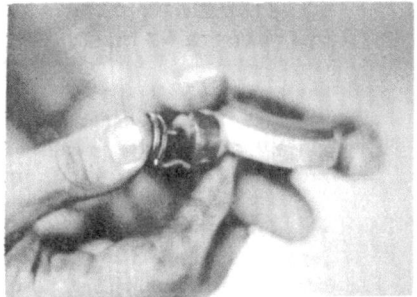

The release bearing is simply held in place by a spring clip at either end of the release fork 'prongs'

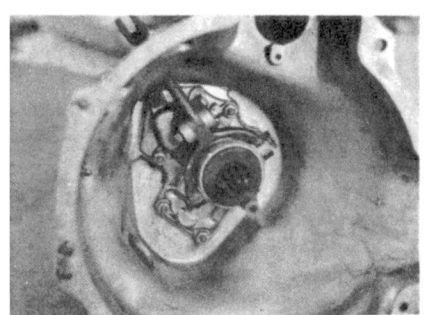

The clutch release fork is held in position by a long bolt and locknut on the inside of the bellhousing

This is a view of a new clutch pressure or cover plate assembly prior to being fitted in place

It is vital that the driven plate is positioned so that the long splined portion on the centre hub faces away from the flywheel

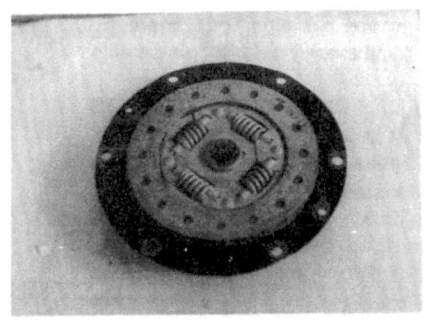

Lay the driven plate on the cover plate with the shortest portion of the splined centre hub facing upwards

Fit the clutch assembly into position by locating the pegs in the pressure plate cover in the small holes in the flywheel

It is quite easy to centralise the clutch driven plate before the cover bolts are tightened down hard, with the aid of a rod and frequent visual checks

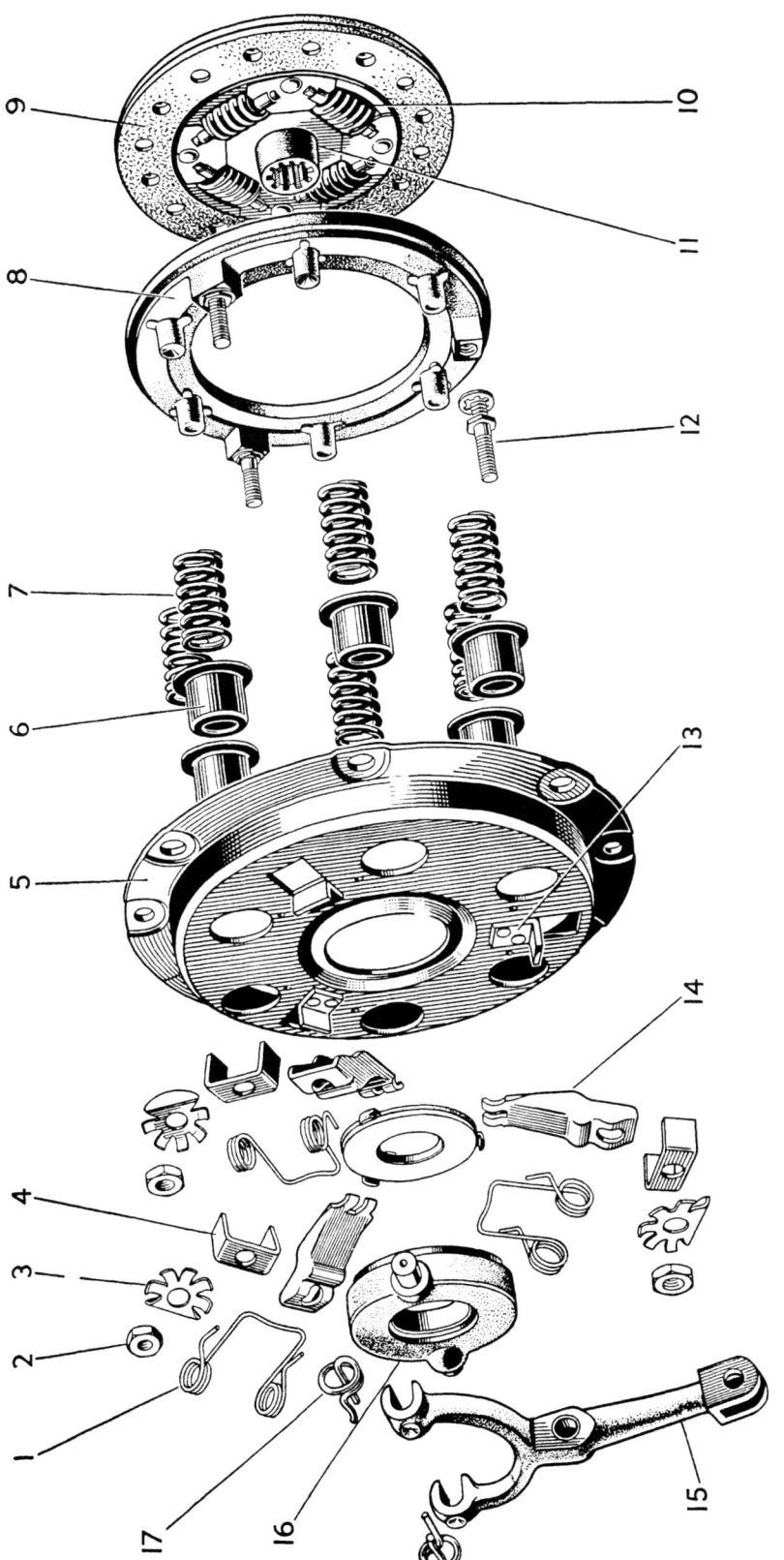

Fig. 5 : 3. An exploded view of the early type of clutch fitted to 948 c.c. models.

1 Anti-rattle spring
2 Adjusting nut
3 Tab washers

4 Bearing plates
5 Clutch cover
6 Flanged cups

7 Thrust springs
8 Pressure plate
9 Clutch driven plate

10 Driven plate springs
11 Splined hub
12 Shoulder stud

13 Fulcrum
14 Release lever
15 Clutch withdrawal lever

16 Release bearing and
    cup assembly
17 Retaining spring

Remove the clutch assembly by unscrewing the six bolts holding the cover to the rear face of the flywheel. Unscrew the bolts diagonally half a turn at a time to prevent distortion to the cover flange.

With all the bolts and spring washers removed lift the clutch assembly off the two locating dowels. The driven plate or clutch disc will fall out at this stage as it is not attached to either the clutch cover assembly or the flywheel.

CLUTCH REPLACEMENT

It is important that no oil or grease gets on the clutch disc friction linings, or the pressure plate and flywheel faces. It is advisable to replace the clutch with clean hands and to wipe down the pressure plate and flywheel faces with a clean dry rag before assembly begins.

Place the clutch disc against the flywheel with the shorter end of the hub, which is the end with the chamfered splines, facing the flywheel. On no account should the clutch disc be replaced with the longer end of the centre hub facing the flywheel as on reassembly it will be found quite impossible to operate the clutch in this position.

Replace the clutch cover assembly loosely on the two dowels. Replace the six bolts and spring washers and tighten them finger-tight so that the clutch disc is gripped but can still be moved.

The clutch disc must now be centralised so that when the engine and gearbox are mated the gearbox input shaft splines will pass through the splines in the centre of the driven plate hub.

Centralisation can be carried out quite easily by inserting a round bar or long screwdriver through the hole in the centre of the clutch, so that the end of the bar rests in the small hole in the end of the crankshaft containing the input shaft bearing bush.

Using the input shaft bearing bush as a fulcrum, moving the bar sideways or up and down will move the clutch disc in whichever direction is necessary to achieve centralisation.

Centralisation is easily judged by removing the bar and viewing the driven plate hub in relation to the hole in the release bearing. When the hub appears exactly in the centre of the release bearing hole all is correct.

Tighten the clutch bolts in a diagonal sequence to ensure that the cover plate is pulled down evenly and without distortion of the flange.

Mate the engine and gearbox, and check that the clutch is operating properly.

CLUTCH DISMANTLING

It is not very often that it is necessary to dismantle the clutch cover assembly, and in the normal course of events clutch replacement is the term used for simply fitting a new clutch disc.

If a new clutch disc is being fitted it is a false economy not to renew the release bearing at the same time. This will preclude having to replace it at a later date when wear on the clutch linings is still very small.

It should be noted here that it is preferable to purchase an exchange clutch cover assembly unit, which has been built up by the manufacturers and properly balanced, rather than to dismantle and build up your existing clutch cover assembly. A special tool is necessary to ensure that the job is done properly.

Presuming that it is possible to borrow from your local B.M.C. agent, clutch assembly tool 18G99A, proceed as follows:

1. Mark the clutch cover, release levers, and pressure plate lugs so that they can be refitted in the same relative positions.
2. Unhook the springs from the release bearing thrust plate and remove the plate and spring.
3. Place the three correctly sized spacing washers provided with the clutch assembly tool on the tool base plate in the positions indicated by the chart (found inside the lid of the assembly tool container).
4. Place the clutch face down on the three spacing washers so that the washers are as close as possible to the release levers, with the six holes in the cover flange in line with the six holes in the base plate.
5. Insert the six bolts provided with the assembly tool through the six holes in the cover flange, and tighten the cover down diagonally onto the base plate.
6. With a suitable punch, tap back the three tab washers and then remove the three adjusting nuts and bearing plates from the pressure plate bolts on early models, and just unscrew the three adjusting nuts on later models.
7. Unscrew the six bolts holding the clutch cover to the base plate, diagonally, and a turn at a time, so as to release the cover evenly. Lift the cover off and extract the six pressure springs and the spring retaining cups.

CLUTCH INSPECTION

Examine the clutch disc friction linings for wear and loose rivets and the disc for rim distortion, cracks, broken hub springs, and worn splines.

It is always best to renew the clutch driven plate as an assembly to preclude further trouble, but, if it is wished to merely renew the linings, the rivets should be drilled out and not knocked out with a punch. The manufacturers do not advise that only the linings are renewed and personal experience dictates that it is far more satisfactory to renew the driven plate complete than to try and economise by only fitting new friction linings.

Check the machined faces of the flywheel and the pressure plate. If either are badly grooved they should be machined until smooth. If the pressure plate is cracked or split it must be renewed, also if the portion on the other side of the plate in contact with the three release lever tips are grooved.

Check the release bearing thrust plate for cracks and renew it if any are found.

Examine the tips of the release levers which bear against the thrust plate, and renew the levers if more than a small flat has been worn on them.

Renew any clutch pressure springs that are broken or shorter than standard.

CLUTCH AND ACTUATING MECHANISM

Examine the depressions in the release levers which fit over the knife edge fulcrums and renew the levers if the metal appears badly worn.

Examine the clutch release bearing in the gearbox bellhousing and if it is worn to within $\frac{1}{16}$ in. of the rim of the metal cup, or if it is cracked or pitted, it must be removed and replaced.

Removal of the clutch release bearing is easily accomplished by pulling off the two retaining springs.

Also check the clutch withdrawal lever for slackness. If this is evident, withdraw the lever and renew the bush.

CLUTCH REASSEMBLY

1. During clutch reassembly ensure that the marked components are placed in their correct relative positions.
2. Place the three spacing washers on the clutch assembly tool base in the same position as for dismantling the clutch.
3. Place the clutch pressure plate face down on the three spacing washers.
4. Position the three release levers on the knife edge fulcrums (or release lever floating pins in the later clutches) and ensure that the anti-rattle springs are in place over the inner end of the levers.
5. Position the pressure springs on the pressure plate bosses.
6. Fit the flanged cups to the clutch cover and fit the cover over the pressure plate in the same relative position as it was originally.
7. Insert the six assembly tool bolts through the six holes in the clutch cover flange and tighten the cover down, diagonally, a turn at a time.
8. Replace the three bearing plates, tag washers, and adjusting nuts over the pressure plate studs in the early units, and just screw the adjusting nuts into the eyebolts in the later models.
9. To correctly adjust the clutch release levers use the clutch assembly tool as detailed below:
   a) Screw the actuater into the base plate and settle the clutch mechanism by pumping the actuator handle up and down a dozen times. Unscrew the actuater.
   b) Screw the tool pillar into the base plate and slide the correctly sized distance piece (as indicated in the chart in the tool's box) recessed side downwards, over the pillar.
   c) Slip the height finger over the centre pillar, and turn the release lever adjusting nuts, until the height fingers, when rotated and held firmly down, just contact the highest part of the clutch release lever tips.
   d) Remove the pillar, replace the actuator, and settle the clutch mechanism as in (a).
   e) Refit the centre pillar and height finger and recheck the clutch release lever clearance, and adjust if not correct.
10. With the centre pillar removed, lock the adjusting nuts found on early clutches by bending up the tab washers.
11. Replace the release bearing thrust plate and fit the retaining springs over the thrust plate hooks.
12. Unscrew the six bolts holding the clutch cover to the base plate, diagonally, a turn at a time and assembly is now complete.

CLUTCH FAULTS

There are four main faults which the clutch and release mechanism are prone to. They may occur by themselves or in conjunction with any of the other faults. They are clutch squeal, slip, spin, and judder.

CLUTCH SQUEAL - DIAGNOSIS & CURE

If on taking up the drive or when changing gear, the clutch squeals, this is a sure indication of a badly worn clutch release bearing. As well as regular wear due to normal use, wear of the clutch release bearing is much accentuated if the clutch is ridden, or held down for long periods in gear, with the engine running. To minimise wear of this component the car should always be taken out of gear at traffic lights and for similar hold-ups.

The clutch release bearing is not an expensive item, but it is difficult to get to, for to renew it it is necessary to separate the engine from the gearbox. If the clutch is being overhauled it is a false economy not to renew the clutch release bearing at the same time.

CLUTCH SLIP - DIAGNOSIS & CURE

Clutch slip is a self-evident condition which occurs when the clutch friction plate is badly worn, the release arm free travel is insufficient, oil or grease have got onto the flywheel or pressure plate faces, or the pressure plate itself is faulty.

The reason for clutch slip is that, due to one of the faults just listed, there is either insufficient pressure from the pressure plate, or insufficient friction from the friction plate to ensure solid drive.

If small amounts of oil get onto the clutch, under the heat of clutch engagement it will be burnt off, in the process gradually darkening the linings. Excessive oil on the clutch will burn off leaving a carbon deposit which can cause quite bad slip, or fierceness, spin and judder.

If clutch slip is suspected, and confirmation of this condition is required, there are several tests which can be made.
1. With the engine in second or third gear and pulling lightly up a moderate incline, sudden depression of the accelerator pedal may cause the engine to increase its speed without any increase in road speed. Easing off on the accelerator will then give a definite drop in engine speed without the car slowing.
2. Drive the car at a steady speed in top gear and, braking with the left leg, try and maintain the same speed by pressing down on the accelerator. Providing the same speed is maintained a change in the speed of the engine confirms that slip is taking place.
3. In extreme cases of clutch slip the engine will race under normal acceleration conditions.

If slip is due to oil or grease on the linings a temporary cure can sometimes be effected by squirting carbon tetrochloride into the clutch. The permanent cure, of course, is to renew the clutch driven

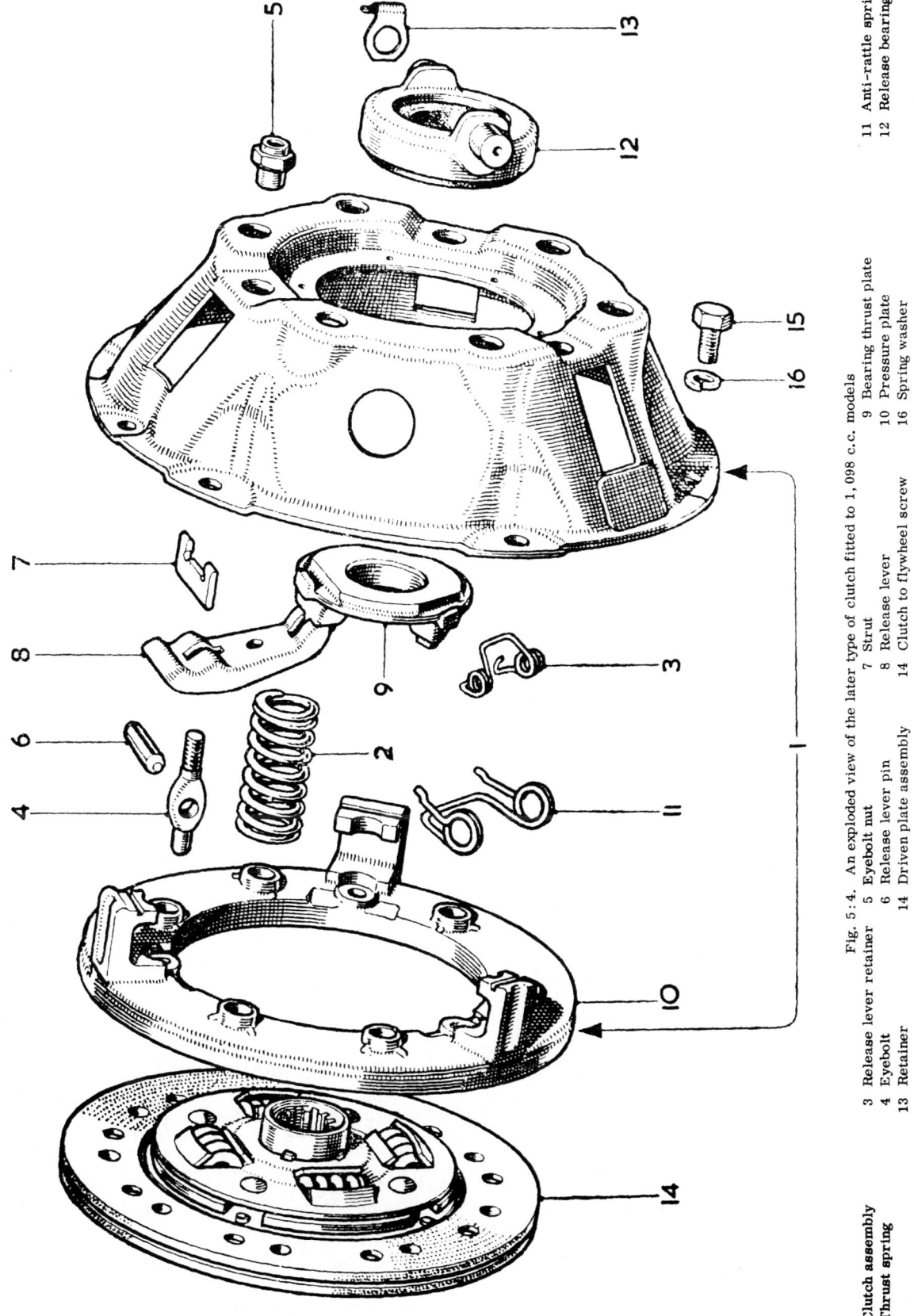

Fig. 5:4. An exploded view of the later type of clutch fitted to 1,098 c.c. models

1 Clutch assembly	3 Release lever retainer	5 Eyebolt nut	7 Strut	9 Bearing thrust plate	11 Anti-rattle spring
2 Thrust spring	4 Eyebolt	6 Release lever pin	8 Release lever	10 Pressure plate	12 Release bearing
	13 Retainer	14 Driven plate assembly	14 Clutch to flywheel screw	16 Spring washer	

CLUTCH AND ACTUATING MECHANISM

plate and trace and rectify the oil leak.

CLUTCH SPIN - DIAGNOSIS & CURE

Clutch spin is a condition which occurs when there is a leak in the clutch hydraulic actuating mechanism where this system of actuation is used, the release arm free travel is excessive, there is an obstruction in the clutch either on the input gear splines, or in the release arm itself, or the oil may have partially burnt off the clutch linings and have left a resinous deposit which is causing the clutch disc to stick to the pressure plate or flywheel.

The reason for clutch spin is that due to any, or a combination of the faults just listed, the clutch pressure plate is not completely freeing from the centre plate even with the clutch pedal fully depressed.

If clutch spin is suspected, the condition can be confirmed by extreme difficulty in engaging first gear from rest, difficulty in changing gear, and very sudden take-up of the clutch drive at the fully depressed end of the clutch pedal travel as the clutch is released. If the clutch has just been stripped and rebuilt and is locked solid the clutch disc has been put in the wrong way round with the long portion of the hub facing forwards towards the flywheel.

Check the release arm free travel. If this is correct examine the clutch master and slave cylinders and the connecting hydraulic pipe for leaks. Fluid in one of the rubber boots fitted over the end of either the master or slave cylinders, where fitted, is a sure sign of a leaking piston seal.

If these points are checked and found to be in order then the fault lies internally in the release mechanism or the clutch, and it will be necessary to remove the clutch for examination.

CLUTCH JUDDER - DIAGNOSIS & CURE

Clutch judder is a self-evident condition which occurs when the gearbox or engine mountings are loose or too flexible, when there is oil on the faces of the clutch friction plate, or when the clutch pressure plate has been incorrectly adjusted.

The reason for clutch judder is that due to one of the faults just listed, the clutch pressure plate is not freeing smoothly from the friction disc, and is snatching.

Clutch judder normally occurs when the clutch pedal is released in first or reverse gears, and the whole car shudders as it moves backwards or forwards.

Remove the clutch assembly by unscrewing the six bolts holding the cover to the rear face of the flywheel. Unscrew the bolts diagonally half a turn at a time to prevent distortion to the cover flange.

With all the bolts and spring washers removed lift the clutch assembly off the two locating dowels. The driven plate or clutch disc will fall out at this stage as it is not attached to either the clutch cover assembly or the flywheel.

FAULT FINDING CHART

Cause	Trouble	Remedy
SYMPTOM:	CLUTCH SLIP	
General wear	Worn clutch linings Worn clutch release bearing Weak or broken thrust springs Weak anti-rattle springs	Remove clutch and fit new centre plate and linings. Fit new clutch release bearing. Remove clutch cover assembly, dismantle and fit new springs. Remove and overhaul clutch assembly.
Damage or dirt Oil or air leaks	Piston seized in clutch slave cylinder Engine backplate bent or distorted Air leak in clutch hydraulic actuating system Oil on clutch centre plate	Overhaul or replace clutch slave cylinder. Remove and straighten backplate. Trace and rectify leak. Bleed clutch system. Remove clutch and fit new centre plate and linings. Rectify oil leak.
SYMPTOM:	CLUTCH DRAG, SPIN, FIERCENESS OR SNATCH	
General wear	Worn centre plate linings Forward end of first motion shaft binding on spigot bush	Remove clutch and fit new centre plate. Examine bush and first motion shaft for wear and renew as necessary.
Damage or dirt	Dirt in clutch hydraulic system Centre plate hub binding on first motion shaft splines Clutch centre plate linings broken Clutch centre plate distorted or damaged Clutch pressure plate broken	Flush out, clean, and bleed system. Clean splines and check for obstruction. Remove clutch, and fit new clutch centre plate. Remove clutch, fit new clutch centre plate. Fit new pressure plate assembly.

FAULT FINDING CHART

Cause	Trouble	Remedy
SYMPTOM:	CLUTCH JUDDER	
General wear	Worn or partially sheared engine or gearbox rubber mountings Propeller shaft to differential bolts loose Rear spring shackles worn Excessive backlash in transmission Rear springs weak or broken	Fit new rubber mountings. Inspect and tighten bolts. Fit new rear spring shackles. Inspect universal joints, rear axle, and mainshaft splines for wear. Replace as necessary. Remove and fit reconditioned springs.
Damage or dirt	Pressure plate not parallel with flywheel face Clutch centre plate bent First motion shaft bent Engine backplate bent or distorted	Remove and overhaul pressure plate assembly. Remove and fit new centre plate and linings. Examine first motion shaft, straighten or fit new shaft. Remove and straighten backplate.
Oil leaks	Oil on clutch centre plate linings	Remove clutch and fit new centre plate and linings. Rectify oil leak.
SYMPTOM:	CLUTCH RATTLE	
General wear	Clutch release bearing loose on clutch release fork Worn clutch release mechanism Excessive backlash in the transmission	Separate engine and gearbox and check and rectify. Overhaul release mechanism and fit new parts as required. Check universal joints, splines, and rear axle for wear. Renew component parts as necessary.
SYMPTOM:	CLUTCH KNOCK	
Components loose or worn	Clutch pressure plate not parallel with flywheel face Splines on first motion shaft or in centre plate hub badly worn First motion shaft bush badly worn Flywheel bolts loose	Remove and overhaul pressure plate assembly. Inspect and renew first motion shaft or centre plate hub. Extract old bush and fit new replacement. Fit new tab washers and tighten bolts securely.

CHAPTER SIX

GEARBOX

SPECIFICATION

Morris Minor 1000 – 948 c.c.

Number of forward speeds	4.
Synchromesh	Second, third, and top gears.
Ratios:	First .. .. 3.628 : 1
	Second .. .. 2.374 : 1
	Third .. .. 1.412 : 1
	Top .. .. 1.000 : 1
	Reverse .. .. 4.664 : 1
Overall ratios:	First .. .. 16.507 : 1
	Second .. .. 10.802 : 1
	Third .. .. 6.425 : 1
	Top .. .. 4.555 : 1
	Reverse .. .. 21.221 : 1
Speedometer drive gear to pinion ratio	..5/13.

Morris Minor 1000 – 1,098 c.c.

Number of forward speeds	4.
Synchromesh	Second, third, and top gears.
Ratios:	First .. .. 3.628 : 1
	Second .. .. 2.172 : 1
	Third .. .. 1.412 : 1
	Top .. .. 1.0 : 1
	Reverse .. .. 4.664 : 1
Overall ratios:	First .. .. 15.276 : 1
	Second .. .. 9.169 : 1
	Third .. .. 5.950 : 1
	Top .. .. 4.220 : 1
	Reverse .. .. 19.665 : 1

GENERAL DESCRIPTION

The gearbox fitted to all models contains four forward gears and reverse. Synchromesh is fitted between second and third gears, and between third and fourth. Early gearboxes have cone synchronisers, plain bearings, and a side cover which is held in place by set bolts. Later gearboxes make use of baulk ring synchromesh, needle roller bearings, and a side cover held in place by nuts and studs. Otherwise the gearboxes are virtually identical.

GEARBOX REMOVAL

The gearbox can be removed in unit with the engine through the engine compartment, as described in detail in Chapter 1. If wished, the gearbox can be separated from the engine at the clutch bellhousing, and removed through the engine compartment after the removal of the engine. As a matter of interest these are the only ways the gearboxes fitted to the Austin Healey Sprite and M.G. Midget can be removed.

In addition to the two methods listed above, on the Morris Minor 1000 it is possible to remove the gearbox from underneath the car with the engine still in place.

The car must first be positioned high enough to enable it to be worked on in reasonable comfort and safety from underneath. If a ramp or pit is not available then jack up the front of the car as high as possible. Safety is vital here, so once the car has been jacked up use chocks to ensure it will not collapse. Ramps or stands onto which the front wheels are driven are ideal.

To remove the gearbox from under the car proceed as follows:-

1. Remove the earth lead from the battery.
2. Unscrew the gearbox drain plug and place a suitable container in place to catch the gearbox oil.
3. Remove the speedometer cable from the side of the gearbox by unscrewing the knurled retaining nut.

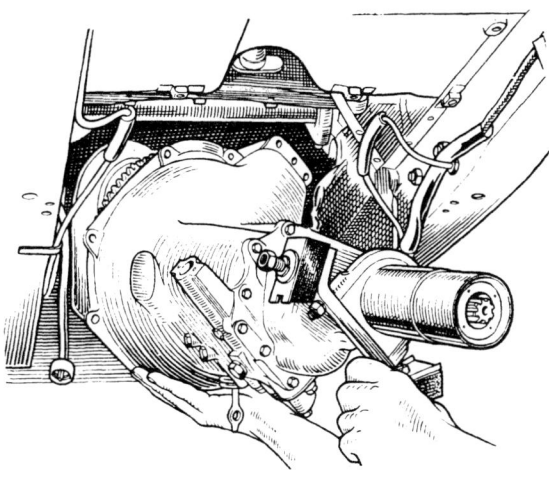

Fig. 6:1. Turn the gearbox slightly clockwise when removing it from under the car

4. Release the distributor spring clips and remove the distributor cover.

5. Unscrew the nut holding the starter cable to the starter motor and detach the cable at the motor.

6. Detach the wire from the oil pressure sender unit.

7. Drain the radiator, unscrew the retaining clips at the thermostat elbow and of the top hose and pull the hose away.

8. If a heater unit is fitted, remove the retaining clips from the heater hoses, and pull the hoses away, after draining the cylinder block and heater unit.

9. Part the exhaust manifold from the exhaust pipe by unscrewing the flange securing nuts, remove the nut and bolt holding the exhaust pipe support bracket to the bellhousing, and tie the exhaust pipe back out of the way.

10. Free the accelerator linkages and choke cable from the carburettor.

11. Pull off the rubber dust cover from the base of the gearlever inside the car, release the three set screws, spring washers, anti-rattle springs, and the gearlever locating peg from the gearlever seat, and lift away the gearlever together with the lever seat cover.

12. Mark the rear axle pinion flange and the rear propeller shaft flange to ensure that they are reassembled in the same relative positions and unscrew the four nuts, bolts, and spring washers holding the propeller shaft to the rear axle and remove the propeller shaft. (Free the flanges by pushing the propeller shaft towards the gearbox to clear the lip on the rear axle flange.)

13. The Morris Minor has a mechanically operated clutch and dismantling should now proceed as follows :-

    a) Remove the clutch pedal return spring and free the clutch relay levers from the operating rods by removing the split pins and anti-rattle washers.

    b) Unscrew the two bolts and spring washers which hold the relay shaft bracket to the main frame. Take off the packing plate, bracket, and bush. Pull the shaft away from the spherical bush, remove the spring, and remove the operating rod from the clutch release arm.

    c) Release the engine steady cable as detailed in Chapter 1.

    d) Remove the gearbox cross member as detailed in Chapter 1.

14. Place a sling round the rear of the engine, or a jack underneath the rear of the sump and take the weight of the engine.

15. Lower the rear of the engine, the front end pivoting on the two front engine mountings, until the bellhousing flange will clear the body when the gearbox is pulled back.

16. Place a suitable chock under the gearbox or a jack to provide the necessary support, and, working underneath the car, unscrew the nuts, bolts, and lockwashers holding the bellhousing to the rear engine plate.

17. Remove the gearbox by pulling it backwards until the input shaft is clear of the clutch hub. Never allow the gearbox to hang suspended on the front shaft, and always have a jack or chock under the gearbox to take the weight while the bellhousing bolts are removed. As the gearbox is removed it must be turned slightly clockwise so that the raised portion will clear the rack and pinion steering tube.

18. Replacement of the gearbox is a straight reversal of the above process. Ensure where the earthing strap has been removed that it is replaced, - the failure of many an engine to start after a gearbox overhaul has been due to this simple ommission.

Fig. 6:1A. Drain the gearbox before removal from the car. The arrow indicates the drain plug

GEARBOX

GEARBOX DISMANTLING

With the gearbox withdrawn it should be placed on a strong bench so as to be comfortable and accessable while being worked on. If a bench is not available then lay the gearbox on the floor, but make sure the latter is clean and dirt free and preferably covered with paper.

To make the sequence of dismantling and rebuilding as easy as possible the text has been keyed to Fig. No. 6:2, except where otherwise stated. Throughout the text the numbers in brackets, i.e. (15) refer to the parts shown in this illustration. Strip the gearbox in the following sequence:-

1. Remove the remote control housing, gasket, and rear extension to the gearbox, by unscrewing the eight nuts and spring washers holding the remote control housing in place, and the nine nuts and spring washers holding the rear extension to the gearbox. To remove the rear extension pull it back a little and then turn it anti-clockwise to enable the control lever to slide out from the fork rod ends.

2. The side cover (13) on early models, was held in place by eight set bolts and spring washers. On later models the side cover was held in place by studs, nuts and spring washers, (3, 15, 16). Remove the set bolts or nuts and take off the side cover and gasket. Turn the gearbox on its side and shake it to free the two springs and plungers from their separate holes in the front edge of the gearbox side cover flange (78, 79).

3. Working from inside the bellhousing (1), prise off the two retaining springs from the clutch release bearing and remove the bearing.

4. Knock back the locking tab (84) on the clutch release arm bolt (82) and remove the nut, spring washer and tab (85, 83, 84). Unscrew the bolt from its housing (9) and withdraw the clutch release arm (80).

5. Unscrew the seven nuts and spring washers (11, 12) inside the bellhousing and pull off the front cover (9) and front cover joint gasket (10). Remove the bearing packing washer (54).

6. On the forward portion of the side cover of the gearbox casing are two plugs. Unscrew the lower of these together with its fibre washer (7, 8). Tilt the gearbox and shake out the reverse plunger and spring (78, 79). Unscrew the upper plug and washer (76, 77).

7. Place the gears in neutral by lining up the slots in the selector rods (66, 70, 68).

8. Turn the gearbox onto its side so that the open side cover faces upwards.

9. Working partially through the drain plug hole, unscrew the reverse fork locating nut (72), the reverse fork locating bolt (71), and remove together with the lockwasher (73).

10. Working through the hole in the side of the gearbox casing, unscrew the locating bolts, lock nuts, and lock washers (72, 73, 71) from the first and second speed fork (67), and the third and fourth speed fork (69).

11. Pull out from the rear of the gearbox the third and fourth speed selector rod (70), the first and second speed selector rod (68), and the reverse selector rod (66), in this order. As the rods are withdrawn the interlock balls (75), and the interlock plunger (74), should emerge from their holes in the front and rear of the gearbox side cover flange. If necessary shake the casing to free them. The rods may be drifted out gently if they prove difficult to remove.

12. Measure the end float of the laygear (26) with a feeler gauge. If the end float exceeds .003 in. then new thrust washers must be refitted on reassembly. If the reading is in excess of .003 in. write it down so that the correctly sized washers can be obtained at a later stage.

13. With a suitable metal rod, drift the layshaft (25) forward out into the bellhousing. The laygear cluster (26) and the two thrust washers (30, 31) will drop to the bottom of the gearbox casing as the drift used to push out the layshaft is withdrawn.

14. The third motion shaft (32) is removed from the rear of the gearbox casing with the large ball bearing (51) and the bearing housing (52) complete as one assembly. Freeing the bearing housing from the gearbox casing is sometimes difficult. Try gently tapping the bearing housing at alternate, diagonally opposite, points from inside the casing. Alternatively, unscrew the third motion shaft nut (59) and remove the distance piece and speedometer gear drive (55, 56). Replace the nut and tap vigorously against its underside. The housing will gradually emerge from the gearbox casing and as soon as it is sufficiently far out, place a puller or levers under the lip of the bearing housing to accelerate the complete removal of the third motion shaft assembly from the gearbox. Take great care not to damage the bearing housing or the gearbox casing during this operation.

15. Insert a metal rod through the large hole in the gearbox casing left by the third motion shaft bearing housing, and locate the end of the rod in the hole in the end of the first motion shaft. Tap the first motion shaft complete with bearing into the bellhousing. Lift out the laygear.

16. Unscrew the reverse shaft set bolt (61) and the spring washer (62) and remove.

17. With a screwdriver, working from the rear of the gearbox casing, turn the slotted end of the reverse shaft (60) and at the same time push it forwards into the gearbox.

18. As the shaft emerges the gear and bush (63) will fall away freely and can then be lifted out.

19. The gearbox is now completely stripped. The component parts should now be examined for wear as detailed later, and the layshaft, first motion shaft, and third motion shaft broken down further, as shown in the section headed 'Gearbox Examination & Renovation'.

REMOTE CONTROL & GEARBOX REAR COVER - DISMANTLING & REASSEMBLY

The remote control assembly and the gearbox rear cover are dismantled easily, after they have

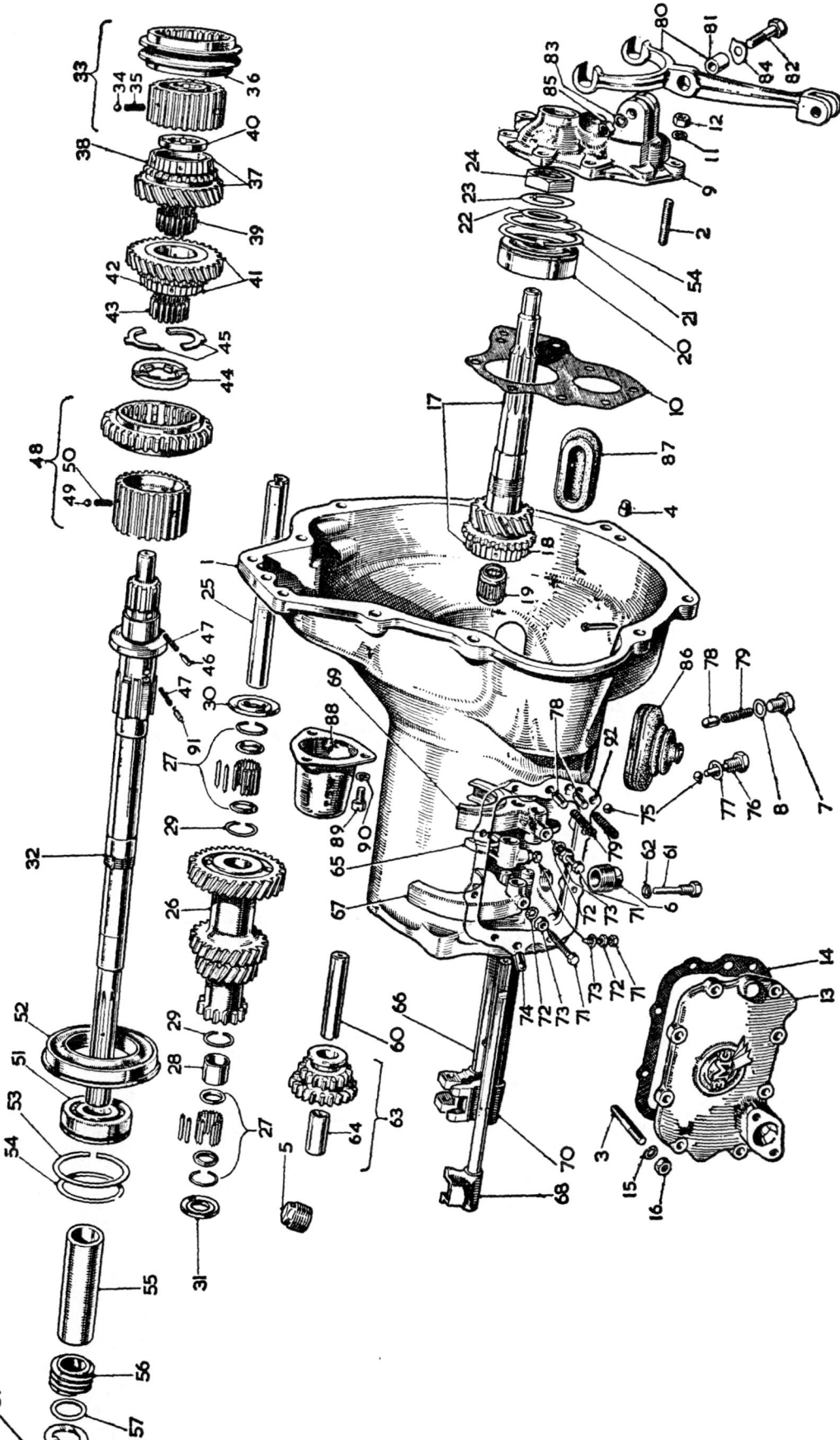

Fig. 6:2. Exploded view of the later type of gearbox with needle roller bearings and baulk ring synchromesh. 1 Gearbox bell housing. 2 Stud for front cover. 3 Stud for front cover. 4 Dowel. 5 Filler plug. 6 Drain plug. 7 Plug for reverse plunger spring. 8 Washer. 9 Front cover. 10 Front cover joint. 11 Spring washer. 12 Nut. 13 Side cover. 14 Joint for side cover. 15 Spring washer. 16 Nut. 17 First motion shaft with cone. 18 Synchronising cone. 19 Needle roller bearing. 20 First motion shaft journal ball bearing. 21 Spring ring. 22 Washer. 23 Lockwasher. 24 Nut. 25 Layshaft. 26 Laygear. 27 Needle roller bearing with spring ring. 28 Distance piece. 29 Spring ring. 30 Thrust washer (front). 31 Thrust washer (rear). 32 Third motion shaft/mainshaft. 33 Third and fourth speed synchroniser. 34 Ball. 35 Spring. 36 Sleeve. 37 Third speed gear with cone. 38 Synchronising cone. 39 Needle roller. 40 Third speed gear locking collar. 41 Second speed gear with cone. 42 Synchronising cone. 43 Needle roller. 44 Splined locking washer. 45 Split washer. 46 Peg for locking collar. 47 Springs for pegs. 48 First speed gear assembly. 49 Ball. 50 Spring for ball. 51 Third motion shaft journal ball bearing. 52 Bearing housing. 53 Spring ring. 54 Bearing packing washer. 55 Third motion shaft distance piece. 56 Speedometer gear. 57 Plain washer. 58 Locking washer. 59 Third motion shaft nut. 60 Reverse gear shaft. 61 Locking screw. 62 Spring washer. 63 Reverse gear wheel and bush. 64 Bush. 65 Reverse fork. 66 Reverse fork rod. 67 First and second speed fork. 68 First and second speed fork rod. 69 Third and fourth speed fork. 70 Third and fourth speed fork rod. 71 Fork locating bolt. 72 Shakeproof washer. 73 Nut. 74 Interlock plunger. 75 Interlock ball. 76 Plug. 77 Washer. 78 Plunger for fork rod. 79 Spring. 80 Clutch withdrawal lever with bush. 81 Bush. 82 Bolt. 83 Spring washer. 84 Locking washer. 85 Nut. 86 Dust cover. 87 Dust cover for bell housing. 88 Starter pinion cover. 89 Screw. 90 Washer. 91 Spring loaded plunger.

97

been removed from the gearbox (see the previous section, para. 1 for details of removal), by following the sequence detailed below. The numbers in brackets refer to Fig. No. 6 : 4.

1. Unscrew the speedometer pinion sleeve (14) and remove together with the pinion and washers (13).

2. To free the control lever (10) from the control shaft (9), unscrew the control shaft locating screw, and to assist removal of the control shaft, which is a push fit in the rear cover, screw the locating screw into the tapped hole at the front end of the shaft, extract the shaft, and lift out the lever.

3. Turn the remote control housing upside down and remove the four bolts and spring washers (21, 22) which hold the bottom cover and gasket (19, 20) in place under the gearlever.

4. If the gearlever (26) has not already been removed, unscrew the three set bolts and spring washers (24, 25) from the gearbox seat cover (23), and remove the anti-rattle spring cap, its washer, spring, and plunger (36, 37, 35, 34) and the lever locating peg (32) before lifting the gearlever and seat cover off. If the plunger and spring are not removed before the gearlever is lifted off, then should they fall into the remote control housing they should be retrieved and placed with their cap until reassembly.

5. Unscrew the reverse plunger cap (38) and remove the reverse plunger spring and ball (40, 39).

6. Remove the rubber ring (27), thrust button (47), and thrust button spring (48), from the rear selector lever (44), and place with the lever after they have been removed, for ease of reassembly.

7. To remove the front (51) and rear (44) selector levers, extract the two welch plugs (31) from either end of the remote control housing, unscrew the set bolt and spring washer from each lever (45, 46, 52, 53) and drift out the remote control shaft (49).

8. To remove the split tapered bush (54) from the selector lever (51), release the circlip holding the halves together.

9. Reassembly is a reversal of the dismantling procedure.

GEARBOX EXAMINATION & RENOVATION

Carefully examine all the component parts starting with the synchronising cones or baulk rings. The cones are copper in colour and are shrunk onto the sides of the second, third, and fourth speed gears. If the ridges are badly worn, or if the cones are loose on their gears, or if the cones are cracked or broken, they must be renewed. It is normal practice to purchase new gears and synchronising cones complete.

If engineering facilities are available it is possible to shrink on new cones to existing gearwheels, and then machine the cones to the correct dimensions. This is highly skilled work, it is most unlikely that the private owner, or the majority of garages have the necessary equipment, and the saving is not really sufficient to make it worthwhile. It is altogether better to purchase either a complete reconditioned

mainshaft or new gears and synchronising units and fit them to the mainshaft yourself.

Examine the gearwheels for excessive wear and chipping of the teeth and renew them as necessary.

If the laygear endfloat is above the permitted tolerance (see para. 12 in the section headed ' Gearbox Dismantling '), the thrust washers must be renewed. The smaller thrust washer fitted at the rear end is available from your local B.M.C. agent in varying thicknesses to compensate for laygear wear. On reassembly end float should not be less than .001 in. The thrust washers are available in the following thicknesses:- .123 to .124 in., .125 to .126 in., .127 to .128 in., and .130 to .131 in.

A needle roller bearing is fitted internally to each end of the laygear. To examine them prise out the retaining clips from each end, and with a finger pull out the outer race, needle rollers, and inner race. At the end of the laygear with the smaller gear, also extract the distance piece and the inner spring rings from both ends. Renew the roller bearings and races, if worn.

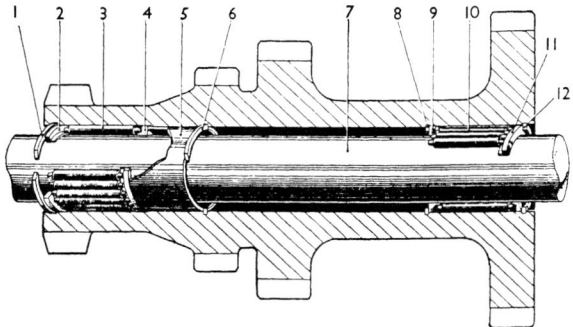

Fig. 6 : 3. A sectioned view of the laygear assembly showing the layout of the needle roller bearings. 1 Spring ring (outer). 2 Outer race. 3 Needle rollers. 4 Inner race. 5 Distance piece. 6 Spring ring (inner). 7 Layshaft. 8 Spring ring (inner). 9 Inner race. 10 Needle rollers. 11 Outer race. 12 Spring ring (outer).

It is helpful to replace the roller bearings round a dummy shaft inside the laygear. Dealing first with the smaller end of the laygear, place it upright with the smaller end at the top and fit the inner spring ring, the distance piece, and slide the new roller bearing, which comes in a cage, into position, ensuring that the ends of the needle rollers enter into the retaining nicks in the bearing end races. Slip the spring retaining ring into the groove. Repeat this procedure for the larger end of the laygear, turning the laygear round, and omitting, of course, the distance piece.

Examine the condition of the main ball bearings, one on the first motion shaft, and the other on the third motion shaft. If there is looseness between the inner and outer races the bearings must be pulled off and renewed.

On the first motion shaft it is necessary to remove the retaining nut and lockwasher before the bearing is pulled. NOTE the position of the spring ring. On refitting a new bearing to the first motion shaft position the tag on the lockwasher in the shaft keyway so that it faces towards the nut.

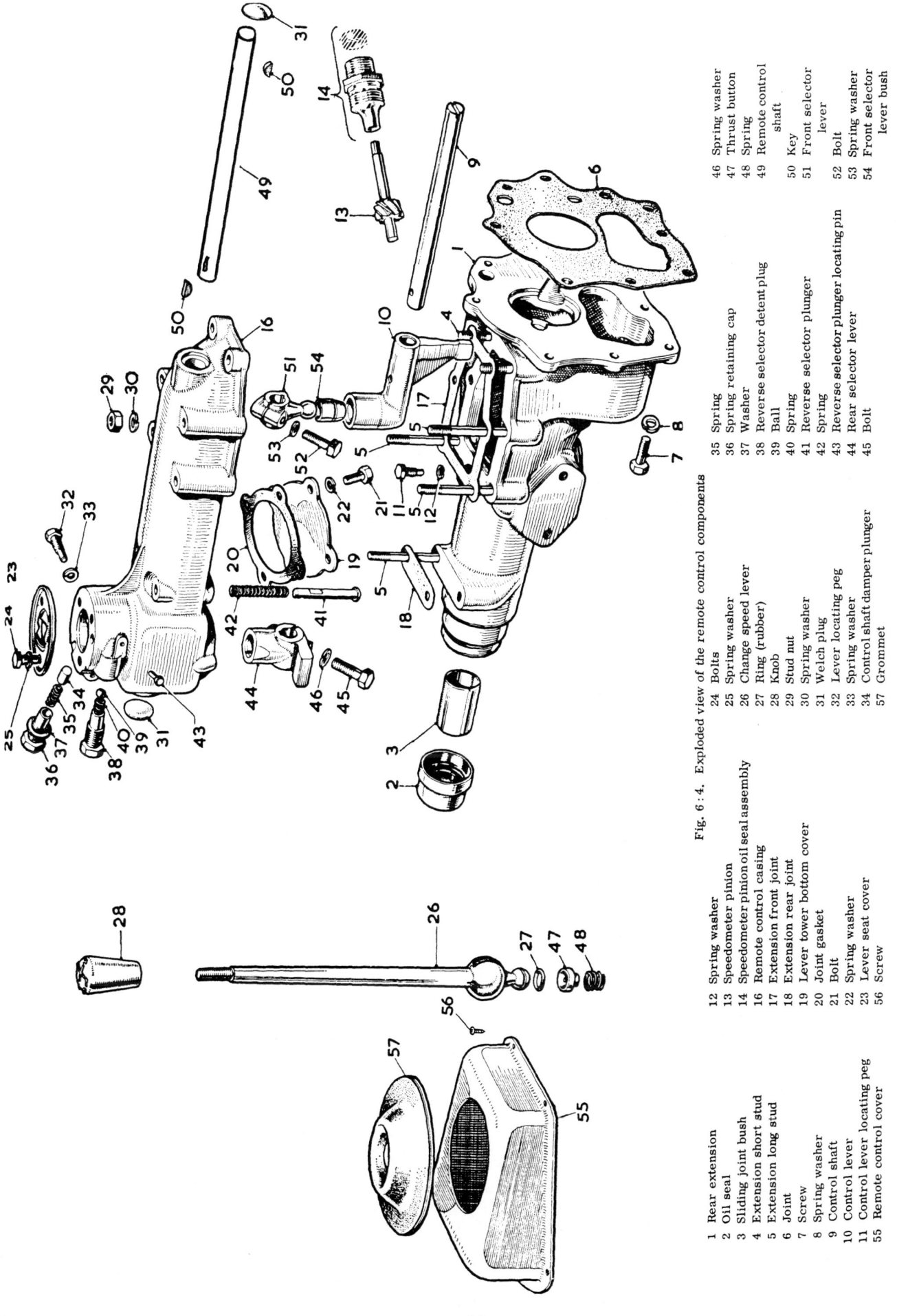

Fig. 6 : 4. Exploded view of the remote control components

1	Rear extension	35	Spring
2	Oil seal	36	Spring retaining cap
3	Sliding joint bush	37	Washer
4	Extension short stud	38	Reverse selector detent plug
5	Extension long stud	39	Ball
6	Joint	40	Spring
7	Screw	41	Reverse selector plunger
9	Control shaft	42	Spring
10	Control lever	43	Reverse selector plunger locating pin
11	Control lever locating peg	44	Rear selector lever
55	Remote control cover	45	Bolt
12	Spring washer	46	Spring washer
13	Speedometer pinion	47	Thrust button
14	Speedometer pinion oil seal assembly	48	Spring
16	Remote control casing	49	Remote control shaft
17	Extension front joint	50	Key
18	Extension rear joint	51	Front selector lever
19	Lever tower bottom cover	52	Bolt
20	Joint gasket	53	Spring washer
21	Bolt	54	Front selector lever bush
22	Spring washer	24	Bolts
23	Lever seat cover	25	Spring washer
56	Screw	26	Change speed lever
		27	Ring (rubber)
		28	Knob
		29	Stud nut
		30	Spring washer
		31	Welch plug
		32	Lever locating peg
		33	Spring washer
		34	Control shaft damper plunger
		57	Grommet

99

On the mainshaft place the shaft in a vice with padded jaws, release the mainshaft nut (59), locking washer (58), speedometer gear (56), and distance piece (55), if this has not already been done, and then pull the bearing housing (52) and bearing (51) off the shaft. The bearing can then be drifted away from its housing.

Examine the first motion shaft spigot bush which should have a clearance of between .002 in. to .003 in. with the third motion shaft. If the clearance is excessive, either the bush or the third motion shaft, depending if either or both are worn, must be renewed. On later gearboxes a needle roller bearing instead of a bush is fitted and must also be examined and renewed as necessary.

It it is wished to renew the synchronisers, or to examine the second and third gear bushes or needle roller bearings the third motion shaft must be dismantled in the following sequence which will ensure the job is done rapidly, correctly, and easily.

EARLY GEARBOXES - CONE SYNCHROMESH, GEAR BUSHES

1. Slide the sleeve (36) together with the third and fourth gear synchroniser (33) off the front end of the third motion shaft.

2. To separate the third and fourth speed synchroniser and the sleeve, wrap a piece of cloth round the synchroniser and press out the sleeve. The cloth will retain the three balls and springs (34, 35) which hold the sleeve to the synchroniser. If a piece of cloth is not wrapped round the synchroniser the balls will fly out and probable become lost.

3. With an electrical screwdriver or piece of thin rod, press down the spring loaded plunger (3 in Fig. No. 6 : 5) through the semi-circular hole at the front of the synchroniser cone and turn the splined locking washer (4) so that a spline holds the plunger down and the ring is so positioned that it can slide forwards off the end of the third motion shaft.

4. Remove the now exposed plunger and spring (3, 2) and slide off the third speed gear and the needle roller bearing on later gearboxes.

5. Slide off the bush interlocking ring and second speed gear. Examine the condition of the second speed gear bush and if worn chisel it off, and sweat on a new bush.

6. Finally, pull off the splined rear thrust washer, the first speed gearwheel, and the second gear synchroniser. The first speed gearwheel is separated from the second gear synchroniser in the same way as previously described in (3) above.

LATE GEARBOXES - BAULK RING SYNCHRO-MESH, NEEDLE ROLLER BEARINGS

1. In addition to the differences already listed at the beginning of the chapter, the third motion shaft is of a quite different design to that used in the early gearboxes. This means that the second and first speed gears have to be taken off the opposite end of the shaft to the third speed gear.

2. Repeat the dismantling process as for early gearboxes down to para. 4. Then proceed as follows:-

3. With the third motion shaft nut, locking washer, speedometer drive gear, distance piece, and bearing already removed, pull off the first speed gear and second speed synchroniser assembly. Separate the synchroniser from the hub as described in (3) in the previous section.

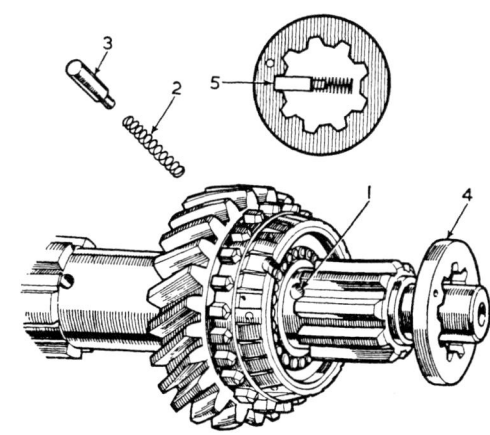

Fig. 6:5. Method of holding the mainshaft gearwheel in place. 1 Hole for locking plunger. 2 Spring. 3 Locking plunger. 4 Locking washer. 5 Locking washer with plunger engaged.

4. With an electrical screwdriver or piece of thin rod press down the spring loaded plunger (31) and turn the splined locking washer (44) so that one of the splines holds the plunger down, and the ring is so positioned that it can slide rearwards off the end of the third motion shaft.

5. Remove the split washer (45) and slide the second speed gear off the end of the third motion shaft complete with needle roller bearing. Examine the needle roller bearing for wear and renew as necessary.

Reassembly of the third motion shaft in both early and late gearboxes is a reversal of the above dismantling procedure.

GEARBOX REASSEMBLY & REPLACEMENT

1. Position the reverse gear (63) in the gearbox and slide the reverse gear shaft (60) into position. Turn the shaft, by means of a screwdriver in the rear slot, until the holes in the shaft and the casing coincide. Insert and tighten down the locking screw and spring washer (61, 62).

2. Turn the gearbox on end, and place the laygear (26) in position, remembering the thrust washers (30, 31) at each end. Place a long rod or tommy bar through the laygear and the holes in either end of the gearbox casing so that on turning the gearbox back, the laygear and thrust washers will not drop to the bottom of the casing.

3. Replace the mainshaft (32) through the rear of the gearbox and tap the bearing housing (52)

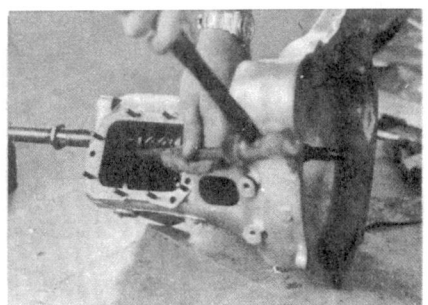

The first step is to dismantle the gearbox. Take care not to damage the mainshaft bearing when drifting it out of the gearbox casing

The first motion shaft complete with bearing is drifted out of the front of gearbox with a rod positioned through the mainshaft bearing hole

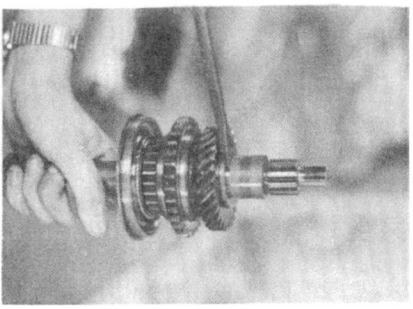

When dismantling the mainshaft examine the bushes for wear and remove and replace them if worn. Later models use needle roller bearings

If the synchronising cones are badly worn or cracked it will be necessary to renew the complete gearwheel. Later models are fitted with baulk ring synchromesh

Fitting new cones to existing gearwheels involves specialised machining operations, and as the gear teeth are bound to be worn a new gearwheel and cone is the best answer

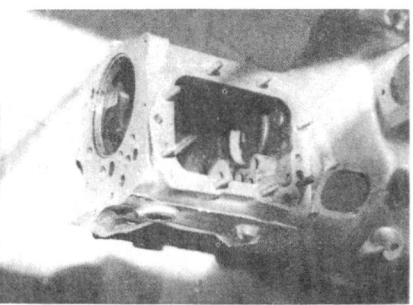

The gearbox casing must be thoroughly cleaned out before replacing the gears and selector rods

First reassemble in the bottom of the gearbox the reverse gear and shaft. The shaft slides into the gearwheel easily

The reverse gearwheel is fitted with the larger end facing the rear of the gearbox

The next step is to fit the roller bearings inside the laygear. There is a set of bearings at each end and fitting can be a fiddly job

The laygear is replaced in the gearbox casing with the large gearwheel towards the front

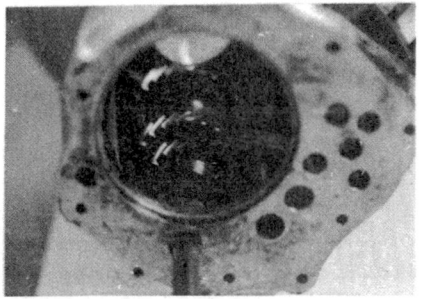

With the laygear resting in the bottom of the gearbox, position the two thrust washers, and hold the laygear and washers in place with a thin rod

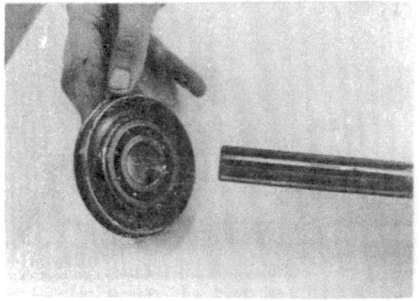

The next step is to reassemble the mainshaft. First fit the mainshaft bearing from the splined end of the shaft

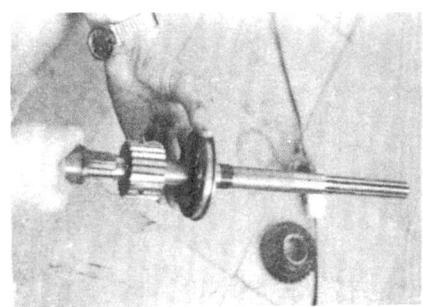

Now fit the second gear synchroniser assembly in place so that the protruding end faces the bearing

Slide the straight cut first speed gear over the second gear synchroniser, and then fit the internally splined thrust washer, second gear bush, and second gear

Next slide the interlocking ring into place so that it mates with the two protrusions on the second gear bush

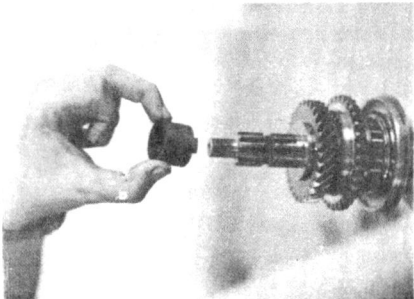

Then fit the third gear bush, with the protrusions facing inwards to mate with the two remaining slots on the interlocking ring

The third gear is then fitted with the synchronising cone facing towards the front of the mainshaft

An internally splined thrust washer is fitted, and turned one spline on the mainshaft circular groove, so as to securely lock the gearwheels in place

The thrust washer is prevented from turning by a spring and locking peg which are pressed into a hole in the mainshaft. Third gear has been omitted for pictorial clarity

Turning the thrust washer slightly allows the peg to spring up into one of the internal spline grooves so locking the washer in place

A good make-shift tool with which to hold the peg down is half a cylinder ring

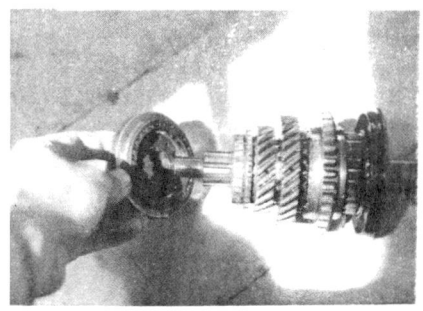

The third and fourth gear coupling sleeve and synchronisers are fitted next

The first motion shaft and the mainshaft fit together in the gearbox as shown above

When the first motion shaft and the mainshaft are correctly engaged in the gearbox they appear as illustrated

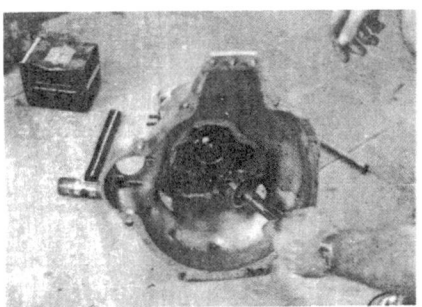

The next step is to drift the first motion shaft into position at the front of the gearbox. Make sure the spring ring rests in the gearbox recess

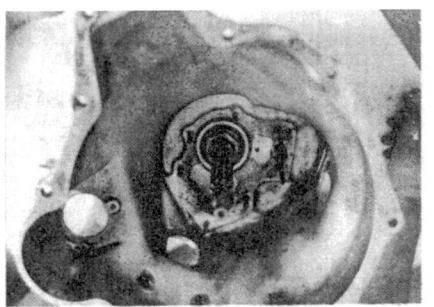

With the first motion shaft firmly in place, the mainshaft is then fitted

Fit the mainshaft through the large hole in the rear of the gearbox casing until it meshes with the first motion shaft

Gently tap down the flat portion of the mainshaft main bearing until it is flush with the end of the gearbox case

The laygear is now brought up into mesh with the mainshaft by pushing the thin rod out with the layshaft. Keep the shaft and rod pressed together until the shaft is fully inserted

The gears are now assembled in the box. The next step is to fit the gear selector forks and selector rods

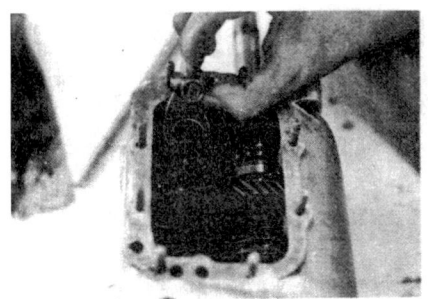

First fit the reverse gear selector fork into position on the front of the reverse gear, with the tapped hole facing the drain plug

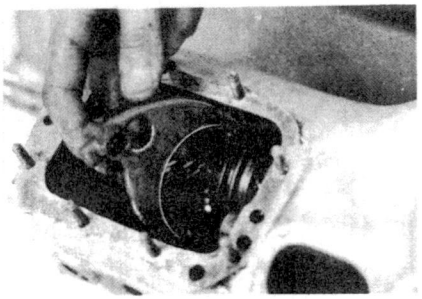

Then place the third and fourth gear selector fork over the third and fourth gear coupling sleeve

The next step is to place the first and second gear selector fork over the first speed gearwheel

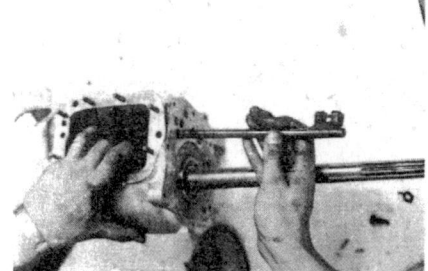

With the open side of the gearbox facing upwards push the reverse gear selector rod in through the lowest selector rod hole in the end of the gearbox casing

The rod passes through the reverse gear selector fork and the hole in the rod must be lined up with the tapped hole in the selector fork

The locking screw can then be fitted to the tapped selector fork through the gearbox drain hole and the locking screw lock nut tightened

103

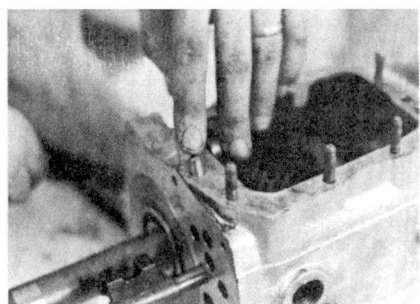

The double ended plunger is then dropped into the hole in the centre of the rear side plate flange

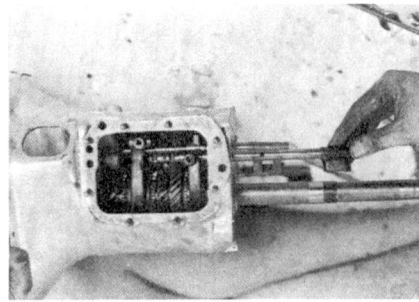

The next step is to insert the 1st and 2nd gear selector rod through the top selector rod hole in the rear of the casing

Line up the hole in the rod with the hole in the selector fork and fit the locking screw and lock nut

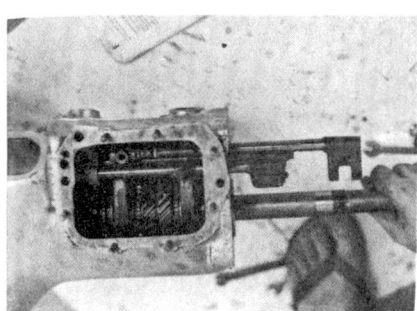

Now fit the 3rd and 4th gear selector rod through the middle selector rod hole. Push the rod in so it just enters the hole in the front of the gearbox

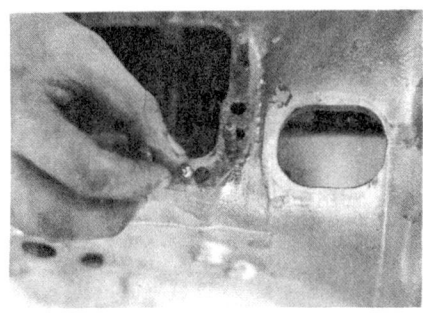

Drop a ball into the hole on the front edge of the side cover flange. Push the ball down hard with a thin rod to centralise the selector rod

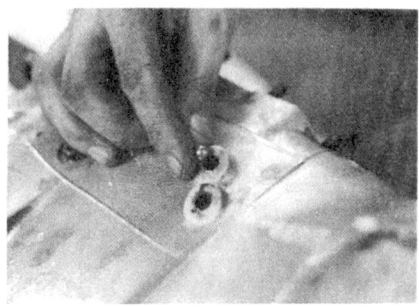

Turn the gearbox over so the drain plug side faces up and drop and ram home a ball in the upper of the two holes illustrated

Now push the 3rd and 4th gear selector rod fully home, line up the holes in the selector rod and fork and fit the locking screw and lock nut

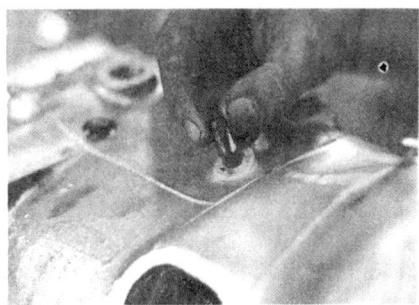

With the gearbox drain plug side up drop the reverse plunger, rounded end first, into the lower of the two holes indicated, and follow it with the spring

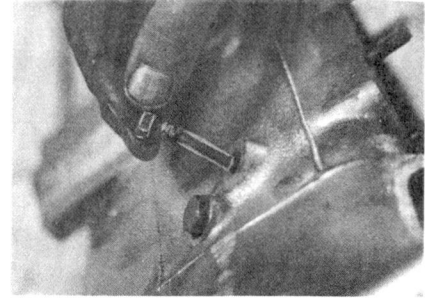

The long-shanked plug blocks the upper hole, and the shorter plug the lower. Make sure new fibre washers are fitted under the plug heads

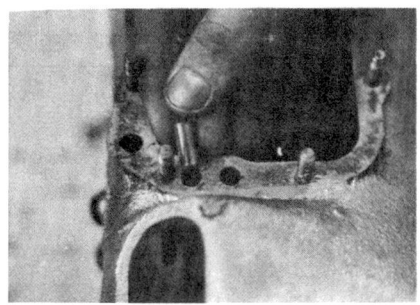

The two remaining plungers are now dropped, rounded ends first, into the two holes in the front side of the side cover flange. Follow each plunger with a spring

The next step is to ensure the side cover flange is clean and to then fit a new gasket

Replace the side cover and screw down the eight securing nuts. Remember to fit the securing washers

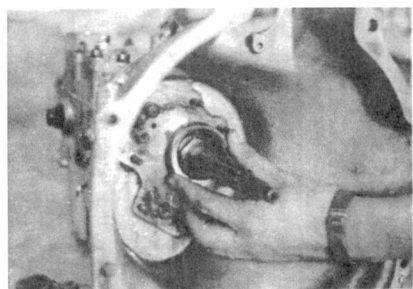

Clean the front face of the gearbox casing inside the bell housing and fit a new gasket

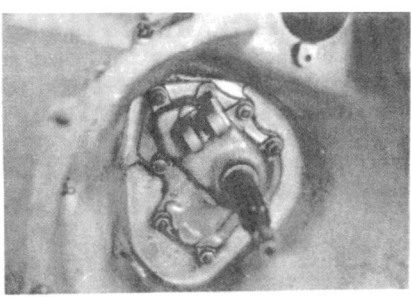

Fit the front cover to the front face of the gearbox and note how the small raised half-moon shaped casting in the lower cover centre covers the raised lip on the layshaft

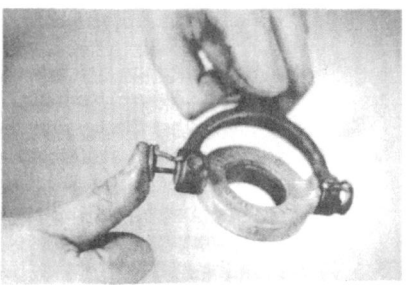

Unless virtually unworn it is a good idea to fit a new clutch release bearing at this stage

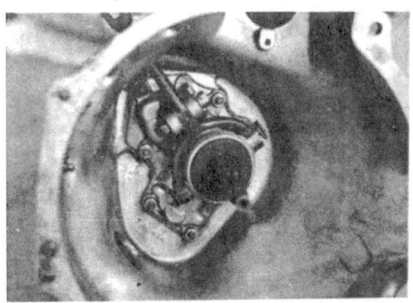

The clutch release arm is held to the front cover by means of a bolt and nut

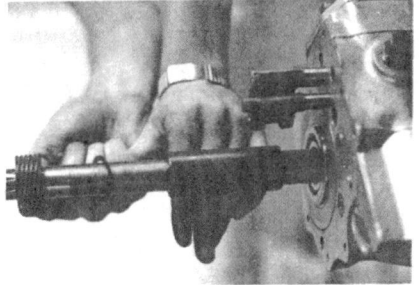

Next fit the distance piece and speedometer drive, to the mainshaft

Tighten the lock nut down, turn up the tag on the outside edge of the lock washer, clean the rear face of the gearbox casing and fit a new gasket

The next step is to fit the gearbox rear extension in place. Tighten down the securing bolts and washers, and ensure the selector rod forks are correctly lined up

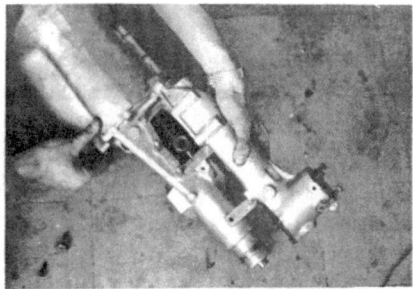

Then fit a new gasket over the studs for the remote control housing and fit the housing in place

Tighten down the eight nuts which hold the remote control housing to the gearbox rear extension. Remember to f i spring washers

Then fit the gearbox support bracket to the gearbox rear housing. When the gearbox is replaced in the car the bracket is secured to the chassis frame

Finally, when the box is back in the car, the gearlever can be fitted as shown above

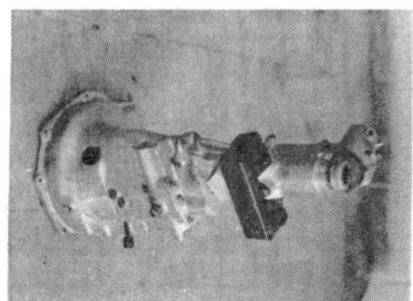

The rebuilt gearbox ready for replacement in the car. Note that some models use different shaped securing brackets

flush with the gearbox casing with a rawhide or plastic headed hammer.

4. Check that the laygear teeth (26) do not foul the first motion shaft bearing housing, and drift the first motion shaft and bearing into place from inside the bellhousing. Ensure that the spring ring (21) is properly located in the groove in the gearbox casing.

5. Oil the layshaft (25) and by judicious manipulation of the rod inside the laygear (26) lift the laygear into mesh with the third motion shaft and then use the layshaft to slide the rod out. Keep the ends of the rod and the layshaft in contact until the layshaft is fully in position to prevent the possibility of one of the thrust washers (30, 31) slipping out.

6. Rotate the half-mooned end of the layshaft (25) so that it will fit into the half-mooned recess in the front cover (9) when the front cover is replaced.

7. Position the reverse fork (65) so that its tapped hole is in line with the gearbox drain hole.

8. Replace the first and second speed fork (67), so that it fits over the first speed gearwheel.

9. Replace the third and fourth speed fork (69) so that it fits over the third and fourth speed coupling sleeve.

10. Place the gearbox on its side so that the hole in the side cover of the casing faces upwards. Insert the reverse fork rod (66) through the lowest hole in the rear of the casing, through the reverse fork, and through the hole in the third and fourth speed fork.

11. Line up the hole in the rod with the hole in the reverse fork and insert and tighten down the locking screw, lockwasher, and locking nut.

12. Insert the double ended interlock plunger (74) into the hole in the middle of the casing side cover rear face (also see Fig. No. 6:6).

13. Insert the first and second speed rod (68) through the top selector rod hole in the rear of the gearbox, through the hole in the first and second

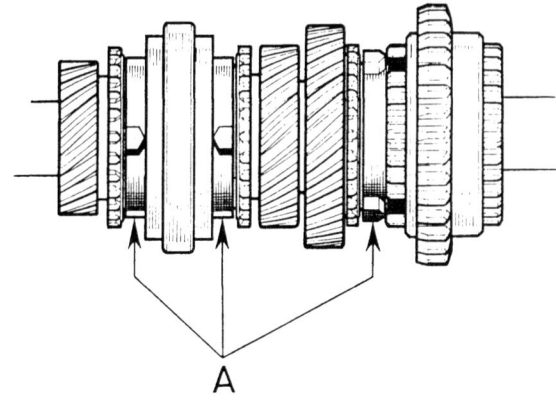

Fig. 6:7. Baulk ring synchronisers (A) instead of cone synchronisers are fitted to later models

speed fork (67) into the hole in the front of the gearbox casing.

14. Lock the fork to the fork rod with the fork locating screw, shakeproof washer, and locknut (71, 72, 73).

15. Insert the third and fourth speed fork rod (70) through the middle selector rod hole in the rear of the gearbox casing, through the hole in the third and fourth speed fork (69), so that the rod just enters in to the hole in the front gearbox casing.

16. With the underside of the gearbox casing facing towards you, and the side cover hole upwards, insert a ball (75) into the hole in the bottom right hand corner of the side flange. Make sure that the ball is firmly against the third and fourth speed rod, and that it is centralised in the slot in the rod by pressing the ball down firmly with a suitable rod. (Also see Fig. No. 6:6).

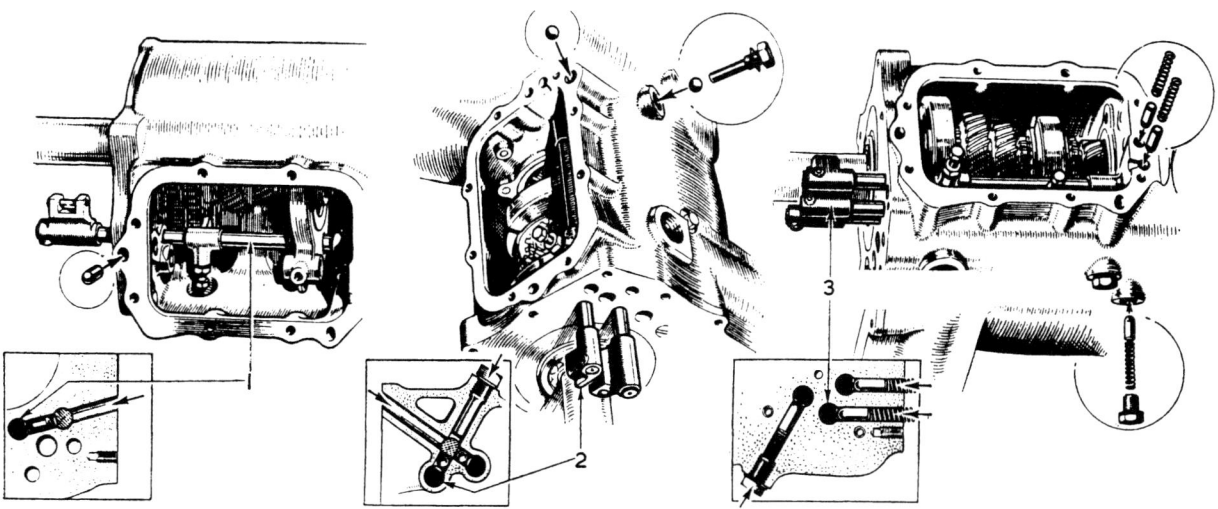

Fig. 6:6. How to fit the selector locking balls, plungers, and springs.
1 Reverse gear for rod. 2 First and second gear fork rod (gearbox upside down). 3 Third and fourth gear fork rod.

17. Turn the gearbox upside down, with the drain plug uppermost and drop the other ball (75) into the hole level with the drain plug ('2' in Fig. No. 6:6) and ensure it rests between the first and second, and third and fourth speed rods. Insert a rod into the hole and press the ball down firmly to centralise the slot in the rod.

18. Push the third and fourth speed rod fully in and lock the fork to the fork rod with the fork locating screw, shakeproof washer, and locknut (71, 72, 73).

NOTE All the rods should be pushed in by hand pressure only. If a rod will not fully enter the casing, centralise the ball in the selector rod slot by pushing firmly on the ball with a suitable rod down the ball's hole. With the ball no longer standing proud of its hole it will be found that the rod can be pushed in easily.

19. Insert the long shanked aluminium plug and fibre washer into the upper hole in line with the drain plug ('2' in Fig. No. 6 : 6).

20. Insert the reverse plunger with its rounded end first into the bottom hole (3) on the underside of the casing. Follow it with the spring, and the plug bolt with a fibre washer under its head.

21. Insert the remaining plungers into the two adjacent holes in the front end of the side cover flange, with their rounded ends first, and place a spring in each hole.

22. Fit the side cover and paper gasket in position over the studs and tighten down the nuts and spring washers diagonally. (Early models make use of spring washers and set bolts).

23. From inside the bellhousing, place the paper front cover gasket (10) in position. With the packing shim (54) held in the front cover bearing recess (9) with a smear of grease. Offer up the cover to the gearbox casing and tighten down the seven nuts and spring washers.

24. At the rear end of the gearbox, position the paper gasket, place an 0.006 in. shim in the rear cover bearing recess, and refit the rear extension. Tighten down the nine long set bolts and spring washers diagonally.

25. Replacement of the gearbox in the car is a reversal of the removal procedure. Replace the drain plug, clean out the gearbox with flushing oil, and fill with the recommended lubricant.
NOTE Although a 0.006 in. packing shim is invariably correct for both the front and rear cover bearing recesses if confirmation is required on this point, proceed as follows:-
a) Measure how much the bearing outer race stands proud of the casing, and how deep the bearing recess is in the cover.
b) Fit the covers without the packing shims, but with the paper gaskets, and tighten down normally.
c) Remove the covers and measure the thickness of the paper gasket.
d) Add together the depth of the bearing recess in the cover and the thickness of the paper gasket. From this total subtract the amount by which the bearing outer race stands proud of the casing. This figure is the correct one to use for the shim thickness.

FAULT FINDING CHART

Cause	Trouble	Remedy
SYMPTOM:	WEAK OR INEFFECTIVE SYNCHROMESH	
General wear	Synchronising cones worn, split or damaged.	Dismantle and overhaul gearbox. Fit new gear wheels and synchronising cones.
	Baulk ring synchromesh dogs worn, or damaged	Dismantle and overhaul gearbox. Fit new baulk ring synchromesh.
SYMPTOM:	JUMPS OUT OF GEAR	
General wear or damage	Broken gearchange fork rod spring	Dismantle and replace spring.
	Gearbox coupling dogs badly worn	Dismantle gearbox. Fit new coupling dogs.
	Selector fork rod groove badly worn	Fit new selector fork rod.
	Selector fork rod securing screw and locknut loose	Remove side cover, tighten securing screw and locknut.
SYMPTOM:	EXCESSIVE NOISE	
Lack of maintenance	Incorrect grade of oil in gearbox or oil level too low	Drain, refill, or top up gearbox with correct grade of oil.
General wear	Bush or needle roller bearings worn or damaged	Dismantle and overhaul gearbox. Renew bearings.
	Gearteeth excessively worn or damaged	Dismantle, overhaul gearbox. Renew gearwheels.
	Laygear thrust washers worn allowing excessive end play	Dismantle and overhaul gearbox. Renew thrust washers.
SYMPTOM:	EXCESSIVE DIFFICULTY IN ENGAGING GEAR	
Clutch not fully disengaging	Clutch pedal adjustment incorrect	Adjust clutch pedal correctly.

CHAPTER SEVEN

PROPELLER SHAFT AND UNIVERSAL JOINTS

GENERAL DESCRIPTION

Drive is transmitted from the gearbox to the rear axle by means of a finely balanced tubular propeller shaft. Fitted at each end of the shaft is a universal joint which allows for vertical movement of the rear axle. Each universal joint comprises a four legged centre spider, four needle roller bearings and two yokes.

Fore and aft movement of the rear axle is absorbed by a sliding spline in the front of the propeller shaft which slides over a mating spline on the rear of the gearbox mainshaft. A supply of oil through very small oil holes from the gearbox lubricates the splines, and a grease nipple is fitted to each universal joint so that the needle roller bearings can be lubricated. Access to the nipple at the front of the propeller shaft is usually through a hole, normally covered by a rubber plug, on the left-hand side of the propeller shaft tunnel, just behind the gearbox. The propeller shaft is a relatively simple component, and to overhaul and repair it is fairly easy.

PROPELLER SHAFT - REMOVAL & REPLACEMENT

1. Jack up the rear of the car, or position the rear of the car over a pit or on a ramp.
2. If the rear of the car is jacked up supplement the jack with support blocks so that danger is minimised should the jack collapse.
3. If the rear wheels are off the ground place the car in gear or put the handbrake on to ensure that the propeller shaft does not turn when an attempt is made to loosen the four nuts securing the propeller shaft to the rear axle.
4. Unscrew and remove the four self-locking nuts, bolts, and securing washers which hold the flange on the propeller shaft to the flange on the rear axle.
5. The propeller shaft is carefully balanced to fine limits and it is important that it is replaced in exactly the same position it was in prior to its removal. Scratch a mark on the propeller shaft and rear axle flanges to ensure accurate mating when the time comes for reassembly.
6. Slightly push the shaft forward to separate the two flanges, and then lower the end of the shaft and pull it rearwards to disengage the gearbox mainshaft splines.
7. Place a large can or a tray under the rear of the gearbox extension to catch any oil which is likely to leak through the spline lubricating holes, when the propeller shaft is removed.
8. Replacement of the propeller shaft is a reversal

of the above procedure. Ensure that the mating marks scratched on the propeller shaft and rear axle flanges line up.

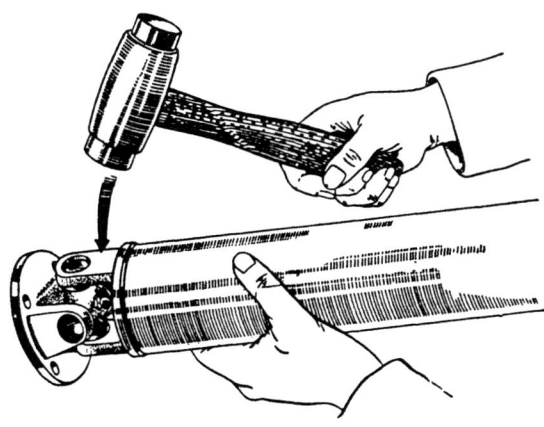

Fig. 7:1. Tap the universal joint to free the bearing

UNIVERSAL JOINTS - INSPECTION & REPAIR

Wear in the needle roller bearings is characterised by vibration in the transmission, 'clonks' on taking up the drive, and in extreme cases of lack of lubrication, metallic squeaking, and ultimately grating and shrieking sounds as the bearings break up.

It is easy to check if the needle roller bearings are worn with the propeller shaft in position, by trying to turn the shaft with one hand, the other hand holding the rear axle flange when the rear universal is being checked, and the front half coupling when the front universal is being checked. Any movement between the propeller shaft and the front and the rear half couplings is indicative of considerable wear. If worn, the old bearings and spiders will have to be discarded and a repair kit, comprising new universal joint spiders, bearings, oil seals, and retainers purchased. Check also by trying to lift the shaft and noticing any movement in the joints.

Examine the propeller shaft splines for wear. If worn it will be necessary to purchase a new front half coupling, or if the yokes are badly worn, an exchange propeller shaft. It is not possible to fit oversize bearings and journals to the trunnion bearing holes.

UNIVERSAL JOINTS - DISMANTLING

1. Clean away all traces of dirt and grease from circlips located on the ends of the spiders, and remove the clips by pressing their open ends

together with a pair of pliers and lever them out with a screwdriver. NOTE If they are difficult to remove tap the bearing face resting on top of the spider with a mallet which will ease the pressure on the circlip.

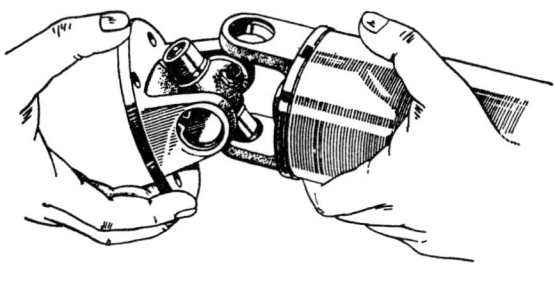

Fig. 7 : 2. Separating the universal joint

2. Hold the propeller shaft in one hand and remove the bearing cups and needle rollers by tapping the yoke at each bearing with a copper or hide faced hammer. As soon as the bearings start to emerge they can be drawn out with your fingers. If the bearing cup refuses to move then place a thin bar against the inside of the bearing and tap it gently until the cup starts to emerge.

3. With the bearings removed it is relatively easy to extract the spiders from their yokes. If the bearings and spider journals are thought to be badly worn this can easily be ascertained visually with the universal joints dismantled.

UNIVERSAL JOINTS - REASSEMBLY

1. Thoroughly clean out the yokes and journals.

2. Fit new cork oil seals and retainers on the spider journals, place the spider on the propellor shaft yoke, and assemble the needle rollers in the bearing races with the assistance of some thin grease.

3. Refit the bearing cups on the spider and tap the bearings home so that they lie squarely in position.

4. Replace the circlips and lubricate the bearings well with a lithium based grease.

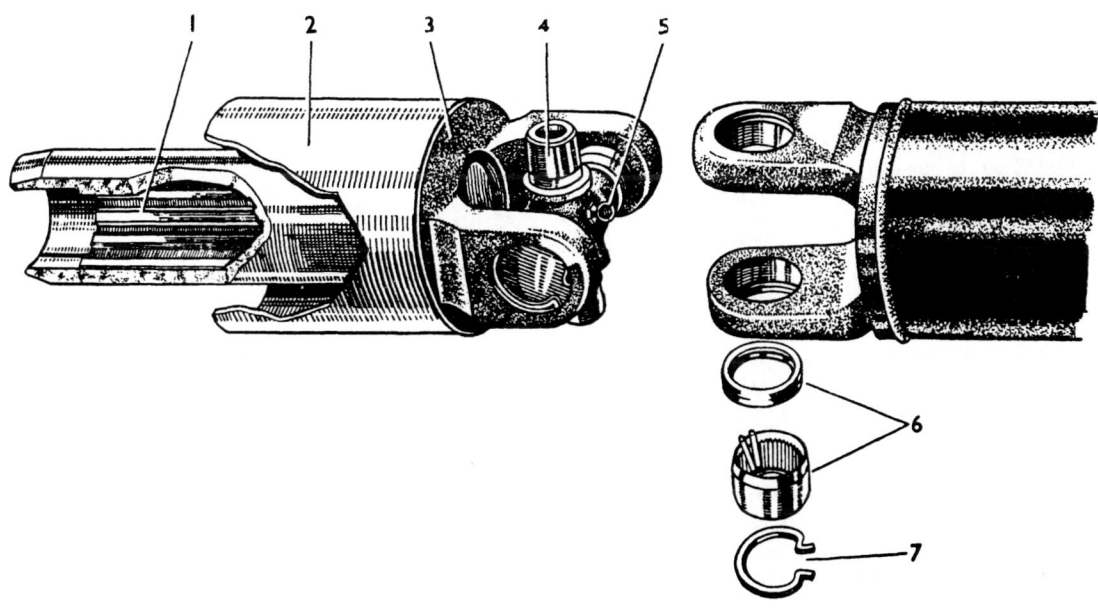

Fig. 7 : 3. Exploded view of the front universal joint. 1 Internal splined end of propeller shaft. 2 Dust cover. 3 Front half coupling. 4 Spider. 5 Lubricating nipple. 6 Needle bearing assembly. 7 Spring ring.

CHAPTER EIGHT

REAR AXLE

SPECIFICATION

The rear axles fitted to the Austin Healey Sprite, **M.G. Midget**, **A.35**, **A.40**, and Morris Minor 1000 are identical to each other except for the axle ratio which varies between the different models.

Weight of axle .. .. 83 lb. (37.64 Kg.).
Type .. .. Three-quarter-floating.
Ratio .. .. 9/38 (4.22 : 1) Austin Healey Sprite & M.G. Midget - 948 & 1,098 c.c.
.. .. 9/41 (4.55 : 1) Morris Minor 1000 - 948 c.c.
.. .. 9/38 (4.22 : 1) Morris Minor 1000 - 1,098 c.c.
.. .. 9/41 (4.55 : 1) Austin A.35 - 948 c.c.
.. .. 9/38 (4.22 : 1) Austin A.35 - 1,098 c.c.
.. .. 9/41 (4.55 : 1) Austin A.40 Mk.I - 948 c.c.
.. .. 9/38 (4.22 : 1) Austin A.40 Mk.II - 1,098 c.c.

GENERAL DESCRIPTION

The rear axle is of the three-quarter-floating type, and is held in place by semi-elliptic springs (except in the case of the early Sprite which was fitted with quarter-elliptic springs and upper suspension rods which acted as radius arms). The semi-elliptic springs provide all the necessary lateral and longitudinal location of the axle. The rear axle incorporates a hypoid crown wheel and pinion, and a two pinion differential. All repairs can be carried out to the component parts of the rear axle without removing the axle casing from the car.

The crown wheel and pinion together with the differential gears are mounted in the differential unit which is bolted to the front face of the banjo-type axle casing.

Adjustments are provided for the crown wheel and pinion backlash; pinion depth of mesh; pinion shaft bearing pre-load; and backlash between the differential gears. All these adjustments may be made by varying the thickness of the various shims and thrust washers.

The axle or half shafts are easily withdrawn and are splined at their inner ends to fit into the splines in the differential wheels. The inner wheel bearing races are mounted on the outer ends of the axle casing and are secured by nuts and lockwashers. The rear wheel bearing outer races are located in the hubs.

REAR AXLE - REMOVAL & REPLACEMENT

1. Remove the rear wheel 'knave plates' and loosen the wheel nuts. In the case of cars with knock-on hub caps, undo the caps a turn.
2. Raise and support the rear of the body and the differential casing with chocks or jacks so that the rear wheels are clear of the ground. This is most easily done by placing a jack under the centre of the differential, jacking up the axle and fitting suitable chocks to support the body.
3. Remove both rear wheels and place the wheel nuts in the knave plates for safe-keeping.
4. If the exhaust pipe runs under the rear axle remove the exhaust pipe and silencer by releasing the appropriate securing nuts and bolts.
5. If check straps are fitted, remove them by unscrewing the nuts and bolts which retain the straps to the body.
6. Free the dampers at their attachment point to the rear axle casing.
7. Disconnect the hand-brake cable at the cable adjustment point.
8. Free the hydraulic brake pipe by releasing the union retaining nut at the point just in front of the differential housing.
9. Undo the nuts and remove them together with the spring washers from the propeller shaft flange bolts. Remove the bolts after having marked the propeller shaft and differential drive flanges to ensure replacement in the same relative positions.
10. Check that the jack is under the differential casing and taking the weight of the rear axle and then unscrew the nuts from under the spring retaining plate. These nuts screw onto the ends of inverted 'U' bolts which retain the axle to the spring. Tap out the 'U' bolts and remove the pad which rests between the spring and the axle bracket. (In the case of early models of the Sprite with quarter-elliptic rear springs, unscrew the nuts from the bolts which hold each of the two radius rods to the brackets on the rear axle, withdraw the bolts, and then unscrew and extract the shackle pins).
11. The axle will now be resting on the jack and can be lowered and removed from the car. Replace-

Jack up and support the rear body, remove the rear wheels, unscrew the two brake drum securing screws, and pull the brake drum off the studs

A phillips screw holds the half shaft to the hub. Undo the screw and pull out the half shaft

Unscrew the four nuts and bolts holding the universal joint to the nose piece flange, remove the nuts from the banjo casing, lift out the nose piece and undo the bearing cap nuts

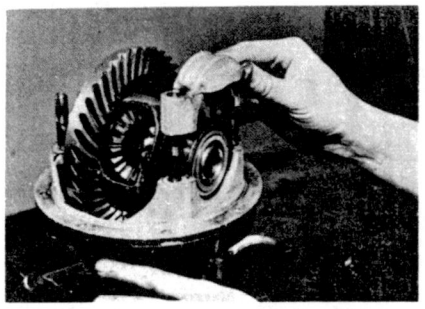

Make sure the caps are marked to ensure correct replacement. If they are difficult to shift tap them gently with a hammer

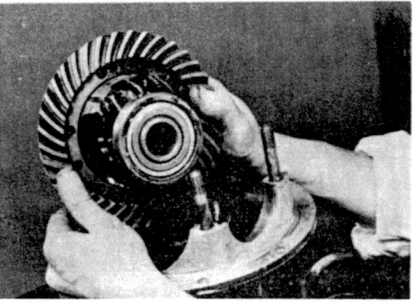

The crown wheel and differential carrier can now be lifted out of the differential case. If difficult to move lever the carrier out with a wooden handle

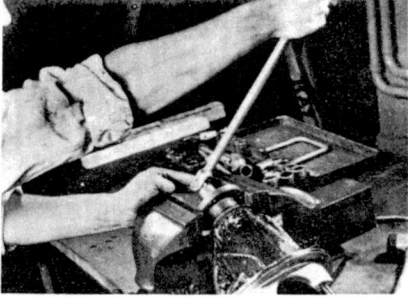

Place the pinion flange in a vice and undo the securing nut. As this is tightened to a torque of 140 lb./ft. it can be difficult to shift

The next step is to pull the pinion flange off the splined pinion shaft

The pinion shaft is removed from the differential nose piece by tapping it with a soft-headed hammer

The pinion bearings are then removed, together with the spanner, which must always be renewed when the bearings are refitted. Fit new bearings if the old ones are worn

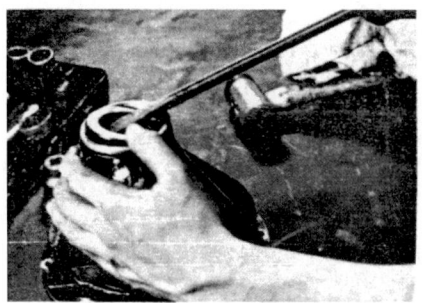

With the aid of a screwdriver, carefully prise out the pinion nose oil seal. Always fit a new one on reassembly

Carefully examine the crown wheel and pinion teeth for wear. The pinion shown here is badly scored and must be replaced

The crown wheel is held to the carrier by six bolts. Bend back the tabs on the locking washers and undo the bolts

The differential carrier can now be lifted away from the crown wheel. Check the condition of the differential gears and if they are worn fit new ones

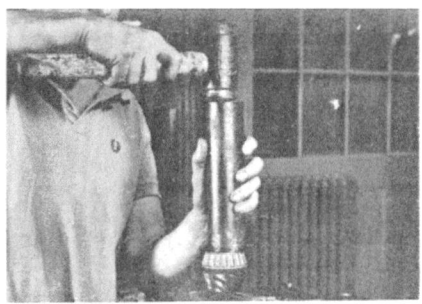

The pinion inner bearing can be driven onto the pinion shaft with the aid of a 14 in. piece of tubing as illustrated

The spacer between the inner and outer pinions must always be renewed on re-assembly. Fit the pinions and inner bearing to the casing and slide on the new spacer

Then fit the outer bearing over the pinion shaft and lubricate the bearings with Castrol Hypoy or a similar lubricant

The next step is to fit a new oil seal. Drive it into place with the aid of a block of wood as illustrated. Make sure the oil seal lip faces inwards

Now fit the pinion flange onto the pinion shaft splines. Oil the inner end of the flange so as not to damage the oil seal

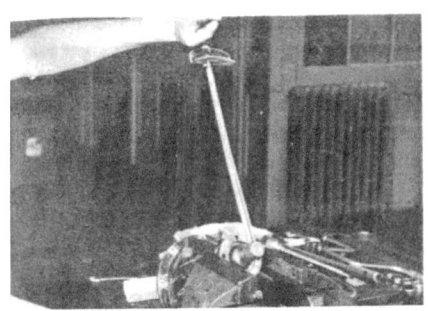

Replace the pinion flange nut and tighten it to a torque of 140 lb./ft.

Preload can be checked with the aid of a spring balance. Measured from one of the flange holes the correct pull should be about 8 lb. before the flange turns

The mating surfaces between the crown wheel and the differential carrier must be absolutely clean. Tighten the six high tensile bolts to a torque of 60 lb./ft.

Wherever possible renew the double ended tab washers. Turn the ends up so as to securely lock the bolts

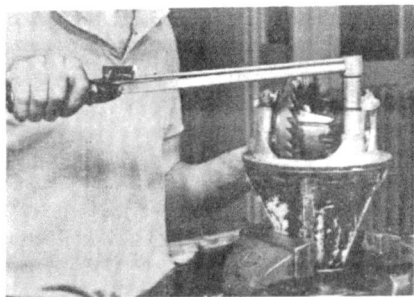

Replace the crown wheel and carrier. Refit the bearing caps correctly, and tighten down the bearing cap nuts to a torque of 65 lb./ft.

The last job before refitting the differential unit to the carrier is to coat the crown wheel with engineers blue and turn it to check it is mating properly with the pinion

ment of the rear axle in the car is a reversal of the above process.

HALF SHAFT - REMOVAL & REPLACEMENT

1. Follow the sequence detailed in paras. 1, 2, and 3, of the preceeding section. (Rear Axle Removal and Replacement). NOTE that if the axle shaft is removed with the car on an even keel it is likely that oil will run out from the differential and contaminate the brake linings. If only one shaft is being removed then jack up that side of the car only. If both shafts are being removed drain the oil from the differential before proceeding further.

2. Release the handbrake and slacken the brake adjusters right off.

3. Unscrew the two Philips-headed countersunk brake drum retaining screws and pull off the brake drum. If necessary tap the brake drums off with a wooden or hide hammer. (On cars fitted with wire wheels it is necessary to bend back the tab washers and unscrew the four nuts from their studs which serve instead of retaining screws).

4. Unscrew the single shaft flange locating screw and pull the half shaft by its flange out from the axle casing. (On cars fitted with wire wheels it is necessary to unscrew the screws holding the hub extension flanges to the hub and pull off the hub extension before the half shaft can be withdrawn.

5. Replacement of the half shafts is a reversal of the above process. Always renew the paper washers to ensure that no oil leaks develop.

REAR HUB - REMOVAL & REPLACEMENT

1. Remove the brake drum and axle shaft as detailed in the preceeding section (Half Shaft Removal and Replacement).

2. Knock back the tab of the locking washer and unscrew the hub retaining nut.

3. Remove the lock washer from the axle casing end by lifting the washer so its key is freed from the locating groove.

4. With a hub puller pull off the hub complete with bearing and oil seal.

5. Replacement is a reversal of the above process but the following points should be noted:-
   a) If fitting a new oil seal, carefully drift it into position before the bearing and ensure that it is placed with the lip facing outwards towards the wheel.
   b) Before replacing the rear bearings lubricate them with high melting-point grease.
   c) Always renew the washer between the hub assembly and the half shaft flange and if making one up ensure that it is cut from paper at least .2 mm. thick.
   d) Remember to knock back the locking tab of the locking washer.

PINION OIL SEAL - REMOVAL & REPLACEMENT

If oil is leaking from the front of the differential nose piece it will be necessary to renew the pinion oil seal. If a pit is not available jack up and chock up the rear of the car. It is much easier to do this job over a pit, or with the car on a ramp.

1. Mark the propeller shaft and pinion drive flanges to ensure their replacement in the same relative positions.

2. Unscrew the nuts from the four bolts holding the flanges together, remove the bolts and separate the flanges.

3. If the oil seal is being renewed with the differential nose piece in position, drain the oil and check that the handbrake is firmly on to prevent the pinion flange moving.

4. Unscrew the nut in the centre of the pinion drive flange. Although it is tightened down to a torque of 140 lb./ft. it can be removed fairly easily with a long extension arm fitted to the appropriate socket spanner. Remove the nut and spring washer.

5. Pull off the splined drive flange, which may be a little stubborn, in which case it should be tapped with a hide mallet from the rear; the pressed steel end cover; and prise out the oil seal with a screwdriver taking care not to damage the lip of its seating.

6. Replacement is a reversal of the above procedure. NOTE that the new seal must be pushed into the differential nose piece with the edge of the sealing ring facing inwards, and take great care not to damage the edge of the oil seal when replacing the end cover and drive flange. Smear the face of the flange which bears against the oil seal lightly with oil before driving the flange onto its splines.

DIFFERENTIAL ASSEMBLY - REMOVAL & REPLACEMENT

If it is wished to renew the differential carrier assembly or to exchange it for a factory reconditioned unit, first remove the axle shafts as detailed in the section headed 'Half Shaft Removal and Replacement' in the previous column.

1. Mark the propeller shaft and pinion flanges to ensure their replacement in the same relative position.

2. Unscrew the nuts from the four bolts holding the flanges together, remove the bolts and separate the flanges.

3. Remove the ring of nuts and spring washers which join the differential nose piece to the axle casing, and pull the nose piece complete with differential assembly out of the casing.

4. Carefully clean down the inside of the axle casing, fit a new nose piece to casing joint, and then fit the exchange or rebuilt differential assembly. Replacement being a reversal of the removal procedure.

5. Refill the differential with the correct grade of oil and run the axle in slowly for the first 500 miles, and then change the oil when it is hot.

DIFFERENTIAL ASSEMBLY - DISMANTLING & EXAMINATION

Most professional garages will prefer to renew the complete differential carrier assembly as a unit if it is worn, rather than to dismantle the unit to renew any damaged or worn parts. To do the job 'according to the book' requires the use of special and expensive tools which the majority of garages do not have, and also, probably, do not have the skilled mechanics who know how these tools should be used.

The primary object of these special tools is to ensure that noise is kept to a minimum. If any increase in noise cannot be tolerated (providing that the rear axle is not already noisy due to a defective part) then it is best to purchase an exchange, built-up differential unit.

If the possibility of a slight increase in noise can be tolerated then it is quite possible to successfully recondition the rear axle without these special tools. The differential assembly should be stripped and examined in the following fashion:-

1. Remove the differential assembly from the rear axle as detailed in the preceeding section.

2. With the differential assembly on the bench begin dismantling the unit by unscrewing the nuts (12, 13, 14) holding the differential bearing caps (10) in place. Ensure that the caps are marked to ensure correct replacement.

3. Pull off the caps and then lever out the differential unit complete with crown wheel and differential gears.

4. Check the differential bearings (16) for side play and if present draw them off from the differential cage (18) together with any shims (17) fitted between the inner ring of each bearing and the cage.

5. Six high tensile steel bolts (26) hold the crown wheel (25) to the differential cage (18). Knock back the tabs of the locking washers (27) and undo and remove the bolts.

6. Professional fitters at B.M.C. garages use a special tool for holding the pinion flange (34) stationary while the nut (35) in the centre of the flange is unscrewed. As it is tightened to a torque of 140 lb./ft. it will require considerable force to move it. As the average owner will not have the use of this tool use the following alternative method. Clamp the pinion flange in a vice and then undo the nut. Any damage caused to the edge of the flange by the vice should be carefully filed smooth.

7. With the nut and spring washer removed, pull off the splined pinion flange (34), (tap the end of the pinion shaft (25) if the flange appears stuck), and remove the pressed end cover and oil seal.

8. Drift the pinion shaft rearwards out of the nose piece. With it will come the inner race and rollers of the rear bearing (29), the bearing spacer (30), and shims. The old bearing spacer can be thrown away as a new spacer which has not been compressed must always be used. The outer race and front bearing (31) will be left in the nose piece. With the pinion shaft removed the rear outer race can be quite easily extracted.

9. The inner race of the front bearing can now be tapped out and then outer race extracted.

10. The inner race of the rear bearing is a press fit on the pinion shaft, and must be drifted off carefully. If the B.M.C. special tool 18G 285 is available this will help the removal of the inner race considerably. Remove the thrust washer (28) under the pinion gear head, and retain for future use.

11. Check the rollers and races for general wear, score marks, and pitting and renew these components as necessary.

12. Examine the teeth of the crown wheel and pinion for pitting, score marks, chipping, and general wear. If a new crown wheel and pinion is required a mated crown wheel and pinion must be fitted. It is asking for trouble to renew one without the other.

13. Tap out the pinion peg (24) from the crown wheel side of the differential cage (18) to free the pinion shaft (23) which is then driven out. NOTE that the hole into which the peg fits is slightly tapered, and the opposite end may be lightly peened over and should be cleared with a $\frac{1}{8}$ in. drill.

14. Extract the pinions, wheels, and thrust washers (21, 19, 20, 22) from the differential cage. Check them for wear and renew as necessary. Replacement of the pinion is a reversal of the above process. NOTE that after the peg has been inserted, the larger end of the hole should be lightly peened over to retain the pin in position.

DIFFERENTIAL ASSEMBLY - REASSEMBLY

1. Replace the thrust washer (28) on the pinion shaft and then fit the inner race of the rear bearing. If the special B.M.C. bearing removal and replacement tool 18G 134 is not available, it is quite satisfactory to drift the rear bearing on with a piece of steel electrical piping 12 to 14 in. long with sufficient internal diameter to just fit over the pinion shaft. With one end of the tube bearing against the race, tap the top end of the tube with a hammer, so driving the bearing squarely down the shaft and hard up against the underside of the thrust washer.

2. Slip a new bearing spacer (30) over the pinion shaft and fit the outer race of the front and rear bearings to the differential nose piece (10).

3. Insert the pinion shaft (25) forwards into the differential nose piece from inside the casing and then drop the front inner bearing race and rollers (31) into place.

4. Lubricate the bearings with the correct grade of rear axle oil. Fit a new oil seal (32) with the edge of the sealing ring facing inwards. A block of wood is useful for ensuring the seal is driven on squarely.

5. With the seal in position, replace the dust cover (33), lubricate the underside of the pinion flange (34) which bears against the oil seal and drive the flange onto the splines with a rawhide hammer.

6. Replace the spring washer (36) and with the flange held securely in a vice tighten the flange nut (35) down to 140 lb./ft.

7. To obtain the correct pinion bearing pre-load it is first essential to have renewed the bearing

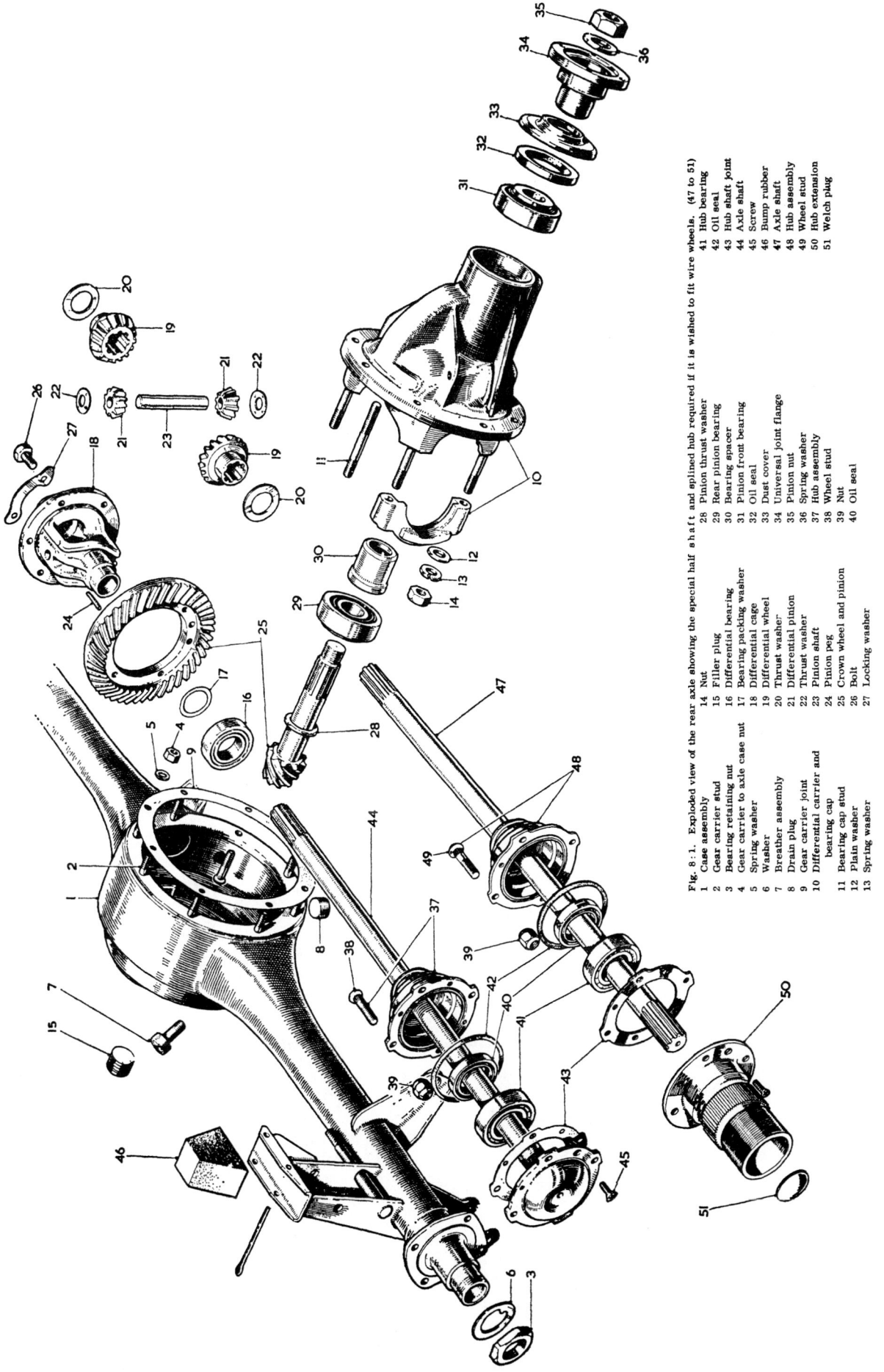

Fig. 8:1. Exploded view of the rear axle showing the special half shaft and splined hub required if it is wished to fit wire wheels. (47 to 51)

1 Case assembly	28 Pinion shaft	41 Hub bearing
2 Gear carrier stud	29 Rear pinion bearing	42 Oil seal
3 Bearing retaining nut	30 Bearing spacer	43 Hub shaft joint
4 Gear carrier to axle case nut	31 Pinion front bearing	44 Axle shaft
5 Spring washer	32 Oil seal	45 Screw
6 Washer	33 Dust cover	46 Bump rubber
7 Breather assembly	34 Universal joint flange	47 Axle shaft
8 Drain plug	35 Pinion nut	48 Hub assembly
9 Gear carrier joint	36 Spring washer	49 Wheel stud
10 Differential carrier and bearing cap	37 Hub assembly	50 Hub extension
11 Bearing cap stud	38 Wheel stud	51 Welch plug
12 Plain washer	39 Nut	
13 Spring washer	40 Oil seal	
14 Nut		
15 Filler plug		
16 Differential bearing		
17 Bearing packing washer		
18 Differential cage		
19 Differential wheel		
20 Thrust washer		
21 Differential pinion		
22 Thrust washer		
23 Pinion shaft		
24 Pinion peg		
25 Crown wheel and pinion		
26 Bolt		
27 Locking washer		

spacer (30). The correct pre-load should be 11 to 13 lb./in. Measure this with a spring balance hooked into one of the drive flange holes. As these holes are $1\frac{1}{2}$ in. from the shaft axis a pull of 8 lb./in. is the correct pre-load figure using this method. If the pre-load is too great use a thinner thrust washer. If too high use a thicker thrust washer. Renew the bearing spacer each time as it must never be compressed twice.

8. Refit the shims (17) and differential bearings (16) to the differential cage (18).

9. Ensure that the crown wheel and cage are scrupulously clean and then bolt the crown wheel (25) to the differential cage flange, tightening the six high tensile steel bolts down to a torque of 60 lb./ft. Turn up the tabs on the locking washers.

10. Measure the backlash at the edge of the pinion flange. The reading should be between $\frac{1}{32}$ in. to $\frac{1}{8}$ in. Also check the meshing of the crown wheel and pinion by smearing engineers blue on the crown wheel and then turning the pinion. The contact mark should appear right in the middle of the crown wheel teeth. If the mark appears on the toe or the heel of the crown wheel teeth then shims must be removed from one side of the differential bearings to the other until the marks are in the correct position.

11. The differential unit can now be refitted to the axle casing.

CHAPTER NINE

BRAKING SYSTEM

SPECIFICATION

Morris Minor 1000 – 948 c.c.

Make	Lockheed.
Footbrake	Hydraulic.
Handbrake	Mechanical (on rear wheels only).
Drum diameter	7 in. (17.78 cm.).
Shoe lining length	6.54 in. (16.6 cm.).
Shoe lining thickness	.198 in. (5.0 mm.).
Shoe lining width	1.22 in. (31.0 mm.).
Number of rivets	10.
Lining material	MR11.

Morris Minor 1000 – 1,098 c.c.

Make	Lockheed.
Footbrake	Hydraulic.
Handbrake	Mechanical (on rear wheels only).
Drum diameter (front)	8 in. (20.3 cm.).
Drum diameter (rear)	7 in. (17.78 cm.).
Total frictional area (front)	73.9 sq.in. (477 sq.cm.).
Total frictional area (rear)	53.6 sq.in. (346 sq.cm.).
Lining material	Ferodo AM8.

DRUM BRAKES - GENERAL DESCRIPTION

The four wheel drum brakes fitted are of the internal expanding type and are operated by means of the brake pedal, which is coupled to the brake master cylinder and hydraulic fluid reservoir.

The front brakes are of the two leading shoe-type, with a separate cylinder for each shoe. The ends of each shoe are able to slide laterally in grooves in the ends of the brake cylinders, so ensuring automatic centralisation when the brakes are applied.

The rear brakes are of the single leading shoe-type, with one brake cylinder per wheel for both shoes. Attached to each of the rear wheel operating cylinders is a mechanical expander operated by the handbrake lever through a bowden cable which runs from the brake lever to a compensator mounted on the underside of the rear axle. Transverse rods run from the compensator to the backplate brake levers. This provides an independent means of rear brake application.

Drum brakes have to be adjusted periodically to compensate for wear in the linings. It is unusual to have to adjust the handbrake system as the efficiency of this system is largely dependent on the condition of the brake linings and the adjustment of the brake shoes. The handbrake can, however, be adjusted separately to the footbrake operated hydraulic system.

The hydraulic brake system functions in the following manner:- On application of the brake pedal, hydraulic fluid under pressure is pushed from the master cylinder to the brake operating cylinders at each wheel, by means of a four way union and steel pipe lines and flexible hoses.

The hydraulic fluid moves the pistons out so pushing the brake shoes into contact with the brake drums. This provides an equal degree of retardation on all four wheels in direct proportion to the pressure applied to the brake pedal. Return springs between each pair of brake shoes draw the shoes together when the brake pedal is released.

DRUM BRAKES - MAINTENANCE

Every 3,000 miles, carefully clean the top of the brake master cylinder reservoir, remove the cap, and inspect the level of the fluid which should be $\frac{1}{4}$ in. below the bottom of the filler neck. Check that the breathing holes in the cap are clear.

If the fluid is below this level, top up the reservoir with Lockheed Super Heavy Duty Brake Fluid, or a fluid which conforms to specification SAE 70 R3. It is vital that no other type of brake fluid is used. Use of a non-standard fluid will result in brake failure caused by the perishing of the special seals in the master and brake cylinders. If topping up becomes frequent then check the metal piping and flexible hosing for leaks, and check for worn brake or master cylinder seals which will also cause loss of fluid.

At intervals of 3,000 miles, or more frequently if pedal travel becomes excessive, adjust the brake shoes to compensate for wear of the brake linings.

At the same time lubricate all joints in the handbrake mechanism with an oil can filled with Castrolite or similar.

DRUM BRAKES - ADJUSTMENT

Before adjusting the brakes remove the hubcaps and check that, where fitted, the holes in the road wheels line up with the adjusting holes in the brake drum which should be covered with a rubber dust excluder plug. If the holes do not line up then slacken the wheel nuts slightly prior to jacking up the car and removing the wheel. NOTE Not all models are fitted with wheels with this access hole. With the car jacked up proceed as follows:-

1. With the wheel whose brake shoes are to be adjusted clear of the ground, remove the rubber or metal plug from the adjuster hole. Remove the road wheel if this blanks off the hole.

2. Turn the wheel until the hole comes opposite one of the adjusting screws. NOTE There are two adjusting screws on the front brakes at 180^{0} to each other, at approximately 8 or 10 o'clock and 2 or 4 o'clock. There is one adjusting screw only on each of the rear brakes and this is positioned at 8 or 4 o'clock. NOTE On later models the rear brakes make use of a square-headed adjuster positioned at the rear of each backplate. This is adjusted in an identical fashion to the previous adjusting screw, but a special spanner with a square hole should be used instead of a screwdriver.

3. Insert a screwdriver in the brake drum hole and turn the adjuster screw clockwise, a notch at a time until the wheel is locked. Turn back the adjuster one notch so the wheel will rotate without binding.

4. Spin the wheel and apply the brakes hard to centralise the shoes. Recheck that it is not possible to turn the adjusting screw further without locking the shoe. NOTE A rubbing noise when the wheel is spun is usually due to dust in the brake drum. If there is no obvious slowing of the wheel due to brake binding there is no need to slacken off the adjusters until the noise disappears. Better to remove the drum and blow out the dust.

5. Repeat this process to the other three brake

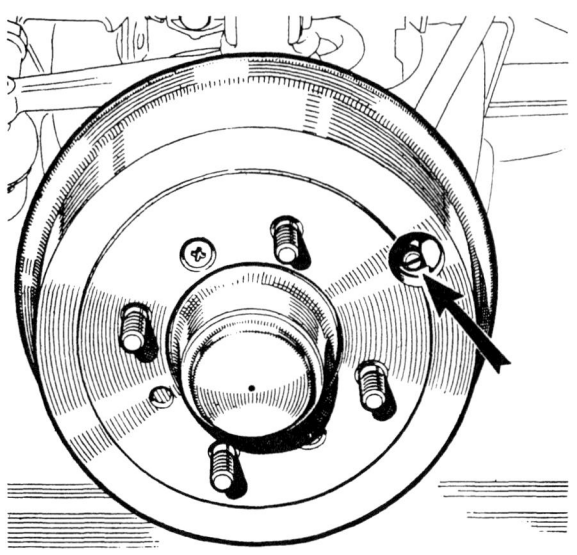

Fig. 9:1. The position of one of the brake shoe adjustment screws

shoes and drums. A good tip is to paint the head of the adjusting screws white which will facilitate future adjustment by making the screw heads easier to see.

BRAKE SYSTEM - BLEEDING

Gather together a clean jam jar, a 9 in. length of tubing which fits tightly over the bleed nipples, and a tin of the correct brake fluid. Then proceed as follows:-

1. Fill the master cylinder and the bottom inch of the jam jar with hydraulic fluid.

2. On the wheel furthest away from the master cylinder, remove the rubber dust cap from the bleed nipple and with a suitable spanner unscrew the nipple $\frac{3}{4}$ of a turn.

3. Place one end of the tube over the nipple and insert the other open end in the jam jar so that it is covered by the fluid.

4. A friend should now pump the brake pedal up and down, slowly, replenishing the master cylinder as necessary, until all air bubbles cease to emerge with the fluid from the end of the tube.

5. Tighten the bleed nipple on the next down stroke, and replace the rubber dust cap.

6. Repeat this process with the other three bleed nipples, finishing up at the nipple nearest the brake master cylinder. NOTE Never use immediately the fluid bled from the hydraulic system to top up the hydraulic reservoir. The fluid should be left to stand for at least 24 hours to allow the minute air bubbles to escape.

DRUM BRAKE SHOE - INSPECTION, REMOVAL, & REPLACEMENT

After high mileages it will be necessary to fit replacement brake shoes with new linings. Refitting new brake linings to old shoes is not always satisfactory, but if the services of a local garage or workshop with brake lining equipment are available, then there is no reason why your own shoes should not be successfully relined.

1. Remove the hub cap, loosen off the wheel nuts, securely jack up the car, and remove the road wheel.

2. Completely slacken off the brake adjustment and take out the one or two set screws, depending on the model, which hold the drum in place. Remove the brake drum. If it proves obstinate tap the rim gently with a soft-headed hammer. The shoes are now exposed for inspection.

3. The brake linings should be renewed if they are so worn that the rivet heads are flush with the surface of the lining. If bonded linings are fitted they must be removed when the material has worn down to $\frac{1}{32}$ in. at its thinnest point.

4. Detach the shoes and return springs by pulling one end of the shoes away from the slot in the closed end of one of the brake cylinders and in the case of rear wheel brakes pull the ends of both shoes out of the pivot post. Allow the return spring to pull the free end of the brake shoe down the side of the brake cylinder and then slide the micram adjuster and mask outwards off the piston head. Repeat this process at the other brake cylinder and then lift both brake shoes away.

5. Thoroughly clean all traces of dust from the shoes, back plates, and brake drums with a dry paint brush and compressed air, if available. Brake dust can cause squeal and judder and it is therefore important to clean out the brakes thoroughly.

6. Check that the pistons are free in their cylinders and that the rubber dust covers are undamaged and in position and that there are no hydraulic fluid leaks. Secure the pistons with wire or string.

7. Prior to reassembly smear a trace of white brake grease to all sliding surfaces. The shoes should be quite free to slide on the closed end of the cylinder and the piston anchorage point. It is vital that no grease or oil comes in contact with the brake drums or the brake linings.

8. Replacement is a straight reversal of the removal procedure, but note the following points:-
    a) Check that when the micram adjusters are replaced they are backed right off.
    b) Ensure that the return springs are in their correct holes in the shoes and lie between them and the backplate.

FLEXIBLE HOSE INSPECTION, REMOVAL & REPLACEMENT

Inspect the condition of the flexible hydraulic hoses leading from the chassis mounted metal pipe to the brake backplates. If any are swollen, damaged, cut, or chaffed, they must be renewed.

1. Unscrew the metal pipe union nuts from its connection to the hose, and then holding the hexagon on the hose with a spanner, unscrew the attachment nut and washer.

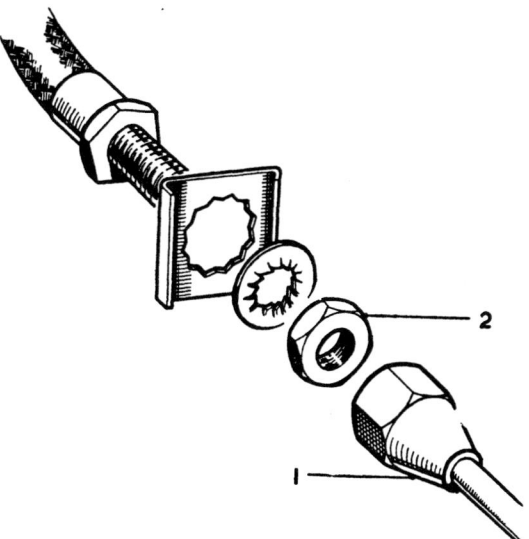

Fig. 9:2. When removing a flexible hose always unscrew the union nut '1' before the attachment nut '2'. Never try to turn the flexible hose

2. The chassis end of the hose can now be pulled from the chassis mounting bracket and will be quite free.

3. Disconnect the flexible hydraulic hose at the backplate by unscrewing it from the brake cylinder. NOTE When releasing the hose from the backplate, the chassis end must always be freed first.

4. Replacement is a straight reversal of the above procedure.

BRAKE SEAL & CYLINDER - INSPECTION & OVERHAUL

If hydraulic fluid is leaking from one of the brake cylinders it will be necessary to dismantle the cylinder and replace the piston rubber and sealing ring. If brake fluid is found running down the side of the wheel, or it is noticed that a pool of liquid forms alongside one wheel and the level in the master cylinder has dropped, proceed as follows:-

1. Remove the brake drums and brake shoes as detailed in the section headed 'Drum Brake Shoe Inspection, Removal & Replacement'.

2. Ensure that all the other wheels and drums are in place and where two brake operating cylinders are fitted to one backplate, as on the front wheels, securely wire the piston in the cylinder which is not leaking. Remove the piston, piston rubber and seal from the leaking cylinder by applying gentle pressure to the foot brake. Place a quantity of rag under the backplate or a tray to catch the hydraulic fluid as it pours out of the cylinder.

3. Inspect the inside of the cylinder for score marks caused by impurities in the hydraulic fluid. If any are found the cylinder and piston will require renewal.

4. If the cylinder is sound thoroughly clean it out with fresh hydraulic fluid.

5. The old rubbers will probably be swollen and visibly worn. Smear the new rubbers with hydraulic fluid and reassemble in the cylinder

the spring, cup filler, cup, piston, sealing ring and dust cover, in that order.

6. Replenish the brake fluid, replace the brake shoes and brake drum, and bleed the hydraulic system as previously detailed.

7. If the cylinder is scored and is to be renewed, remove the flexible hose as detailed in the section 'Flexible Hose Inspection, Removal & Replacement.

8. In the case of two leading shoe front brakes disconnect the pipe between the two brake cylinders and remove complete with the banjo adaptors. Unscrew from the backplate the two set bolts and spring washers which retain each cylinder in place. The cylinders are now free. Replacement is a direct reversal of this process.

9. In the case of early models with single leading shoe rear brakes remove the bolt which secures the banjo adaptor to the wheel cylinder. Disconnect the handbrake lever rod at the backplate. Move the backplate handbrake lever until its shoulder clears the backplate. Then move the brake operating cylinder forward, turn it about its forward end, and extract the rear end from the slot. To remove the cylinder, move it backwards, so clearing its forward end from the backplate. Reassembly is a direct reversal of this process.

10. In the case of the rear brake assemblies on later models, remove the hydraulic pipe, the flexible cable, bleed screw, and circlip from the cylinder boss which protrudes through the backplate. With the brake drum and brake shoes removed the cylinder can now be released. Reassembly is a direct reversal of this process.

DRUM BRAKE BACKPLATE REMOVAL & REPLACEMENT

1. In the case of the front brakes the backplate can be removed after disconnecting the flexible pipe, by removing the four backplate securing bolts and washers.

2. In the case of the rear brakes the backplate securing bolts can be removed and the backplate lifted away after:-
   a) The road wheels, brake drum, handbrake lever rod, and hydraulic pipe have been disconnected.
   b) The half shaft and hub assembly have been removed as detailed in Chapter 8.

3. Replacement in both cases is a straight reversal of the above.

HANDBRAKE ADJUSTMENT

If the handbrake requires adjustment it is more than likely that the footbrake will require adjustment also. Excess travel in the footbrake is compensated by adjusting the brake shoes, this automatically compensates for excess travel in the handbrake lever also.

Never try to adjust the handbrake to compensate for wear on the rear brake linings. It is very seldom that the handbrake will require adjustment, and that only after very high mileages due to slight stretching

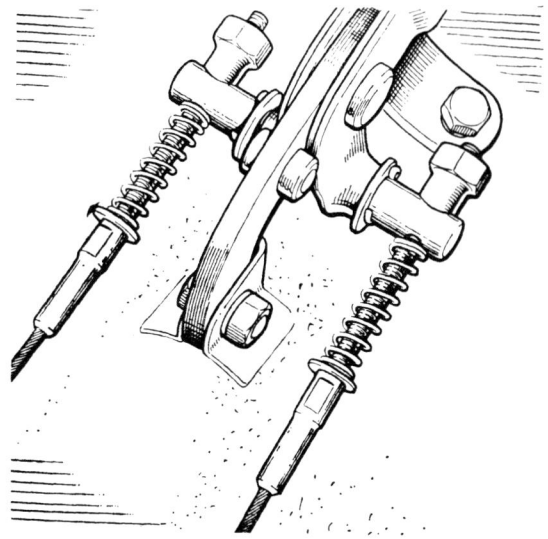

Fig. 9:3. The rear brakes should be adjusted by turning the adjusting screws in the rear brake drums. Only turn the anchorage nuts on the handbrake lever trunnion to take up cable stretch after a considerable mileage

of the cable. Usually it is badly worn rear brake linings that lead to excessive handbrake travel. If the rear brake linings are in good condition or have been recently renewed and the handbrake tends to reach the end of its ratchet travel before the brake come on, adjust the handbrake as follows:-

1. Lock the rear brake shoes by rotating the adjustment screw as far as it will turn clockwise.

2. Apply the handbrake on the third or fourth notch of its ratchet.

3. Remove the slackness in the cable by turning the adjusting nuts on the handbrake lever trunnion. DO NOT OVERTIGHTEN the cables or the rear brakes will bind.

4. Release the handbrake and check that neither of the rear wheels are binding. A certain resistance due to the differential gears is natural.

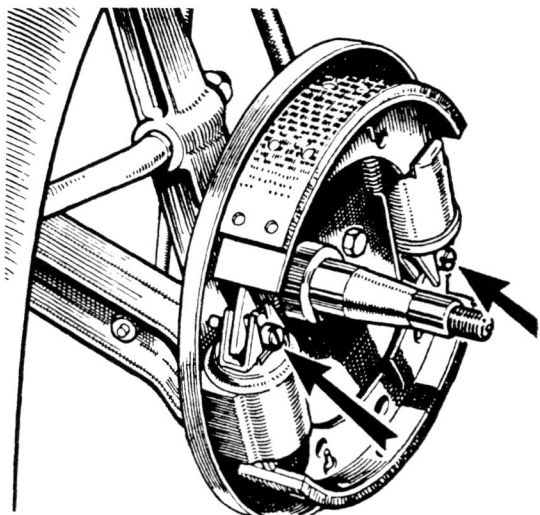

Fig. 9:4. The location of the adjusting screws (arrowed) on the front brake backplate. The brake drum has been removed for clarity

Remove the hub cap, loosen the wheel nuts, and jack up the car. Remove the wheel nuts placing them in the hub cap, and pull off the wheel

The front brakes are of the two leading shoe type with adjusting screws at the 10 o'clock and 4 o'clock or 8 o'clock and 2 o'clock positions

Tighten the screws in turn until the drum is locked and then slacken off each adjusting screw one click

To remove the drum to inspect the condition of the brake shoe linings, undo the two screws holding the drum in place

Turn the adjusting screws fully anti-clockwise and pull the drum off evenly. A little judicious tapping with a rawhide mallet will help here

Pull the drum completely away which exposes the brake shoes and brake cylinders

Carefully remove all traces of brake dust by wiping the drum and linings with a clean cloth. Excessive brake dust can cause squeal and judder.

If it is wished to remove the brake shoes for relining or replacement lift one end of the shoe with a screwdriver and slide out the adjuster

Now repeat this process and remove the other adjuster

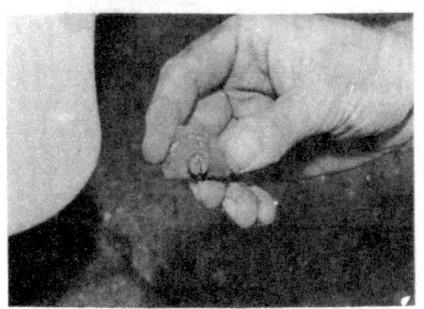

The adjusters slide in and out of a wide slot in the open end of each brake actuating cylinder. The other end of the shoe slides in a narrow slot in the closed end of the cylinder

Unhook the springs holding the brake shoes together after noting the hole into which each hook of the spring fits

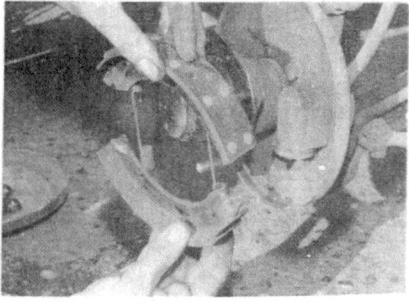

When replacing the brake shoes ensure the coil portion of the pull off springs faces the backplate

BRAKING SYSTEM

MASTER CYLINDER - REMOVAL & REPLACEMENT

The master cylinder on the Morris Minor is mounted underneath the floor on the driver's side and the master cylinder cap is exposed when the carpet in front of the driver's seat is lifted. A spanner has to be used to unscrew the filler cap from the master cylinder. If it is wished to remove the master cylinder from the car, proceed as follows:-

1. Remove the front carpet and also the driver's seat, gear lever knob and the rubber boot at the base of the gearlever.
2. Unscrew the brass bolts from the gearbox floor panel and lift out the panel.
3. The master cylinder is secured in place by two bolts, and prior to their removal it is necessary to remove the torsion bar which otherwise covers them, as described in Chapter 11.
4. Unhook the return spring and extract the split pin and washer from the rear end of the clutch rod.
5. Unscrew the nut on the clutch lever pedal cotter pin two turns and tap the cotter pin to free it. Completely unscrew the nut and extract the pin.
6. Unscrew the speedometer cable from the gearbox casing.
7. Extract the brake and clutch pedal cross shaft from the clutch and brake pedals.
8. Unscrew the banjo union at the rear of the master cylinder to free the hydraulic pipes to the front and rear brakes.
9. Unhook the brake pedal return spring from the chassis frame, and lift out the master cylinder complete with brake pedal.
10. Remove the rubber boot from the flange on the end of the master cylinder and pull the push rod and brake pedal from the forward end of the master cylinder.
11. Replacement is a direct reversal of the above sequence. Ensure that the clearance of the foot pedal is correct as described on page 124, and bleed the system, as previously detailed.

MASTER CYLINDER - DISMANTLING & REASSEMBLY

To avoid spilling the hydraulic fluid from the brake reservoir, remove the drain plug at the rear of the reservoir and empty the contents into a clean jam jar for future use. Press the piston into the cylinder and remove the retaining circlip at the cylinder mouth. Remove the piston stop, secondary cup, piston, dished washer, master cup, spring seat, piston return spring, and valve body, cup, and washer in that order, from the master cylinder.

The rubber secondary cup can be removed from the piston by carefully pulling it over the end flange. Inspect the condition of the master and secondary cups and if they are swollen, distorted, or damaged in any way they must be renewed. Inspect the master cylinder walls for scoring. If score marks are present it will be necessary to purchase a replacement master cylinder.

Thoroughly clean all the parts with hydraulic brake fluid and then reassemble the parts to the master cylinder.

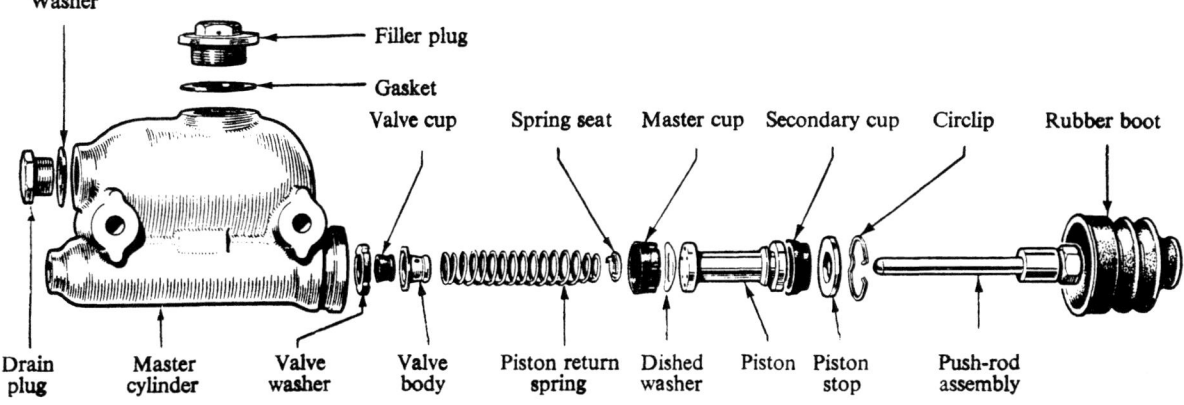

Fig. 9:5. Exploded view of the brake master cylinder

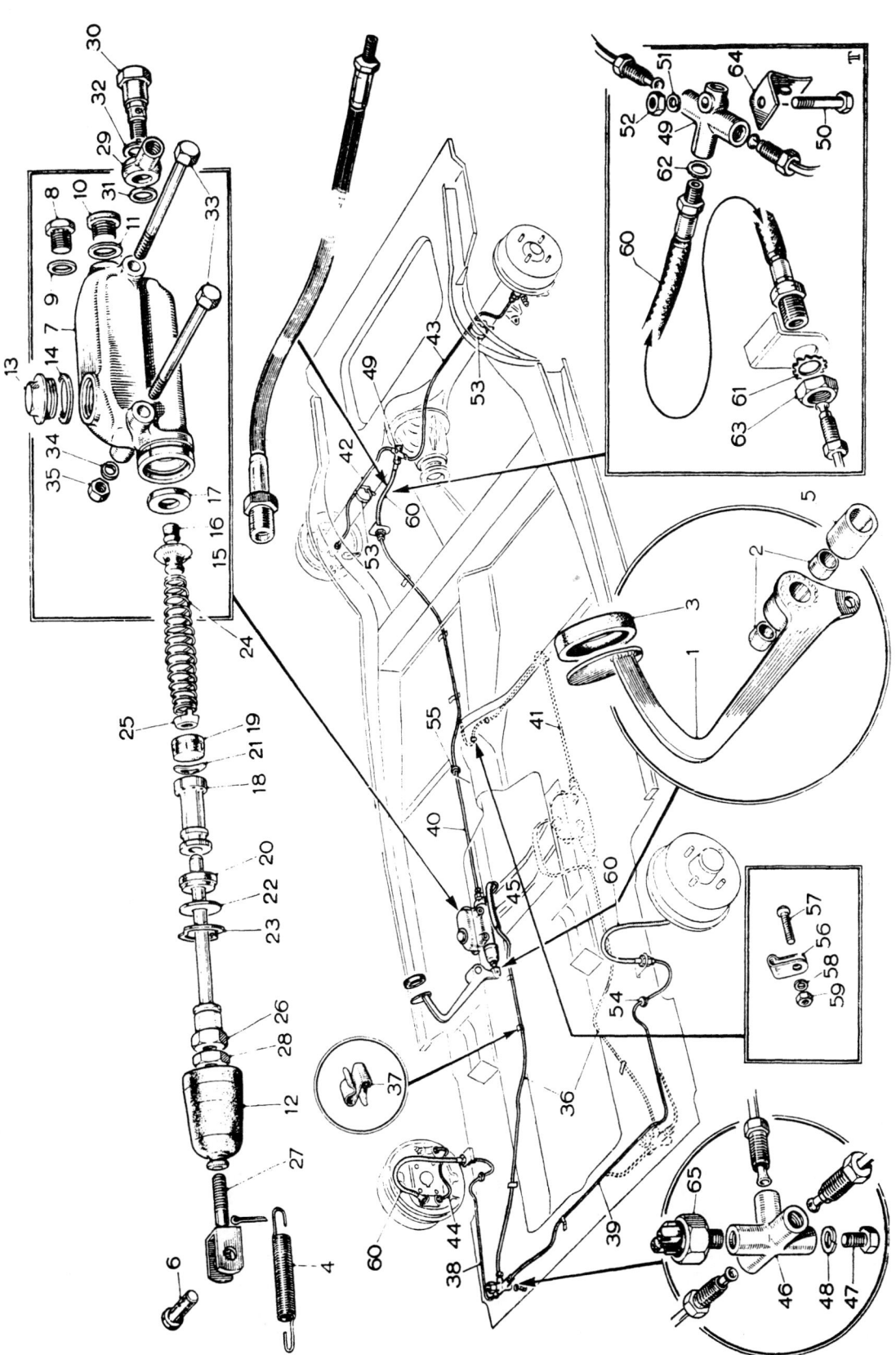

Fig. 9 : 6. Exploded view and layout of the Morris Minor 1000 braking system. 1 Brake pedal. 2 Bush for pedal shaft. 3 Rubber pad. 4 Return spring. 5 Spacer. 6 Clevis pin to master cylinder. 7 Master cylinder and tank. 8 Drain plug (earlier). 9 Gasket (earlier). 10 Drain plug (later). 11 Gasket (later). 12 Rubber boot. 13 Filler plug. 14 Gasket. 15 Body—valve assembly. 16 Cup—valve assembly. 17 Washer—valve assembly. 18 Piston. 19 Cup—main. 20 Cup—secondary. 21 Washer—dished. 22 Washer for retainer. 23 Circlip for retainer 24 Piston return spring. 25 Retainer. 26 Push rod. 27 Yoke—push rod. 28 Locknut for yoke. 29 Banjo connection. 30 Bolt for banjo connection. 31 Gasket for banjo bolt (small 32 Gasket for banjo bolt (large). 33 Bolt—master cylinder to frame. 34 Spring washer for nut. 35 Nut for bolt. 36 Pipe—master cylinder to three-way front. 37 Clip—pipe to longitudina member. 38 Pipe—three-way to R.H. front. 39 Pipe—three-way to L.H. front. 40 Pipe—master cylinder to rear hose. 41 Pipe—master cylinder to rear hose. 42 Pipe—hose to R.H. rear. 43 Pipe—hose to L.H. rear. 44 Pipe—cylinder bridge. 45 Sleeve—pipe protecting (rubber). 46 Three-way piece (front). 47 Screw for front three-way piece. 48 Sprin washer for screw. 49 Three-way piece for rear axle. 50 Bolt for rear axle three-way piece. 51 Spring washer for nut. 52 Nut for bolt. 53 Strap—pipe to rear axle. 54 Grommet fo front wheel arch. 55 Grommet for centre cross member. 56 Clip—pipe to cross member. 57 Screw for clip. 58 Spring washer for nut. 59 Nut for screw. 60 Hose. 61 Washer. 6 Gasket. 63 Locknut. 64 Bracket for rear hose. 65 Switch for stop light.

The parts should be reassembled in reverse order to that in which they were removed. All the parts should be lubricated with brake fluid before reassembly, especially the two rubbers (master and secondary cups).

The secondary cup should be stretched over the end flange of the piston with the cup's lip pointing towards the inner drilled end of the piston. Ensure that the cup is properly fitted by working it round its groove. The master cup is also fitted with the lip facing towards the rear end of the master cylinder.

Before fitting the piston to the master cylinder and after inserting the main cup, it is most important that the thin dished copper washer is fitted with its convex side resting against the piston head. If this washer is omitted it is likely that the transfer holes in the end of the piston will become blocked in due course. If no washer was found on dismantling the master cylinder, to obviate any possibility of future trouble, it is important that one is now fitted.

Complete the reassembly of the master cylinder by replacing the piston stop and refitting the circlip to its groove in the cylinder base. Check that the master cylinder is working properly by filling the reservoir with clean hydraulic fluid and then pushing the master cylinder push rod down several times (the return spring returns it automatically). If all is well hydraulic fluid should emerge from the outlet hole at the third or fourth stroke.

BRAKE PEDAL ADJUSTMENT

To ensure that no brake binding occurs due to the main cup covering the by-pass port it is vital that there is a certain amount of free movement between the master cylinder pushrod and the master cylinder piston. Under normal circumstances there is no need to touch this adjustment throughout the life of the car, but, if the adjustment has been disturbed by a previously ignorant owner then it will be necessary to reset it. This is done by altering the effective length of the pushrod by adjusting the nuts until there is $3/4$ in. of free movement at the pedal. If the pedal is depressed by hand the point at which the resistance of the piston in the master cylinder is met is quite obvious.

BRAKE DRUM DUST SEALS

Early models make use of a wheel with a small hole which when correctly positioned, covers the brake shoe adjustment hole in the brake drum, the hole normally being covered with a rubber grommet to prevent the ingress of dust and dirt. From car No. 228267, seals were used that were held in place by the wheel. On later models a strengthened wheel was fitted which had no brake shoe adjustment hole and it is vital that the original grommet is never used with these wheels as they will not allow the wheel to seat properly against the brake drum. The brake drum dust seals that should be fitted with the later wheels have part Nos. ACA 5404 for brake drums with oval holes, and ACA 5377 for brake drums with round holes.

FAULT FINDING CHART

Cause	Trouble	Remedy
SYMPTOM:	PEDAL TRAVELS ALMOST TO FLOORBOARDS BEFORE BRAKES OPERATE	
Leaks and air bubbles in hydraulic system	Brake fluid level too low	Top up master cylinder reservoir. Check for leaks.
	Wheel cylinder leaking	Dismantle wheel cylinder, clean, fit new rubbers and bleed brakes.
	Master cylinder leaking (Bubbles in master cylinder fluid)	Dismantle master cylinder, clean, and fit new rubbers. Bleed brakes.
	Brake flexible hose leaking	Examine and fit new hose if old hose leaking. Bleed brakes.
	Brake line fractured	Replace with new brake pipe. Bleed brakes.
	Brake system unions loose	Check all unions in brake system and tighten as necessary. Bleed brakes.
Normal wear	Linings over 75% worn	Fit replacement shoes and brake linings.
Incorrect adjustment	Brakes badly out of adjustment	Jack up car and adjust brakes.
	Master cylinder push rod out or adjustment causing too much pedal free movement	Reset to manufacturer's specification.
SYMPTOM:	BRAKE PEDAL FEELS SPRINGY	
Brake lining renewal	New linings not yet bedded-in	Use brakes gently until springy pedal feeling leaves.
Excessive wear or damage	Brake drums badly worn and weak or cracked	Fit new brake drums.
Lack of maintenance	Master cylinder securing nuts loose	Tighten master cylinder securing nuts. Ensure spring washers are fitted.
SYMPTOM:	BRAKE PEDAL FEELS SPONGY & SOGGY	
Leaks or bubbles in hydraulic system	Wheel cylinder leaking	Dismantle wheel cylinder, clean, fit new rubbers, and bleed brakes.
	Master cylinder leaking (Bubbles in master cylinder reservoir)	Dismantle master cylinder, clean, and fit new rubbers and bleed brakes. Replace cylinder if internal walls scored.
	Brake pipe line or flexible hose leaking	Fit new pipeline or hose.
	Unions in brake system loose	Examine for leaks, tighten as necessary.
SYMPTOM:	EXCESSIVE EFFORT REQUIRED TO BRAKE CAR	
Lining type or condition	Linings badly worn	Fit replacement brake shoes and linings.
	New linings recently fitted - not yet bedded-in	Use brakes gently until braking effort normal.
	Harder linings fitted than standard causing increase in pedal pressure	Remove linings and replace with normal units.
Oil or grease leaks	Linings and brake drums contaminated with oil, grease, or hydraulic fluid	Rectify source of leak, clean brake drums, fit new linings.
SYMPTOM:	BRAKES UNEVEN & PULLING TO ONE SIDE	
Oil or grease leaks	Linings and brake drums contaminated with oil, grease, or hydraulic fluid	Ascertain and rectify source of leak, clean brake drums, fit new linings.
Lack of maintenance	Tyre pressures unequal	Check and inflate as necessary.
	Radial ply tyres fitted at one end of car only	Fit radial ply tyres of the same make to all four wheels.
	Brake backplate loose	Tighten backplate securing nuts and bolts.
	Brake shoes fitted incorrectly	Remove and fit shoes correct way round.
	Different type of linings fitted at each wheel	Fit the linings specified by the manufacturers all round.
	Anchorages for front suspension or rear axle loose	Tighten front and rear suspension pick-up points including spring anchorage.
	Brake drums badly worn, cracked or distorted	Fit new brake drums.

BRAKING SYSTEM

Cause	Trouble	Remedy
SYMPTOM:	BRAKES TEND TO BIND, DRAG, OR LOCK-ON	
Incorrect adjustment	Brake shoes adjusted too tightly Handbrake cable over-tightened Master cylinder push rod out of adjustment giving too little brake pedal free movement	Slacken off brake shoe adjusters two clicks. Slacken off handbrake cable adjustment. Reset to manufacturer's specifications.
Wear or dirt in hydraulic system or incorrect fluid	Reservoir vent hole in cap blocked with dirt Master cylinder by-pass port restricted - brakes seize in 'on' position Wheel cylinder seizes in 'on' position	Clean and blow through hole. Dismantle, clean, and overhaul master cylinder. Bleed brakes. Dismantle, clean, and overhaul wheel cylinder. Bleed brakes.
Mechanical wear	Brake shoe pull off springs broken, stretched or loose	Examine springs and replace if worn or loose.
Incorrect brake assembly	Brake shoe pull off springs fitted wrong way round, omitted, or wrong type used	Examine, and rectify as appropriate.
Neglect	Handbrake system rusted or seized in the 'on' position	Apply 'Plus Gas' to free, clean and lubricate.

CHAPTER TEN

ELECTRICAL SYSTEM

SPECIFICATION

	Early Minor 1000	Late Minor 1000
Battery		
Type: Home	GTW7A or BT7A	BT7A
Export	GTZ7A or BTZ7A	BTZ7A
Voltage or capacity at 20 hour rate	12-volts, 43 amp/hr.	
Dynamo		
Type	Lucas C39 PV2	Lucas C40-1
Cutting in speed	1,050 to 1,200 r.p.m. ..	1,200 to 1,400 r.p.m.
Maximum output	13.5 volts, 19 amps ..	13.5 volts, 22 amps
Field resistance	6.1 ohms	6.1 ohms
Starter Motor		
Type	Lucas M.35 G.1 Four brush	
Control Box		
Type	Lucas RB 106/1 or 106/2	Lucas RB 106/2
Cut in voltage	12.7 to 13.3 volts.. ..	12.7 to 13.3 volts
Drop off voltage	9 to 10 volts..	8.5 to 11 volts
Reverse current	3 to 5 amps	3 to 5 amps
Windscreen Wiper		
Type	Lucas DR2	Lucas DR3A
Normal running current	2.3 to 3.1 amps at 12 volts	
Armature resistance	.34 to .41 ohms	.28 to .35 ohms
Field resistance	12.8 to 14 ohms	8 to 9.5 ohms
Fuse Unit		
Type (2 live, 2 spare fuses)	Lucas SF6	Lucas 4FJ
Fuses	50 amp (AUX) & 35 amps	2 by 35 amps
.. ..	(AUX, IGN) or 2 by 35 amps	
Flashing Indicator Unit		Lucas FL5

BULBS	B.M.C. Part No.	Volts	Watts.	B.M.C. Part No.	Volts	Watts.
Headlamps	BFS 354	12	42/36	13H 496	12	60/45
Sidelamps	BFS 989	12	6	BFS 989	12	6
Tail/stop lamps	BFS 380	12	21/6	BFS 380	12	21/6
Front and rear flasher - all models	BFS 382	12	21	Same as Early Model		
Panel lamps - all models	BFS 987	12	2.2	"		
Roof lamp - all models	BFS 254	12	6	"		
Number plate lamp - all models	BFS 989	12	6	"		
Ignition warning lamp, Oil) pressure warning lamp,) Headlamp main beam warning) lamp, Direction indicator) warning lamp)	BFS 987	12	2.2	"		

GENERAL DESCRIPTION

The electrical system is of the 12-volt type and the major components comprise: a 12-volt 43-amp/hour battery of which the positive terminal is earthed; a voltage regulator and cut-out; a Lucas dynamo which is fitted to the front right-hand side of the engine and is driven by the fan belt from the crankshaft pulley wheel; and a starter motor which is fitted to the end plate and gearbox bellhousing on the right-hand side of the engine.

The six plate 12-volt battery supplies a steady supply of current for the ignition, lighting, and other electrical circuits, and provides a reserve of electricity when the current consumed by the electrical equipment exceeds that being produced by the dynamo.

The dynamo is of the two brush type and works in conjunction with the voltage regulator and cut-out. Two types of dynamo were fitted, the type fitted to your car depending on when it was manufactured. Early models made use of the Lucas C39 PV 2 unit, while later models made use of the virtually identical C40-1 unit which has a slightly higher output. The dynamo is cooled by a multi-bladed fan mounted behind the dynamo pulley, and blows air through cooling holes in the dynamo end brackets. The output from the dynamo is controlled by the voltage regulator which ensures a high output if the battery is in a low state of charge or the demands from the electrical equipment high, and a low output if the battery is fully charged and there is little demand from the electrical equipment.

BATTERY - REMOVAL & REPLACEMENT

1. Disconnect the positive and then the negative leads from the battery terminals by slackening the retaining nuts and bolts, or by unscrewing the retaining screws if these are fitted.
2. Remove the battery clamp and carefully lift the battery out of its compartment. Hold the battery vertical to ensure that none of the electrolyte is spilled.
3. Replacement is a direct reversal of this procedure. NOTE Replace the negative lead before the earth (positive) lead and smear the terminals with petroleum jelly (vaseline) to prevent corrosion. NEVER use an ordinary grease as applied to other parts of the car.

BATTERY MAINTENANCE & INSPECTION

Normal weekly battery maintenance consists of checking the electrolyte level of each cell to ensure that the separators are covered by $1/4$ in. of electrolyte. If the level has fallen, top up the battery using distilled water only. Do not overfill. If the battery is overfilled or any electrolyte spilled immediately wipe away the excess as electrolyte attacks and corrodes any metal it comes into contact with very rapidly.

As well as keeping the terminals clean and covered with petroleum jelly, the top of the battery, and especially the top of the cells, should be kept clean and dry. This helps prevent corrosion and ensures that the battery does not become partially discharged by leakage through dampness and dirt.

Once every three months remove the battery and inspect the battery securing bolts, the battery clamp plate, tray, and battery leads for corrosion (white fluffy deposits on the metal which are brittle to touch.) If any corrosion is found, clean off the deposits with ammonia and paint over the clean metal with an anti-rust/anti-acid paint.

At the same time inspect the battery case for cracks. If a crack is found, clean and plug it with one of the proprietary compounds marketed by firms such as 'Holts' for this purpose. If leakage through the crack has been excessive then it will be necessary to refill the appropriate cell with fresh electrolyte as detailed later. Cracks are frequently caused to the top of the battery cases by pouring in distilled water in the middle of winter AFTER instead of BEFORE a run. This gives the water no chance to mix with the electrolyte and so the former freezes and splits the battery case.

If topping up the battery becomes excessive and the case has been inspected for cracks that could cause leakage, but none are found, the battery is being overcharged and the voltage regulator will have to be checked and reset.

With the battery on the bench at the three monthly interval check, measure its specific gravity with a hydrometer to determine its state of charge and condition of the electrolyte. There should be very little variation between the different cells and if a variation in excess of 0.025 is present it will be due to either:-
a) Loss of electrolyte from the battery at some time caused by spillage or a leak resulting in a drop in the specific gravity of the electrolyte, when the deficiency was replaced with distilled water instead of fresh electrolyte.
b) An internal short circuit caused by buckling of the plates or a similar malady pointing to the liklihood of total battery failure in the near future.

The specific gravity of the electrolyte for fully charged conditions at the electrolyte temperature indicated, is listed in Table A. The specific gravity of a fully discharged battery at different temperatures of the electrolyte is given at Table B.

TABLE A

Specific Gravity - Battery fully charged

1.268 at 100°F or 38°C electrolyte temperature
1.272 at 90°F or 32°C   "   "
1.276 at 80°F or 27°C   "   "
1.280 at 70°F or 21°C   "   "
1.284 at 60°F or 16°C   "   "
1.288 at 50°F or 10°C   "   "
1.292 at 40°F or 4°C   "   "
1.296 at 30°F or -1.5°C   "   "

TABLE B

Specific Gravity - Battery full discharged

1.098 at 100°F or 38°C electrolyte temperature
1.102 at 90°F or 32°C   "   "
1.106 at 80°F or 27°C   "   "
1.110 at 70°F or 21°C   "   "
1.114 at 60°F or 16°C   "   "
1.118 at 50°F or 10°C   "   "
1.122 at 40°F or 4°C   "   "
1.126 at 30°F or -1.5°C   "   "

ELECTROLYTE REPLENISHMENT

If the battery is in a fully charged state and one of the cells maintains a specific gravity reading which is 0.025 or more lower than the others, and a check of each cell has been made with a voltage meter to check for short circuits (a four to seven second test should give a steady reading of between 1.2 to 1.8 volts), then it is likely that electrolyte has been lost from the cell with the low reading at some time.

Top the cell up with a solution of 1 part sulphuric acid to 2.5 parts of water. If the cell is already fully topped up draw some electrolyte out of it with a pipette. The total capacity of each cell is $3/4$ pint. When mixing the sulphuric acid and water NEVER ADD WATER TO SULPHURIC ACID - always pour the acid slowly onto the water in a glass container. IF WATER IS ADDED TO SULPHURIC ACID IT WILL EXPLODE. Continue to top up the cell with the freshly made electrolyte and then recharge the battery and check the hydrometer readings.

BATTERY CHARGING

In winter time when heavy demand is placed upon the battery, such as when starting from cold, and much electrical equipment is continually in use, it is a good idea to occasionally have the battery fully charged from an external source at the rate of 3.5 to 4 amps. Continue to charge the battery at this rate until no further rise in specific gravity is noted over a four hour period. Alternatively a trickle charger charging at the rate of 1.5 amps can be safely used overnight. Specially rapid 'boost' charges which are claimed to restore the power of the battery in 1 to 2 hours are most dangerous as they can cause serious damage to the battery plates through overheating. While charging the battery note that the temperature of the electrolyte should never exceed 100°F.

DYNAMO - ROUTINE MAINTENANCE

Routine maintenance consists of checking the tension of the fan belt, and lubricating the dynamo rear bearing once every 6,000 miles.

The fan belt should be tight enough to ensure no slip between the belt and the dynamo pulley. If a shrieking noise comes from the engine when the unit is accelerated rapidly then it is likely that it is the fan belt slipping. On the other hand, the belt must not be too taut or the bearings will wear rapidly and cause dynamo failure or bearing seizure. Ideally $1/2$ in. of total free movement should be available at the fan belt midway between the fan and the dynamo pulley. To adjust the fan belt tension slightly slacken the three dynamo retaining bolts, and swing the dynamo on the upper two bolts outwards to increase the tension, and inwards to lower it. It is best to leave the bolts fairly tight so that considerable effort has to be used to move the dynamo; otherwise it is difficult to get the correct setting. If the dynamo is being moved outwards to increase the tension and the bolts have only been slackened a little, a long spanner acting as a lever placed behind the dynamo with the lower end resting against the block works very well in moving the dynamo outwards. Retighten the dynamo bolts and check that the dynamo pulley is correctly aligned with the fan belt.

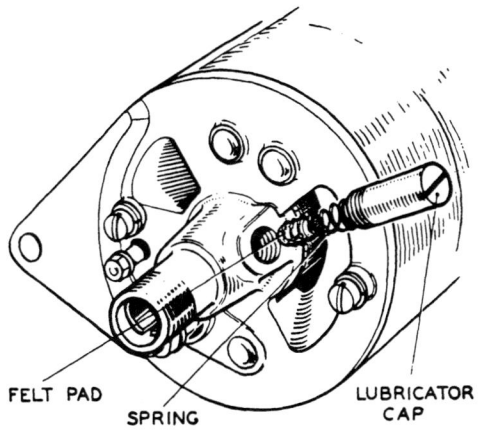

Fig. 10:1. An exploded view of the rear dynamo bearing early wick-type lubricator.

Lubrication of early model Lucas C39 PV2 dynamos consists of unscrewing the lubricator cap from the end bracket, removing the spring and felt pad from the cap, half filling the cap with high melting point grease, replacing the spring and felt pad in the cap, and screwing home the cap to the dynamo. Lubrication on the C40-1 dynamo consists of inserting three drops of S.A.E. 30 engine oil in the small oil hole in the centre of the commutator end bracket. This lubricates the rear bearing. The front bearing is pre-packed with grease and requires no attention.

DYNAMO - TESTING IN POSITION

If, with the engine running no charge comes from the dynamo, or the charge is very low, first check that the fan belt is in place and is not slipping. Then check that the leads from the control box to the dynamo are firmly attached and that one has not come loose from its terminal. The lead from the 'D' terminal on the dynamo should be connected to the 'D' terminal on the control box, and similarly the 'F' terminals on the dynamo and control box should also be connected together.

Disconnect the leads from terminals 'D' and 'F' on the dynamo and then join the terminals together with a short length of wire. Attach to the centre of this length of wire the negative clip of a 0-20 volts voltmeter and run the other clip to earth. Start the engine and allow it to idle at approximately 750 r.p.m. At this speed the dynamo should give a reading of about 15 volts on the voltmeter. There is no point in raising the engine speed above a fast idle as the reading will then be inaccurate.

If no reading is recorded then check the brushes and brush connections. If a very low reading of approximately 1 volt is observed then the field winding may be suspect. On early dynamos it was possible to remove the dynamo cover band and check the dynamo and brushes in position. With the Lucas C40-1 windowless yoke dynamo, currently fitted to all models, the dynamo has to be removed and dismantled before the brushes and commutator can be attended to.

If the voltmeter shows a good reading then with the temporary link s t i l l in position connect both leads from the control box to 'D' and 'F' on the dynamo ('D' to 'D' and 'F' to 'F'). Release the lead from the 'D' terminal at the control box end and clip one lead from the voltmeter to the end of the cable, and the other lead to a good earth. With the engine running at the same speed as previously, an identical voltage to that recorded at the dynamo should be noted on the voltmeter. If no voltage is recorded then there is a break in the wire. If the voltage is the same as recorded at the dynamo then check the 'F' lead in similar fashion. If both readings are the same as at the dynamo then it will be necessary to test the control box.

DYNAMO - REMOVAL & REPLACEMENT

1. Slacken the two dynamo retaining bolts, and the nut on the sliding link, and m o v e the dynamo in towards the engine so that the fan belt can be removed.

2. Disconnect the two leads from the dynamo terminals. NOTE if the ignition coil is mounted on top of the dynamo, remove the high tension wire from the centre of the coil by unscrewing the knurled nut, and unscrew the nuts holding the two low tension wires in place.

3. Remove the nut from the sliding link bolt, and remove the two upper bolts. The dynamo is then free to be lifted away from the engine.

4. Replacement is a reversal of the above procedure. Do not finally tighten the retaining bolts

and the nut on the sliding link until the fan belt has been tensioned correctly. (See para. 2 of 'Dynamo Routine Maintenance').

5. If it is wished to fit a replacement dynamo, check the identification marks which will be found on the yoke, and quote these to your local B.M.C. or Lucas agent prior to handing the dynamo in to ensure a replacement is available.

LYNAMO - DISMANTLING & REASSEMBLY

1. Remove the dynamo pulley after unscrewing the nut and lockwasher which retains it to the armature shaft. (It is not necessary to do this if only the brushes and commutator are to be examined).

2. From the commutator end bracket remove the nuts, spring, and flat washers from the field terminal post.

3. Unscrew the two through bolts and remove them together with their spring washers.

4. Take off the commutator end bracket, and remove the driving end bracket complete with the armature.

5. Lift the brush springs and draw the brushes out of the brush holders. Unscrew the screws and lockwashers holding the brush leads to the commutator end bracket.

6. The bearings need not be removed, or the armature shaft separated from the drive end bracket unless the bearings or the armature are to be renewed. If it is wished to remove the armature shaft from the drive end bracket and bearing

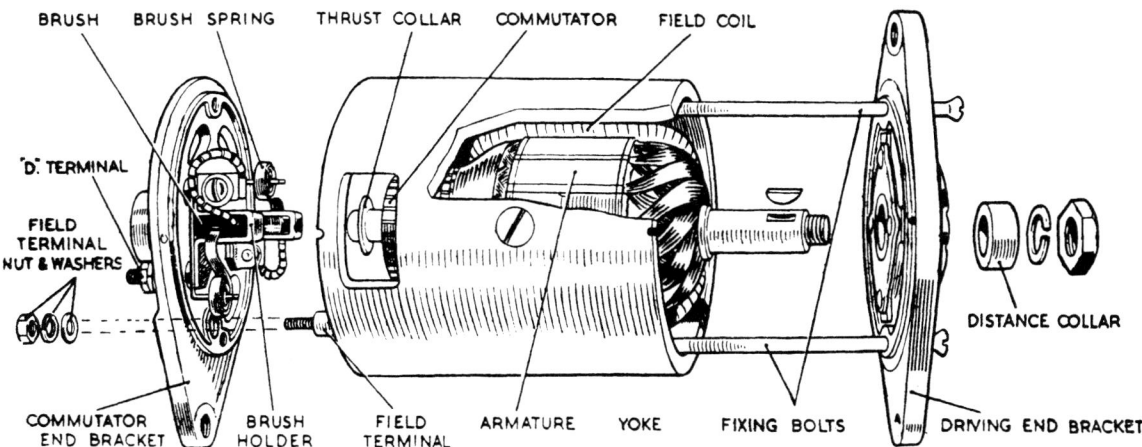

Fig. 10:2. Exploded view of the Lucas dynamo fitted to early models

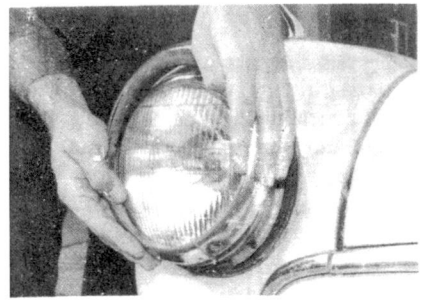

To adjust the headlights or to fit a new bulb just undo the screw at the base of the headlight rim and then turn and pull it off

The headlight is adjusted by the three screws indicated

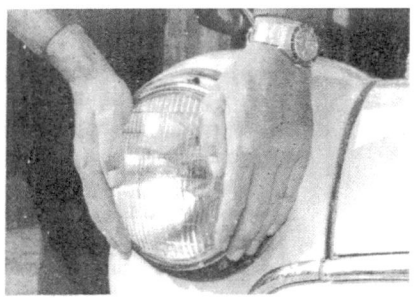

To remove the light unit press it in slightly against the small springs behind the adjusting screws, at the same time twisting it anti-clockwise

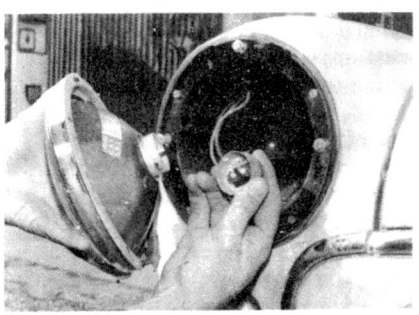

To disconnect the light unit completely turn the bayonet fitting anti-clockwise and pull it away from the reflector

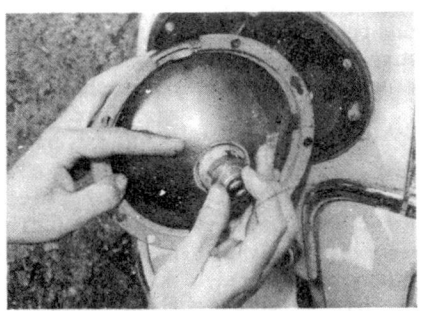

The bulb can now be removed. Note that there is always a notch in the base of the bulb which must line up with the ridge in the bulb holder

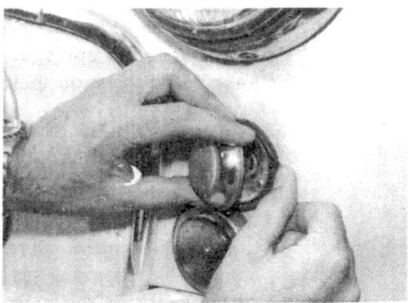

To remove a sidelight, peel back the rubber retaining ring as indicated (use a screwdriver if the rubber is very stiff) and lift out the glass cover and securing ring

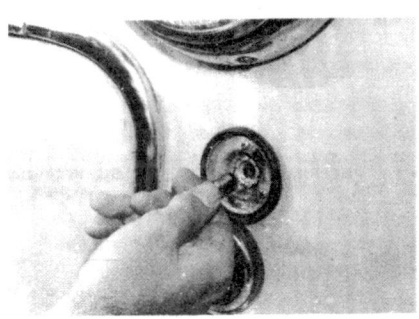

The bulb is a simple bayonet fitting and its removal and replacement should present no problems

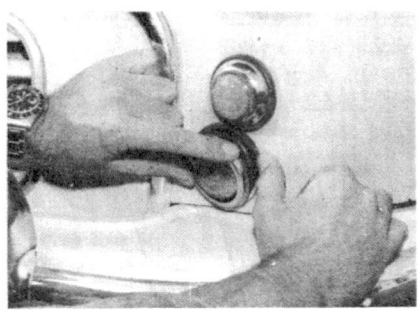

On models with separate flashers, first peel back the outer rubber retaining ring and remove the circular chromium plated ring

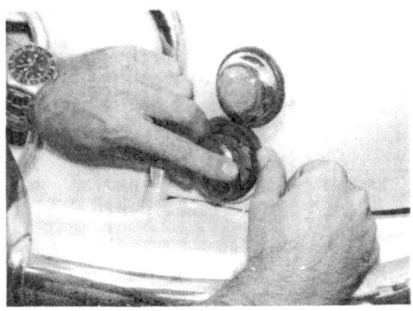

Then pull back the inner rubber ring and lift out the glass cover

The bulb, like the side light, is a simple bayonet fitting and can be removed and replaced easily

To renew one of the rear bulbs first unscrew the two screws, one at the top and one at the bottom, of the rear light cover

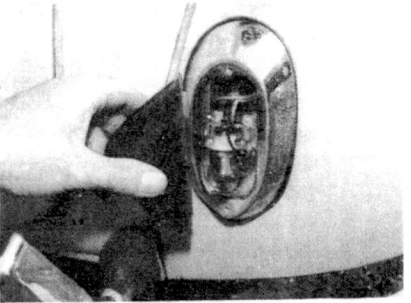

With the screws removed the cover can then be lifted away to give access to the bulbs

(and this is necessary for bearing renewal) then the bearing retaining plate must be supported securely, and with the woodruff key removed the shaft pressed out of the end bracket.

7. When a new armature is fitted or the old one replaced, it is most important that the inner journal of the ball bearing is supported by a steel tube of suitable diameter so that no undue strain is placed on the bearing as the armature shaft is pressed home.

8. Reassembly is a straight reversal of the above process. A point worth noting is that when fitting the commutator end plate with brushes attached, it is far easier to slip the brushes over the commutator if the brushes are raised in their holders and held in this position by the pressure of the springs resting against their flanks rather than on their heads.

DYNAMO - INSPECTION & REPAIR

First check the brushes for wear. Any brush on early C39 type dynamos less than $^{11}/32$ in. long and $^{9}/32$ in. long on the C40 unit, must be replaced. Check that the brushes move freely and easily in their holders by removing the retaining springs and then pulling gently on the wire brush leads. If either of the brushes tend to stick in their holders clean the brushes with a petrol moistened rag and if still stiff, lightly polish the sides of the brush with a very fine file until the brush moves quite freely and easily in its holder.

If the brushes are but little worn and are to be used again then ensure that they are placed in the same holders from which they were removed. Check the tension of the brush springs with a spring balance. The tension of the springs when new was 20 to 25 oz. on the C39 dynamo and the springs should be renewed if the tension falls below 15 oz. On the C40 unit the tension, new, was 30 oz. falling to 13 oz. when the brush was sufficiently worn to warrant replacement.

Secondly, check the condition of the commutator. If the surface is dirty or blackened, clean it with a petrol damped rag. If the commutator is in good condition the surface will be smooth and quite free from pits or burnt areas, and the insulated segments clearly defined.

If, after the commutator has been cleaned pits and burnt spots are still present, then wrap a strip of glass paper round the commutator and rotate the armature.

In extreme cases of wear the commutator can be mounted in a lathe and with the lathe turning at high speed, a very fine cut may be taken off the commutator. Then polish the commutator with glass paper. If the commutator has worn so that the insulators between the segments are level with the top of the segments, then undercut the insulators to a depth of $^{1}/32$ in. (.8 mm.). The best tool to use for this purpose is half a hacksaw blade ground to the thickness of the insulator, and with the handle end of the blade covered in insulating tape to make it comfortable to hold.

Thirdly, check the armature for open or short

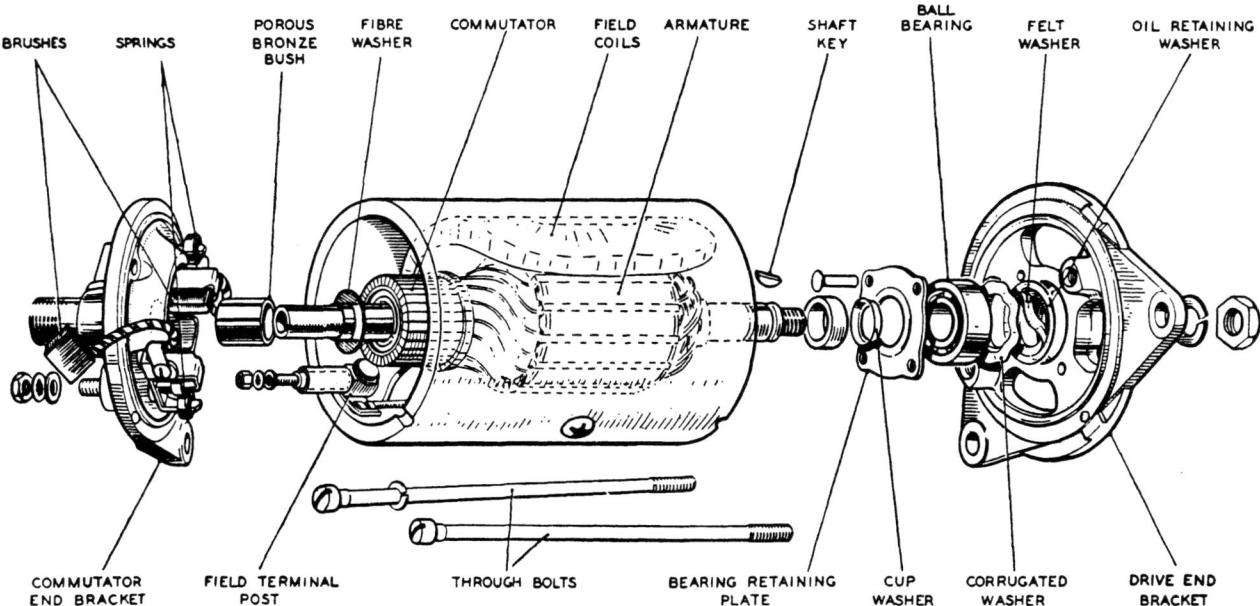

Fig. 10:3. Exploded view of the Lucas windowless yoke dynamo fitted to later models

circuited windings. It is a good indication of an open circuited armature when the commutator segments are burnt. If the armature has short circuited the commutator segments will be very badly burnt, and the overheated armature windings badly discoloured. If open or short circuits are suspected then test by substituting the suspect armature for a new one.

Fourthly, check the resistance of the field coils. To do this, connect an ohmmeter between the field terminal and the yoke and note the reading on the ohmmeter which should be about 6 ohms. If the ohmmeter reading is infinity this indicates an open circuit in the field winding. If the ohmmeter reading is below 5 ohms this indicates that one of the field coils is faulty and must be replaced.

Field coil replacement involves the use of a wheel operated screwdriver, a soldering iron, caulking and riveting and this operation is considered to be beyond the scope of most owners. Therefore, if the field coils are at fault either purchase a rebuilt dynamo, or take the casing to a reputable electrical engineering works for new field coils to be fitted.

DYNAMO BEARINGS - INSPECTION, REMOVAL & REPLACEMENT

With the dynamo partially stripped down, check the condition of the bearings. They must be renewed when wear has reached such a state that they allow visible side movement of the armature shaft. A bush bearing is fitted to the commutator end bracket and a ball bearing to the drive end bracket. To renew the bush bearing proceed as follows:-

1. With a suitable extractor pull out the old bush from the commutator end bracket. Alternatively screw a $\frac{3}{8}$ in. tap into the C39 bush and a $\frac{5}{8}$ in. tap into the C40 bush and pull out the bush together with the tap.
2. NOTE when fitting the new bush bearing that it is of the porous bronze type, and it is essential that it is allowed to stand in S.A.E.30 engine oil for at least 24 hours before fitment.

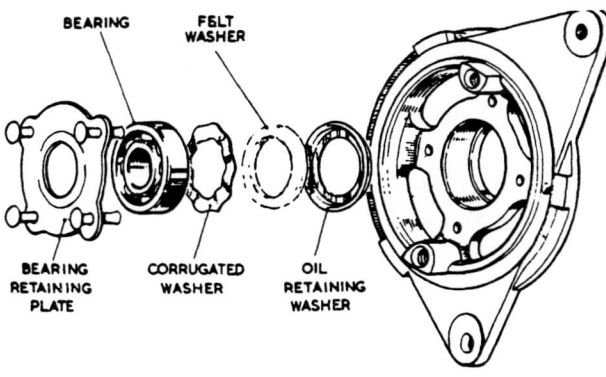

BEARING **FELT WASHER**

BEARING RETAINING PLATE **CORRUGATED WASHER** **OIL RETAINING WASHER**

Fig. 10:4. Exploded view of the dynamo front end bracket and bearing assembly

3. Carefully fit the new bush into the end plate, pressing it in until the end of the bearing is flush with the inner side of the end plate. If available press the bush in with a smooth shouldered mandrel the same diameter as the armature shaft.

To renew the ball bearing fitted to the drive end bracket remove the armature from the end bracket as detailed in the section headed 'Dynamo Dismantling and Reassembly', and then proceed as follows:-

1. Drill out the rivets which hold the bearing retainer plate to the end bracket and lift off the plate.
2. Press out the bearing from the end bracket and remove the corrugated washer, felt washer, and oil retaining washer from the bearing housing.
3. Thoroughly clean the bearing housing, and the new bearing and pack with high melting-point grease.
4. Place the oil retaining washer, felt washer, and corrugated washer in that order in the end bracket bearing housing, and then press in the new bearing.
5. Replace the plate and fit new rivets opening out the rivet ends to hold the plate securely in position. (NOTE that on the C40 dynamo the rivets are fitted from the outer face of the end bracket).

STARTER MOTOR - GENERAL DESCRIPTION

The starter motor is mounted on the right-hand lower side of the engine end plate, and is held in position by two bolts which also clamp the bellhousing flange. The motor is of the four field coil, four pole piece type, and utilises four spring-loaded commutator brushes. Two of these brushes are earthed, and the other two are insulated and attached to the field coil ends.

STARTER MOTOR - TESTING ON ENGINE

If the starter motor fails to operate then check the condition of the battery by turning on the headlamps. If they glow brightly for several seconds and then gradually dim, the battery is in an uncharged condition.

If the headlamps glow brightly and it is obvious that the battery is in good condition then check the tightness of the battery wiring connections (and in particular the earth lead from the battery terminal to its connection on the bodyframe). Check the tightness of the connections at the relay switch and at the starter motor. Check the wiring with a voltmeter for breaks or shorts.

If the wiring is in order then check that the starter motor switch is operating. To do this press the rubber covered button in the centre of the relay switch under the bonnet. If it is working the starter motor will be heard to 'click' as it tries to rotate. Alternatively check it with a voltmeter.

If the battery is fully charged, the wiring in order, and the switch working and the starter motor fails to operate then it will have to be removed from the car for examination. Before this is done, however, ensure that the starter pinion has not jammed in mesh with the flywheel. Check by turning the square end of armature shaft with a spanner. This will free the pinion if it is stuck in engagement with the flywheel teeth.

STARTER MOTOR - REMOVAL & REPLACEMENT

1. Disconnect the battery earth lead from the positive terminal.
2. Disconnect the starter motor cable from the terminal on the starter motor end plate.
3. Remove the distributor as detailed in Chapter 4.
4. Unscrew the two starter motor bolts after removing the starter motor dirt deflector where this is fitted.
5. Lift the starter motor out of engagement with the teeth on the flywheel ring.
6. Replacement is a straight reversal of the removal procedure.

STARTER MOTOR - DISMANTLING & REASSEMBLY

With the starter motor on the bench, loosen the screw on the cover band and slip the cover band off. With a piece of wire bent into the shape of a hook, lift back each of the brush springs in turn and check the movement of the brushes in their holders by pulling on the flexible connectors. If the brushes are so worn that their faces do not rest against the commutator, or if the ends of the brush leads are exposed on their working face, they must be renewed.

If any of the brushes tend to stick in their holders then wash them with a petrol moistened cloth and, if necessary, lightly polish the sides of the brush

with a very fine file, until the brushes move quite freely in their holders.

If the surface of the commutator is dirty or blackened, clean it with a petrol dampened rag. Secure the starter motor in a vice and check it by connecting a heavy gauge cable between the starter motor terminal and a 12-volt battery.

Connect the cable from the other battery terminal to earth on the starter motor body. If the motor turns at high speed it is in good order.

If the starter motor still fails to function or if it is wished to renew the brushes, then it is necessary to further dismantle the motor.

1. Lift the brush springs with the wire hook and lift all four brushes out of their holders one at a time.
2. Remove the terminal nuts and washers from the terminal post on the commutator end bracket.
3. Unscrew the two through bolts which hold the end plates together and pull off the commutator end bracket. Also remove the driving end bracket which will come away complete with the armature.

At this stage if the brushes are to be renewed their flexible connectors must be unsoldered and the connectors of new brushes soldered in their place. Check that the new brushes move freely in their holders as detailed above. If cleaning the commutator with petrol fails to remove all the burnt areas and spots then wrap a piece of glass paper round the commutator and rotate the armature. If the commutator is very badly worn remove the drive gear as

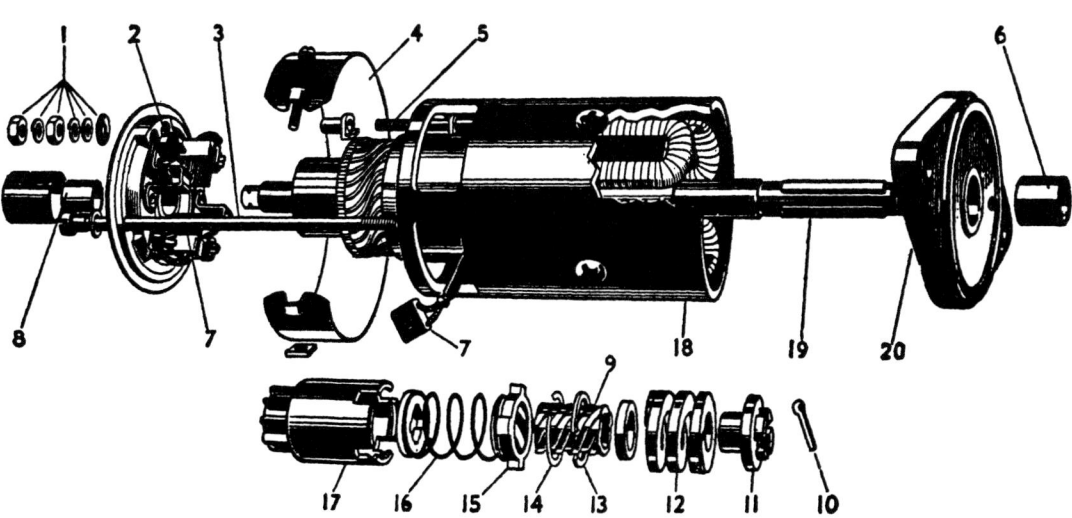

Fig. 10:5. Exploded view of the starter motor and starter motor drive

1	Terminal nuts and washers	5	Terminal post	9	Sleeve	13	Retaining ring	17	Pinion and barrel
2	Brush spring	6	Bearing bush	10	Split pin	14	Washer	18	Yoke
3	Through-bolt	7	Brushes	11	Shaft nut	15	Control nut	19	Armature shaft
4	Band cover	8	Bearing bush	12	Main spring	16	Restraining spring	20	Driving end bracket

detailed in the following section. Then mount the armature in a lathe and with the lathe turning at high speed, take a very fine cut out of the commutator and finish the surface by polishing with glass paper. DO NOT UNDERCUT THE MICA INSULATORS BETWEEN THE COMMUTATOR SEGMENTS.

With the starter motor dismantled, test the four field coils for an open circuit. Connect a 12-volt battery with a 12-volt bulb in one of the leads between the field terminal post and the tapping point of the field coils to which the brushes are connected. An open circuit is proved by the bulb not lighting.

If the bulb lights, it does not necessarily mean that the field coils are in order, as there is a possibility that one of the coils will be earthing to the starter yoke or pole shoes. To check this, remove the lead from the brush connector and place it against a clean portion of the starter yoke. If the bulb lights the field coils are earthing. Replacement of the field coils calls for the use of a wheel operated screwdriver, a soldering iron, caulking and riveting operations and is beyond the scope of the majority of owners. The starter yoke should be taken to a reputable electrical engineering works for new field coils to be fitted. Alternatively, purchase an exchange Lucas starter motor.

If the armature is damaged this will be evident after visual inspection. Look for signs of burning, discolouration, and for conductors that have lifted away from the commutator. Reassembly is a straight reversal of the dismantling procedure.

STARTER MOTOR DRIVE - GENERAL DESCRIPTION

The starter motor drive is of the outboard type. When the starter motor is operated the pinion moves into contact with the flywheel gear ring by moving in towards the starter motor.

If the engine kicks back, or the pinion fails to engage with the flywheel gear ring when the starter motor is actuated no undue strain is placed on the armature shaft, as the pinion sleeve disengages from the pinion and turns independently.

STARTER MOTOR DRIVE - REMOVAL & REPLACEMENT

1. Extract the split pin from the shaft nut on the end of the starter drive.
2. Holding the squared end of the armature shaft at the commutator end bracket with a suitable spanner, unscrew the shaft nut which has a right-hand thread, and pull off the mainspring.
3. Slide the remaining parts with a rotary action off the armature shaft.
4. Reassembly is a straight reversal of the above procedure. Ensure that the split pin is refitted.

NOTE It is most important that the drive gear is completely free from oil, grease and dirt. With the drive gear removed, clean all the parts thoroughly in paraffin. UNDER NO CIRCUMSTANCES OIL THE DRIVE COMPONENTS. Lubrication of the drive components could easily cause the pinion to stick.

STARTER MOTOR BUSHES - INSPECTION, REMOVAL & REPLACEMENT

With the starter motor stripped down check the condition of the bushes. They should be renewed when they are sufficiently worn to allow visible side movement of the armature shaft.

The old bushes are simply driven out with a suitable drift and the new bushes inserted by the same method. As the bearings are of the phosphor bronze type it is essential that they are allowed to stand in S.A.E. 30 engine oil for at least 24 hours before fitment.

CONTROL BOX - GENERAL DESCRIPTION

The control box comprises the voltage regulator and the cut-out. The voltage regulator controls the output from the dynamo depending on the state of the battery and the demands of the electrical equipment, and ensures that the battery is not overcharged. The cut-out is really an automatic switch and connects the dynamo to the battery when the dynamo is turning fast enough to produce a charge. Similarly it disconnects the battery from the dynamo when the engine is idling or stationary so that the battery does not discharge through the dynamo. Ordinary screw-type terminals are used on early Lucas control boxes but later modified RB106/2 types make use of Lucar connectors.

CUT-OUT & REGULATOR CONTACTS - MAINTENANCE

Every 12,000 miles check the cut-out and regulator contacts. If they are dirty or rough or burnt place a piece of fine glass paper (DO NOT USE EMERY PAPER OR CARBORUNDUM PAPER) between the cut-out contacts, close them manually and draw the glass paper through several times.

Clean the regulator contacts in exactly the same way, but use emery or carborundum paper and not glass paper. Carefully clean both sets of contacts

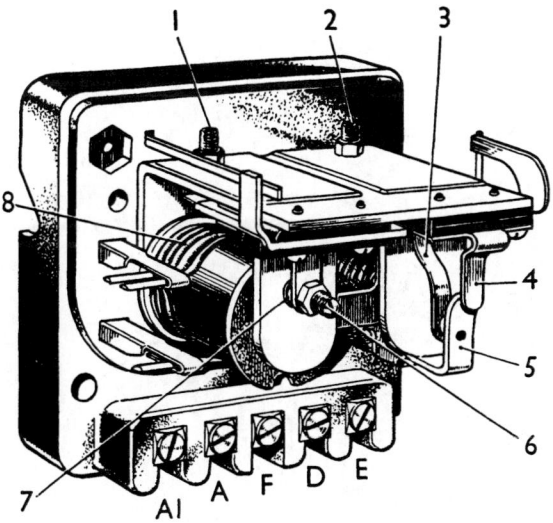

Fig. 10:6. The control box fitted to early models. 1 Regulator adjusting screw. 2 Cut-out adjusting screw. 3 Fixed contact blade 4 Stop arm. 5 Armature tongue and moving contact. 6 Regulator moving contact. 7 Fixed contact. 8 Regulator series windings.

from all traces of dust with a rag moistened in methylated spirits.

VOLTAGE REGULATOR ADJUSTMENT

If the battery is in sound condition, but is not holding its charge, or is being continually overcharged, and the dynamo is in sound condition, then the voltage regulator in the control box m u s t be adjusted.

Check the regulator setting by removing and joining together the cables from the control box terminals A1 and A. Then connect the negative lead of a 20-volt voltmeter to the 'D' terminal on the dynamo and the positive lead to a good earth. Start the engine and increase its speed until the voltmeter needle flicks and then steadies. This should occur at about 2,000 r.p.m. If the voltage at which the n e e d l e steadies is outside the limits listed below, then remove the control box cover and turn the adjusting screw in the illustration, clockwise, a quarter of a turn at a time to raise the setting, and a similar amount, anti-clockwise, to lower it.

Air Temperature	Type RB 106/1 Open circuit voltage	Type RB 106/2 Open circuit voltage
10°C or 50°F	16.1 to 16.7	16.1 to 16.7
20°C or 68°F	15.8 to 16.4	16.0 to 16.6
30°C or 86°F	15.6 to 16.2	15.9 to 16.5
40°C or 104°F	15.3 to 15.9	15.8 to 16.4

It is vital that the adjustments be completed within 30 seconds of starting the engine as otherwise the heat from the shunt coil will affect the readings.

CUT-OUT ADJUSTMENT

Check the voltage required to operate the cut-out by connecting a voltmeter between the control box terminals 'D' and 'E'. R e m o v e the control box

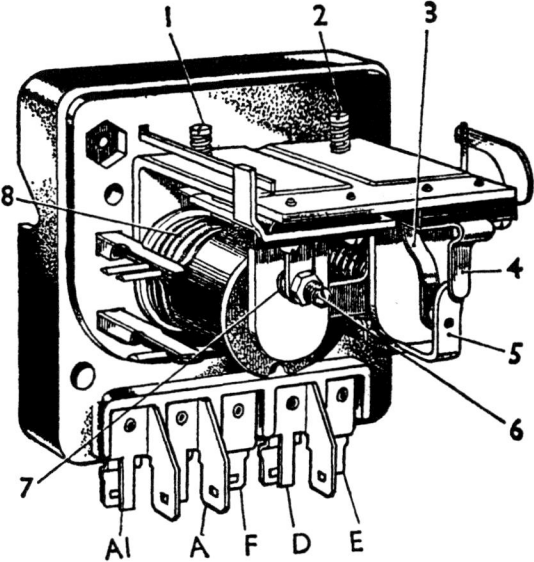

Fig. 10:7. The control box fitted to l a t e r models with Lucar connectors. 1 Regulator adjusting screw. 2 Cut-out adjusting screw. 3 Fixed contact blade. 4 Stop arm. 5 Armature tongue and moving contact. 6 Regulator fixed contact screw. 7 Regulator moving contact. 8 Regulator series windings.

cover, start the engine and gradually increase its speed until the cut-outs close. This should occur when the reading is between 12.7 to 13.3 volts. If the reading is outside these limits turn the cut-out adjusting screw in the illustration a fraction at a time clockwise to raise the voltage, and anti-clockwise to lower it. To adjust the drop off voltage bend the fixed contact blade carefully. The adjustment to the cut-out should be completed within 30 seconds of starting the engine as otherwise heat build-up from the shunt coil will affect the readings.

If the cut-out fails to work, clean the contacts, and if there is still no response renew the cut-out and regulator unit.

FUSES - GENERAL

Two fuses are fitted to a separate fuse holder positioned adjacent to the control box. The f u s e marked A1 - A2 protects the electrical items such as the horn and lights, which function irrespective of whether the ignition is on or not.

The fuse marked A3 - A4 protects the ignition system and items which only operate when the ignition system is switched on. i.e. the stop lights, f u e l gauge, flasher unit, and windscreen wiper motor.

If e i t h e r of these fuses blow due to a short circuit or similar trouble, t r a c e and rectify the cause before renewing the fuse.

In later models a 10 amp fuse is fitted in the pilot and tail light circuit and is fitted in a tube located in the wiring loom beneath the regulator. To expose the fuse, twist and press i n one end then pull the assembly apart and remove the fuse.

FLASHER CIRCUIT - FAULT T R A C I N G & RECTIFICATION

The actual flasher unit is enclosed in a small cylindrical metal container located in the engine compartment. The unit is actuated by the direction indicator switch.

If the flasher unit fails to operate, or works very slowly or very rapidly, check out the flasher indicator circuit as detailed below before assuming there is a fault in the unit itself.

1. Examine the direction indicator bulbs front and rear for broken filaments.
2. If the external flashers are working but the internal flasher warning light has ceased to function check the filament of the warning bulb and replace as necessary.
3. With the aid of the wiring diagram check all the flasher circuit connections if a flasher bulb is sound but does not work.
4. In the event of total direction indicator failure check the A3 - A4 fuse.
5. With the ignition turned on check that current is reaching the flasher unit by connecting a voltmeter between the 'plus' or 'B' terminal and earth. If this test is positive connect the 'plus' or 'B' terminal and the 'L' terminal and operate the flasher switch. If the flasher bulb lights up the flasher unit itself is defective and must be replaced as it is not possible to dismantle and repair it.

WINDSCREEN WIPER MECHANISM - MAINTENANCE

Renew the windscreen wiper blades at intervals of 12,000 miles, or more frequently if necessary.

The cable which drives the wiper blades from the gearbox attached to the windscreen wiper motor is pre-packed with grease and requires no maintenance. The washer round the wheelbase spindle can be lubricated with several drops of glycerine every 6,000 miles.

WINDSCREEN WIPER MECHANISM - FAULT DIAGNOSIS & RECTIFICATION

Should the windscreen wipers fail to park or park badly then check the limit switch on the gearbox cover. Loosen the four screws which retain the gearbox cover and place the projection close to the rim of the limit switch in line with the groove in the gearbox cover. Rotate the limit switch anti-clockwise 25° and tighten the four screws retaining the gearbox cover. If it is wished to park the windscreen wipers on the other side of the windscreen rotate the limit switch 180° clockwise.

Should the windscreen wipers fail, or work very slowly, then check the current the motor is taking by connecting up a 1-20 volt voltmeter in the circuit and turning on the wiper switch. Consumption should be between 2.3 to 3.1 amps.

If no current is passing through check the A3 - A4 fuse. If the fuse has blown replace it after having checked the wiring of the motor and other electrical circuits serviced by this fuse for short circuits. If the fuse is in good condition check the wiper switch and the current operated thermostat by substitution.

If the wiper motor takes a very high current check the wiper blades for freedom of movement. If

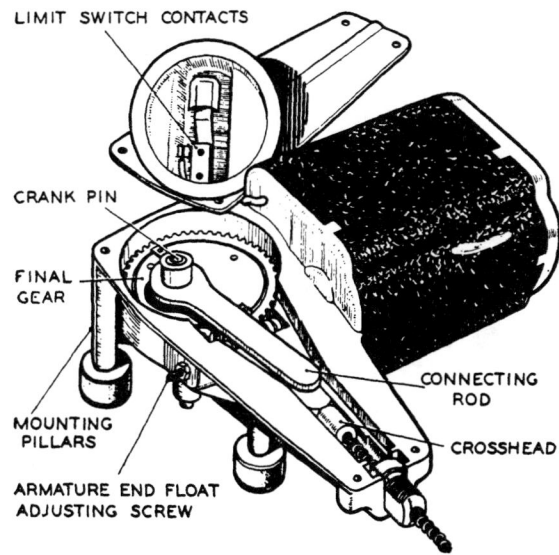

Fig. 10:9. The windscreen wiper gearbox cover removed, showing the limit switch contacts

this is satisfactory check the gearbox cover and gear assembly for damage and measure the armature end float which should be between .008 to .012 in. (.20 to .30 mm.). The end float is set by the adjusting screw. Check that excessive friction in the cable connecting tubes caused by too small a curvature is not the cause of the high current consumption.

If the motor takes a very low current ensure that the battery is fully charged. Check the brush gear after removing the commutator end bracket and ensure that the brushes are bearing on the commutator. If not, check the brushes for freedom of movement and if necessary renew the tension spring. Check the armature by substitution if this unit is suspected.

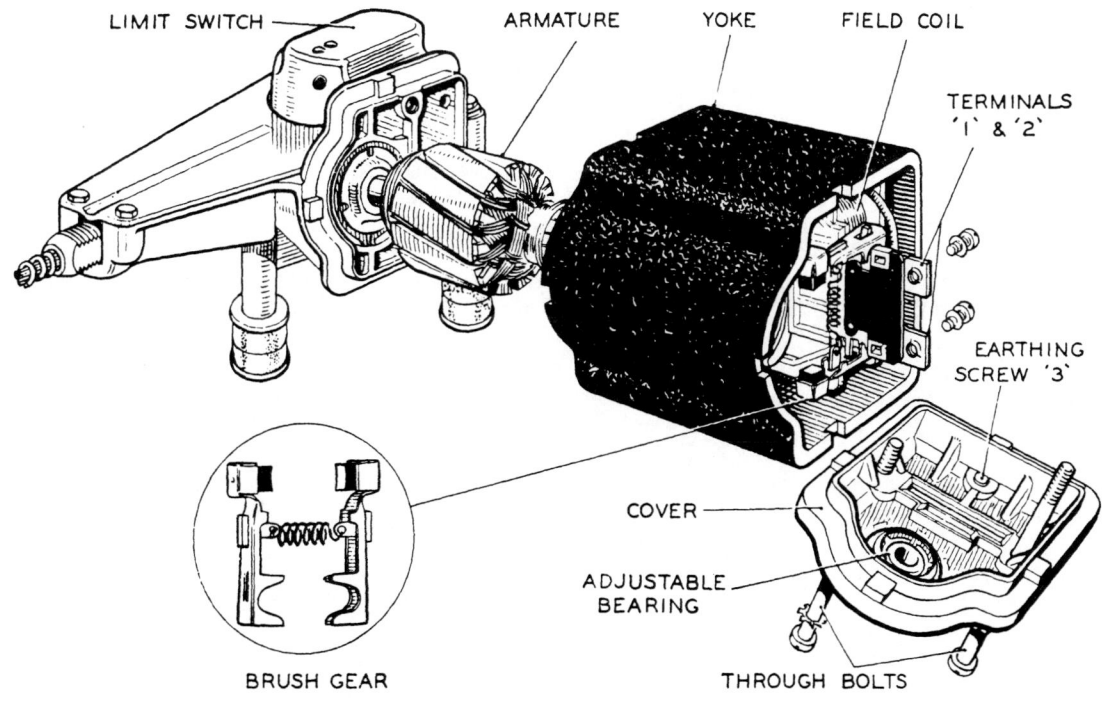

Fig. 10:8. A view of the windscreen wiper motor partly dismantled

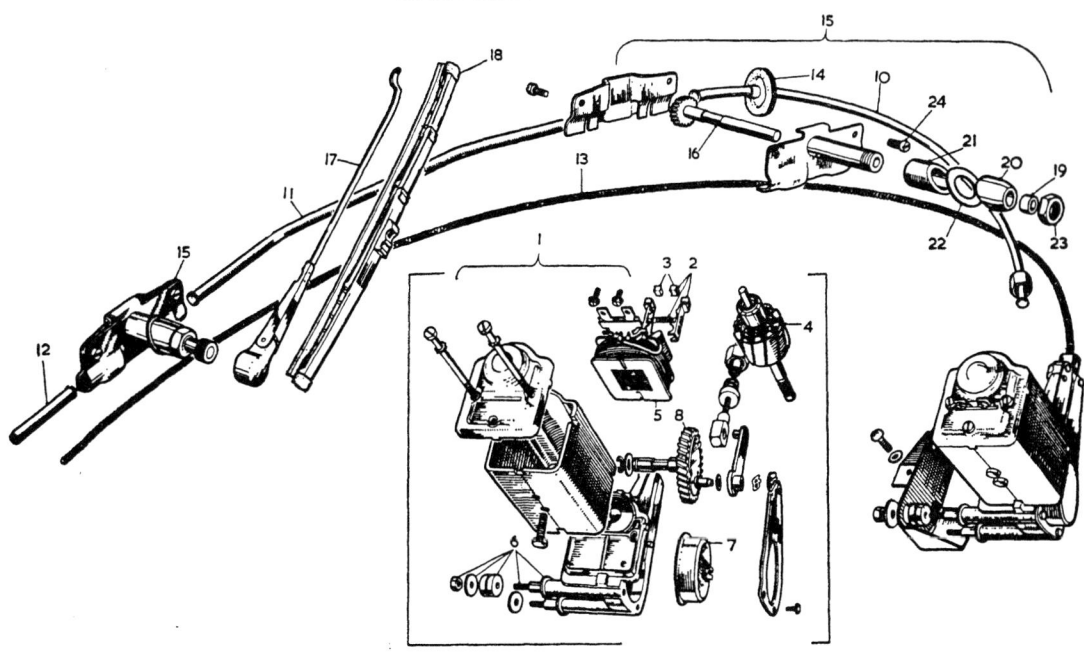

Fig. 10:10. Exploded view of the complete windscreen wiper mechanism

1	Windshield wiper motor	7	Parking switch	13	Cross-head and rack assembly
2	Brush gear	8	Gear and shaft	14	Grommet
3	Brush	10	Motor to wheelbox outer casing	15	Wheelbox
4	Armature	11	Wheelbox to wheelbox outer	16	Spindle and gear
5	Field coil		casing	17	Wiper arm
6	Fixing parts	12	Wheelbox extension outer casing	18	Wiper blade

19	Rubber tube spindle
20	Front bush
21	Rear bush
22	Rubber washer
23	Nut
24	Cover screw

WINDSCREEN WIPER MOTOR, GEARBOX, & WHEELBOX REMOVAL & REPLACEMENT

1. Remove the windscreen wiper arms by lifting the blades, carefully raising the retaining clip and then pulling the arms off the splined drive shafts.

2. Disconnect the electrical cables from the wiper motor and release the outer cable from the gearbox housing.

3. Unscrew and remove the three nuts and spring washers which hold the wiper motor in position and lift off the motor complete with cable rack.

4. The windscreen wiper arm wheelboxes are located immediately underneath the splined drive shafts over which the wiper arms fit. To remove these wheelboxes release the cable rack outer casings by slackening the wheelbox cover screws. Remove the external nut, bush, and washer from the base of the splines and pull out the wheelboxes from under the fascia.

5. Replacement is a straight reversal of the above sequence but take care that the cable rack emerges properly and that the wheelboxes are correctly lined up.

HORN - FAULT TRACING & RECTIFICATION

If the horn works badly or fails completely, check the wiring leading to it for short circuits and loose connections. Check that the horn is firmly secured and that there is nothing lying on the horn body.

If the fault is not an external one remove the horn cover and check the leads inside the horn. If these are sound, check the contact breaker contacts. If these are burnt or dirty, clean them with a fine file and wipe all traces of dirt and dust away with a petrol moistened rag. Test the current consumption of the horn which should be between 3 and $3\frac{1}{2}$ amps.

ELECTRICAL SYSTEM
FAULT FINDING CHART

Cause	Trouble	Remedy
SYMPTOM:	STARTER MOTOR FAILS TO TURN ENGINE	
No electricity at starter motor	Battery discharged	Charge battery.
	Battery defective internally	Fit new battery.
	Battery terminal leads loose or earth lead not securely attached to body	Check and tighten leads.
	Loose or broken connections in starter motor circuit	Check all connections and tighten any that are loose.
	Starter motor switch or solenoid faulty	Test and replace faulty components with new.
Electricity at starter motor: faulty motor	Starter motor pinion jammed in mesh with flywheel gear ring	Disengage pinion by turning squared end of armature shaft.
	Starter brushes badly worn, sticking, or brush wires loose	Examine brushes, replace as necessary, tighten down brush wires.
	Commutator dirty, worn, or burnt	Clean commutator, recut if badly burnt.
	Starter motor armature faulty	Overhaul starter motor, fit new armature.
	Field coils earthed	Overhaul starter motor.
SYMPTOM:	STARTER MOTOR TURNS ENGINE VERY SLOWLY	
Electrical defects	Battery in discharged condition	Charge battery.
	Starter brushes badly worn, sticking, or brush wires loose	Examine brushes, replace as necessary, tighten down brush wires.
	Loose wires in starter motor circuit	Check wiring and tighten as necessary.
SYMPTOM:	STARTER MOTOR OPERATES WITHOUT TURNING ENGINE	
Dirt or oil on drive gear	Starter motor pinion sticking on the screwed sleeve	Remove starter motor, clean starter motor drive.
Mechanical damage	Pinion or flywheel gear teeth broken or worn	Fit new gear ring to flywheel, and new pinion to starter motor drive.
SYMPTOMS:	STARTER MOTOR NOISY OR EXCESSIVELY ROUGH ENGAGEMENT	
Lack of attention or mechanical damage	Pinion or flywheel gear teeth broken or worn	Fit new gear teeth to flywheel, or new pinion to starter motor drive.
	Starter drive main spring broken	Dismantle and fit new main spring
	Starter motor retaining bolts loose	Tighten starter motor securing bolts. Fit new spring washer if necessary.
SYMPTOM:	BATTERY WILL NOT HOLD CHARGE FOR MORE THAN A FEW DAYS	
Wear or damage	Battery defective internally	Remove and fit new battery.
	Electrolyte level too low or electrolyte too weak due to leakage	Top up electrolyte level to just above plates
	Plate separators no longer fully effective	Remove and fit new battery.
	Battery plates severely sulphated	Remove and fit new battery.
Insufficient current flow to keep battery charged	Fan/dynamo belt slipping	Check belt for wear, replace if necessary, and tighten.
	Battery terminal connections loose or corroded	Check terminals for tightness, and remove all corrosion.
	Dynamo not charging properly	Remove and overhaul dynamo.
	Short in lighting circuit causing continual battery drain	Trace and rectify.
	Regulator unit not working correctly	Check setting, clean, and replace if defective.
SYMPTOM:	IGNITION LIGHT FAILS TO GO OUT, BATTERY RUNS FLAT IN A FEW DAYS	
Dynamo not charging	Fan belt loose and slipping, or broken	Check, replace, and tighten as necessary.
	Brushes worn, sticking, broken, or dirty	Examine, clean, or replace brushes as necessary.
	Brush springs weak or broken	Examine and test. Replace as necessary.
	Commutator dirty, greasy, worn, or burnt	Clean commutator and undercut segment separators.

	Armature badly worn or armature shaft bent	Fit new or reconditioned armature.
	Commutator bars shorting	Undercut segment separations.
	Dynamo bearings badly worn	Overhaul dynamo, fit new bearings.
	Dynamo field coils burnt, open, or shorted.	Remove and fit rebuilt dynamo.
	Commutator no longer circular	Recut commutator and undercut segment separators.
	Pole pieces very loose	Strip and overhaul dynamo. Tighten pole pieces.
Regulator or cut-out fails to work correctly	Regulator incorrectly set	Adjust regulator correctly.
	Cut-out incorrectly set	Adjust cut-out correctly.
	Open circuit in wiring of cut-out and regulator unit	Remove, examine, and renew as necessary.

Failure of individual electrical equipment to function correctly is dealt with alphabetically, item by item, under the headings listed below:

FUEL GAUGE

Fuel gauge gives no reading	Fuel tank empty!	Fill fuel tank.
	Electric cable between tank sender unit and gauge earthed or loose	Check cable for earthing and joints for tightness.
	Fuel gauge case not earthed	Ensure case is well earthed.
	Fuel gauge supply cable interrupted	Check and replace cable if necessary.
	Fuel gauge unit broken	Replace fuel gauge.
Fuel gauge registers full all the time	Electric cable between tank unit and gauge broken or disconnected	Check over cable and repair as necessary.

HORN

Horn operates all the time	Horn push either earthed or stuck down	Disconnect battery earth. Check and rectify source of trouble.
	Horn cable to horn push earthed	Disconnect battery earth. Check and rectify source of trouble.
Horn fails to operate	Blown fuse	Check and renew if broken. Ascertain cause.
	Cable or cable connection loose, broken or disconnected	Check all connections for tightness and cables for breaks.
	Horn has an internal fault	Remove and overhaul horn.
Horn emits intermittent or unsatisfactory noise	Cable connections loose	Check and tighten all connections.
	Horn incorrectly adjusted	Adjust horn until best note obtained.

LIGHTS

Lights do not come on	If engine not running, battery discharged	Push-start car, charge battery.
	Light bulb filament burnt out or bulbs broken	Test bulbs in live bulb holder.
	Wire connections loose, disconnected or broken	Check all connections for tightness and wire cable for breaks.
	Light switch shorting or otherwise faulty	By-pass light switch to ascertain if fault is in switch and fit new switch as appropriate.
Lights come on but fade out	If engine not running battery discharged	Push-start car, and charge battery.
Lights give very poor illumination	Lamp glasses dirty	Clean glasses.
	Reflector tarnished or dirty	Fit new reflectors.
	Lamps badly out of adjustment	Adjust lamps correctly.
	Incorrect bulb with too low wattage fitted	Remove bulb and replace with correct grade
	Existing bulbs old and badly discoloured	Renew bulb units.
	Electrical wiring too thin not allowing full current to pass	Rewire lighting system.

ELECTRICAL SYSTEM

Cause	Trouble	Remedy
Lights work erratically - flashing on and off, especially over bumps	Battery terminals or earth connection loose Lights not earthing properly Contacts in light switch faulty	Tighten battery terminals and earth connection. Examine and rectify. By-pass light switch to ascertain if fault is in switch and fit new switch as appropriate.
WIPERS		
Wiper motor fails to work	Blown fuse Wire connections loose, disconnected, or broken Brushes badly worn Armature worn or faulty Field coils faulty	Check and replace fuse if necessary. Check wiper wiring. Tighten loose connections. Remove and fit new brushes. If electricity at wiper motor remove and overhaul and fit replacement armature. Purchase reconditioned wiper motor.
Wiper motor works very slowly and takes excessive current	Commutator dirty, greasy, or burnt Drive to wheelboxes too bent or un-lubricated Wheelbox spindle binding or damaged Armature bearings dry or unaligned Armature badly worn or faulty	Clean commutator thoroughly. Examine drive and straighten out severe curvature. Lubricate. Remove, overhaul, or fit replacement. Replace with new bearings correctly aligned. Remove, overhaul, or fit replacement armature.
Wiper motor works slowly and takes little current	Brushes badly worn Commutator dirty, greasy, or burnt Armature badly worn or faulty	Remove and fit new brushes. Clean commutator thoroughly. Remove and overhaul armature or fit replacement.
Wiper motor works but wiper blades remain static	Driving cable rack disengaged or faulty Wheelbox gear and spindle damaged or worn Wiper motor gearbox parts badly worn	Examine and if faulty, replace. Examine and if faulty, replace. Overhaul or fit new gearbox.

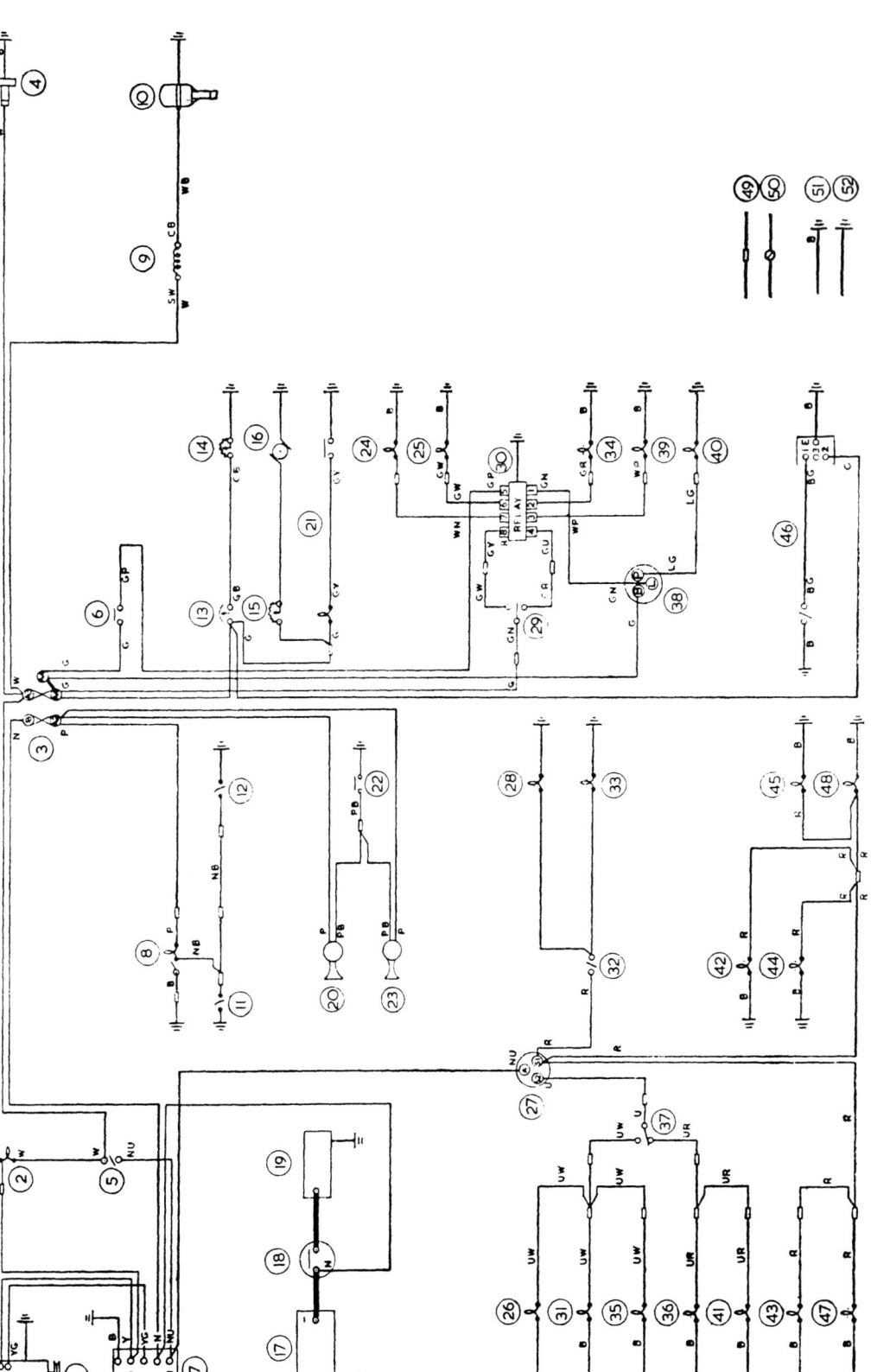

Fig. 10 : 11. Wiring diagram for early models with flashing indicator control. 1 Dynamo. 2 Ignition warning light. 3 Fuse unit. 4 Fuel pump. 5 Ignition switch. 6 Stop lamp **switch.** 7 Control box. 8 Interior light and switch (when fitted)—earthed to control box terminal 'E'. 9 Ignition coil. 10 Distributor. 11 Courtesy light switch (when fitted). 12 Courtesy light switch (when fitted). 13 Fuel gauge. 14 Fuel tank unit. 15 Heater rheostat (when fitted). 16 Heater (when fitted). 17 12-volt battery. 18 Starter switch. 19 Starter motor. 20 Horn. 21 Oil pressure warning light and switch. 22 Horn push. 23 Horn. 24 R.H. rear flasher and stop lamp. 25 R.H. front flasher. 26 Main beam warning light. 27 Lighting switch. 28 Panel light. 29 Flasher switch. 30 Relay. 31 R.H. headlight main beam. 32 Panel light switch. 33 Panel light. 34 L.H. front flasher. 35 L.H. headlight main beam. 36 R.H. headlight dip beam. 37 Dipper switch. 38 Flasher unit. 39 L.H. rear flasher and stop lamp. 40 Flasher warning light. 41 L.H. headlight dip beam. 42 R.H. tail lamp. 43 L.H. sidelamp. 44 L.H. tail lamp. 45 Number plate lamp. 46 Screen wiper switch and motor—earthed to control box terminal 'E'. 47 R.H. sidelamp. 48 Number plate lamp. 49 Snap connectors. 50 Terminal blocks or junction box. 51 Earth connections made via cable. 52 Earth connections made via fixing bolts.

CABLE COLOUR CODE

B Black	N Brown	P Purple	S Slate	Y Yellow	D Dark
U Blue	G Green	R Red	W White	L Light	M Medium

NOTE When a cable has two colour code letters the first denotes the main colour and the second denotes the tracer colour

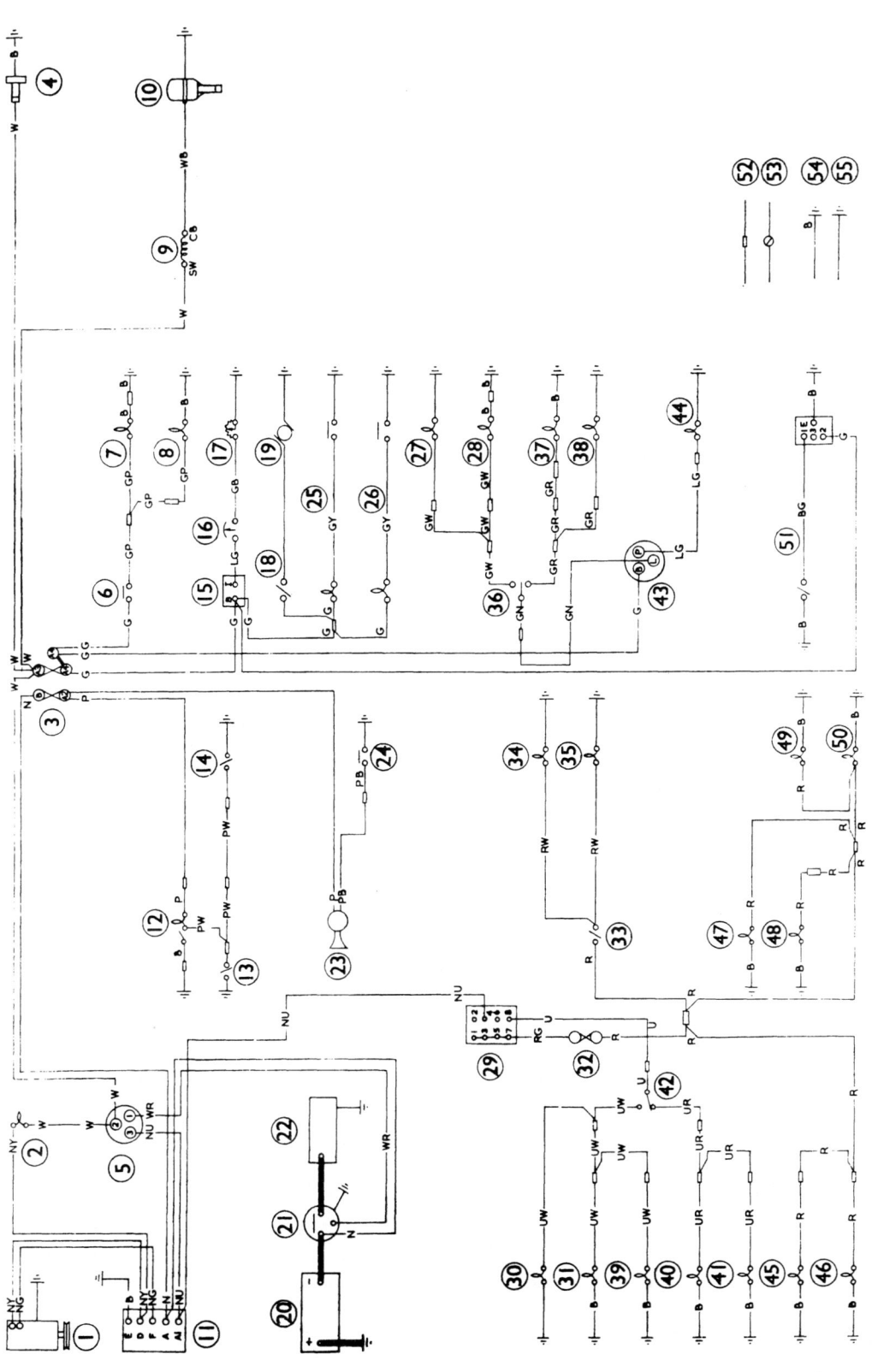

Fig. 10 : 12. Wiring diagram for later models with separate flashing equipment. 1 Dynamo. 2 Ignition warning light. 3 Fuse unit. 4 Fuel pump. 5 Ignition and starter switch. 6 Stop lamp switch. 7 R.H. stop lamp. 8 L.H. stop lamp. 9 Ignition coil. 10 Distributor. 11 Control box. 12 Interior light and switch (when fitted). 13 Courtesy light switch (when fitted). 14 Courtesy light switch (when fitted). 15 Instrument voltage stabiliser. 16 Fuel gauge. 17 Fuel tank unit. 18 Heater switch (when fitted). 19 Heater (when fitted). 20 12-volt battery. 21 Starter solenoid switch. 22 Starter motor. 23 Horn. 24 Horn push. 25 Oil filter warning light and switch. 26 Oil pressure warning light and switch. 27 R.H. front flasher. 28 R.H. rear flasher. 29 Lighting switch. 30 Main beam warning light. 31 R.H. headlamp main beam. 32 Line fuse (10 amp). 33 Panel light switch. 34 Panel light. 35 Panel light. 36 L.H. rear flasher. 38 L.H. front flasher. 39 L.H. headlamp main beam. 40 R.H. headlamp dip beam. 41 L.H. headlamp dip beam. 42 Dipper switch. 43 Flasher unit. 44 Flasher warning light. 45 L.H. pilot lamp. 46 R.H. pilot lamp. 47 R.H. tail lamp. 48 L.H. tail lamp. 49 Number plate lamp. 50 Number plate lamp. 51 Windscreen wiper switch and motor—earthed to control box terminal 'E'. 52 Snap connectors. 53 Terminal blocks or junction box. 54 Earth connections made via cable. 55 Earth connections made via fixing bolts.

NOTE Twin number plate lamps fitted to Traveller models only

CABLE COLOUR CODE

B Black	N Brown	P Purple	S Slate	Y Yellow	L Light
U Blue	G Green	R Red	W White	D Dark	M Medium

NOTE When a cable has two colour code letters the first denotes the main colour and the second denotes the tracer colour

143

CHAPTER ELEVEN

SUSPENSION – DAMPERS – STEERING

SPECIFICATION

FRONT SUSPENSION & STEERING

Camber	Nil (1° on models with rubber top link bushes).
Castor angle	.. .. 3°.
King pin inclination	8½° (7½° on models with rubber top link bushes).
Turns of steering wheel — lock to lock	.. .. 2.6.
Track	.. ..50⅝ in. (1.284 m.).
Turning circle	.. .. R. H. 33 ft. 1 in. (10.09 m.).
	.. .. L. H. 32 ft. 11 in. (10.04 m.).
Wheelbase	.. ..86 in. (218.44 cm.).
Ground clearance	.. .. 6¾ in. (17 cm.).
Tyre size	.. .. 5.00/5.20 — 14.
Tyre pressures: (Normal with two passengers	.. .. .. Front: 22 lb./sq.in. (1.6 kg./cm.²).
(	.. .. Rear: 22 lb./sq.in. (1.6 kg./cm.²).
(Fully loaded with four passengers and ..	.. Front: 22 lb./sq.in. (1.6 kg./cm.²).
(luggage	.. Rear: 24 lb./sq.in. (1.7 kg./cm.²).

SPRINGS

Type: Front	.. .. Torsion bar.
Rear	.. .. Semi-elliptic.
Working load: Front	.. .. .. 462 lb. (209.5 kg.).
Rear	.. .. .. 440 lb. (199.6 kg.).
Length: Rear	.. .. 43.5 in. (110.5 cm.).
Width: Rear	.. .. 1½ in. (38.1 mm.).
Number of leaves: Rear	.. .. 7.
Thickness of leaves: Rear	.. ..⁷/32 in. (5.56 mm.).
Free camber: Rear .. .. 3.5 in. (88.9 mm.); models with second-type axle 4.125 in. (10.5 cm.).
Working camber: Rear .28 in. (7.1 mm.) negative; models with second-type axle .34 in. (8.6 mm.) positive.

HYDRAULIC DAMPERS

Type	.. .. Armstrong double-acting.

REAR SPRINGS (from Car No. 680464)

Number of leaves	.. .. .. 5.
Thickness of leaves	.. ¼ in. (6.35 mm.).
Free camber	.. 4.22 in. (10.72 cm.).
Working camber	.78 in. (19.84 mm.) positive

STEERING

Type	.. Rack and Pinion.
Ratios	.. 2.4 turns lock to lock.
Toe-in	..³/32 in. (2.5 mm.).

GENERAL DESCRIPTION

The independent front suspension is of the built-up lower wishbone, longitudinal torsion bar, and single upper link type. The rear axle is located by means of semi-elliptic springs with shackles at the rear, the front end being attached to the body by anchor pins. Rubber bushes are used extensively in the suspension front and rear.

The torsion bars are attached to the bodyframe and are adjustable so that the ride level of the car can be restored to normal as the springs or torsion bars settle.

Armstrong double acting lever-type hydraulic dampers are fitted front and rear, the levers on the front dampers acting as the upper links for the front suspension.

Rack and pinion steering is fitted which requires 2½ turns lock to lock for a 33 ft. turning circle.

The rear end of the helically toothed pinion protrudes from the rack housing and is splined and engages with the end of the steering column to which it is held by a clamp bolt.

Rotating the steering wheel turns the pinion which in turn moves the rack sideways in the required direction. Tie-rods at each end of the rack operate the steering levers via exposed and rubber gaitered ball joints. The steering gear is adjustable for back-lash and end float.

FRONT & REAR SUSPENSION - MAINTENANCE

The 6 nipples on the front suspension should be greased at intervals of 3,000 miles with a grease gun filled with Castrolease L.M. or similar. Grease nipples are located as follows:- One on each steering tie-rod outer ball joint (Total 2): One at the top and bottom of each stub axle assembly (Total 4): When lubricating the stub axle nipples jack the front of the car up to take the weight off the king pins.

The securing nuts on the rear spring 'U' bolts should be checked for tightness at intervals of 6,000 miles and the springs cleaned and wiped with an oily rag. Check for broken leaves, loose shackles, and worn shackle bushes at the same time.

FRONT & REAR DAMPERS - MAINTENANCE

At intervals of 6,000 miles thoroughly clean the area in the vicinity of the damper filler plug; unscrew the plug; and check the level of the hydraulic fluid which should be just below the filler plug threads. Replenish the dampers as necessary with 'Armstrong Super Thin Shock Absorber Oil', or if not available, any good quality mineral oil of S.A.E. 20/20 W specification.

In the case of the rear dampers, to do the job properly means removing the dampers, placing them upright in a vice, and working the damper arm up and down while filling them to remove all air bubbles.

At the same time check the tightness of the bolts which hold the damper units to the body frame, and if loose tighten to a torque of 25 to 30 lb./ft. Ensure the cheese-headed screws on the gear damper cover plates are kept well tightened down to ensure no leaks occur.

Fig. 11:1. Carefully clean round the damper filler orifice and top up at the recommended intervals

RACK & PINION STEERING - MAINTENANCE

The upward facing nipple on the left-hand side of the rack housing should be given 10 strokes with the grease gun filled, not with grease, but with

Fig. 11:2. The rear dampers should be removed and held vertical during the topping-up process

Castrol Hypoy or any extreme pressure E.P. 90 oil, at intervals of 12,000 miles. Check the rubber gaiters for damage and leaks and keep the securing clips tight. As the inner ball joints are enclosed within the gaiters the oil in the steering housing lubricates them without the need for lubricating nipples as on the outer ball joints. Your local B.M.C. agent should check the toe-in at intervals of 6,000 miles.

To get at the rack and pinion lubricating nipple, pull back the toeboard carpet on the passenger's side and remove the rubber plug which normally seals the nipple access hole in the toeboard.

INSPECTING THE SUSPENSION, STEERING, & DAMPERS FOR WEAR

To check for wear in the outer ball joints of the tie-rods place the car over a pit, or lie on the ground looking at the ball joints, and get a friend to rock the steering wheel from side to side. Wear is present if there is play in the joints.

To check for wear in the rubber and metal bushes jack up the front of the car until the wheels are clear of the ground. Hold each wheel in turn, at the top and bottom and try to rock it. If the wheel rocks continue the movement at the same time inspecting the upper trunnion link rubber bushes, and the rubber bushes at the inner ends of the wishbone and wish-bone tie-bar for play.

If the wheel rocks and there is no side movement in the rubber bushes then the king pins and metal bushes will be worn. Alternatively, if the movement occurs between the wheel and the brake backplate, then the hub bearings require replacement. The rubber bushes can be renewed by the owner.

Sideplay or vertical or horizontal movement of the upper link or damper arm relative to the damper body is best checked with the outer end of the damper arm freed from the upper trunnion link. If play is present the damper bearings are worn and a replacement damper should be purchased. How well the dampers function can be checked by bouncing the car at each corner. After each bounce the car should return to its normal ride position within 1 to 1¼ up-and-down movements. If the car continues to move up-and-down in decreasing amounts it means that either the shock absorbers require topping up, or, if they are already full, that the dampers are worn and must be replaced.

The dampers cannot be adjusted without special tools and must therefore not be dismantled but exchanged with your local B. M. C. agent for replacement units.

Excessive play in the steering gear will lead to wheel wobble, and can be confirmed by checking if there is any lost movement between the end of the steering column and the rack. Rack and pinion steering is normally very accurate and lost motion in the steering gear indicates a considerable mileage or lack of lubrication.

The outer ball joints at either end of the tie-rods are the most likely items to wear first, followed by the rack ball joints at the inner end of the tie-rods.

TORSION BAR ADJUSTMENT

If it can be seen that one side of the car has dropped slightly, (e.g. If the car is frequently driven with only the driver in it, the bar on the right-hand side will probably settle more than the bar on the left), normal ride height can be restored by adjusting the lever on the end of the torsion bar in relation to the adjuster plate which covers a vertical slot in the chassis. In extreme cases the lever is removed from the end of the torsion bar and replacing the former one spline down on the torsion bar will raise the car approximately $1\frac{1}{2}$ in. The correct height setting can be found with the car standing on perfectly level ground by measuring the distance of the fulcrum pin (53) on the outer end of the wishbone arm vertically to the ground, and then measuring the distance of the inner fulcrum pin (49) vertically to the ground. The difference between these two measurements should be $1\frac{5}{8}$ in. (4.1 cm.).

The torsion bars are adjusted by following the procedure given below. All numbers in brackets refer to Fig. 11:4.

1. Remove the hub cap on the side on which the torsion bar is to be adjusted, slacken the road wheel nuts, jack up the front of the car by the body, and remove the road wheel. Place a support under the body, remove the jack and place it under the outer end of the rear built-up wishbone arm (43). Raise the jack until the underside of the damper arm is $\frac{1}{4}$ in. clear of the rubber rebound stop.

2. Unscrew the nut, bolt, and washer (69, 70, 71), which holds the end of the wishbone tie-bar (61) to the wishbone fork (65) and pull the tie-bar (61) clear.

3. Remove the nuts and washers (52, 50, 57, 56, 66, 67) holding the front wishbone arm (42) to the rear wishbone arm (43) and remove the front arm.

4. Remove the lower link fulcrum pin (53) from the lower link (8) and lower the jack under the wishbone arm until the torsion bar spring is fully extended.

5. Loosen the nut and washer (76, 77) at the rear of the torsion bar (72).

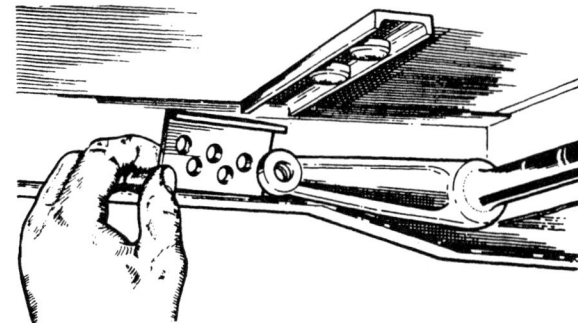

Fig. 11:3. The graduated holes in the adjuster plate cover the slot in the chassis for torsion bar adjustment

6. Remove the bolt (79) holding the end of the torsion bar lever (73) to the adjuster plate (78), the bolt also passing through the slot in the chassis, after noting in which hole in the plate the bolt was inserted.

7. Each successive lower hole in the adjuster plate (which is moved sideways so that the various holes line up with the slot in the chassis) raises the car $\frac{1}{4}$ in. and each higher hole in the adjuster plate lowers it $\frac{1}{4}$ in.

8. To obtain the desired alteration in height move the adjuster plate so the correct hole is in line with the slot in the chassis and insert the bolt into the slot and adjuster plate hole. Ensure the washer (80) is located between the adjuster plate and the torsion bar lever (73), replace the spring washer (81) and do up the nut (82). If there are insufficient holes left in the adjuster plate to raise the car the required amount, then slide the lever (73) forward off the splines on the torsion bar, and turn the lever down the required amount, remembering that each spline represents $1\frac{1}{2}$ in. of increase in body height.

9. Reassembly is now a straight reversal of the removal procedure.

TORSION BAR - REMOVAL & REPLACEMENT

1. Carry out the procedure detailed in paras. 1 to 6 in the previous section.

2. Screw the nut (76) off the end of the torsion bar (72) and remove the washer (77).

3. Slide the torsion bar lever (73) forward off the splines on the torsion bar (72) and pull off the washers (74, 75).

4. Pull off the forward splined end of the torsion bar from the splines in the wishbone arm (43) and lower the lever to the ground.

5. Replacement is a straight reversal of this process. NOTE Ensure on reassembly that the bevel on the slotted retaining washer (74) faces the torsion bar lever (73) and that the shoulder on the lever locating washer (75) fits into the hole on the chassis frame.

REAR SEMI-ELLIPTIC SPRINGS - REMOVAL & REPLACEMENT

1. Remove the wheel cap, loosen the wheel nuts, and jack up the side of the car from which the spring is to be removed.

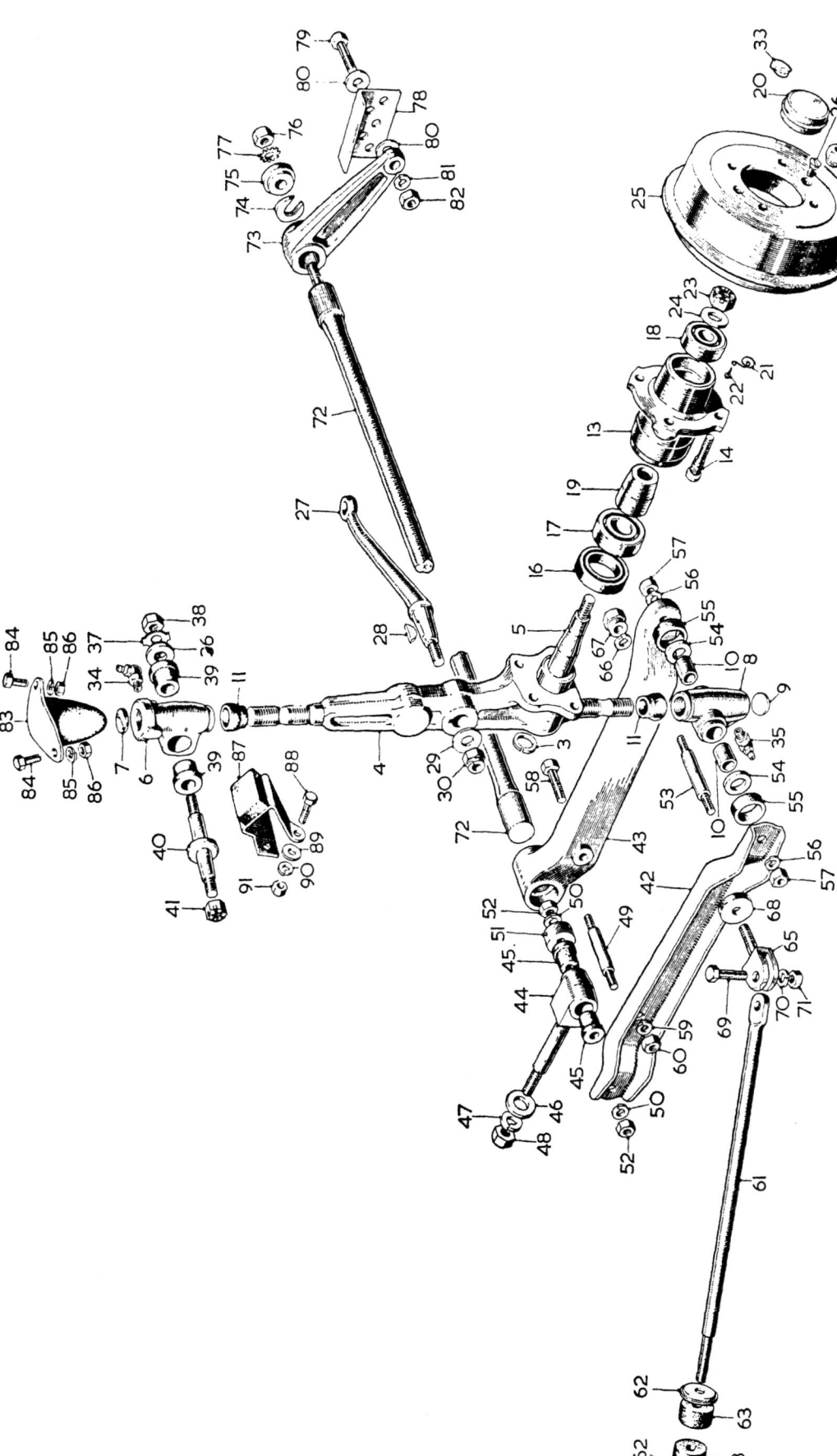

Fig. 11 : 4. Exploded view of the Morris Minor 1000 front suspension. 3 Circlip. 4 King pin and stub axle—L.H. 5 Stub axle—L. H. 6 Upper link. 7 Plug. 8 Lower link—L.H. 9 Plug. 10 Bush. 11 Seal (rubber). 13 Hub assembly. 14 Wheel nut. 15 Nut for wheel stud. 16 Hub oil seal. 17 Inner bearing. 18 Outer bearing. 19 Bearing distance piece. 20 Cap. 21 Spring —anti-static (when radio is fitted). 22 Screw for spring (when radio is fitted). 23 Nut—L. H. thread (to stub axle). 24 Washer for nut. 25 Brake drum. 26 Screw. 27 Steering arm— L.H. 28 Key—to swivel pin. 29 Washer for swivel pin. 30 Nut for swivel pin. 33 Dust seal—brake. 34 Lubricator for upper link. 35 Lubricator for lower link. 36 Washer for rear pivot. 37 Tab washer for rear pivot. 38 Nut for rear pivot. 39 Bush for upper link (rubber). 40 Damper arm pivot bolt. 41 Nut for front pivot. 42 Wishbone arm—front. 43 Wishbone arm—rear. 44 Eyebolt. 54 Bush for eyebolt (rubber). 46 Washer—eyebolt adjusting. 46 Lock washer—eyebolt to frame. 48 Nut—eyebolt to arms. 50 Spring washer for fulcrum pin. 51 Spigot pivot (rear). 52 Nut for fulcrum pin eyebolt. 53 Lower link fulcrum pin. 54 Thrust washer for link fulcrum pin. 55 Sealing ring for link fulcrum pin. 56 Spring washer for fulcrum pin nut. 57 Nut for link fulcrum pin. 58 Bolt—rear arm to front. 59 Spring washer for nut. 60 Nut for bolt. 61 Wishbone tie-bar. 62 Cup washer. 63 Bush to frame(rubber). 64 Slotted nut. 65 **Wishbone fork.** 66 Spring washer for nut. 67 Nut for fork. 68 **Washer for fork nut.** 69 Bolt—to fork. 70 Spring washer for nut. 71 Nut for bolt. 72 Torsion bar. 73 Torsion bar lever. 74 Washer—lever locating. 75 Washer—lever retaining. 76 Nut. 77 Washer for nut. 78 Adjuster plate. 79 Bolt—lever to frame. 80 **Washer for bolt.** 81 Spring washer for nut. 82 **Nut for bolt.** 83 **Bump rubber assembly.** 84 Screw to wheel arch. 85 Spring washer for nut. 86 Nut for screw. 87 Re- bound check bracket assembly. 88 **Screw—to wheel arch.** 89 Plain washer for screw. 90 Spring washer for nut. 1 Nut for screw.

2. Unscrew the wheel nuts and lift away the wheel.
3. Place a suitable support under the rear cross-body member as close to the rear of the spring as possible and remove the jack.
4. Reposition the jack under the axle casing close to the spring so that the rear axle is well supported, but the spring not compressed.
5. Unscrew the four lock nuts from the two inverted 'U' bolts.
6. Unscrew the rear shackle nuts and remove the shackle pins and plates.
7. Unscrew the nut and washer from the anchor pin in the front eye of the spring, drive the pin out and remove the spring.
8. If any of the shackles or the rubber bushes are worn they must be replaced together with the pins if they too show signs of wear. Replacement is a straight reversal of the dismantling process. Do not fully tighten the shackle pin nuts until the car has been lowered onto the ground and the spring is in its normal position. If this is not done the rubber bushes will require frequent replacement.

FRONT DAMPERS - REMOVAL & REPLACEMENT

1. Loosen the road wheel securing nuts on the side from which the damper is to be removed, apply the handbrake, and jack up the front of the car by the body.
2. Remove the road wheel, place a support under the body and remove the jack, place the jack under the outer end of the wishbone arm and raise the jack until the damper arm is clear of the rebound stop.
3. Pull out the split pin and unscrew the castellated nut (41) on the end of the damper arm pivot bolt (40).
4. Knock back the damper body lock washer retaining tags and remove the four bolts holding the damper to the chassis frame.
5. Tap the damper arm forwards off the tapered pivot bolt (40) and remove the damper.
6. Replacement is a straight reversal of the removal process.

REAR DAMPERS - REMOVAL & REPLACEMENT

It is not necessary to jack up the rear of the car for removal of the rear dampers if a pit or ramp is available. Otherwise jack up, and firmly support the rear of the car.

1. To remove a damper unscrew the nut and spring washer from the bolt which holds the damper arm to the link arm; remove the two nuts and spring washers from the damper securing bolts and remove the bolts; thread the lever over the link arm bolt and so remove the damper.
2. Keep the damper upright to prevent air getting into the operating chamber. Reassembly is a straight reversal of the removal procedure.

FRONT HUBS - REMOVAL & REPLACEMENT

The front hubs are not adjustable and if wear is detected (play between the road wheel and backplate) the hubs will have to be removed and new bearings

fitted. A hub extractor is required for this job and your local B.M.C. garage will probably be willing to lend or hire you one.

1. Slacken the road wheel nuts, jack up the car, and remove the road wheel.
2. Unscrew the brake drum retaining screws and pull off the brake drum.
3. Lever off the hub cap, extract the split pin, and unscrew and remove the castellated nut and locating washer.
4. Use a hub extractor to pull the complete hub assembly off the stub axle. If the inner bearing remains on the stub axle shaft it must be pulled off with a hub bearing remover. Frequently, the inner race of the inner bearing is left in position and if this occurs it is in the long run easiest to remove the brake backplate on drum braked cars to ease the removal of the race.
5. Carefully tap out the distance piece and outer bearing with a suitable drift, and then drift out the inner bearing and oil seal from the inside of the hub. The hub is now completely dismantled.
6. Replacement is a direct reversal of the removal sequence but the following points should be noted:
   a) The bearings and the space between them must be lubricated with Castrolease L.M. grease or similar.
   b) The sides marked 'thrust' on the inner and outer bearings must face towards the bearing distance piece.
   c) The oil seal lip should face the inner bearing.
   d) The castellated nut should be tightened to 55 to 65 lb./ft.
   e) Wipe away excess grease and half-fill the hub retaining cap.

OUTER BALL JOINT - REMOVAL & REPLACEMENT

If the tie-rod outer ball joints are worn it will be necessary to renew the whole ball joint assembly as they cannot be dismantled and repaired. To remove a ball joint, free the ball joint shank from the steering arm and mark the position of the lock nut on the tie-rod accurately to ensure near-accurate toe-in on reassembly.

Slacken off the ball joint lock nut, and holding the tie-rod by its flat with a spanner, to prevent it from turning, unscrew the complete ball assembly from the rod. Replacement is a straight reversal of this process. Visit your local B.M.C. agent to ensure that toe-in is correct.

FRONT SUSPENSION STUB AXLE & KING PIN - REMOVAL & REPLACEMENT

1. Carry out the procedure detailed in paras. 1 to 4 of the section headed 'Torsion Bar Adjustment' on page 146.
2. Disconnect the flexible hydraulic pipe from the brake backplate as detailed on page 119.
3. Remove the split pin from the castellated nut on the tie-rod to steering arm ball joint and unscrew the nut three turns. Hit the head of the nut with a soft-faced hammer to drive the shank of the ball joint out of the steering arm

(31). Remove the nut and pull the tie-rod away.

4. To disconnect the upper link (6) from the damper arm, release the tab washer (37), and unscrew the rear pivot nut (38). Remove the castellated nut (41) and drive the damper arm pivot bolt (40) from the damper arm.

5. Replacement is a straight reversal of the removal sequence but the following two additional points should be followed on early models. On late models with rubber bushed upper links paras. 6 and 7 do not apply. See para. 7 of the section headed 'Stub Axle & King Pin Dismantling & Reassembly' below.

6. Check that the lower and upper links (6, 8) which screw onto each end of the king pin (4) are so screwed on that the pivot bolts have maximum clearance on each side in the waisted portion of the king pin. To achieve this, line up the king pin recess with the hole in the link, insert the bolt, and screw the link as far as it will turn in each direction which will be between 2 and 3 turns. When the extent of the travel with the bolt fitted is known turn the link to the middle position. This will give maximum clearance.

7. Plain type pivot bolts must have an end clearance on reassembly of .002 in. (.05 mm.) which is measured with a feeler gauge between the damper arm and the link. Adjustment is made by tightening or loosening the large 9/16 in. nut a flat at a time. Ensure the link is firmly against the nut to ensure that the reading between the damper arm and the link is correct.

STUB AXLE & KING PIN - DISMANTLING, INSPECTION, & REASSEMBLY

Remove the stub axle assembly from the car as detailed in the previous section and then proceed as follows:-

1. Remove the rubber bushes (39), washers (54), sealing rings (55), and the lower link bushes (10) from the upper and lower links.

2. Unscrew the top and bottom links (6, 8) from the king pin (4), noting that the left-hand king pin has a left-hand thread.

3. Check the rubber bushes and sealing rings for wear, distortion, or damage. Examine the top link and the top link pin for wear. Examine the faces of the lower washers (54) which should be flat and parallel. If any of these items are suspect they must be replaced.

4. Examine the threads of the links for wear and renew them if there is excessive slackness when fitted to the king pin.

5. If the threads at either end of the king pin are worn, remove the hub (see page 148 for details) and the brake backplate by unscrewing the four retaining bolts.

6. Take the king pin to your local Morris agent who will be able to recut the thread .015 in. (.38 mm.) undersize using the special B.M.C. die nut (Part No. 18G 305A) and to supply new undersize bushes which are painted yellow and have the following part numbers:-

Right-Hand Upper King Pin Link	AJA 4005
Right-Hand Lower King Pin Link	AJA 4009
Left-Hand Upper King Pin Link	AJA 4006
Left-Hand Lower King Pin Link	AJA 4010

7. Reassembly is a straight reversal of this process. NOTE That when refitting upper links which are rubber bushed the link should be screwed into the king pin as far as it will go and then turned back one turn so the lug faces towards the engine. The pivot pin rubber bush retaining nut (38) should not be finally tightened until the front wheels are resting on the ground to prevent excess wear in the bush.

FRONT WHEEL ALIGNMENT

The front wheels are correctly aligned when they turn in at the front 0 to 1/8 in. (0 to 3mm.). (Optimum setting 3/32 in. (2.5 mm.). Adjustment is effected by loosening the lock nut on each tie-rod ball joint, and the clips on the gaiters, and turning both tie-rods equally until the adjustment is correct.

This is a job that your local B.M.C. Agent must do, as accurate alignment requires the use of expensive base bar or optical alignment equipment.

If the wheels are not in alignment, tyre wear will be heavy and uneven, and the steering will be stiff and unresponsive.

STEERING WHEEL - REMOVAL & REPLACEMENT

Unscrew the small screw from the side of the steering wheel boss where this is fitted, and prise off the motif cap from the centre of the steering wheel with a small screwdriver. With a suitable socket spanner, unscrew the nut which retains the wheel to the steering column.

Remove the nut, and on later models the retaining washer under it, and pull the wheel off the splines on the column. Replacement is a simple reversal of this process.

STEERING COLUMN BUSH - RENEWAL

If there is any play in the steering column in a vertical direction this is invariably due to a worn felt bush which is fitted between the top of the inner and outer steering columns. The bush is replaced after removing the steering wheel and prising the old bush out. The new bush should be soaked in heavy oil and slid into place.

STEERING COLUMN - REMOVAL & REPLACEMENT

1. Disconnect the battery by removing the lead from the positive terminal.

2. Disconnect the wires from the horn and direction indicators at their snap connectors under the fascia.

3. Remove the steering wheel as detailed previously.

4. Unscrew the two domed nuts and remove the washers from the screws on the support bracket under the fascia. Take off the lower half of the bracket together with the screws and the padded strip.

5. On early models the horn and direction indicator switch can be removed after unscrewing the screw on the end of the direction indicator switch, and the nut, washer, and bolt holding the unit in place.

6. On later models the horn is actuated by the horn button in the centre of the steering wheel and the direction indicator switch is removed as follows. Unscrew the three chrome screws holding the indicator switch cover to the indicator unit and slide the cover off the end of the steering column. Unscrew two screws holding the switch clamp to the column and lift off the switch at the same time pulling the indicator wires through the grommetted hole in the fascia.

7. Remove the clamp bolt from the lower end of the steering column.

8. Pull the column away from the splines on the end of the steering gear pinion and lift the column out of the car.

9. Replacement is a straight reversal of this process but ensure the mark on the pinion spline is in line with the gap in the clamp bracket on the end of the column with the wheels in the straight-ahead position.

RACK & PINION BACKLASH - ADJUSTMENT

Backlash between the pinion and the rack can be taken up by means of an adjustment between the rack damper cap, and the rack housing. If backlash is present adjust the rack damper in the following manner. Numerical references in brackets refer to Fig. 11:3

1. Disconnect the outer ends of the steering tie-rods (19) by knocking out the tie-rod ball joint shanks from the holes in the steering arms.

2. Unscrew the damper cap (5) and remove the spring (4) and shims (6).

3. Refit the damper cap together with the plunger (3), but without the spring (4) and the shims (6).

4. Tighten the damper cap until it requires about a 3 oz. pull at the steering wheel rim to turn the wheel.

5. Measure the gap between the underside of the damper cap and the rack housing with a feeler gauge, and add to this figure a clearance figure of .002 to .005 in. (.05 to .127 mm.). The total figure represents the thickness of the shims that must be fitted under the cap. Shims are available in thicknesses of .003 in. and .010 in. (.76 and .254 mm.).

6. Remove the cap, replace the spring, fit the necessary shims and tighten the cap down firmly. Reconnect the tie-rod ball joints to the steering arms and note the improvement when the car is taken on the road.

PINION END FLOAT - ADJUSTMENT

1. Disconnect the outer ends of the steering tie-rods (19) from the steering arms by driving out the tie-rod ball joint shanks from the holes in the arms.

2. Remove the bolt (60) at the splined lower end of

the steering column, and free the column from the splines on the pinion.

3. Unscrew the bolts (14) retaining the pinion housing (12) in place and remove the shims (13). Remove the housing and bolt it down without the shims so there is no pinion end float.

4. Measure the gap between the pinion housing and the rack housing with a feeler gauge and add to this figure between .002 to .005 in. (.05 to .13 mm.). The total figure represents the thickness of the shims that must be fitted between the pinion and rack housings. Shims are available in thicknesses of .003, .005, and .010 in. (.76, .13, and .254 in.).

RACK & PINION STEERING GEAR - REMOVAL & REPLACEMENT

1. Unscrew the nut and remove the bolt from the clamp on the lower end of the steering column.

2. Slacken the two bolts which hold the steering column bracket cap in place and pull back the column from the spline on the steering gear pinion.

3. Remove the split pin from the castellated nut on top of each of the two tie-rod to steering arm ball joints and unscrew the nuts three turns. Hit the head of the nut with a soft-faced hammer to drive the shank of the ball joint out of the steering arm. Remove the nut and pull the tie-rods complete with ball joints, away.

4. Lift the rack and pinion out of the car. Replacement is a straight reversal of this process but do not tighten the rack housing bolts until the column clamp bolt is tightened. Take the car to your local B.M.C. Agent to have the toe-in checked.

RACK & PINION - DISMANTLING & REASSEMBLY

1. Mark the position of the lock nuts (30) on the tie-rods (19) so the toe-in is approximately correct on reassembly.

2. Release the lock nuts (30) and screw off the ball joints.

3. Unscrew the clips (33, 34) holding the rubber gaiters (32) to the rack housing (1) and tie-rods, drain the oil from the housing and remove the gaiters.

4. Unscrew and remove the damper cap (5), spring (4), plunger (3), and shim (6).

5. Unscrew and remove the secondary damper cap (9), spring (8), plunger (7), and washer (10).

6. Unscrew and remove the two bolts (14), from the pinion housing (12), and remove the housing shims (13), pinion (11), and bottom thrust washer (17).

7. Each inner tie-rod ball joint is locked to a slot in the end of the rack (2) by means of tabs on a lock washer (31) and also in three places to the ball housing. Prise out these tabs to free the tie-rod ball joint housing.

8. Unscrew the ball joints from the rack with a mole wrench or the special B.M.C. tie-rod 'C'

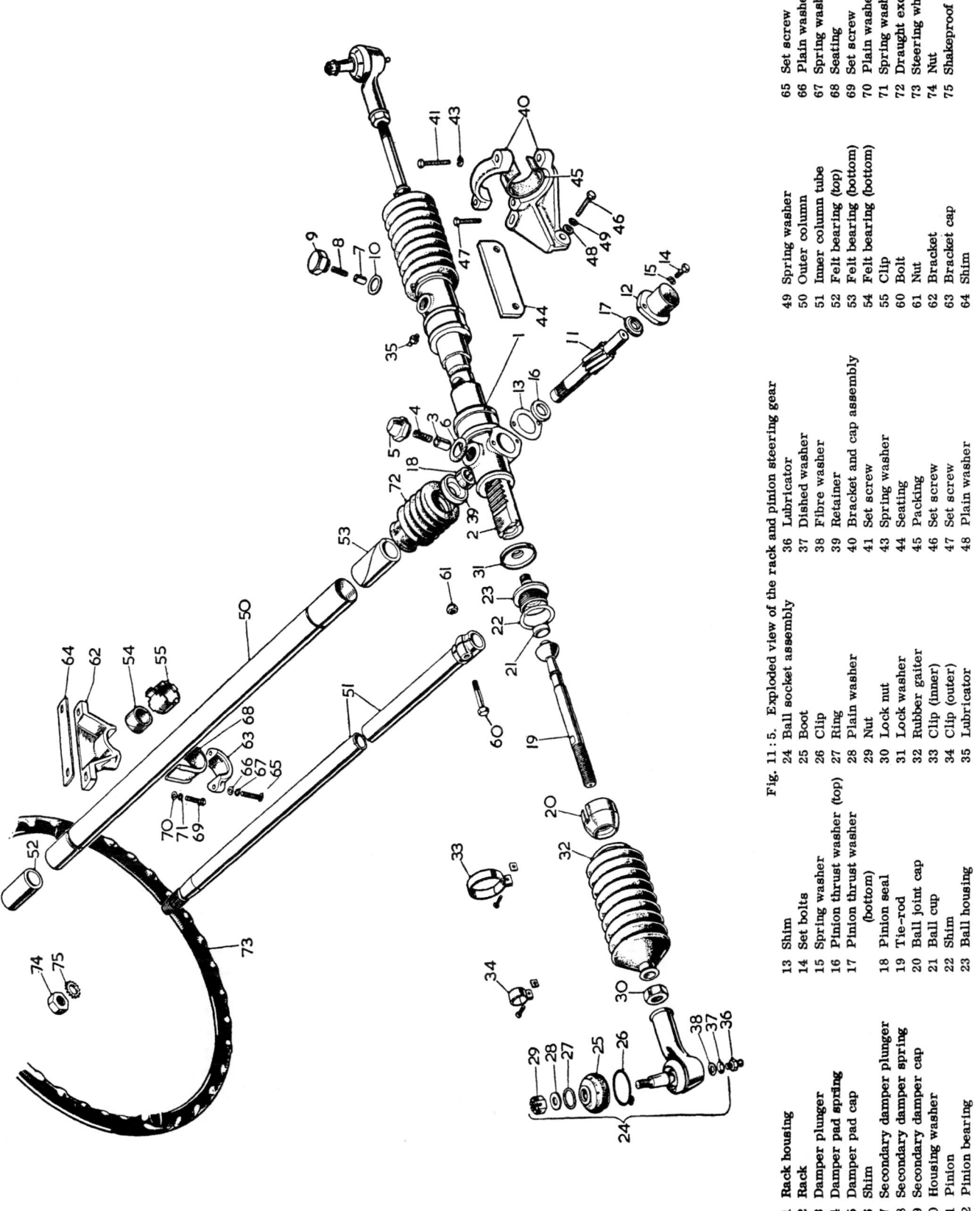

Fig. 11 : 5.   Exploded view of the rack and pinion steering gear

1 Rack housing	24 Ball socket assembly	49 Spring washer	65 Set screw
2 Rack	25 Boot	50 Outer column	66 Plain washer
3 Damper plunger	26 Clip	51 Inner column tube	67 Spring washer
4 Damper pad spring	27 Ring	52 Felt bearing (top)	68 Seating
5 Damper pad cap	28 Plain washer	53 Felt bearing (bottom)	69 Set screw
6 Shim	29 Nut	54 Felt bearing (bottom)	70 Plain washer
7 Secondary damper plunger	30 Lock nut	55 Clip	71 Spring washer
8 Secondary damper spring	31 Lock washer	60 Bolt	72 Draught excluder
9 Secondary damper cap	32 Rubber gaiter	61 Nut	73 Steering wheel
10 Housing washer	33 Clip (inner)	62 Bracket	74 Nut
11 Pinion	34 Clip (outer)	63 Bracket cap	75 Shakeproof washer
12 Pinion bearing	35 Lubricator	64 Shim	
13 Shim	36 Lubricator		
14 Set bolts	37 Dished washer		
15 Spring washer	38 Fibre washer		
16 Pinion thrust washer (top)	39 Retainer		
17 Pinion thrust washer (bottom)	40 Bracket and cap assembly		
18 Pinion seal	41 Set screw		
19 Tie-rod	43 Spring washer		
20 Ball joint cap	44 Seating		
21 Ball cup	45 Packing		
22 Shim	46 Set screw		
23 Ball housing	47 Set screw		
	48 Plain washer		

spanner if this can be borrowed. To examine the condition of the joints, unscrew the ball joint cap (20) from the ball housing (23). Ensure the shims (22) are kept with the correct joint.

9. Examine the condition of the ball on the end of the tie-rod (19), and the cup (21) which should be renewed if worn.

10. Remove the lock washers and extract the rack from the pinion end of the rack housing. Clean the rack and pinion and carefully examine the condition of the teeth. If they are worn, pitted, or chipped, new items should be fitted. Renew the rubber gaiters if they are cracked, split, or perished.

11. On reassembly, which is a straight reversal of the dismantling sequence, use new lock washers, adjust the backlash and end float as previously detailed, and check that the rack ball joints fit tightly but are free to move. If they are excessively loose or tight adjustment can be made by varying the thickness of the shims (22) between the ball joint cap (20) and the ball housing (23). The following sized shims are available .002, .003, .005, and .010 in. (.05, .076, .13, and .254 mm.).

12. After fitting the rack and pinion in place fill it with 10 fl. oz. of S.A.E.140 extreme pressure oil such as Castrol Hypoy.

FAULT FINDING CHART

Cause	Trouble	Remedy
SYMPTOM:	STEERING FEELS VAGUE, CAR WANDERS AND FLOATS AT SPEED	
General wear or damage	Tyre pressures uneven Dampers worn or require topping up Spring clips broken Steering gear ball joints badly worn Suspension geometry incorrect Steering mechanism free play excessive Front suspension and rear axle pick-up points out of alignment	Check pressures and adjust as necessary. Top up dampers, test, and replace if worn. Renew spring clips. Fit new ball joints. Check and rectify. Adjust or overhaul steering mechanism. Normally caused by poor repair work after a serious accident. Extensive rebuilding necessary.
SYMPTOM:	STIFF & HEAVY STEERING	
Lack of maintenance or accident damage	Tyre pressures too low No grease in king pins No oil in steering gear No grease in steering and suspension ball joints Front wheel toe-in incorrect Suspension geometry incorrect Steering gear incorrectly adjusted too tightly Steering column badly misaligned	Check pressures and inflate tyres. Clean king pin nipples and grease thoroughly. Top up steering gear. Clean nipples and grease thoroughly. Check and reset toe-in. Check and rectify. Check and readjust steering gear. Determine cause and rectify (Usually due to bad repair after severe accident damage and difficult to correct).
SYMPTOM:	WHEEL WOBBLE & VIBRATION	
General wear or damage	Wheel nuts loose Front wheels and tyres out of balance Steering ball joints badly worn Hub bearings badly worn Steering gear free play excessive Front springs loose, weak or broken	Check and tighten as necessary. Balance wheels and tyres and add weights as necessary. Replace steering gear ball joints. Remove and fit new hub bearings. Adjust and overhaul steering gear. Inspect and overhaul as necessary.

CHAPTER TWELVE

BODYWORK AND UNDERFRAME

MAINTENANCE - BODYWORK & UNDERFRAME

The condition of your car's bodywork is of considerable importance as it is on this that the second hand value of the car will mainly depend. It is very much more difficult to repair neglected bodywork than to renew mechanical assemblies. The hidden portions of the body, such as the wheel arches and the underframe and the engine compartment are equally important, though obviously not requiring such frequent attention as the immediately visible paintwork.

Once a year or every 12,000 miles, it is a sound scheme to visit your local main agent and have the underside of the body steam cleaned. This will take about 1½ hours and costs about £2. All traces of dirt and oil will be removed and the underside can then be inspected carefully for rust, damaged hydraulic pipes, frayed electrical wiring and similar maladies. The car should be greased on completion of this job.

At the same time the engine compartment should be cleaned in the same manner. If steam cleaning facilities are not available then brush 'Gunk' or a similar cleanser over the whole engine and engine compartment with a stiff paint brush, working it well in where there is an accumulation of oil and dirt. Do not paint the ignition system and protect it with oily rags when the Gunk is washed off. As the Gunk is washed away it will take with it all traces of oil and dirt, leaving the engine looking clean and bright.

The wheel arches should be given particular attention as undersealing can easily come away here and stones and dirt thrown up from the road wheels can soon cause the paint to chip and flake, and so allow rust to set in. If rust is found, clean down to the bare metal with wet and dry paper, paint on an anti-corrosive coating such as Kurust, or if preferred, red lead, and renew the paintwork and undercoating.

The bodywork should be washed once a week or when dirty. Thoroughly wet the car to soften the dirt and then wash the car down with a soft sponge and plenty of clean water. If the surplus dirt is not washed off very gently, in time it will wear the paint down as surely as wet and dry paper. It is best to use a hose if this is available. Give the car a final washdown and then dry with a soft chamois leather to prevent the formation of spots.

Spots of tar and grease thrown up from the road can be removed with a rag dampened with petrol.

Once every six months, or every three months if wished, give the bodywork and chromium trim a thoroughly good wax polish. If a chromium cleaner is used to remove rust on any of the car's plated parts remember that the cleaner also removes part of the chromium, so use sparingly.

MAINTENANCE - UPHOLSTERY & CARPETS

Remove the carpets and thoroughly vacuum clean the interior of the car every three months, or more frequently if necessary. Beat out the carpets and vacuum clean them if they are very dirty. If the headlining or upholstery is soiled apply an upholstery cleaner with a damp sponge and wipe off with a clean dry cloth.

MINOR BODY REPAIRS

At some time during your ownership of your car it is likely that it will be bumped or scraped in a mild way, causing some slight damage to the body. Major damage must be repaired by your local B.M.C. agent, but there is no reason why you cannot successfully beat out, repair, and respray minor damage yourself. The essential items which the owner should gather together to ensure a really professional job are:-

a) A plastic filler such as Holts 'Cataloy'.
b) Paint whose colour matches exactly that of the bodywork, either in a can for application by a spray gun, or in an aerosol can.
c) Fine cutting paste.
d) Medium and fine grade wet and dry paper.

Never use a metal hammer to knock out small dents as the blows tend to scratch and distort the metal. Knock out the dent with a mallet or rawhide hammer and press on the underside of the dented surface a metal dolly or smooth wooden block roughly contoured to the normal shape of the damaged area.

After the worst of the damaged area has been knocked out, rub down the dent and surrounding area with medium wet and dry paper and thoroughly clean away all traces of dirt.

The plastic filler comprises a paste and a hardener which must be thoroughly mixed together. Mix only a small portion at a time as the paste sets hard within five to fifteen minutes depending on the amount of hardener used.

Smooth on the filler with a knife or stiff plastic to the shape of the damaged portion and allow to thoroughly dry - a process which takes about six hours. After the filler has dried it is likely that it will have contracted slightly so spread on a second layer of filler if necessary.

Smooth down the filler with fine wet and dry paper wrapped round a suitable block of wood and continue until the whole area is perfectly smooth and it is impossible to feel where the filler joins the rest of the paintwork. Spray on from an aerosol can, or with a spray gun, an anti-rust undercoat, smooth down with wet and dry paper, and then spray on two coats of the final finishing using a circular motion. When thoroughly dry polish the whole area with a fine cutting paste to smooth the resprayed area into the remainder of the wing and to remove the small particles of spray paint which will have settled round the area. This will leave the wing looking perfect, with not a trace of the previous unsightly dent.

MAJOR BODY REPAIR

Because the body is built on the monocoque principle and is integral with the underframe, major damage must be repaired by competent mechanics with the necessary welding and hydraulic straightening equipment.

If the damage is serious it is vital that the bodyshell is in correct alignment, as otherwise the handling of the car will suffer and many other faults such as excessive tyre wear, and wear in the transmission and steering, may occur. The B.M.C. produce a special alignment jig and to ensure that all is correct a repaired car should be checked on this jig.

Alternatively, with the bodyshell jacked up off a level floor a series of measurement checks can be carried out to determine whether misalignment is present or not. Start by dropping a plumb line from the front and centre of each of the front suspension torsion bars to the floor, and mark the spot. Repeat this from the outside of the rear spring support members. Carefully determine the centre line by scribing two arcs on the floor between 'A' and 'D' as shown in Fig. 12:3.

HINGES & LOCKS - MAINTENANCE

Once every six months or 6,000 miles the door, bonnet, and boot hinges should be oiled with a few drops of engine oil from an oil can. The door striker plates can be given a thin smear of grease to reduce wear and ensure free movement.

BUMPERS - REMOVAL & REPLACEMENT

The front bumpers can be removed after undoing the two brackets which are held to the body frame by nuts, bolts, and spring washer. The bumper bar is held to each bracket by bolts, distance washers, spring washers and nuts. The rear bumpers are attached to the rear of the bodyframe in an identical fashion. Replacement is a straight reversal of this process.

WINDSCREEN - REMOVAL & REPLACEMENT

If it is wished to renew the sealing rubbers round the windscreen or to fit a new windscreen, first cover the bonnet with a thick blanket. The next step is to lift the wiper blades away from their splined spindle.

The weatherstrip surrounding the windscreen is attached to the body with the aid of adhesive. To break this joint run a knife round the windscreen between the body and the weatherstrip.

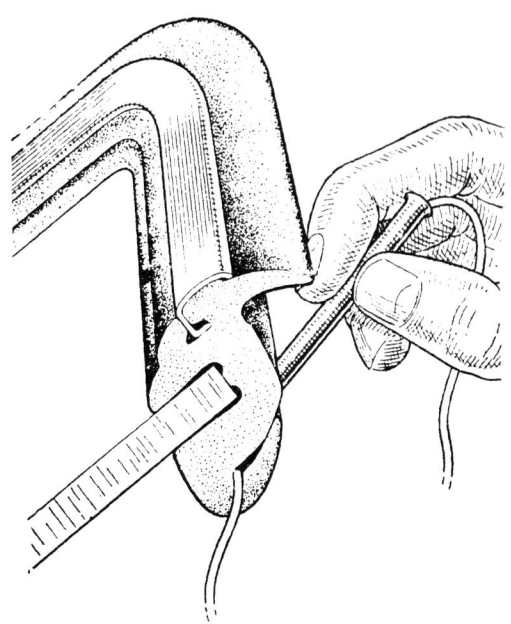

Fig. 12:1. A piece of brake piping is ideal for threading the cord into the body flange channel of the rubber seal

To force the weatherstrip away from the body frame, hit the inside top area of the glass smartly with the palm of your hand. Support the outside area of the glass at the same time. As soon as the weatherstrip has come away at one spot it is quite easy to work the remainder away from the body and to then remove it complete with the windscreen glass.

Replacement commences by fitting the windscreen glass to the inner channel of the weatherstrip. Start

Fig. 12:2. The four screws which, when loosened, allow the piston of the striker plate and pin socket to be altered

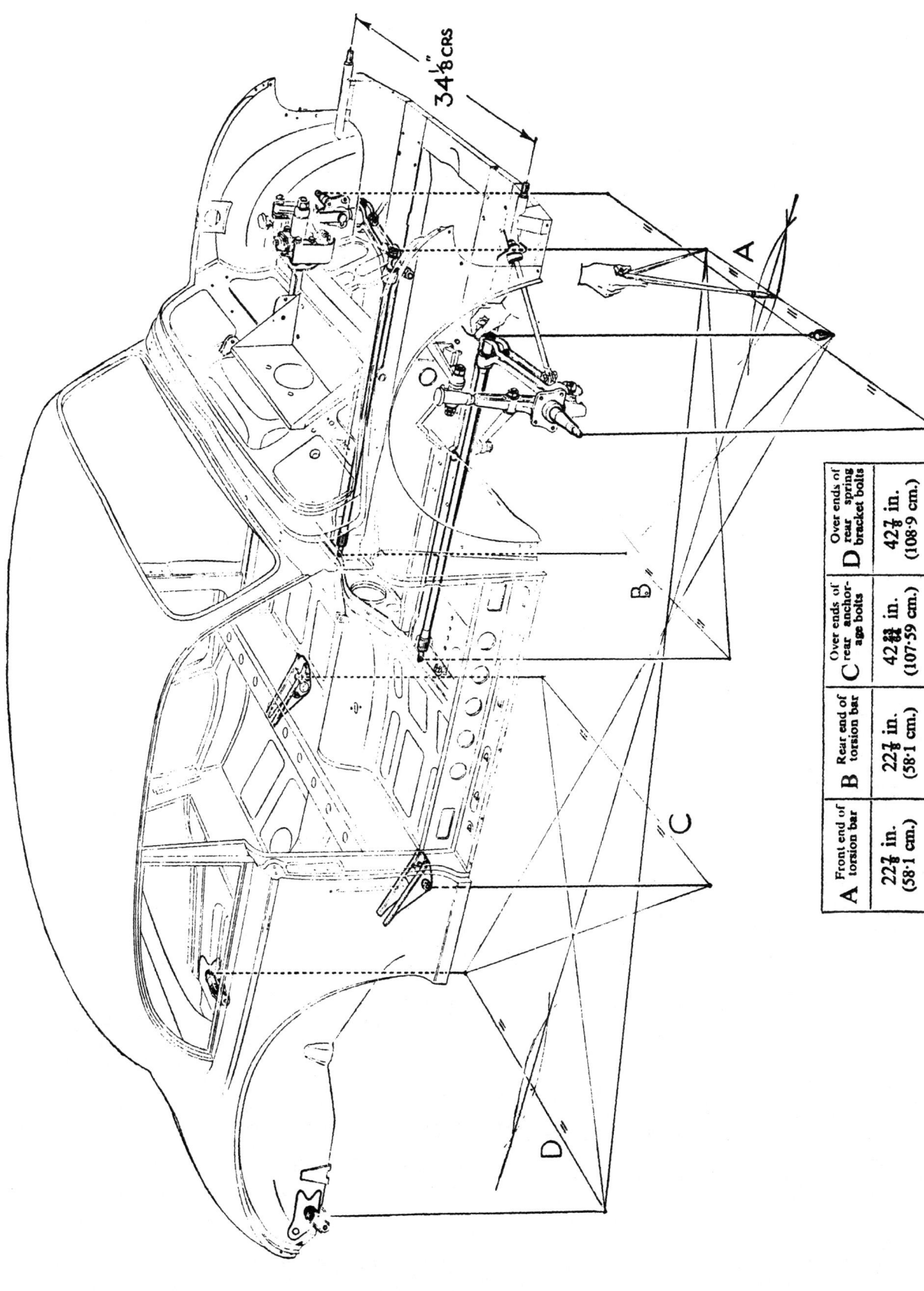

A Front end of torsion bar	**B** Rear end of torsion bar	**C** Over ends of rear anchorage bolts	**D** Over ends of rear spring bracket bolts
22⅞ in. (58·1 cm.)	22⅞ in. (58·1 cm.)	42¹⅜ in. (107·59 cm.)	42⅞ in. (108·9 cm.)

34⅛″CRS

Fig. 12:3. The Morris Minor can be checked for horizontal alignment by a system of diagonal measurement checks from points projected onto a level floor by means of a plumb-bob. Then establish a centre line with a large pair of compasses. Body distortion will show up if any of the diagonals fail to intersect on the centre line or if there are considerable differences in the same measurements from one side to another

at one end of the glass and carefully work the weatherstrip into position.

The next step is to thread two pieces of string round the outer channel of the weatherstrip. The windscreen complete with weatherstrip, is fitted to the body from outside the car. Press the windscreen and weatherstrip against the windscreen body frame. Pull out the string from the inside of the weatherstrip, and then from the outside. As the string is pulled away the rubber weatherstrip will peel over the windscreen body flange, so holding the windscreen firmly to the body.

With the windscreen properly in position coat a suitable adhesive between the weatherstrip rubber and the windscreen, and the weatherstrip rubber and the body on the outside of the car. This will seal the windscreen and ensure no leaks develop.

REAR WINDOW - REMOVAL & REPLACEMENT

The rear window is removed and replaced in a similar manner to the windscreen, but is taken out and refitted from inside rather than from the outside of the car. The other difference is that only one piece of string is used and this is pulled away outside the car while an assistant presses the glass in place from inside the car.

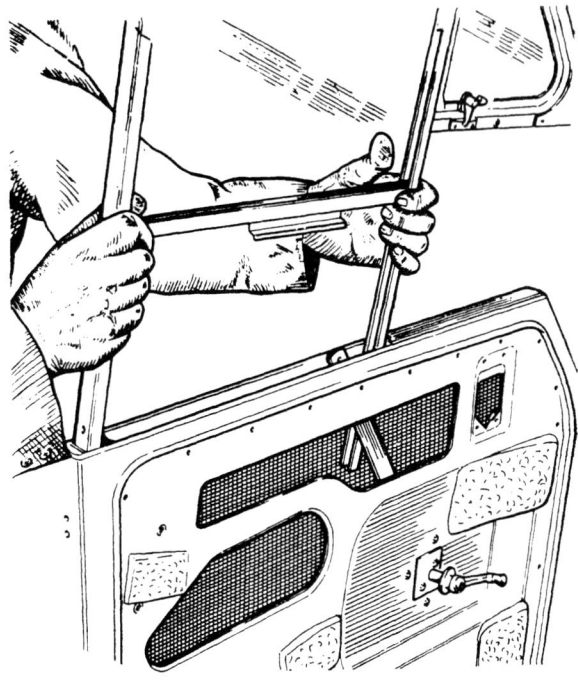

Fig. 12:5. The door window frame lifts out easily as shown

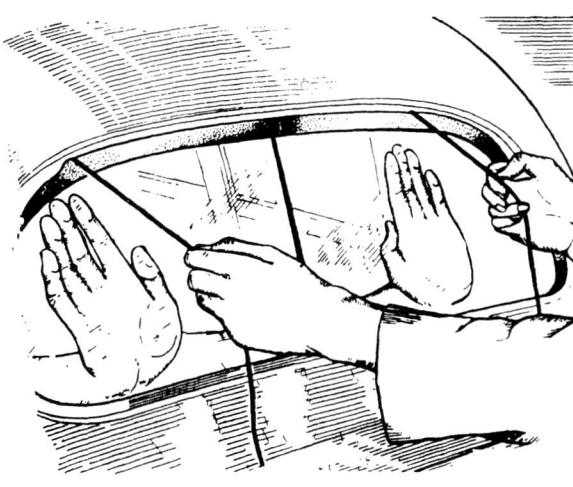

Fig. 12:4. The rear window is fitted from inside the car, a piece of string lifting the flange of the rubber seal into place as shown in the illustration

DOOR GLASS - REMOVAL & REPLACEMENT

First, remove the interior door handle and the window winding handle. Then carefully prise away the trim, with a screwdriver, from the door panel to which it is held by a number of spring clips. Pull away the rubber grommets located at the edge of the door and unscrew the three bolts which hold the door glass channel guide in place.

Unscrew the nut and bolt which holds the lower end of the glass channel guide to the door, and remove the two bolts from underneath the ventilator panel.

Wind up the window until it is possible to disengage the window winder arm from the lift channel. The window, complete with surround can then be lifted clear of the car, and the glass removed from the window frame.

Replacement is a straight reversal of the dismantling procedure. Make sure that the sealing rubber is placed underneath the ventilator frame when the frame and glass is replaced on the doors.

DOOR HANDLE & LOCK - REMOVAL & REPLACEMENT

Remove the door glass and surrounding frame as detailed in the previous section.

Pull out the split pin, spring, and the flat washer which hold the lock plunger to the remote control link. Undo and remove the three Phillips screws which hold the handle and lock in place, and lift out the assembly from the door.

On two-door models fitted with an interior safety catch pull out the spring clip and remove the door locking lever. When the handle and lock assembly has been removed it is most important that the locking lever and retaining spring clip are immediately replaced. Otherwise, if the lock assembly is turned upside down, the locking bolt will fall out. On the latest models the locking bolt is held in with a pin and will not pull out unless the pin is removed.

Replacement is a straight reversal of the removal sequence.

WINDOW WINDER MECHANISM - REMOVAL & REPLACEMENT

First, remove the interior door handle and the window winder handle. Then carefully prise away the trim from the door with a screwdriver.

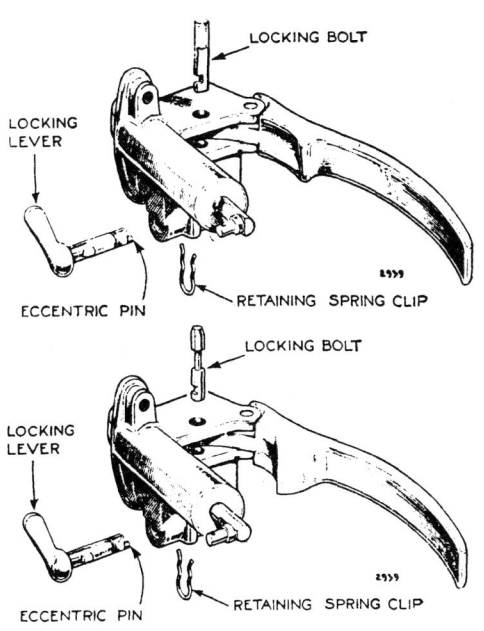

Fully close the window and then unscrew the four bolts and spring washers which hold the window winding mechanism to the door frame.

Disengage the window winder arm from the lift channel at the bottom of the window glass, and work it between the door panel and the window glass guide channel.

The window winder mechanism can then be removed from the large aperture at the bottom of the door.

Replacement is a straight reversal of the dismantling process.

STRIKER PLATE - ADJUSTMENT

If a door is not closing properly it will be necessary to adjust the lock striker plate on the door pillar. To do this slacken the two Phillips screws which hold the plate in position, and move the plate in the required direction. Retighten the securing screw.

If the door will not remain closed in the closed position it will be necessary to adjust the socket plate located below the lock striker plate. It is adjusted in an identical fashion to the lock striker plate.

ASH FRAMEWORK PRESERVATION – MORRIS TRAVELLER

With time it is likely that the wooden framework on the traveller will become darker. To restore it to its original condition sand down the remaining varnish from the wood, bleach the wood to restore its colour, and then apply several coats of varnish.

INDEX

INDEX

Zeitfracht Medien GmbH
Ferdinand-Jühlke-Straße 7
99095 Erfurt, Deutschland
produktsicherheit@kolibri360.de